SECOND EDITION

Why They Call It Politics

A Guide to America's Government

SECOND EDITION

Why They Call It Politics

A Guide to America's Government

Robert Sherrill

*Under the General Editorship of
James David Barber, Duke University*

HARCOURT BRACE JOVANOVICH, INC.

New York   Chicago   San Francisco   Atlanta

© 1972, 1974 by Harcourt Brace Jovanovich, Inc.

All rights reserved. No part of this publication may be reproduced or transmitted in any form or by any means, electronic or mechanical, including photocopy, recording, or any information storage and retrieval system, without permission in writing from the publisher.

ISBN: 0-15-596001-6

Library of Congress Catalog Card Number: 73-21080

Printed in the United States of America

Drawings by Julio Fernández

Acknowledgments for chapter opening quotes

p. 2 Ronald Steel, *Imperialists and Other Heroes* (Random House, Inc., 1971); © 1971 by Ronald Steel.
p. 76 © 1971 by The New York Times Company. Reprinted by permission.
p. 108 Joseph Clark, *Congress: The Sapless Branch* (Harper & Row, 1964).
p. 156 Reprinted by permission from TIME, The Weekly Newsmagazine; Copyright Time Inc.
p. 190 From Emmet John Hughes, *The Living Presidency* (Coward, McCann & Geoghegan, Inc., 1973); © 1972, 1973 by Emmet John Hughes.
p. 226 (1) From *Corporate Power in America*, edited by Ralph Nader and Mark J. Green. Copyright © 1973 by Ralph Nader. Reprinted by permission of Grossman Publishers.
(2) © 1973 by The New York Times Company. Reprinted by permission.
p. 314 William Safire, *The New Language of Politics* (Random House, Inc., 1968); © 1968 by William Safire.

Acknowledgments

For advice and criticism in this edition, my thanks to James David Barber, Duke University; Donald F. Cate, College of San Mateo; and Clement T. McGuire, San Jose City College. Needless to say, I did not heed them on every point, and any errors that remain are all my own. Virginia Joyner Williamson, who must certainly be one of the finest as well as one of the most demanding editors in the business, proved it with scholarship and stubbornness and physical durability. My thanks to these others who made the project easier: to Everett Sims for unfailing optimism, Tom Williamson for wit, Harrison C. Griffin for sobriety, Irene Pavitt for needed finickiness, Harry Rinehart for high design, Julio Fernández for lowdown art, Mary Sherrill for not telling who really wrote the book, and most especially Bill Tackett for finally repaying me for all those evenings I plied him with coffee.

Robert Sherrill

Contents

Foreword

About 2:30 A.M. on June 17, 1972, Washington, D.C. police entered the offices of the Democratic National Committee in the Watergate office-apartment complex and caught five men burglarizing the place and attempting to bug the telephones in the DNC chairman's office.

That was the beginning of what Senator Charles Percy, a Republican from Illinois, called, with some restraint, "the darkest scandal in American political history."[1] Over the next two years newspaper, grand jury, and Congressional investigations uncovered the most weird series of political activities ever put together. Many, if not most, of the activities were traced back to sources either in the White House or in what was called the Committee for the Re-Election of the President (CREEP), which had been set up to keep President Richard Nixon in office and was headed by officials recently resigned from the Nixon Cabinet and subcabinet.

In addition to the five burglars caught on the spot, two White House staff members were also convicted of being directly involved in the burglary. That was just the beginning. By the time the Watergate scandal had been uncovered to its fifth layer of dirt—and it seemed by then that the layers were beyond counting—top officials in the White House or at CREEP were found to have inspired not only several other burglaries, but also the burning of incriminating evidence by the acting director of the FBI; the issuance of false letters to suggest that one of the leading Democratic contenders for the presidential nomination was a racist and two other leading contenders had misbehaved sexually; the use of the FBI to gather data on political opponents and "radicals"; the planting of FBI provocateurs in antiwar groups to encourage them to violence and thereby discredit Senator George McGovern, the Democratic presidential nominee and a leading opponent of the Vietnam war; plans to bomb or set fire to the Brookings Institution, a center of academic criticism of some of Nixon's policies; and the compilation of a list of two hundred "White House enemies," who might be subjected to special harassment by the Internal Revenue Service and to character assassination (one black congressman was targeted for notoriety because he supposedly "likes white women"). There was also—by what smacked very heavily of extortionist techniques—the solicitation of an enormous campaign slush fund from corporation executives and industrialists who did business with the government and who were fearful of suffering reprisals if they did not kick through.

The men charged with these sometimes criminal and always unethical actions gave excuses that made their behavior seem all the more ominous. They said that they had countenanced burglaries and spying and the suspension of civil liberties because they thought these were necessary for "national security"—the very excuse, some observers recalled, that had been used by the Hitler faction in its rise to power in Germany. Others in the inner White House circle excused their actions by saying that they felt President Nixon's reelection was necessary to "save the country"—a singular evaluation of one politician in a democracy. One who gave this as his excuse was John Mitchell. At the very time he was the United States Attorney General, the highest officer of the law in the land, Mitchell was associating with—if not encouraging, as some have charged—men whom he knew to be planning felonies. He admitted that he had obstructed justice and lied under oath, both felonies. Moreover, documents obtained by the *New York Times* indicate that in 1970 President Nixon himself approved a domestic espionage plan, parts of which he had been warned were "clearly illegal." The plan included burglary, monitoring private phone conversations, and opening private mail.

Writers began using extravagant words and phrases not often directed toward the White House: "Gestapo" (Mary McGrory), "tide of Nazism" (Carl T. Rowan), "the Sun King" (Anthony Lewis). Even Barry Goldwater, conservative Republican senator from Arizona, referred to the Watergate events as growing out of "a Gestapo frame of mind."[2]

But for a long while the American people, a majority of whom apparently were desperate to hold onto their faith in government, refused to believe that the Watergate burglary and the auxiliary political dirty tricks could be traced to anybody but a few kooks on the fringe of the Republican party. By mid-1973, however, after the Senate select committee on the Watergate scandal had been shoveling the compost out of the White House stables for a couple of months, the faith of the public had begun to evaporate. By June most national polls showed that between two-thirds and three-quarters of the populace believed not only that some of the highest officials in the Nixon Administration had personally supervised the scandalous activities but that President Nixon himself had helped in the cover-up of the scandals.[3]

So deeply implicated was the entire Republican party hierarchy, by ignorance and inefficiency if not by complicity, that the political scene in Washington took on an air of surrealism, a weird and almost frightening atmosphere. Democratic partisans who ordinarily would have rushed in with heavy-handed criticism of the President restrained themselves, afraid that if they pulled the wrong thread too hard the whole fabric of government would fall apart. The corruption seemed that imbedded and wholesale.

At first the talk of impeachment was made only in a general, scholarly way—a "what if" kind of discussion. But by October 1973, before Nixon had completed the first year of his second term, the House hopper was beginning to bulge with serious resolutions calling for his impeachment. The last straw that October came when Nixon fired Archibald Cox, the special prosecutor for the Watergate case. Cox had been promised total independence in his work, but he ran into a brick wall when he tried to pry some secret tapes out of the President to find out whether Nixon was involved in the Watergate cover-up. Also fired at the same time (technically they resigned), because they refused to participate in helping to get rid of Cox, were Attorney General Elliot P. Richardson and Deputy Attorney General William P. Ruckelshaus.

Chaos had come to the executive branch, and many felt that at last radical steps were called for. Congressmen from such relatively civilized areas as San Francisco reported their mail running 2000 to 1 in favor of impeachment, and even congressmen from the South—ordinarily an area faithful to the President during his contest with investigative reporters—reported mail running 30 or 40 to 1 in favor of impeachment.

By the end of the year, Washington conversations turned not so much on a discussion of *whether* Nixon should resign or be impeached, but *when* one or the other would take place. The House appropriated $1 million for an impeachment probe.

Perhaps even more significant was the grave erosion of Establishment support. Columnist Joseph Alsop, the voice of the Establishment, and Republican Senator Edward Brooke urged that Nixon resign. So did the *New York Times*, the *Los Angeles Times*, the

Denver Post, and *Time* magazine. And so did George Meany, boss of the Establishmentarian AFL-CIO, who only a year earlier had been a golfing crony of Nixon's.

At first the proposals for impeachment were made with the supposition, of course, that Vice President Spiro Agnew was on hand to pick up the reins and carry on. Even some liberal Democrats thought he would be an improvement; they predicted that he might establish a coalition government with the Democrats. But that prospect of a return to relative normalcy was dashed when it was discovered that Agnew was under investigation for participating in bribes and kickbacks as a Maryland official. Within a matter of weeks after that disclosure, Agnew resigned as Vice President and pleaded *nolo contendre* to violating federal income tax laws. Thereupon Washington was plunged into more wrangling and debate over whether a President who seemed a likely candidate for impeachment should be permitted to nominate his own potential successor (Congressman Gerald Ford).

And so it went, apparently an endless series of shock waves from political tremors that shook the federal capital on such a regular basis that reporters and historians, much less the general public, could hardly keep up with events.

To say the least, the public's spirit had not needed that kind of bludgeoning. Even without Watergate, people had a low enough opinion of the federal government. The slump in political faith had been developing for a long time. In 1964, the Institute for Social Research found that two-thirds of the Americans sampled in a national poll thought they could trust the government most of the time. In the fall of 1972, as the first Nixon Administration came to a conclusion, less than half (45 percent) had that much faith.[4] And at that time the Watergate scandal was still mostly buried.

It isn't just that the people seem to think the politicians and bureaucrats and judges in Washington have ceased to function; rather, they feel that the government is functioning for somebody other than the general public. With the smog of the latest scandals beginning to obscure the outlines of the White House and the Capitol, a cross section of Americans told pollster Louis Harris in June 1973 that they felt abandoned and cheated: 69 percent said they felt that "large corporations have a great deal of influence" in Washington, but only 7 percent said they thought "the average citizen" had much clout in federal decision-making. Sixty percent had great confidence in Ralph Nader, but only 24 percent thought that the politicians in Washington were listening to him. Fifty-six percent greatly respected women's rights groups, but only 7 percent thought the organized women's groups had much influence in Washington. In short, many typical Americans were convinced that the government had slipped out of their hands—if they had ever, in fact, had a good grip on it.

Occasionally over the last few years there has been a dramatic contrapuntal expression of this discontent, as on the morning of March 1, 1971, when a bomb exploded in one of the men's rooms in the United States Capitol. The same morning, the *Washington Post* carried a Louis Harris poll showing that 63 percent of the American people had given the Ninety-first Congress a negative rating—a new low—and 59 percent had given the President a negative rating for his job in dealing with domestic programs.

Although very few Americans approved of the bomber's methods for showing his unhappiness, obviously the violent and the nonviolent agreed in their estimation of those who run the federal government. Disenchantment is widespread; cynicism is epidemic; disillusionment is a way of life among the electorate. Within a few months after the bombing, a Roper Organization poll (July 8, 1971) showed that two-thirds of the American people believed that their country had lost its proper sense of direction. And a poll by Gallup (June 26, 1971) showed that 47 percent— nearly one out of every two, and a majority of those with an opinion—felt that unrest and divisions among the people would likely lead to "a real breakdown in this country."

These feelings reach to the top and are acknowledged there. "Most Americans," President Nixon said in his 1971 State of the Union address, "are simply fed up with government at all levels." More precisely, they are fed up with the *manner* in which they are governed, an attitude singularly aggravated by the Nixon Administration in subsequent years. And if the governed are fed up, so are some of those who govern. Senator Mark Hatfield of Oregon, a dissident member of the President's party, expressed this feeling: "I've worked within the system all my life, and I believe in our system. But when I look at what we need to do, and I see how much time it takes, how hard you have to shove to get the slightest response, I have to agree some days with the kids who say it may not be enough. It may not be enough. . . ."[5]

Another who decided it may not be enough but that he had certainly had enough of it was Senator Harold Hughes, Iowa Democrat. After only one term in the Senate, Hughes declared in 1973 that he would not run for reelection but would become a lay preacher because "government will change for the better only when people change for the better in their hearts."

The remarkable aspect of the present discontent is that it is being voiced as much by people inside the channels of power as it is by those outside.

Writers and journalists who hobnob with the great and the near-great ordinarily tend to view this as the best of all possible systems of government, if for no other reason than that the men who run it supply them with juicy gossip and flattering inside information and sometimes even treat them to a lunch at one of Washington's cushy restaurants. When pessimism besets these scribes, the evidence of decay becomes ominous indeed. Thus we ignore at our peril the gloom of such men as Stewart Alsop and Walter Lippmann, confidants of Presidents. Wrote Alsop: "The late Everett McKinley Dirksen used to compare the system . . . to an unsinkable scow. 'Congress,' he would sonorously proclaim, 'is like an old waterlogged scow. It doesn't go far. It doesn't go fast. But it doesn't sink.' Not only Congress, but the whole American system of government seems to go less and less far, less and less fast. There are more and more people who are so frustrated and infuriated by it that they would like to see it sink."[6]

And almost at the same time the nation's most venerable columnist, Lippmann, was contributing this to the dirge:

> The things that have to be done—say, saving the environment—need a government in order to be done. Yet, with the number of people participating, government is increasingly impossible. When the American Constitution was adopted, about 5 percent of the population voted, no more. And that was 5 percent of very few people. Now 70-80 percent of the people take part in questions of enormous complexity. Solution? There is no solution. It's like finding a solution to the question why fish came onto the land. You can be certain that anybody who thinks he has a solution doesn't know what he's talking about.[7]

To be sure, some of their pessimism may be explained by personal complaints: Lippmann was old, and Alsop was physically ailing, and neither was being courted by the mighty as he once had been. But the rest of it is quite in tune with the unease and disaffection of the general electorate.

These feelings run so deeply through some elements of the electorate that there is even vague talk of revolution. Not much, but some talk of this sort. And, ironically, it is here that one finds the most encouragement for salvaging the present system and improving it and moving ahead. The hope stems from the fact that even those with the best reason to think in rebellious terms—the blacks—are generally led by men who ultimately concede that no matter how satisfying it is to talk of physically throwing out the rascals, reality lies elsewhere, sanity lies elsewhere, improvement lies elsewhere: and that elsewhere is within the context of constitutional politics. Violent revolution, says Julian Bond, should not be dismissed as an impossibility, but it should be recognized as an improbability for several reasons, one of the most important being that "those who order society are usually able to keep it stable by allowing minimal reforms, so that even oppression can become bearable."[8] While dreaming of revolution, says Bond, blacks should go immediately to work to set up a political movement.

Many militant black leaders agree. Stokely Carmichael, for example, urges his followers "to take over all of the political institutions inside our community: the police station, the judicial system, the board of education, the welfare system, especially the education system, because education is nothing but an ideology. . . . Overt, open confrontation, however, is no longer the way. We're going to organize politically to take them over."[9] If disgust with the system could have overturned it, the blacks would have been victorious long ago; but they are practical people, and they know that not much of a revolutionary army can be raised with welfare checks; so, to bring about change, they turn to the power levers at hand. Former Black Panther leader Bobby Seale donned his business suit in 1973 and won enough votes to make the run-off election for mayor of Oakland (which he then lost).

All challenges to the system—except the violent ones that result in the subtraction of civil liberties—are probably for the good. It's high time that all our basic political assumptions were reexamined. We have done ourselves, our government, and our traditions a great disservice by jumbling together various pieces of holiday rhetoric—innocently offered at the time as no more than rhetoric—and reassembling them over the years as though they were reality. "Government of, by, and for the people with liberty and justice for all"—it sounds very pretty. But it is hard to find. The resulting cynicism among the growing number of Americans who have a sophisticated awareness of what is going on at the federal level can only be dispelled by candidly discussing our government as a very defective process. On paper, the goals may be high and the framework of the government may be as perfect as any ever devised;

but the machinery does not live up to its political platform guarantees, and the operation of it is a constant repair job.

At its most efficient, our government could not be described more honestly than as "a process of making things—including itself —less defective." Just less defective. If we approach our subject in this spirit we will be radical only in the sense that we will be returning to the radical historical roots of our government. A reading of *The Federalist* papers, for example, will show that those wonderful harangues by Hamilton, Madison, and Jay offered the Constitution only as the best guide through some rough governmental terrain. They did not peddle the Constitution as a way to escape the roughness or as a magical formula for making the roughness disappear. As we approach the nation's two hundredth anniversary, there is surely no more patriotic way to celebrate the occasion than to subject the constitutional machinery of government to a new appraisal to see where the weakest parts are, why the breakdowns are occurring, and why at times the terrain seems almost impassable.

This book is critical of politics as it operates at the federal level today, and critical of many politicians and bureaucrats for their style of operating. Criticism can become tedious, however, unless it is made with the background acknowledgment that we are talking not about scientific absolutes, but about the imperfect human shaping of a sometimes too plastic ideal.

Even while thrashing them with well-deserved scorn and damnation, we must bear in mind that the men and women who run the government are, pardon the expression, human beings. And many are very fascinating human beings. They are subject to exhaustion, anger, greed, lust, and all the other impulses that make life worth chronicling. When Senators Strom Thurmond and Ralph Yarborough wrestled on the floor outside a committee room in 1964, they were expressing more than a difference in ideology. And the same can be said for the encounter the previous year when Congressman Henry Gonzalez hit Congressman Ed Foreman for calling him "pinko." And the same can be said for Senator Kenneth B. McKellar, eighty at the time, when he punched two newsmen in one day for writing about him as "old."

Before man had government, he had instincts and glands, and whether we like it or not in this sophisticated age, instincts and glands still have much to do with what is produced in Washington. When Hal Holbrook was preparing for a television series based on the mythical life of a "Senator Hays Stowe," he spent many hours talking with real senators to get a feel for the job. One senator told him privately that he "hated" having to deal with his constituents.

"In come John Doe and Mary Doe and eight little Does expecting to see you," he explained. "They're on vacation and he's in Bermuda shorts and the kids are mad and tired. When they lean back on that sofa to rest and visit and you've got to make a speech that night and you're not prepared and the mail is stacking up, you just can't imagine the feeling that comes over you. It's almost intolerable. But you've got to see them."[10]

The textbook legend is that politicians are afraid to show this distaste for the public; but thousands of tourists who have visited the offices of their congressmen can testify to a more irritating reality. In the past decade the size of congressional staffs has multiplied several times, as the politicians have ringed themselves with concentric walls of well-paid but often surly receptionists, clerks, and secretaries whose primary function, it sometimes seems, is to keep the electorate at a distance.

Nervousness, exhaustion, psychotic arrogance, irritation with the public—these have their effects on the shaping of the legislation that runs the country. And the appetites and gross pleasures that touch the lives of barbers and clerks touch also the lives of the mighty. F. R. Pettigrew, who spent two terms in the United States Senate at the turn of the century, wrote of President Cleveland:

> My seat was the first seat on the main aisle. Grover Cleveland was brought in by two or three men and placed in a chair right across the aisle from me. He was still stupidly intoxicated, his face was bloated, and he was a sight to behold. He did not seem to know what was occurring, but looked like a great lump of discolored flesh.

Alas, even demon rum still lives in Washington and has his influence—small influence—on the outcome of things. It is said, for example, that a senator, who normally would have voted against the measure, cast the deciding vote in 1971 in favor of the quarter-billion-dollar Lockheed Aircraft loan because he was soused. One of the more instructive exchanges at the Senate's Watergate hearings was the debate between committee kibitzers and White House aide John Ehrlichman over whether he had played fair by using as campaign material the drinking habits of several Democratic incumbents.

If nothing else, the purpose of this book is to encourage candor and discourage cant. A democratic government in the final analysis comes down to a great many very human beings who aren't especially fond of one another, jostling and shoving with the common hope that each will come out on top. But it can't be done. One of the oldest clichés describes politics as the "art of the possible." It means that not everyone has the same ideal, and when ideals clash, compromises must be made. It is a bad description in many ways. Politics is no art; the majority of men who practice politics are seldom driven by high ideals—they are driven by what they call "practicalities," among which the lower biases of their constituents rank rather high. The concept of compromise is usually perverted into an apology for selling the people out.

Admitting all that and more, one still shouldn't be too self-critical. That way, one loses perspective and becomes tediously whining and guilt-paralyzed. If our political leaders leave something to be desired, let us not forget that it has always been this way and we have somehow survived.

> Of the two great parties which at this hour almost share the nation between them, I should say that one has the best cause, and the other contains the best men. The philosopher, the poet, or the religious man, will of course wish to cast his vote with the democrat, for free-trade, for wide suffrage, for the abolition of legal cruelties in the penal code, and for facilitating in every manner the access of the young and the poor to the sources of wealth and power. But he can rarely accept the persons whom the so-called popular party propose to him as representatives of these liberalities. They have not at heart the ends which give to the name of democracy what hope and virtue are in it. The spirit of our American radicalism is destructive and aimless: it is not loving; it has no ulterior and divine ends, but is destructive only out of hatred and selfishness. On the other side, the conservative party, composed of the most moderate, able and cultivated part of the population, is timid, and merely defensive of property. It vindicates no right, it aspires to no real good, it brands no crime, it proposes no generous policy; it does not build, nor write, nor cherish the arts, nor foster religion, nor establish schools, nor encourage science, nor emancipate the slave, nor befriend the poor, or the Indian, or the immigrant. From neither party, when in power, has the world any benefit to expect in science, art, or humanity, at all commensurate with the resources of the nation.

Ralph Waldo Emerson wrote that in 1844. One must take note of his extravagances; the differences between the two parties were not so black and white then. Nor are they now. But in general the *deficiencies* were accurately noted, and they have not changed much in the more than a century intervening between Emerson's complaints and the ones heard today—that either the politicians take little thought before they rush in with their passionate reforms, or they have no passions and no reforms to offer. The defects of the government and of the politicians and bureaucrats who run it may be more critical today simply because of the pressure of people and the pressure of time. But if the nation was able to survive the Whig President and the Congress of Emerson's day, there is reason to hope that life will go on in a reasonably acceptable way despite the Congresses and the bureaucracy and the courts and the Johnsons and the Nixons and their successors of our time, although some of what follows may lead the reader to think differently.

Read it with this reminder from the most American of philosophers, Will Rogers:

> We've been staggering along now about 155 years under every conceivable horse thief that could get into office and yet here we are, still going strong. I doubt if Barnum's circus has housed as many different kinds of species as has been in our government employ during its existence. As bad as they are they can't spoil it and as good as they are they can't help it. So as bad as we are, we are better off than any other nation. So what's the use to worry?

That preachment may be a bit too easy-going to allow for progress; indeed, what applied to the relatively simple world in which that was said, the world of 1930, no longer applies so certainly today. But it is worth coming back to from time to time as an antidote for the illness of political melancholy.

SECOND EDITION

Why They Call It Politics

A Guide to America's Government

Presidency I:
The Most Powerful
Politician in the World

*The changes that are necessary to reform this society
are not going to be accomplished by a single charismatic
leader miraculously striking forth to solve our problems.
We have wasted too much time waiting for leaders,
watching them fail to keep their promises, and then mourning
what they might have been once they have disappeared.
It is a delusion to put much faith in a leader, and it is
an evasion of responsibility. In a society where men
are truly free, they need not seek salvation in their leaders.
Happy the land, as Brecht once wrote, that needs no hero*

Ronald Steel, Imperialists and Other Heroes

When George Romney, President Nixon's first Secretary of Housing and Urban Development, stepped down after four years in office, he departed with one of his characteristically candid judgments: "You don't get basic reform unless you have a crisis. We have no means by which we can deal with sensitive problems to the point that the public understands them and they can be dealt with before a crisis occurs."[1]

If the accuracy of that statement is evident in domestic matters—if it takes riots, run-away inflation in the supermarket, and

taxpayers' revolts to arouse the adrenalin of reform on the home scene—it takes even more to achieve it in foreign affairs: namely, it takes unwelcome wars. Of these, the most unwelcome of all are those the people can't understand—neither how we got into them nor why they are being fought. These are "presidential wars," which the public is asked to accept on faith in the constitutional preeminence of the Chief Executive in foreign affairs as well as on faith that "he is acting on information that you don't have."

These two assumptions have been raised to the level of religion within the White House itself. An aura of all-mightiness sometimes hangs over White House pronouncements, both those made by the worshipful staff and those made by Himself. "The Presidency 'stands across the path of those who mistakenly assert that democracy must fail because it can neither decide promptly nor act vigorously.' That office is now occupied by a man with a talent for power," said Billy Don Moyers. "If he fails, we all fail. If he succeeds, we all succeed."

Mr. Moyers, the East Texas boy who put aside ambitions in the Baptist ministry to serve an equally difficult master, Lyndon Johnson, might not express his view of LBJ quite so extravagantly today, but as special assistant to the President he was being paid to say things like that in 1966. It was the era when another aide, Jack Valenti, described the President as a superman "with extra glands." President Johnson must have seen himself in much the same way, for, in response to what he considered a trivial inquiry, he rebuked a reporter, "Why do you come and ask me, the leader of the Western world, a chickenshit question like that?"

Those lively days evolved under President Nixon into a sometimes subtler and often more pious kind of Big Daddyism, expressed by Nixon in such offhand remarks as, "The average American is just like the child in the family."[2] The fervency of the 1966-era Moyers was echoed by Nixon aide Jeb Stuart Magruder when he excused his part in the 1972 election scandals on the grounds that "it was important that Mr. Nixon win 'at all costs' to save the country"—which sounds very much as if he looked on the President as divinely chosen.

The disasters of foreign affairs, especially under recent Democratic administrations, have made the nation less tolerant of those swaggering remarks. In the short term of John Kennedy, liberals in increasing numbers were beginning to wonder if perhaps major alterations should be made in the structure of government to keep a sluggish and backward Congress from nullifying the best hopes of our best Presidents.* But with the advent of Lyndon Johnson, demand for reform took a different direction. To some extent— usually overrated—this reaction was to LBJ's engulfing personality, which, coming after the smooth and languid administration of John Kennedy, was enough to frighten Georgetown matrons. A much more reasonable explanation for the reaction was the presidentially created war in Southeast Asia, which, although begun by Kennedy, was not brought to its full grotesque scope until after the election of Johnson.

A slow awakening came with the destruction of the domestic budget, as a result of war-born inflation and waste, and with the body count in Southeast Asia. When the longest war in American history officially limped to a semiconclusion in early 1973, the bodies were stacked like statistical cordwood: U.S. combat dead— 45,943; U.S. dead from noncombat causes (accidents, illnesses)— 10,298; U.S. missing—1333; U.S. wounded—303,616; South Vietnamese combat deaths during the U.S. period—166,429; South Vietnamese wounded—453,039; North Vietnamese and Vietcong combat dead—937,562; civilians killed—415,000; civilians wounded —935,000.

Overwhelmed by these numbers, accumulated during a war that was often questioned on constitutional as well as moral and strategic grounds, many people of both liberal and conservative persuasion began seriously to reexamine the office of the Presidency, where American participation in the war was hatched, and to wonder if the description offered by Moyers, of a relationship by which the entire nation (or at least its reputation) could rise or fall on the luck or mischief of one man, might not be uncomfortably close to the truth. The war had been joined and prolonged by three Presidents, three very human beings,† but the terrible cost was not, to put it mildly, borne by them but by the whole nation, and some wondered if it would ever fully recover.

---

* This was the motivating worry, for example, in James MacGregor Burns's *The Deadlock of Democracy* (Englewood Cliffs, N.J.: Prentice-Hall, 1963).

† Just how human was discovered in late 1972 when Dr. Max Jacobson, well-known for administering the powerful stimulant known as "speed" to famous patients, admitted that he had accompanied President Kennedy to Vienna in 1961 when the President participated in a summit conference with Soviet Premier Nikita Khrushchev. Jacobson admits he gave Kennedy shots, but he will not say what they were. Mrs. Kennedy also found the obliging doctor useful. So, eleven years after the fact, the nation learned that some of its war-and-peace diplomacy may have been conducted by a President who was feeling like Superman, thanks to amphetamines.

Is He Too Powerful?

The popular question has become once again what it traditionally was in this country, except for one brief period: Does the President have too much power?* The Bricker Amendment of the 1950s, which would have prevented the Chief Executive from making treaties and executive agreements with foreign governments, was condemned by liberals as an embarrassingly reactionary proposal—prompted by some of the international antics of their beloved FDR. But since the time of LBJ they have found themselves talking very much the same as conservatives of an earlier era.

In the last year of Johnson's term, Sir Denis W. Brogan, a noted British historian who is something of an authority on American politics, summed it up like this:

> Vietnam is now the third-biggest war in American history. It is one that's been fought without any kind of declaration—no United Nations resolution, no recognition that there's a war on. . . . Consequently the people begin to look at the Presidency and ask: "Is this what we want? Is this what James Madison wanted? Is this what even Lincoln, the greatest aggrandizer of the Presidency, dared to do in the Civil War?" So there is an attack on the Presidency which I think arises from the fact that the Presidency now is seen as dangerous, as potentially dangerous—not as the great saving, unifying institution which it has been in the past, but as the dangerous institution which has got to be cut down to size.[3]

Considering the way our thirty-seven Chief Executives have performed in the job, the debate on the power of the Presidency does not on the surface make much sense. Few historians would rate more than ten Presidents as "strong"—Jackson, Polk, Lincoln, Cleveland, Theodore Roosevelt, Wilson, Franklin Roosevelt, Truman, perhaps Kennedy, and Johnson—and usually for no better reason than their eagerness to call out the Army and draw blood, either in military adventures or as strikebreakers (Cleveland). No more than three or four at the most could be rated as strong if the criterion was the pushing of domestic reforms. Two-thirds of our past Presidents, viewing themselves primarily as ribbon-cutters, were thoroughly intimidated by what they considered much more

---

* So that there will be no misunderstanding of what follows, the author's position is that the Presidency offers far too much power in foreign affairs for occupants of the White House who are thoughtless or arrogant. But in domestic affairs *no* President—especially an imaginative one—has half as much power as he needs. There is nothing new in this position, of course.

powerful congressional prerogatives; far from desiring to swell the office, they were uncomfortable at the thought of exercising power.

During the depression of 1873, President Grant surrendered his authority without firing a shot: "It is the duty of Congress to devise the method of correcting the evils which are acknowledged to exist, and not mine."

Another of America's least memorable Presidents, Franklin Pierce (1853–57), had taken an even deader position. He concluded that neither he *nor* Congress should do anything to correct evils. Although one might have supposed he would be sympathetic to the legislation, since his own wife was mentally unbalanced most of her adult life, he vetoed a law passed by Congress to establish insane asylums somewhat superior to the ones existing at that time (commonly the inmates were caged or chained) with the withering explanation:

> I readily, and I trust feelingly, acknowledge the duty incumbent on us all, as men and citizens, and as among the highest and holiest of our duties, to provide for those who, in the mysterious order of Providence, are subject to want and diseases of body or mind, but I cannot find any authority in the Constitution for making the federal government the great almoner of public charity throughout the United States.

And that bleak philosophy was perpetuated by succeeding Presidents down to 1933 and the advent of Franklin D. Roosevelt. In the interim, other spiritless pronouncements were issued from the White House.

With unemployment at 12 percent of the national work force in 1921—the highest in this century, except for the unemployment rate of the 1930s—President Warren G. Harding looked the situation over thoughtfully and, with the kind of fatalism that has marked most presidential decision-making, decided that assisting the jobless unfortunates in any way, including the manipulation of the economy in their behalf, was not a federal responsibility. Eight years later, with steam gushing out of Wall Street's safety valve and the seams beginning to give, President Herbert Hoover modestly excused himself from action, saying he had "no authority to stop booms." Eisenhower's two terms were marked by three sharp recessions, but his only contribution to helping solve them was to urge people to go out and buy more commodities. For men like these, the question of the power quantity available to the Presidency was beside the point.

The minority of assertive Presidents measured their power—or lack of it—in long periods of frustration and anger, usually triggered by the sight of their programs disappearing in the swamp of geriatrics and obstreperousness and parochialism on Capitol Hill. "By God," cried Theodore Roosevelt, on the verge of a tantrum, "I'd like to have 16 or 20 lions to set loose in the Senate." In recent decades an increasingly ponderous and independent bureaucracy has joined Congress in frustrating activist Presidents, until the latter have been stung to crassly bitter summations of their impotence. "They talk about the power of the President," said Harry Truman, "they talk about how I can just push a button to get things done. Why, I spend most of my time kissing somebody's ass."[4]

Shortly after his swearing in, following Kennedy's assassination, Johnson approached key members of Kennedy's staff and begged them to stay on and help him, arguing for their transferred loyalty with an irrefutable logic: "I'm the only President you've got." Although the statement was probably supposed to convey no more than the uncharacteristic humility he felt at the moment, in its simplicity it nicely sums up the problem every President confronts throughout the easy days as well as in the crises—that there is only one of him. The President is singular. He is our only national politician. He is the only politician whose constituency is total. He is the only politician whose decision-making powers are neither duplicated elsewhere nor shared with somebody else as an equal.

The problems he deals with are generally no different from the problems that ricochet around all federal halls, the same problems Congress wrestles with in a more lumbering fashion, but in dealing with these problems only the President can justifiably have on his desk (as President Truman had) a sign proclaiming with as much resignation as pride: "The buck stops here." Sir Denis, the British historian quoted earlier, agrees: "The President is a 'monarch,' in the strict sense of the term: It's a one-man show. The power cannot be delegated nor be given to committees. It can be abandoned—the President may be idle—but nobody else gets the power; it just is lost for the time being."[5]

Because of this singularity, we wrap the Presidency in a cocoon of pomp and myth and mystique that is no doubt very satisfying to the ego of the man in the job and in fact augments enormously the powers he has by law. But this deference also keeps him from serving the nation with the openness and efficiency that the job deserves, for the most harmful misconception of the President is that his singularity somehow gives him a power that is total and, since he is above the people, a power that to a degree is inherently against them. This is a common feeling among both Americans and foreign students of our government (thus Sir Denis' use of the word *monarch*). Although partly it was a desire by right-wingers to reach back a few years and deliver an insulting wallop to the memory of Franklin D. Roosevelt, who had had the gall to break tradition by being elected four times, it was also the national monarchophobia that pushed through the Twenty-second Amendment to the Constitution in 1951 to limit the President to no more than two terms. Coincidentally, by automatically making every second-termer a lame duck, the amendment robs the President of a great deal of the influence that he would need to carry out his constitutional role.*

The fear that our top politician will somehow be able to perpetuate himself indefinitely gets no support from experience. The electorate in its caution, or in its fickleness, has permitted only thirteen Presidents (Washington, Jefferson, Madison, Monroe, Jackson, Lincoln, Grant, Cleveland, McKinley, Wilson, FDR, Eisenhower, and Nixon) out of thirty-seven to serve even a second term, much less get a hereditary grip on the post.

With this safe history behind us, why, then, the persistent concern over whether the President may be too powerful?

The concern is understandable, considering the libertarian nature of the American people. We revere champions, but we dislike the boss. We are passionately orthodox, but we rebel against those who impose orthodoxy. As a people we have regrettably indulged ourselves in romantic admiration for the wheelers and dealers of politics at the neighborhood and state levels—the Mayor Daleys and the Boss Crumps and the Mayor Curleys and the Huey Longs—but, at the same time, we suspect and fear and even hate the respectable attributes that smack of national monarchy. To the colonists, one-man rule meant monarchy, which was, in turn, synonymous with tyranny; most Americans still use the two words interchangeably. With the degrading rule of George III so fresh in

---

* The longer a President is in office—that is, the closer he comes to the probable termination of his service—the less power he has to swap with the power brokers in Congress. Even before the second term was made automatically lame duck, Presidents had their problems maintaining the muscle of their office. After the passage of the Social Security Act in 1935, FDR carried little weight with Congress except in military matters, although he served ten more years.

their memories, it is understandable that the leaders of the new nation were too quick to see clues of a return to monarchy in some aspects of the new government. The Constitution frightened Patrick Henry. "It squints towards monarchy," he warned. "Your President may easily become king."

A reading of *The Federalist* papers—written in 1787 and 1788 to soothe the myriad fears of the populace in respect to governmental bugaboos—reveals that no other problem was so vexing as that of the Presidency. It was this office and what Hamilton called the constant "aversion of the people to monarchy" that the opponents of the new Constitution found most useful in promoting unrest. Hamilton accurately pointed out—using an argument any schoolboy could develop today—that opponents were dealing heavily in fiction when they likened the Presidency to the British Crown of that day, since the Presidency was a four-year term, whereas the Crown was hereditary; the President's veto of legislation could be overridden by a two-thirds vote of both houses, whereas the king's negation of parliamentary acts was final; the President had nothing to do with the nation's mode of worship (unless a predilection for visiting Catholic priests at midnight, as LBJ sometimes did, or holding a round robin of interdenominational services in the White House, as Nixon has done, influences the people), whereas the king was head not only of the British state but also of the British church; and the President could be removed by congressional impeachment and trial, whereas the king could only be removed by assassination or banishment.*

---

* Adding the procedure for impeachment to the Constitution was favored by Benjamin Franklin for the very reason that otherwise assassination would be the only way left to get rid of a Chief Executive who was judged to be wrecking the country. Yet Americans have cheated on the Constitution and have treated their Presidents to the decencies of democratic unhappiness only once, when an effort was made to impeach and convict Andrew Johnson (it failed by one vote). At this writing, Congress is contemplating the impeachment of Nixon, but it still has a long way to go. For the most part, Americans have dealt with their Presidents as though they were monarchs, removing four of them from power by assassination and attempting to remove three others in that fashion.

Regrettably, the result has been to force the President farther from the people. He fears them. The Secret Service force that protects him from the people has been more than doubled since 1963. Its budget is up tenfold. He rides among the people in a car built like a tank. An impregnable model was produced for him in 1972, by Ford Motor Company, at a reported cost of $500,000. It weighs five tons and has quarter-inch armor plate all around, oversized bulletproof tires, bulletproof glass with a hydraulic bubble roof, hand boards and fold-down running boards for Secret Service men, a two-way

Some of Hamilton's assurances regarding presidential powers and presidential plain living have not held up, and these are the points that so often raise talk of the monarchical qualities of the office.

The most obvious miscalculation on Hamilton's part was in hooting at those who raised the specter of a President with "imperial purple flowing in his train . . . [or] seated on a throne surrounded with minions and mistresses, giving audience to the envoys of foreign potentates in all the supercilious pomp of majesty . . . decorated with attributes superior in dignity and splendor to those of the king of Great Britain."

The Pomp of the Presidency

The splendor that Hamilton thought so ridiculous to imagine has in fact arrived. Acknowledging that as things go in the world of potentates the Presidency isn't a bad place to serve, Nixon said, with a smile of candor, "We're roughing it pretty nicely." It's getting nicer all the time.

There were always elements of pomp around the President;

---

radio, a telephone, and a trunkful of electronic equipment. Ford, which is under contract to keep two such vehicles available at all times, is very proud of its product; an executive claims, "It is as strong as a tank. It is so strong that a bomb would only roll it over." (Unfortunately for the auto's reputation, it was dented when it collided with a bicycle on August 7, 1972; the bike wasn't hurt.) Even when the President goes to his "informal" quarters at Camp David he goes with great caution. Referring to the double steel fence around Camp David's two hundred acres, plus the guard of forty-eight Marines who patrol the area night and day, plus the cleared "no-man's land" along the perimeter, a White House aide understandably assessed the Presidential retreat as "the nearest thing we have to a medieval castle with a moat and foot guards." Indeed, Charles the Bald was not so protected. The White House is bathed in protective floodlights at night. There are bulletproof guardhouses at the gates. In 1963, higher fences were put up around the White House. New restrictions were placed on visitors.

Such defenses are a recent phenomenon. Even until the 1930s the White House was almost unguarded. Security was so easygoing in President Hoover's time that sightseers sometimes wandered into Hoover's private rooms by error. Until the turn of this century, thousands of Americans felt that there was no way to usher in the New Year quite like dropping by the White House to shake the President's hand—sometimes the line stretched for blocks. How distantly innocent that all seems today. Now there is distrust on both sides. Fearing the people, the President becomes more physically remote and seemingly more mentally aloof. The people, in turn, fear this aloofness as a sign of self-aggrandizement.

but stark plainness was, for a long time, also present. If Washington loved to move grandly among the citizenry in a regal coach pulled by six horses or on a white stallion with leopard-skin housing, the populace cannot be said to have encouraged this kind of ego, nor did many of Washington's successors seek to present themselves so regally as he. When Thomas Jefferson took the oath of office on March 4, 1801, he "dressed plainly and without ostentation" for the occasion, walked from his boarding house to the Capitol (accompanied only by two men who would be in his Cabinet), and delivered his Inaugural Address only to members of Congress. Then he walked back to his boarding house for supper, only to find that all the chairs were taken and that no one offered to surrender his place at the table to the new President. From that egalitarian era the United States moved, in 172 years, to an Inaugural at which the grandstand alone cost $425,000, the whole works cost $4 million, and after which there were five "galas" attended by 37,000 guests, some of whom paid $125 per folding chair to watch either President Nixon dance or seventy-year-old Hollywood stars crack political jokes.

Whether or not it has been in the right direction is perhaps debatable, but U.S. Presidents have come a long way since 1853, when Franklin Pierce moved into a White House so ill-equipped that he could find only a single candle to light his way to bed, which on that first night was a mattress on the floor. Calvin Coolidge thought it not at all beneath his dignity to retire from the White House to a $36-a-month rented duplex. When Harry and Bess Truman left the White House for the last time, they went to the railroad station and paid their own fares back to Independence, Missouri; not until Truman had been out of office six years did Congress decide that all Presidents and their widows deserved to be paid a pension. It was a far cry from the way Lyndon Johnson, only sixteen years later, was moved into luxurious retirement—flown back to Texas in the presidential plane and given $450,000 to draw on for "transitional expenses."

Mr. Nixon's salary is $200,000 a year—on which, because of deductions, he paid virtually no taxes ($792 in 1970, and $878 in 1971)—plus a $50,000 expense account, plus endless perquisites. A hundred years ago the President earned $5000 a year less than the First Lady's press secretary earns today ($30,000).

But the taxpayer, willingly or not, also occasionally gets billed for some items he may not have expected. In 1973 it was discovered that Nixon had quietly drawn on the federal budget to

Some of the more sentimental chroniclers of life in the White House insist that a President can be lonely, which of course is possible, but President Nixon sometimes overspent his social budget by $100,000 before the year was half up. During the first fourteen months of his administration, Nixon entertained 50,000 people in the White House—more than any other President—at a cost of $25 a person for state dinners and "something less than" $10 a person for reception-buffets. Johnson's record for entertaining in one year was 26,000 guests; Eisenhower's record was a reclusive 3200.

In a style that would have satisfied ancient kings, President Nixon's entrance into the East Room of the White House for state dinners was sometimes marked by fanfare from lines of red-coated Marine trumpeters, their gleaming instruments draped with banners that lacked only heraldic symbols to be complete. On state occasions he was usually attended by his troubadours and minstrels—the Army Strolling Strings, Sea Chanters, Marine Fanfare Group, Air Force Chorus, and Airmen of Note.

It is the physical aspects of the Presidency that observers are most likely to interpret as monarchical. When George Reedy, President Johnson's former press aide, likened life in the White House to "the life of a court," he first mentioned by way of explanation that everything in that establishment is focused on "the material needs and the desires of a single man." The material needs. By that he meant everything "from the very latest and most luxurious jet aircraft to a masseur constantly in attendance to soothe raw presidential nerves."*

Even more important, however, he is treated with all of the reverence due a monarch. No one interrupts a presidential contemplation for anything less than a major catastrophe somewhere on the globe. No one speaks to him unless spoken to first. No one invites him to "go soak your head" when his demands become petulant and unreasonable.†

* Of the half-dozen jets in the presidential fleet, the latest cost $10 million and has seven compartments. Unfortunately, the arrangement of these seven compartments, decorated in early 1973 at a cost of $2 million, did not suit Mrs. Nixon; so in late 1973 the compartments were rearranged and redecorated at a cost of $285,000. Our Caesars are very proud of their chariots. One of the first gadgets that President Eisenhower demonstrated to Kennedy while showing his successor around the White House was the button to summon a helicopter to the south lawn. Ike punched, and lo, there it came.
† Nor, apparently, are they inclined to dissuade him from a course that he is determined to follow. Lyndon Johnson once said:
If you have all the information, you don't make many mistakes. So many people and I disagree, but they wouldn't if we had the same information.

pay for all sorts of luxurious equipment at his personal Cali
and Florida homes, and also at the Bahamas island retreat c
of his cronies. How much? The White House started off by s
it had dipped into the public's pocket for only a few tho
dollars to pay for "security" equipment. But shortly thereaft
truth was revealed; nearly $10 million had been spent on e
thing from swimming pools to golf carts to ice-makers to d
tive pillows.[6]

Nixon does not allow these vacation homes to stand
During the first four and a half years of his reign, he spen
days at Key Biscayne, Florida, and 224 days at San Clemente,
fornia (for a total of 371 days, or a cost of $25,000 a day f
taxpayers' renovation, but that does not count maintenance
also "escaped" to Camp David, a presidential hideaway in the N
land mountains near Washington, for a total of 120 visits. So, d
the first four and a half years, he was away from Washingtor
days—the greatest disappearing act of any President of this g
ation.

The cost of pomp, as well as the cost of living, keeps in
ing. A hundred years ago the cost of operating the White H
was only $13,800 a year. Today the cost is $70 million. Pres
Hoover got by with a staff of forty-two. Although he pror
during his campaign that he would have a "small staff," i
first term Nixon found it necessary to jump his personnel fron
to 548 (the new payroll: $9.1 million annually), and that d
count the carpenters, plumbers, electricians, flower arran
housekeepers, butlers, cooks, doormen, pantry maids, and
handymen ($1.1 million a year), or the gardeners, caretakers, s
masons, and other outdoor workers ($200,000 a year).*

The $9.1 million payroll did not include the staff costs o
National Security Council, an adjunct to the White House ($
million), or the $3.1 million for the White House police and a "
fidential" share of the Secret Service's $45 million budget, or
$700,000 for the Vice President's thirty-nine staffers, or the
million for special projects, or the $1 million "emergency fund
Nixon could not claim thriftiness at least he could claim simpli
the previous Republican President, Dwight Eisenhower, wound
with a staff of 1200, more than twice the number who serve Ni

---

* All head counts must be judged in terms of an insight given by C
Coolidge. *New York Times* correspondent Arthur Krock asked Pres
Coolidge, "How many people work for you in the White House?" He rep
"About half of them."

Many of our Presidents have had skin that was kingly thin and likely to bruise under the slightest criticism. Often they, or their courtiers, respond with amusing overkill. After Speaker Carl Albert had made a speech in which he said that Nixon had "gotten away with murder on economic issues," Nixon's advisers tried to persuade then-House Minority Leader Gerald Ford to denounce Albert on the floor "for calling Nixon a murderer."

But it was the physical aspects, even the bodily aspects, of royalty that Reedy kept coming back to, the fact that

> the President was not to be jostled by a crowd—unless he elected to subject himself to do so during those moments when he shed his role as chief of state and mounted the hustings as a candidate for reelection. The ritual of shaking hands with the President took on more and more the coloration of the medieval "king's touch" as a specific for scrofula.[7]

He exaggerates, but there is enough truth in what he says to make one wonder. Not only do plain people not touch the body of the President, they must not even touch those things that touch his body. Two young Marines assigned as guards to the presiden-

---

I've seen it time and time again that when we get in these meetings, by and large, if they have the same facts, a decision is relatively easy. The problem is getting the facts. I keep reading about various viewpoints that my men have. I've never heard some of them. I go around the table and ask each man. I've never had a meeting in which I didn't go around the table.

One can just hear the yesses whistling down through the years. But were those trusted aides, smothered with "all the information" that was available to the White House, telling him what they honestly believed? The above quote was taken from *Life* magazine (July 5, 1968). Adjacent to the statement was a picture of Johnson and some of his advisers in the White House "situation room." Pictured with LBJ were Clark Clifford, Llewellyn Thompson, Nicholas Katzenbach, Dean Rusk, Marvin Watson, McGeorge Bundy, and Walt Rostow. Only a few years after that picture was taken, and after the Johnson regime had ended, three of those seven men—Clifford, Katzenbach, Bundy—had decided the United States should pull out of Vietnam. What new information could they have obtained on the outside that they did not have in that inner sanctum? Or had they simply relearned how to say no?

Like kings of old, modern Presidents do not appreciate their sharp-tongued Beckets and Luthers; knowing this, ministers who enjoy the companionship of Presidents do not try to prick their consciences. The preeminent example of this is the Reverend Billy Graham, the favored minister of Johnson and Nixon. Often during the Vietnam war, the Reverend Graham said that Jesus had been a hawk and would have supported the administrations' war policies; after that conflict ended, the Reverend Graham acknowledged that he had had "grave questions" about it from the very beginning. (*New York Times*, January 21, 1973.)

tial mountain retreat at Camp David were severely reprimanded for swimming in the President's pool. Perhaps he felt it was permanently tainted, for he later built a *second* pool for his personal use at Camp David.

Also reminiscent of medieval kings who took their retinue and scepter and movable throne and other regal gewgaws with them as they moved about their kingdoms, Presidents carry along the glitter of state on their travels. When Lyndon Johnson traveled abroad, he often took along White House china and crystal for entertaining chiefs of state. Nixon topped that on his trip to Rumania by airlifting not only State Department china, White House crystal, and vermeil flower bowls for the luncheon he gave dignitaries of that country, but also the White House maître d', five butlers, twenty-six stewards, and the all-American menu: Florida crab mousse, roast sirloin of beef Colorado, bouquetiere vegetables California, New Mexico tomato salad, New Jersey blueberries, petit fours, and demitasse.*

But even on a routine trip within the United States, just a little "get-away" trip to San Clemente or Key Biscayne, Nixon would consider himself untended if he were not accompanied by as many as two hundred persons, including his staff and their wives, his valet and dog handler, half a dozen Navy mess stewards, several chauffeurs, eight White House switchboard operators, and Mrs. Nixon's hairdresser. Gear accompanying him will include a couple of limousines aboard one of three big jets that go on every trip, a communications system that includes eighteen telephones and two teletypewriters, and a supply of Nixon's blood type. Plus food and toys and whimsical luxuries to pass the time, lest he be bored.[8] For every week Nixon is away from Washington, it costs the taxpayers an estimated $200,000 in travel expenses alone.

British observers are especially likely to see tufts of ermine in the White House. Henry Fairlie has written of definite trends in the Presidency toward "Caesaro-papism," which he called "the most refined of all absolutist systems." The specter of religious absolutism joined to political absolutism is an interesting twist.

* The Vice President travels regally, too. Spiro Agnew's around-the-world trip in 1971 was made in four 707s carrying 141 in his party plus 11 newsmen, with a fifth cargo plane carrying two bulletproof limousines. The trip cost $1.2 million. But who's to say it was ill-spent? African leaders treated Agnew to the spectacle of fornicating rhinos in Kenya and allowed him to feed sugar cubes to Gladys, a baboon.

Although tenuous, parallels do exist between American Presidents who on leaving office carry away tons of their sacred papers, around which they build self-aggrandizing monuments called libraries,* and the Pharaohs of Egypt and Caesars of Rome and Fathers of the Catholic Church who built pyramids and temples of various kinds to enshrine sacred writings, sacred relics, and sacred bones.

Nixon dreams of enshrining his earthly records (including, presumably, the secret tapes he made of telephone and face-to-face conversations he had with unsuspecting visitors) in an $8 million library—a dream momentarily blighted by the fact that Watergate seriously eroded fund-raising for the library and by the additional unhappy fact that four of the seven members of the library's board of trustees were either indicted by the courts or banished by Nixon for their part in the 1972 election skulduggery.

So sacred is every presidential word presumed by his coterie (a presumption often shared by the President, no doubt) that nothing is considered so trivial as to be cast aside. Thus on Nixon's visit to China, the White House press officials dutifully recorded for posterity, and Xeroxed for the press corps, such momentous pronouncements as these: on viewing the Great Wall of China: "I think that you would have to conclude that this is a great wall"; on viewing the mountains overshadowing the city of Hangchow, immortalized by Marco Polo: "It looks like a postcard"; on viewing through a magnifying glass a minute piece of ivory on which a verse by Mao Tse-tung was inscribed: "Art is my weakness." Experienced reporters were caught up in the apostolic mood to such an extent that when Mrs. Nixon said "Hi there" to a pair of pandas in the Peking Zoo, Hugh Sidey of *Time-Life* hastened to take down her greeting.

---

* Louis Heren, chief correspondent in Washington for the *Times* of London, related the result of this modern temple-building:

> The day after the [Kennedy] inauguration, when the new President and his embryonic staff arrived in the White House, fresh and eager to establish the New Frontier, they found to their consternation that the cupboard was bare. All the files had been emptied; not a state paper remained to suggest what had happened while they were campaigning, or when they were still in distant university common rooms or up on the Hill. All the papers had gone to stock Eisenhower, Truman, and Roosevelt libraries, on the monarchical principle that state papers are the personal property of the ruler's family. One can argue of course that it is nice to start afresh; at least there will be more room for the new President's papers. It is a charming idea, but it presents some obstacles to the continuity of government. ("The King's Men," *Harper's* [February 1965].)

But perhaps the truest note of "Caesaro-papism" is struck in the presidential pretension that the occupant of that office can annul words once spoken, can in effect obliterate an event. Two striking examples of this occurred in 1973. One had to do with the case of Ernest Fitzgerald, who had been discharged from his civil service job in the Pentagon after publicly disclosing a multibillion-dollar overrun in the cost of the C-5A Air Force transport plane. Fitzgerald, arguing that he had been fired without cause and that this was a violation of civil service regulations, insisted that he get his job back. The Pentagon, claiming that Fitzgerald had not been fired but that a "reduction in force" had wiped out his job, insisted that he had no claim to employment by the government. At his January 13, 1973, news conference Nixon said: "I was totally aware that Mr. Fitzgerald would be fired or discharged or asked to resign. I approved it. . . . No, this was not a case of some person down the line deciding he should go. It was a decision that was submitted to me. I made it and I stick by it."

This repudiated the Pentagon's contention that Fitzgerald had not been fired and, in effect, upheld his claim for legal reinstatement in the job. When somebody in the Pentagon brought this to Nixon's attention, he announced that in his previous utterance he had "misspoke"; that is, his words should be wiped from the pages of history.[9]

The most amazing job of obliterating the record came on April 17, 1973, when Nixon announced through his press aide that "all previous White House statements about the Watergate case are 'inoperative' "—thus wiping out, at least to President Nixon's satisfaction, the dozens of denials of White House complicity that he had made personally or through his press aides over the previous ten months.

If one sticks strictly to outward trappings and presumptuous "ego trips," one may construct a persuasive argument about the monarchical quality of the Presidency. But of his substantive powers, only one—more through tradition and the accidental attrition of congressional power than through law—approaches the absolutism of a monarch.

The Scepter in Foreign Policy

This is his power to make treaties and agreements with other countries and to make (not declare) war, or, putting them together:

his right to create foreign policy. Hamilton assured readers of *The Federalist* papers that

> the President is to be commander-in-chief of the army and navy of the United States. In this respect his authority would be nominally the same with that of the king of Great Britain, but in substance much inferior to it. It would amount to nothing more than the supreme command and direction of the military and naval forces, as first general and admiral . . . while that of the British king extends to the *declaring* of war and to the raising and *regulating* of fleets and armies—all which, by the Constitution under consideration, would appertain to the legislature.

That assurance lost its validity long ago. In the first year of our nation's life, there were less than one thousand soldiers in the Army and no Navy at all, so if the President had wanted to make war he would first have had to persuade Congress of the need to recruit fighters. But when the Chief Executive has a sizable standing Army and Navy at his disposal, he easily manages to get around the need for formally declaring war. Invariably a President who uses troops without consulting Congress will excuse himself with one or several of the following arguments: He will say there was precedent for the action—that for more than one hundred years other Presidents had done the same thing. (He will conveniently forget to mention, though, that military action taken by unilateral executive decision in the nineteenth century usually did not involve conflicts with foreign states.) He will say that he is operating under the nineteenth-century "neutrality theory" for the protection of United States citizens or property caught in foreign tumult. He will say there was a "sudden attack." Or he will say that he is acting under a "collective security" treaty with another nation.

Sometimes these excuses have chain reactions. When Lyndon Johnson sent combat troops to South Vietnam he invoked the "collective security" excuse. When he began the bombing raids against North Vietnam he invoked the "sudden attack" excuse. When Nixon sent troops into Cambodia without consulting Congress* he invoked, retroactively, a contorted version of the "neu-

---

* The view of the world from the level of the Senate apparently is quite different from what it is at the august level of the Presidency. When President Truman, without getting the approval of Congress as he had promised to do, sent troops to Europe to support our commitment under the NATO alliance, Nixon, then a senator, was among those who voted for and passed a resolution saying that "no ground troops in addition to . . . four divisions should be sent to Western Europe in implementation of Article 3 of the North Atlantic Treaty

trality theory"—that is, he claimed to have taken the action to protect United States citizens in South Vietnam.

Without asking for the approval of Congress, Presidents have sent troops into Southeast Asia, Korea, Lebanon, and into a dozen South American and Carribean island dominions in this hemisphere. Between 1798 and 1800 John Adams fought an undeclared, limited war against France. Jefferson sent our ragtag Navy after the Barbary pirates in 1801. Wilson, with no congressional authority, sent troops into Mexico in 1914. From 1900 to the outbreak of the Second World War, United States military forces were used in a dozen "expeditions" and "interventions."

Somewhat cynically, Major General Smedley D. Butler of the Marine Corps recalled this glorious period of our history in a letter to the editor of *Common Sense* on November 19, 1933: "I helped make Mexico, and especially Tampico, safe for American oil interests, I helped make Haiti and Cuba a decent place for the National City Bank boys to collect revenue in. I helped Nicaragua for the international banking house of Brown Brothers. I brought light to the Dominican Republic for American sugar interests. I helped make Honduras 'right' for American fruit companies."

When Truman took us into the Korean War in 1950, he did so without congressional approval. Eisenhower arbitrarily dispatched Marines to Lebanon in 1958. Kennedy, without consulting Congress, used the Navy to blockade Cuba during the missile crisis of 1962 and eased us into the South Vietnam war by a progressively larger commitment of "advisory" troops. Johnson continued the operation with enthusiasm. Additionally, in 1966 Johnson made a major, and subsequently much criticized, invasion of the Dominican Republic with 23,000 troops, without the consent of Congress. President Nixon, without notifying Congress, much less asking its approval, sent troops into Cambodia in 1970 and into Laos in 1971 to establish them as active battlefield extensions of the Vietnam war.

Again without consulting Congress, Nixon in the closing weeks of 1972 unleashed such a torrent of bombs on North Vietnam's civilian centers that even such a sedate Republican conserva-

---

without further congressional approval." The only President in this generation to adhere to the need for advice from Congress was Eisenhower; in 1954 when he was urged to send troops to South Vietnam to help the French, he said he would not do so without approval from Congress. Lyndon Johnson, then Democratic Majority Leader, and other key senators advised him against the troop commitment, and Eisenhower did not push it further.

tive as Senator William Saxbe concluded that the President "appears to have left his senses."* And without consulting Congress or many of his own White House advisers, earlier in that year Nixon decided to take the step Lyndon Johnson had shied away from as too risky—the mining of the harbor at Haiphong. In 1973, with the war presumably over, he launched daily bombing raids on Cambodia to assist the corrupt ruler of that nation—once again, needless to say, without notifying Congress of his plans. By that time Nixon doubtless felt accustomed to operating in Cambodia on his own. In March 1969, just two months after taking office, he launched a top-secret, fourteen-month bombing campaign in Cambodia that involved 3630 B-52 raids. Congress didn't find out about that little presidential adventure until 1973. Perhaps presidential decisions to enter new wars should be separated from presidential decisions to expand wars, but they are of the same arbitrary pattern.

Since the beginning of the republic, the President has interpreted his constitutional role as Commander-in-Chief in such a way as to involve the United States in more than two hundred foreign military adventures, only five of which were declared wars. Apparently this is something in which our Presidents take pride: hanging from standards behind the President's desk are more than two hundred streamers commemorating these military campaigns. Indulging a presidential whim to hunt pirates is one thing, but that sort of itch in the nuclear age can get a nation in trouble, and it raises an extremely relevant question: Is such power constitutional?

Saul K. Padover replies:

> The answer is that it is not patently unconstitutional. There is nothing in the Constitution that says that the President may not wage war abroad at his discretion. The Constitution merely states that only Congress can "declare" war. But it does not say that a war has to be "declared" before it can be waged. Vietnam is the culmination of this long-accumulating Executive power in the military domain. Where it differs from preceding Presidential commitments of armed forces abroad without war declaration is in scale—in numbers of troops committed, worldwide consequences and soaring casualties. There is obviously a considerable difference between the three small frigates and one sloop of war that Jefferson dispatched against the Barbary pirates in 1801, and the current deployment

---

* Nixon no doubt did not agree, but he apparently was not offended, for in the fall of 1973 he nominated Saxbe to become his Attorney General. Saxbe later corrected the quote: "What I really said," Saxbe told reporters, "was, 'He must be out of his f—— mind.'" (*Newsweek*, November 12, 1973.)

[of half a million men] in Vietnam. However, the principle of Presidential discretion in the use of force abroad remains the same.[10]

Many others, not so tolerant as Padover, would be inclined to agree with Henry Steele Commager, who testified before the Senate Foreign Relations Committee on March 8, 1971:

> Five times in the past ten years presidents have mounted major military intervention in foreign nations without prior consultation with the Congress: The Bay of Pigs, the invasion of the Dominican Republic, the attacks on North Vietnam, Cambodia, and Laos. None of these now appears to have represented a genuine emergency; none was in response to attacks on the United States which implacably required immediate military reaction. None therefore appears to meet the requirements for the exercise of war powers by the President formulated by the makers of the Constitution.

When strong Presidents are questioned sharply by Congress because of such excursions, they talk back just as sharply. Claiming that two United States destroyers had been attacked by enemy seacraft in the Tonkin Gulf, off Indonesia, on August 4, 1964, President Johnson sought and obtained open-end authority from Congress to pursue the war in South Vietnam in any manner he thought proper. Later, when it was discovered that Johnson had played up this highly questionable "encounter" with the enemy for no apparent reason but to obtain war powers from Congress, the Senate Foreign Relations Committee, feeling duped, summoned Undersecretary of State Nicholas Katzenbach to give an explanation of the executive department's attitude. Katzenbach, rather crisply and without the slightest sign of humility, informed the committee that the constitutional provision reserving to Congress the right to declare war had become "outmoded in the international arena."*

Knowing President Johnson's habit of looking over the shoulder of anyone who testified for the executive department, the committee members realized that they were hearing the saucy rebuttal

---

* On July 28, 1970, Katzenbach, out of office, appeared again before the committee, this time to urge repeal of the Tonkin Gulf Resolution, which gave the President full support for any action he thought necessary in the Vietnam war. In this way he hoped to take away what he now called the President's only legal excuse for being in Southeast Asia, thus repudiating his former argument. Which goes to show, perhaps, that the Undersecretary of State is used not for his brain but as a messenger boy. His brain is called back into service after he returns to private life.

of Johnson himself. And if they had any lingering doubts about it, Johnson dispelled them in a speech in Omaha when he said—referring to the constitutional provision that he seek congressional advice and consent in foreign policy matters—"There are many, many who can recommend, advise, and sometimes a few of them consent. But there is only one that has been chosen by the American people to decide."

In the same vein, Nixon through White House Communications Director Herbert G. Klein responded to congressional complaints about lack of consultation in 1973. Said Klein: "The President feels that he is fully accountable for battlefield tactics and he is fully accountable for negotiations and the key thing . . . is not whether you reveal it at a given moment but whether you reveal it at all. . . . It is simply not appropriate for a President to do things by committee. . . ."[11]

When Nixon decided to mine the Haiphong harbor and go hell-for-leather in the bombing of North Vietnam in 1972, he met with congressional leaders only to tell them what he had decided, in a Hannibalian style that closed out all discussion: "I've crossed the Rubicon. The die is cast." Hugh Sidey reconstructed the decision-making process on that occasion: "State and Defense and the CIA expressed their worries. But, locked in his own convictions, by Saturday Nixon was in his lonely crow's nest at Camp David writing his own speech. On Sunday he finished it. And though he held deliberations all day Monday, his mind was fully made up."[12] So much for consultation with the experts.

The exercise of executive prerogatives in militant foreign policy is increasingly the result of ideology—to "contain communism" or to protect our "vital interests" or to block the "international communist conspiracy"—and therefore more dangerous because it is explained by nebulous philosophies rather than, as so often in the past, by the clear (if questionable) desire to protect American lives or American property. And sometimes presidential explanations approach the surreal, as when Nixon explained why he had launched the heaviest bombing attack up to that time in the air warfare on North Vietnam, a nation without an air force: "They spit in our eye in Paris. What else can we do?"[13]

President Johnson argued that in the Vietnam conflict he was only meeting his obligations under the SEATO Treaty, but his spokesmen made it clear that a President does not need treaties to excuse his sending troops. Secretary of State Dean Rusk stated in 1966 that "no would-be aggressor should suppose that the absence of a defense treaty, congressional declaration, or United States military presence, grants immunity to aggression."

Rusk's use of the phrase "United States military presence" points up a further extension of the quasi-treaty powers available to the President. Aside from the regional and bilateral mutual-defense treaties that now oblige us to go to the rescue of forty-two nations around the world, and aside from the untold number of "executive agreements" with such noble bastions of autocracy as Spain and Libya, we have also made commitments simply by the presence of our military personnel and armaments. At last count, we had 132 major military installations in foreign countries. Half our troops are either overseas or are on ships at sea. Their presence is a promise, a treaty, a compact.

The practical relationship between nations can be measured in much the same way as the relationship between members of a family. If a man and woman live together and have children and share the perils of domesticity, this signifies a deeper commitment than does the existence of a mere marriage license (or domestic treaty). And, as a special report of the Senate Foreign Relations Subcommittee on United States Commitments Abroad noted in December 1970: "Overseas bases, the presence of elements of United States armed forces, joint planning, joint exercises, or extensive military assistance programs represent to host governments more valid assurances of United States commitment than any treaty agreement. The placement of nuclear weapons in a foreign country automatically creates—in itself constitutes—a new relationship between that country and the United States."

But to blame the President for the various methods by which we have become heavily entangled overseas is going a bit too far. Congress has been only too proud of the mutual-security pacts that proliferated around the world, under the presidential hand, since the Second World War. Even the seemingly extravagant extension of presidential powers through the war in South Vietnam was no more than the American people and their federal representatives had long been tacitly encouraging, or at least tempting, the Chief Executive to do.

Perhaps more to the point, he was only doing what the most important spokesmen on the Senate Foreign Relations Committee had encouraged. When the war in South Vietnam turned sour, Senator Fulbright hastened to argue that the Senate had been duped into the passage of the Tonkin Gulf Resolution. But in this argument we see the arrogance of contrived ignorance attempting to match, too late, what Fulbright has called the presidential arrogance of power. Like most of his colleagues, Fulbright has enjoyed the spectacle of American troops marching through other countries—so long as the excursion went well. In a lecture at Cornell University in 1961, with the Democrats just resuming control of the White House but before our military forces had more than a toe in the swamp of Vietnam, Fulbright argued that "for the existing requirements of American foreign policy we have hobbled the Presidency by too niggardly a grant of power." He suggested that the President could do a much better job of directing our military forces and deciding when to use them for "taming, or containing," selected enemies around the world than would "a decentralized, independent-minded, and largely parochial-minded body of legislators."[14] Cynics could be forgiven for concluding that the senator from Arkansas withdrew his support of that position in the case of Vietnam, not because of a reinterpretation of the Constitution, but because he simply was not pleased with the outcome of the latest presidential adventure.

Men who are more candid and more apt at self-criticism than Fulbright have begun to question their own roles in encouraging the Chief Executive to follow his whim in foreign policy. Hans Morgenthau says he used to "implore a succession of Presidents to assert their constitutional powers against Congress as long as I disagreed with the foreign policies to which Congress appeared to be committed," but that since 1965 "I would have welcomed the influence that Congress, the Senate or, for that matter, any other agency of government could have exerted in order to change the course of American foreign policy."[15]

When learned people have played along with the President in the old ad hoc game of armed interference in foreign governments, and when the supposed watchdog Senate Foreign Relations Committee has played along most of the time as well, the "strength" of the Presidency can hardly be held wholly to blame for things when they go to pot. This is a truth that has even begun to trickle through the consciousness of the politicians themselves. Writing with the new-found wisdom that comes to defeated presidential candidates, Senator George McGovern allowed as how it was all very well to talk about Congress's regaining its power in foreign affairs, but that

> if we are willing to concede the President dictatorial authority
> where we happen to agree with him, as liberals have tended to do
> over the years, we will have little chance of tying his hands when
> we do not. Examine the broad grants of power we pushed through

with a Roosevelt, a Truman, a Kennedy, or a Johnson in the White House, and you will see why many of us in the Congress understand how Dr. Frankenstein must have felt when *his* creation ran amok.[16]

Another assurance on which Hamilton missed the mark has to do with the President's treaty-making powers. The eighteenth-century king of Great Britain was "the sole and absolute representative of the nation in all foreign transactions," and as such "can of his own accord make treaties of peace, commerce, alliance, and of every other description." Hamilton promised that the presidential powers had been nipped far short of that by the constitutional provision that the President could make treaties *only with the advice and consent of the Senate,* providing two-thirds of the senators present concurred.

It hasn't worked out that way. In the first place, the formal writing of treaties has become almost an insignificant element in foreign policy. By the time an aggressive President gets through announcing policies (Monroe Doctrine, Truman Doctrine, Johnson's and Nixon's Asian doctrines) and making handshake commitments and agreements with foreign potentates and recognizing or refusing to recognize new regimes (which he has the power to do), the making of formal treaties is reduced to almost an antiquated function.

There is one other ploy available to the President, which Morgenthau has explained in this fashion:

> One-third of the members of the Senate plus one have the veto power over the foreign policies of the President insofar as they have taken the form of international treaties. The Senate has indeed made ample use of that power, the defeat of the Treaty of Versailles being the outstanding example. "A treaty entering the Senate," wrote Secretary of State Hay, summing up his bitter experience, "is like a bull going into the arena. No one can say just how and when the final blow will fall. But one thing is certain—it will never leave the arena alive."
>
> In response to this risk, a succession of Presidents have evaded this constitutional requirement by substituting for treaties executive agreements, which do not require the concurrence of the Senate. Furthermore, executive agreements have as much legal standing as treaties. Thus in 1939, 10 treaties were concluded by the United States as over against 26 executive agreements. The corresponding figures for the following years are eloquent: 1940: 12–20, 1941: 15–39, 1942: 6–52, 1943: 4–71, 1944: 1–74, 1945: 6–54; then 1963: 9–248, 1964: 13–231, 1965: 5–197, 1966: 10–242, 1967: 10–218, 1968: 57–266.[17]

Some of the most important foreign alignments and deals in modern times have been made by Presidents without consulting the Senate. Among the major early ones were the destroyer-for-bases exchange (Lend Lease) with Britain in 1940, the Atlantic Charter in 1941, the Yalta agreement in 1944, and the Potsdam agreement in 1945.

Occasionally the President throws the Senate a bone, while reserving the meat for himself and his personal advisers and sometimes for the State Department. A startling contrast of this sort was seen in the fall of 1970 when President Nixon concluded an executive agreement with Spain that extended some questionably valuable American base rights in that country in exchange for a security pact and many millions of dollars (the State Department was fuzzy about just how much money was involved). Meanwhile the Senate was being permitted to consider the trivial American-Mexican treaty for "Recovery of Returned or Stolen Archeological, Historical and Cultural Property."

The executive agreements are sometimes ethically questionable as well as functionally a bust. President Johnson secretly agreed to pay millions of dollars to the Philippines, South Korea, and Thailand if they would send soldiers to fight beside our men in South Vietnam, pretending to be volunteer allies. This was the first time in our history that the United States hired mercenaries. And how did these hired guns perform? By and large, they did not perform at all, or they performed so poorly as to be the butt of jokes. This inglorious agreement inevitably produced its shadiness. For $35 million the Philippine government agreed to send 2200 noncombat troops, but crooked Philippine politicians skimmed $4 million of this into their own pockets. As for the Philippine troops, they performed most notably as customers of the American PX's in Saigon.

The presidential broken-field running around treaties is pretty dramatic when described in statistics like those supplied by Morgenthau. Less dramatic but perhaps even more important is the whimsical way in which Presidents interpret treaties. One of our supposedly most respected treaties is the United Nations Charter. Article 33 of Chapter 6 commands: "The parties to any dispute, the continuance of which is likely to endanger the maintenance of international peace and security, shall first of all, seek a solution by negotiation, inquiry, mediation, conciliation, arbitration, judicial settlement, resort to regional agencies or arrangements, or other peaceful means of their own choice." The Southeast

Asia Treaty Organization, to which we also belong, restates the obligation to pursue negotiations by the UN formula.

Now, a treaty is not supposed to be taken lightly. In fact, Article VI of the Constitution commands that "all Treaties made . . . under the Authority of the United States, shall be the supreme Law of the Land." Yet Kennedy made no effort to negotiate the Vietnam trouble or to obtain arbitration from the UN or any other source before he sent troops to participate in the war. Johnson's record for avoiding negotiations was even uglier. According to Edward S. Herman and Richard DuBoff, in their well-documented survey of America's Vietnam policy through 1966:

> It has been firmly established that during the fall of 1964, prior to the escalation of the war by the Johnson administration in February 1965, Hanoi was ready to discuss and negotiate, but the United States twice refused outright. On one occasion it refused even to name its own terms. . . . North Vietnam responded both to President Johnson's April 7, 1965, call for discussions and to the bombing lull of mid-May 1965. Although Hanoi's counter proposals were rejected by Washington as unacceptable, United States spokesmen acknowledged in August that these replies were in fact a reasonable starting point for discussions.[18]

Despite President Johnson's publicly repeated offers to "go anywhere, any time" to negotiate with the North Vietnamese to end the war, there is evidence that at least until the last year of his term Johnson several times, either accidentally—if accidents can happen so often—or purposefully, escalated the offensive against the north in just the right way and at just the right time to disrupt what seemed to be promising peace initiatives.*

In foreign affairs there is endless debris of this sort to prove that when the President decides to operate independent of national rules and treaty restrictions, he simply does so. Furthermore, the Supreme Court helped to build an even higher wall around this dangerous presidential privilege when, in 1936 (in the often referenced case of *United States v. Curtiss-Wright Export Corporation*), it talked of "the very delicate, plenary, and exclusive power of the President as the sole organ of the federal government in the field of international relations," and conceded that in external affairs "the President alone has the power to speak or listen as a representative of the nation."

* For more on this, see David Kraslow and Stuart H. Loory, *The Secret Search for Peace in Vietnam* (N.Y.: Random House, 1968).

Note that the date on the court ruling is 1936—six Presidents ago. So the question arises: Why the sudden concern over the President's whimsical power in foreign affairs? Part of the answer, as already indicated, lies in the disastrous results of some of his recent decisions. But probably some of the answer also lies in the *context* of his decision-making today. Although past decisions may not have been any better, there used to be something comforting in the thought that the Department of State had a major part in making them. The good old antiquated, cumbersome Department of State, with its eleven thousand workers wrestling with red tape. It is said that instructions from the State Department in Washington to an ambassador overseas may require as many as twenty-seven signatures before they can be dispatched and that processing the message in a week's time is considered speedy. In that sprawling inefficiency, many see a democratic safeguard. When so many people are involved, they are bound to counteract each other's recklessness; if the policies that emerge from an eleven thousand-man department are not especially brilliant, at least most Machiavellian impulses will have been smothered in the crush. That, at least, was the comforting theory even in the days when John Foster Dulles, the last powerful Secretary of State, was in fact dispensing some dopey and dangerous policy.

In recent years, however, the State Department has been virtually excluded from the foreign policy decision-making context. Since the advent of Kennedy, that context has been reduced almost to the White House itself, with the Pentagon a necessary adjunct because of its specialized data. The centralization of the process is so extreme, indeed, that it has an undemocratic aura. The State Department under Kennedy fell into disuse; under Johnson its vitality continued to decline, even though he included Secretary of State Dean Rusk among his trusted advisers; and for the first four and a half years under Nixon the department became virtually a haunted house. Nixon made the creation of foreign policy a one-man show—one man, surrounded by his tight little White House circle of national security advisers under the direction of urbane, omnipresent Henry Kissinger. The Secretary of Defense could usually claim a place in that circle but the Secretary of State hardly ever.

If any occasion signified the new centralization, it was when President Nixon, in February 1969, signed the document that laid down America's foreign policy for the 1970s. At that White House ceremony Henry Kissinger was present; so were a dozen of his faceless assistants. But not Secretary of State William P. Rogers. Like a good scout, he was off in Ghana handling a routine chore. When Nixon visited China he took both Kissinger and Rogers, but while Kissinger and some of his aides sat in with Nixon at the principal meetings with Mao Tse-tung and Chou En-lai, Rogers was shunted away in tea-drinking ceremonies with second-level Chinese dignitaries. And in mid-May 1973, while Kissinger was in Moscow engaged in delicate negotiations with Soviet party leader Leonid Brezhnev and in Paris negotiating with Hanoi's Le Duc Tho, Rogers was off on a routine nine-nation tour of Latin America.

In the fall of 1973 Rogers stepped down, and Kissinger was named Secretary of State. Most observers interpreted this not as an upgrading of the status of the State Department, but as a further upgrading of the status of Kissinger and as a crystallization of what had become known as the "Nixinger" foreign policy operation. The real meaning of Kissinger's appointment was best indicated by Herblock in an editorial cartoon showing Kissinger and a female figure labeled "State Department" presenting themselves to a city hall clerk to obtain a marriage license. They were pushing a baby carriage in which rode a very large infant who was the spitting image of Kissinger.

The moral was quite sound. In taking his new job Kissinger was legitimizing not the State Department but his own foreign policy offspring. Kissinger had been privy to the secret—and some say unconstitutional—air warfare in Cambodia and to the secret Marine engagements in Laos that were carried out without congressional approval; he had been largely responsible for the misrepresentation of this country's position in the India-Pakistan war; and he had authorized, if he had not outright requested, wiretappings on thirteen government officials, including some members of his own staff, and four newsmen, all of whom were supposedly his personal friends. Yet at his confirmation hearings before the Senate Foreign Relations Committee, the senators seemed content with his assurances that he could not imagine anything arising in the future that would prompt him again to engage in duplicity and deceit in his dealings with Congress. Perhaps the reason the senators were willing to take that promise at face value and confirm his appointment was that by doing so they at last had Kissinger in a position where they could at least question him. When he had been on the White House staff, he could (and often did) hide behind that ubiquitous wall called "executive privilege." As Secretary of State he could be summoned to appear before the congressional foreign affairs committees. He might not tell them much when he got there, but he could be summoned. It was the kind of crumb that Congress had grown accustomed to living off of.

Of Restrictions, Resolutions, and Impeachment

By 1973 even many of the hawks in Congress were frightened and irritated by the presidential military escapades and all their seemingly endless variations. Something would have to be done, a majority of members concluded. So something, but not much, was done: culminating three years of effort, Congress passed a war powers bill requiring the President to stop a war started by the White House within sixty days unless Congress gives its approval by then. However, the new law allows the President to continue his war another thirty days if he feels it "necessary to protect U.S. forces." Within those ninety days Congress can stop the war by passing a concurrent resolution that would not be submitted to the President for possible veto.* It was a wobbly law, and perhaps even a dangerous one. Some critics argued that instead of limiting the President, it actually wrote into law powers that he previously had not had under the Constitution.

But Nixon and his advisers felt, in the words of the White House press release, that the new law "seriously undermines this nation's ability to act decisively and convincingly at times of international crisis." Nixon vetoed the bill, but for the first time in 1973 —after eight previous failures—Congress overrode a presidential veto. Those who shrink from the idea of limiting the President's war power are usually still smitten by the old romantic notion of gunboat diplomacy, the kind of diplomacy that President Truman relished. For a group of Columbia University students, he described one such incident from his own time in the White House:

> I heard—at least word came to my office—that Tito wanted to come to Trieste. I said to myself, "Oh, yeah?"
> I called in the Chief of Naval Operations and I said to him,

---

* These restrictions on the President's emergency war powers won the approval of none other than McGeorge Bundy, national security adviser to President Kennedy and President Johnson. There's no reformer like a reformed sinner.

"Admiral, how long would it take to get the Mediterranean fleet
into the Adriatic?" And he responded, "Three days."

I called in my Chief of Staff, Eisenhower . . . and I said to him,
"Eisenhower, how long would it take to get three divisions to the
Brenner Pass?" . . . and he said, "Three days, sir."

So I called up Tito, and I said, "You coming into Trieste?"
He didn't come.[19]

It may be colorful pageantry—Truman with his forces able to
strike in three days' time and ready to move at his command—but
it is rather primitive to think of coping in this manner with the
Trieste issue, one of the most hotly contested issues between
Yugoslavia and Italy. And even if this were the best course to
follow, it could have been carried out just as effectively with the
consent of Congress.

But as Arthur Schlesinger, Jr., has argued, futility probably
awaits those who try to solve substantive problems by structural
means—at least at this far remove from the Constitution's origin.
He, for one, sees more hope for reform in the dashing of certain
institutional myths to which Congress has contributed as much as
the President—the myth, especially, that the President must know
what he is doing and should not be challenged, because he has
access to intelligence and military reports that are not available to
the rest of us. Schlesinger recommends that we—including Congress
—stop being cowed by "top secret cables," for,

> as one who has had the opportunity to read such cables at various
> times in my life, I can testify that 95 percent of the information
> essential for intelligent judgment is available to any careful reader
> of the New York Times. Indeed, the American government would
> have had a much wiser Vietnam policy had it relied more on the
> Times; the estimate of the situation supplied by newspapermen
> was consistently more accurate than that supplied by the succes-
> sion of ambassadors and generals in their coded dispatches.[20]

And if the press's information is not better, it is often,
strangely, just as good as that available to the innermost councils
of government. During the India-Pakistan confrontation in late
1971, the highest level spy and military nabobs gathered to decide
on the United States' position in the dispute. Here were men like
Richard M. Helms, director of the CIA; Admiral Thomas H.
Moorer, chairman of the Joint Chiefs of Staff; General William C.
Westmoreland of the Joint Chiefs; and Kissinger. Some profound
plotting went on, no doubt? Alas, not so. When minutes of the

meetings were leaked to columnist Jack Anderson, the truth was embarrassingly plain: "Mr. Helms indicated that we do not know who started the current action. . . ." ". . . there are conflicting reports from both sides. . . ." Etc. The experts apparently had no better information about the war than the press, and the press acknowledged that it was dreadfully ignorant about the whole fuss. No such admissions came from government leaders, however.

Schlesinger's advice has been echoed by George Reedy, President Johnson's first press secretary, who told the Senate Foreign Relations Committee in April 1971 that the executive department's legendary information-gathering machinery is "basically a multiplier and it multiplies misinformation as well as information." Even a person who works closely with the President, he said, can never be sure "whether he is acting on information, misinformation, verified data, questionable data, or just plain hunch."*

But suppose precise laws were imposed on the President as to how far he could go without consulting Congress—what assurance would that give of genuinely restricting him? The evidence is all too clear, and too voluminous, that Congress will invariably submit to the President's every wish if he only trots out the flag in the name of "our fighting boys" or refers to mysterious enemies just

---

* Nor can the experts be certain when they are motivated more by the energy of involvement than by objective reason. After he had left the federal government, Adam Yarmolinsky, one of the resident intellectuals of the Kennedy and Johnson administrations, was asked how some of the nation's best thinkers could participate in planning that resulted in such a disaster as the Vietnam war. He replied, "Once you become involved in action, you are a less good question asker." When the liberal brain trust accepted certain foreign policy premises as inevitable, says Yarmolinsky, "That is when we stopped thinking like intellectuals." (*Washington Post*, February 27, 1972.) And stop they did, making them—because they operated under the pose of objectivity—perhaps the most dangerous group in Washington.

As for the President himself, there occasionally come clues from those around him that he is pitifully lacking in more than a surface awareness of what is going on in the world. Certainly he is in no unique position to determine, by himself, where armies of men should be risked. In an interview with Saul Pett of the Associated Press, Kissinger was asked how he found Nixon to work with in foreign affairs. He replied: "He is very systematic and thoughtful. When you talk to him about a country you don't have to explain where it is or who its leaders are and its problems. He knows it. He's probably been there. He has a feel about it. And then he chews the problem over and over." (*Washington Post*, August 23, 1970.) *You don't have to explain where a country is.* Far from being a description of a foreign affairs genius, that endorsement could not be counted on to get an ordinary person more than an apprenticeship in the State Department.

over the horizon. In recent years Congress has not shown itself able to withstand a President's argument that to give him less power in war than he desires is to "tuck tail" and "cop out." With no more than these catch phrases to support his requests, President Johnson recruited Senator Fulbright not only to back the Tonkin Gulf Resolution but indeed to lead the fight for its approval. The ease with which Presidents psych members of Congress into going along with their wishes was acknowledged by Representative Dante Fascell of Florida, a veteran member of the House Foreign Affairs Committee: "The sheer impetus and power of the Presidential commitment in a national emergency is well known; mix in the weight of the Presidential request to the Congress for the expedited consideration; sprinkle liberally with the equally well known attitude of the President's party and the Congress to 'rally 'round the flag.' Result—a predictable legislative approval of the Presidential action achieved in an almost automatic cycle."[21]

Its dismal record shows only too clearly that, having been stampeded into passing its responsibilities to the Chief Executive, Congress is painfully slow in admitting its error and even slower in trying to correct its botched jobs. Before expecting much relief from Congress, one should remember that not in modern times has either house reduced the budget for an armed action in which U.S. troops were involved, although congressmen are well aware that closing the purse would be the quickest and surest way to reduce the scope of the foreign adventure. Not until Nixon had withdrawn all U.S. ground troops from Southeast Asia did the House of Representatives timidly cut off funds for the administration's bombing action in Cambodia. This was one decade after the first U.S. bomb was dropped on Southeast Asia. All the horses having been brought home, the alert members of the House were then ready to shut the barn door. Understandably unintimidated by this action, Nixon's spokesmen said they would carry on the bombing raids with or without approval from Congress—and with or without specifically authorized money. On the Senate side, Mike Mansfield, Montana Democrat, mumbled something about this attitude raising a "constitutional crisis," but neither he nor any other senator seemed willing to engage the White House in a showdown fight over the matter. Consequently, the White House bluffed its way into getting congressional approval for a "final" one-hundred-day bombing orgy.

One possible way of guaranteeing that a President will not

run wild in his generalissimo role is to oil the machinery of impeachment and use it on the very next President who performs his duties grossly contrary to what Congress conceives as the national interest. Many will receive this as a crude suggestion; but there is really no reason why a job that the voters hand out on a regular schedule should not be taken back on an irregular ad hoc schedule when they dislike the results. No portion of the Constitution is fairer or more democratic than Article II, Section 4, which gives the ultimate power to change the government to the people through their federal representatives; it provides that "The President, Vice President and all civil Officers of the United States, shall be removed from Office on Impeachment for, and Conviction of, Treason, Bribery, or other high Crimes and Misdemeanors." That last phrase keeps the situation loose, since it can be made to mean just about anything you want it to mean. In the impeachment of President Andrew Johnson in 1867 for high crimes and misdemeanors, the House of Representatives was instructed to consider as a crime "anything highly prejudicial to the public interest," or "the abuse of discretionary powers from improper motives or for an improper purpose."

At the height of the Watergate exposé in mid-1973, President Nixon stated that he would take responsibility for the misconduct of those members of his White House staff who had been implicated in the buggings, burnings, and assorted dirty tricks of the 1972 election. Should that responsibility have resulted in his impeachment and ouster? If Congress felt that Nixon had helped cover up the scandal, would that be grounds? If he refused to surrender the secret tapes he had taken of conversations in his White House office, as the Senate investigators demanded, would that be grounds? How about his establishment of a secret security force within the White House, seemingly to usurp the statutory tasks of the FBI and the CIA? Or his secret bombing of Cambodia? Would his refusal to spend billions of dollars appropriated by Congress and specified by Congress to be spent in a certain way by a certain time appear to violate the constitutional powers of Congress so gravely as to call for his impeachment? Nixon's conduct has raised the question more often than that of any other President of modern times.

In 1970, Kenneth O'Donnell, one of the intimates of the White House in President Kennedy's tenure, disclosed in a *Life* magazine article that Kennedy had concluded by 1963 that our participation in the Vietnam war was wrong. O'Donnell claims that Kennedy intended to pull our troops out completely but meant to delay this action until 1965 because he was afraid that to do so sooner would hurt his chances for reelection.

O'Donnell's version of Kennedy's Vietnam intentions has not been confirmed by any other member of the Kennedy clique. But assuming for the moment that O'Donnell knew what he was talking about, we can reasonably ask: Had Kennedy lived and had his reasoning been discovered, should he have been impeached and tried? Risking the lives of thousands of American soldiers only for political gain—could this be fairly indicted as "the abuse of discretionary powers from improper motives or for an improper purpose"?

According to the *New York Times'* interpretation of the Pentagon Papers, "for six months before the Tonkin Gulf incident in August, 1964, the United States had been mounting clandestine military attacks against North Vietnam while planning to obtain a Congressional resolution that the Administration regarded as the equivalent of a declaration of war."[22]

But an emotional incident was needed. It was created when the U.S. destroyer *Maddox*, on an intelligence patrol in the Gulf of Tonkin, fired on North Vietnamese PT boats and received return fire (one bullet hit but did not damage the *Maddox*; it was hardly enough to escalate a war). This seemed to be a suitably sensitive area, so two days later the *Maddox* was sent back in, this time accompanied by the destroyer *Turner Joy*.

On the night of August 4, some members of the destroyers' crews thought—or said they thought—they were being attacked by enemy craft. No one actually identified enemy vessels on that pitch-black night. A great deal of shooting took place, but so far as can be proved, *all* of it came from our own ships. There is considerable reason to believe that the blips on the destroyers' sonar screens were as close as the enemy "threat" ever came and that the only serious encounter was with hysteria. Details transmitted to Washington by the destroyers' officers made it clear that they really didn't know what had happened.

Yet the White House—backed by the Pentagon and the State Department—inflated the encounter into a critical international situation. They were assisted by such willing suckers as the *Time* reporter who wrote (using data conveniently put in his hands by the Pentagon):

The night glowed eerily with the nightmarish glare of air-dropped flares and boats' searchlights. For 3½ hours the small boats [of the North Vietnamese] attacked in pass after pass. Ten enemy torpedoes sizzled through the water. Each time the skippers, tracking the fish by radar, maneuvered to evade them. Gunfire and gun smells and shouts stung the air. Two of the enemy boats went down. Then, at 1:30 A.M., the remaining PTs ended the fight, roared off through the night to the north.[23]

Most, if not all, of that is pure hogwash. The White House conveyed similarly inaccurate information to Congress, and on the basis of that information Congress, by a vote of 502 to 2, gave President Johnson carte blanche "to take all necessary steps, including the use of armed force"—and the main act of the tragedy of Vietnam was under way. Later, newsmen discovered that Johnson had been carrying in his pocket for weeks a draft of the total power resolution, just waiting for the right opening. The people, the press, the Congress were all tricked.

Does that sound like an impeachable situation?

The question is academic, of course, because not until Johnson had been out of office more than a year did the Senate even work up enough energy to vote its repudiation of the Tonkin Gulf Resolution. Yet weak as the voice of dissent was in Congress, it was stronger by ratio than the public voice of dissent; symbolically, voters turned out of office the two senators (Gruening and Morse) who voted against the Tonkin Gulf Resolution. It was the weak insistence from within Congress, not the public's even weaker complaint, that persuaded the Johnson Administration periodically to try a bombing pause. As late as the spring of 1968 the electorate was still urging Congress—by a ratio of 52 percent to 30 percent, according to a Harris poll—to pursue the Vietnam conflict, even if it meant ignoring the tragedy of the slums. The reason doubtless had something to do with the chilly observation of Dr. Arthur Burns, chairman of the Federal Reserve Board: "The military-industrial complex has acquired a constituency including factory workers, clerks, secretaries, even grocers and barbers."[24] Adds Jack Raymond, the former *New York Times* Pentagon reporter: "The military budget provides $6000 for flowers for American battle monuments. Flower growers, too, can be part of the military-industrial complex."[25]

In short, so long as the economy was booming (and there was an unparalleled run of prosperity during the Johnson Administration), it would have taken a foreign policy disaster of unimaginable proportions to turn the public—or its more shining image, Congress —to thoughts of impeachment on account of a war concocted by a President.

The electorate didn't resoundingly declare that it wanted the government to get out of Vietnam until the Nixon Administration (partly as a result of "winding down the war") had drawn the nation into its deepest recession in a decade, throwing some aircraft manufacturing cities like Seattle and Wichita into a real depression. In 1969 the hard-hat construction workers were beating up young people who dared to parade on behalf of peace. By 1971 the hard hats, many of them unemployed, were joining antiwar demonstrations. Not until they had the leisure of waiting in line for their unemployment checks did many people feel the shame of the My Lai massacre and pause to question the morality of spreading the war (into Cambodia and Laos) with the excuse of wanting to shorten it.

Since it hardly improves politics to denounce a President for doing something a majority of his constituents for so long considered to be manly and patriotic, perhaps we must come back finally to some vague far-off dream that—by education or voodoo or some other as yet untried method—the American people, the ultimate source of presidential power, will become less supportive of the worst impulses of our generals and hard-line diplomats.

Henry Steele Commager was right on target when he said:

> Abuse of power by Presidents is a reflection, and perhaps a consequence, of abuse of power by the American people and nation. For almost two decades now we have misused our vast power. We misused our economic power, not least in associating economic with military assistance and military with economic support, and in imposing economic sanctions against nations who did not see eye to eye wth us about trade with our "enemies." We misused our political power by trying to force neutrals onto our side in the cold war and by bringing pressure on the nations of Latin America to support our short-sighted policy of excluding China from the United Nations. We have grossly misused our political power—if it may be called that—by planting the CIA in some 60 countries to carry on its work of subversion. We have misused our military power in forcing our weapons on scores of nations around the globe, maintaining military organizations and alliances like NATO and SEATO —the first of which has outlived its usefulness, the second of which never had any usefulness to begin with. And we are now engaged in a monstrous misuse of power in waging war on a distant people that does not accept our ideology. . . .

As we have greater power than any other nation, so we should display greater moderation in using it and greater humility in justifying it. . . . In the long run, then, the abuse of the executive power cannot be separated from the abuse of national power.[26]

But the changing of the national character by lecturing to the people and praying for them to lay aside their ugly impulses is, to say the least, a long-range, almost metaphysical goal. Meanwhile, it will do no harm to inquire further into the question of how we as a nation developed such a militant frame of mind.

Cold War,
National Security,
and the Military

*Our government has kept us in a perpetual state
of fear—kept us in a continuous stampede of patriotic fervor—
with the cry of a grave national emergency. . . . Yet,
in retrospect, these disasters seem never to have happened,
seem never to have been real.*

General Douglas MacArthur, mid-1957,
quoted in The Military-Industrial Complex

When Soviet Communist Party Chairman Leonid
Brezhnev visited Washington in the summer of 1973 to strengthen
business ties with the United States and to take one more timid
step toward a modest disarmament program, he lifted his glass of
vodka and proclaimed, "So far as Russia is concerned, the Cold
War is over."

This was good diplomacy if not exactly factual. With more
than two decades of entrenched suspicions and innate hostilities to
overcome, the United States and Russia will need far more than

the flush of good feelings at a banquet to do the job. But the wheel of history does seem to be moving slowly, at last, after all those years of being frozen in a battlefield rut somewhere between Washington and Moscow. It's a nostalgic moment.

On April 25, 1945, American and Russian troops had met on the banks of the River Elbe and embraced. The two great powers of the world, allies then, had come together, severing forever the Third Reich. But within two years the governments of the United States and the Soviet Union were totally wary, viewing each other as the primary enemy. In February 1946, less than a year after the meeting at the Elbe, Soviet Premier Joseph Stalin spoke of the impossibility of peace, with the communist bloc threatened by "the present capitalist development of the world economy." To some, this sounded very much like the preamble to a declaration of war against the United States, which had emerged from the Second World War as the only nation strong enough to stop the Soviet's expansionary ambitions.

For the next dozen years—and especially during such periods as the Soviet blockade of Berlin in 1948—the possibility of open combat between the two countries was constant. So grim was the atmosphere that any proposal for dealing with the Russians short of nuclear war was hailed as moderate. This was the response to the anonymous article in the now-famous July 1947 issue of *Foreign Affairs* (subsequently it came out that the author was George F. Kennan, chargé d'affaires at the American Embassy in Moscow), in which it was predicted that "the Soviet pressure against the free institutions of the Western world is something that can be contained by the adroit and vigilant application of counter-force at a series of constantly shifting geographical and political points . . . but which cannot be charmed or talked out of existence." This proposal of mere "containment" rather than a policy of annihilation of the Russian people was hailed as the talk of a peace-maker.

By comparison with the way some other important presidential advisers were talking, it was. While the Soviet Union moved aggressively to dominate Eastern Europe, the United States began in 1947 to pour money first into Greece and Turkey (the first action under the Truman Doctrine to "support free peoples who are resisting attempted subjugation by armed minorities or by outside pressures") and later into sixteen Western European countries (this, the Marshall Plan, pumped $12 billion into the Western European economy in three years).

By 1950 Western Europe, which was impoverished at the conclusion of the Second World War and for that reason willing to consider communist plans for recovery, was fat enough to be content with its great capitalist benefactor. Through its financial aid, the United States had achieved a kind of sullen stalemate with the Soviet Union. Those in the Pentagon who urged that the United States launch a "preventive" nuclear attack on Russia—urgings that were still heard even after it was learned in September 1949 that Russia had discovered how to build the atomic bomb—were no longer able to get as many followers.*

The "containment" policy—although it was itself aggressive, tremendously expensive, and risky—was built around the hope that if we managed to stall long enough without actually going to war with the Soviet Union, somehow the passage of time would soften the Soviet heart and open the Iron Curtain, permitting the two powers to coexist in peace if not in friendship. There was much that was rotten in the containment policy: it rationalized our supporting any government, even the most inhuman right-wing dictatorship, so long as it was anticommunist; and it accustomed American leaders to sticking their "dirty, bloody, dollar-crooked fingers" (in General David Shoup's phrase) into the affairs of other countries. But for all that, containment was not a hot war. Although it was a policy that strengthened Europe by a threatening presence—the militarily well-equipped and well-manned North Atlantic Treaty Organization—it was mainly operative through economic assistance, on which the Truman Administration prepared to rely.

The Truman containment policy was not good enough, not dynamic enough, however, for President Eisenhower's messianic Secretary of State, John Foster Dulles. Dulles had promised

---

*In his book *Neither Liberty Nor Safety: A Hard Look at U.S. Military Policy and Strategy* (N.Y.: Holt, 1966), General Nathan F. Twining, who had served as chairman of the Joint Chiefs of Staff from 1957 to 1960, recounts how the National Security Council set up a national security policy, approved by Truman in April 1950, in which the concept of "containment" was reaffirmed. But this concept had some stiff competition, writes Twining, from those who advocated the "pre-emptive action" of clobbering Russia with atomic bombs, the theory being that "the world would become much too dangerous to live in if the Soviet Union were allowed time to develop a nuclear arsenal. While preventive war may be considered immoral, a much greater immorality would result if we were to allow our enemies to destroy our values and inherit the world." At that NSC meeting in 1950, says Twining, the hit-them-first argument "was presented and defended by some very dedicated Americans. However, the Administration ruled out this course of action."

through the Republican platform of 1952 to bring about "the end of the negative, futile and immoral policy of 'containment' which abandons countless human beings to a despotism and godless terrorism which in turn enables the rulers to forge the captives into a weapon for our destruction." For "containment" he substituted the policy of "liberation"—liberation for the countries within the Soviet sphere of influence.

Fortunately, Dulles' policy was more bluff than substance. But his publicly stated willingness to push diplomacy to the brink of nuclear war and let it hang there indefinitely instilled a tone of recklessness in American foreign policy that still is heard all too clearly. Despite the newly opened relations with Red China, including our support of that nation's entry into the United Nations; despite the continuing negotiations between the United States and Russia to reduce slightly the level of stockpiled armaments before both nations are bankrupted; despite the clinking of cocktail glasses and the exchange of smiles and diplomatic pleasantries in Peking and Moscow and Washington; despite the much warmer commercial ties between our big businessmen and communist bloc markets —the Pentagon's budget not only continues to increase but is excused with the argument that our two primary enemies in the mid-1970s are the same ones as in 1950, Communist China and Russia, that basically neither is any less of a threat than it was a quarter century ago, and that anyone who argues otherwise is teetering dangerously on the brink of treason. Long ago our military foreign policy was frozen in that chesty posture. Glowering and sullen and suspicious and armed to the teeth, the United States has met the communist bloc midway on the high wire of militarism; neither side is willing to back up, and there is no evident way to go around. If either shoves or strikes a blow, both will fall. So they stand there, flexing their muscles, cursing each other, but afraid to move. That is peace in our time.

It is what Winston Churchill, one of its creators, called a "balance of terror." According to former Deputy Secretary of Defense Cyrus Vance, who testified at Senate disarmament subcommittee hearings in 1967, if the Soviet Union unleashed its atomic might on us first, 120 million Americans would die. If we struck first, the Soviets would still be able to kill 100 million Americans. "Let me say simply," Vance concluded, "that nobody can win a nuclear war. Until such time as a practical and feasible disarmament agreement can be worked out, this balance of terror must be maintained."

Politics of Fear

Living in terror, feeling threatened from all directions, our foreign-policy-makers have responded in a way that is to them quite logical: they have planned for simultaneous attacks from every direction. It is impossible to say just exactly how long this has been the official assumption of our policy-makers, but at least we have it on record since 1964. At that time Secretary of Defense Robert McNamara admitted in testimony before the House Armed Services Committee that all preparations in the foreign policy field were aimed toward the contingency of an all-out conventional ground attack by the Soviet Union in Europe, a *simultaneous* threat of the same action by Communist China in Asia, and a small-scale intervention of our troops (a "half" war) in some neighboring area, such as the Dominican Republic.

Since our leaders think in terms of multiwars, it is inevitable that munitions-makers and generals have sometimes been our diplomats in fact. "The extent of military penetration into the civilian hierarchy after World War II was without precedent in American history," writes Colonel James A. Donovan (U.S. Marine Corps, retired). "In 1948, it was estimated that one hundred and fifty military men occupied important policy-making posts in civilian government."[1]*

---

* Presidential reliance on military advice in the making of foreign policy had actually begun shortly before the Second World War. Indeed, Roosevelt's strange enthusiasm for military guidance in foreign policy matters was so intense that it even made the admirals and generals uneasy. The Second World War saw the generals about as active in the diplomatic drawing room as on the battlefield. As Adam Yarmolinsky points out:

> General Eisenhower managed relations with the French regime in North Africa, and later he handled negotiations for Italy's surrender. Other American military commanders functioned with even greater political independence. Communication with De Gaulle was as much the responsibility of Admiral Harold R. Stark, the commander of American naval forces in Europe, as of any American ambassador. And in the Far East, General MacArthur, General Joseph Stilwell, and General Albert Wedemeyer dealt with the British Dominions, the Republic of China, and the Chinese Communists as the ranking representatives of the United States. Field commanders and their staffs had much to do with determining which foreign policy issues would be raised in Washington. The service staffs and committees of the Joint Chiefs recommended solutions. After the President made a decision, his instructions went back to the field commanders. From beginning to end, military men were involved in wartime foreign policy. (*The Military Establishment: Its Impacts on American Society* [N.Y.: Harper, 1971].)

Truman had so much distrust of the military that he probably would have put them back on the drill field where they belonged, but the Korean War once again made the White House feel it should counsel with the military on

Despite the frequent alarms sounded by prominent military leaders immediately after the Second World War that another conflict was imminent, the nation was tired of fighting and did not immediately respond. Colonel William H. Neblett, a former national president of the Reserve Officers' Association, who was in the Pentagon during this period, recalls: "Generals and admirals, colonels and captains spoke throughout the land at every meeting to which they could wangle an invitation. Reams of statements of generals and admirals for press and radio were ground out for them by the civilian publicity experts, employed at the Pentagon. ... The Pentagon line was that we were living in a state of undeclared emergency, that war with Russia was just around the corner."[2]

But this strategy didn't work. The defense budget was cut, and Congress refused to pass the universal-military-training bill, which would have ensured a permanent peacetime conscription to support the brass pyramid left over from the war. So a series of false alarms was prepared—and used with effective results.

First came an intelligence report from the Army that, as the *Chicago Tribune* related, "pictured the Soviet Army as on the move when actually the Soviets were redistributing their troops to spring training stations." Whether this report actually frightened Truman or whether he only pretended it did, on March 17, 1948, he went before a joint emergency session of Congress to demand action on the Marshall Plan and Universal Military Training and Selective Service. Although members of Congress were later privately told that the Russian build-up was a phony, the frightened impression left with the general public was never corrected, and the fires were stoked in April and again in June 1948 by General Omar Bradley,

---

foreign policy. Eisenhower, being a military man, was not in awe of them and in some ways held them at arm's length. Yet the influence of the military remained strong. For four decisive years, 1953 to 1957, the second most powerful man on Eisenhower's foreign policy advisory team was the chairman of the Joint Chiefs of Staff, Admiral Arthur W. Radford (the most powerful being Secretary of State John Foster Dulles). And throughout the 1950s and 1960s, writes Yarmolinsky, "the NATO command played a central role both in posing foreign policy issues and in championing particular policies," as did headquarters command in every sector of the world. The Defense Department has more personnel in military missions in fifty countries than the State Department has embassy and consulate personnel (the ratio is 8 to 5), and the military missions can afford to live more luxuriously. "United States ambassadors abroad," Yarmolinsky asserts, "have to ask for rides in the military attachés' aircraft, and State Department officials at home have to ask for rides in their Pentagon colleagues' official automobiles."

Army Chief of Staff, who said on both occasions that war with the Soviet Union was quite possible.* General Lucius D. Clay, American commander in Berlin, warned that war could break out with "dramatic suddenness."

The Army allowed its reserve ranks to wither; it set small quotas for the enlistment of minority races; it assigned thousands of troops to useless jobs in offices and kitchens, and in other ways did all it could to make it appear that its fighting strength had slipped to a dangerous low and that voluntary enlistments could not be depended on to supply the men it needed. Thus on June 24, 1948, a bill to extend the draft for two years became law. The nation had a peacetime conscription program thereafter, until July 1973, when the draft was shelved and a voluntary Army was set up.†

Of paramount importance in developing an atmosphere within the country that could make peacetime conscription possible was the announcement by President Truman on September 23, 1949, that "within recent weeks" the Russians had achieved an atomic explosion. Public reaction varied from jitters to panic. Newspapers contributed their share to the hysterics, and Charles E. Wilson, who had been recruited by Truman as Civil and Defense

---

* This and much other information relating to the early Cold War in this chapter depends heavily on John M. Swomley, Jr., *The Military Establishment* (Boston: Beacon Press, 1964).

† However, young men still had to register and the Selective Service bureaucracy was retained—just in case enough volunteers did not turn out to keep the military services at scheduled strength. The end of the draft was accompanied by an increase in personnel costs that threatened to sink the military budget. In an effort to lure enough volunteers into uniform, base pay went up radically —it was four times as generous in 1973 as it had been in 1964 ($78 a month in 1964; $332 in 1973). Yet there was so little interest in joining up that recruiters began cheating: falsifying birth records, falsifying jail records, falsifying school records—all in an effort to let undesirables or unqualified people enlist. That scandal was accompanied in mid-1973 by the discovery that the brass were grossly misusing many of the men they did lure into uniform: 970 admirals, generals, and navy captains were using 1722 enlisted men (costing the taxpaying public $21.3 million) as gardeners, baby sitters, bartenders, car washers—in other words, as their personal servants.

Experts also estimated that the volunteer forces, although costing four times more, were so sloppily managed that the Pentagon got 25 percent less combat capability for its money than it had ten years earlier. For each combat trooper, the Army had two soldiers in "back up" and "support" capacity, which was about as wasteful a use of manpower as the Pentagon could concoct. More to the point, the Army simply could not account for employment of nearly 22 percent of its personnel. It could not tell Congress *what* these 205,280 Army personnel were doing. (Budget appraisal of Senator McGovern, p. 37; *New York Times*, February 13, 1972.)

Mobilization Director, praised the American Newspaper Publishers Association at its 1951 dinner in words that candidly referred to the manipulation of the economy: "If the people were not convinced that the free world is in mortal danger, it would be impossible for Congress to vote the vast sums now being spent to avert that danger. . . . With the support of public opinion as marshaled by the press, we are off to a good start."

No doubt the nation's acquiescence to a foreign policy of terror can be accounted for by the fact that it was convenient and profitable for civilians at all levels to go along, applauding the permanent distortion of the federal budget to accommodate the military and placidly adjusting their lives to the first peacetime draft, the imposition of strictures in the name of national security, and the subjugation of academic freedom and free enterprise to military industry.

The Military-Industrial-Political Complex

Whether or not it was wise to encase our foreign policy so heavily in fear will never be known, because our foreign policy cannot be judged alone. The same fear that produced and cultivated that policy also produced and cultivated much of our civilian economy. The corrupt exploitation of the economy for defense purposes left most Americans unable to judge whether their foreign "enemies" were truly their enemies or were only necessary symbols for the perpetuation of a way of life, a way of defense, that they did not know how to get rid of.

With the end of the Second World War, the defense industries were faced with a crisis of influence, for never in American history had a war been settled without an accompanying diminution of the arms industry and of the military establishment. To counteract this anticipated slump, steps were taken to integrate the military with big business. When the end of the war was in sight in January 1944, Charles E. Wilson, then president of General Electric, told the Army Ordnance Association that the national goal must be "a permanent war economy," which could be best begun if every key defense industry named a special liaison official, with the commission of a reserve colonel, to serve with the armed forces. In the same year, Navy Secretary James Forrestal helped organize the National Security Industrial Association to assure a clublike approach to industry's dealings with the military.

Other associations included the Aerospace Industries Association. Every arm of the military now has its own special civilian alumni organization—the Association of the United States Army, the Navy League, the Marine Corps League, and the Marine Corps Association—which serve as powerful lobbies and as links between the defense industry and Congress.

But of course the establishment of intricate Pentagon-industrial liaison was not the end of it. A much more productive part of the arrangement was in the military's contracting for even that portion of weapons production that it had customarily handled itself before the Second World War; that is, not only did it now rely on private industry for the production of weapons, the military also turned to private industry to think up new weapons, to test them, to keep them in shape.

Adam Yarmolinsky, who was an assistant to Defense Secretary Robert McNamara, writes:

> Former Pentagon efficiency expert A. E. Fitzgerald claimed that the Air Force, which gained status as a separate service in 1947, "deliberately avoided creation of an in-house capability for the missile age because it wanted to create a big, well-heeled constituency of scientists, organized labor, and industry. It knew that such a constituency would push successfully to keep defense spending high and the Air Force in business." Whether it acted out of such Machiavellian motives, or simply for reasons of greater efficiency, the Air Force in the 1950s began to move far ahead of its sister services in the dominant field of aerospace weaponry, partly by brilliant development of this simple idea—later emulated by the Army and Navy—of nurturing a network of private research and development contractors whose "free enterprise" credentials look the curse off the lavish use of public moneys.[3]

Sufficient money to cement this liaison has never been difficult to obtain; seldom has there been even hesitation on the part of Congress to spend whatever the Pentagon requested, and more. If there is trimming of the military budget, it usually follows the pattern of the reduction made by the House Armed Services Committee in the fiscal 1972 budget—a reduction of less than one-tenth of 1 percent of the total requested by the Pentagon.

For a generation, when Pentagon spending has been discussed, it has been as a central element in our economy. In 1948: "If the international situation had not taken a turn for the worse this spring we would be inclined to take a serious view of the business situation" (*Journal of Commerce*). In 1951: "The defense boom is a guaranteed boom in spite of cut back talk" (*U.S. News & World Report*). In 1952: "A truce will make the predicted slide almost certain. . . . Failure of cease-fire efforts could be a stimulant" (*Business Week*).[4]

This, too, has for years been the open language of the politician. In a campaign speech at the Bell Aircraft plant in Niagara Falls, on September 28, 1960, John Kennedy said: "I think we can use defense contracts to strengthen the economy as well as strengthen the country. In any case if we are successful [in the election], we will try to distribute defense contracts fairly so that it protects the United States and protects the economy."

The General Dynamics plant in Fort Worth, Texas, where 10,000 were employed to produce the trouble-ridden F-111 fighter-bomber, was scheduled to close down at the end of 1971. Then money was slipped into the budget to keep the plant in production at least through 1972, an election year; the next year Pentagon officials admitted they neither needed nor wanted any more F-111s and intended to shut the plant down by the end of 1974—which would at least keep Texas politicians off the hook through one more election. The reaction to the new shutdown threat, as voiced by Congressman Olin E. Teague, whose district housed the defense plant, had little to do with national defense. "We have thousands of Texans employed in this industry and if the Air Forces stick to their determination not to buy any more F-111s after 1974," he grumped, "the unemployment rate in Ft. Worth is going to be pretty brutal. I have an obligation and a privilege to fight for full employment among my constituents."[5]

The political and economic—not defense—nature of so-called defense work was heavily underscored again in 1973 when Nixon announced that he was closing 40 bases and cutting back 219 other military facilities, eliminating 16,600 military and 26,200 civilian jobs over the following year. The move seemed to make good sense, considering that the nation, for the first time in a generation, was not in either a hot or cold war. But there was one strange fact about these cutbacks: two-thirds would have to be absorbed by Massachusetts, the only state to vote for Democratic presidential candidate George McGovern in the 1972 election, and Rhode Island, which has a solidly Democratic slate in Congress and which had given Nixon one of his narrowest margins of victory in 1972. Both states had severe unemployment problems already (Massachusetts, 7.2 percent, fourth highest in the nation, and

Rhode Island, 6.4 percent).* The rationale of Nixon's thrift emphasis in those two states was best seen by comparison. As *Newsweek* (April 30, 1973) pointed out: "Michigan—the home of Senate Minority Whip Robert Griffin and a number of antiquated military bases—came away untouched. And Pennsylvania's Republican leader in the Senate, Hugh Scott, almost gleefully took credit for saving the Philadelphia Naval Shipyard—and winning a net gain there of 1,000 jobs as well. 'I think,' said Scott dryly, 'that being the party's leader in the Senate was helpful.' "

There was another phony aspect of Nixon's "economy" move. The 30,000 or so civilians that the Pentagon claimed to be dropping from the payroll in fiscal 1974 were being replaced by 31,000 ex-soldiers as they became civilians; most of these men who participated in the byplay of just taking off uniforms and putting on civvies were, of course, officers.[6]

Insignificant adjustments in the defense budget have the power to create or wipe out small towns and to make even large towns respond in boom-or-bust ways. When the Army Ordnance Depot (530 workers) was shut down in Igloo, South Dakota (population 1700), several years ago, the community simply went out of existence. Other small towns have disappeared like this as the result of a scratch through some line in a military appropriations bill.

T. Coleman Andrews, former Commissioner of the Internal Revenue Service, told a group of businessmen in 1960, "If the Soviets should present a sincere and reliable proposal for peace, it would throw us into an industrial tailspin the like of which we have never dreamed."[7] With the defense budget now twice as large as it was when he made that prediction, the tailspin would be even

* Rhode Island Republican leaders felt just as betrayed as the Democrats, but their objections had nothing to do with national defense. Taking out a full-page ad in the *Washington Post* on May 23, 1973, James L. Taft, Jr., mayor of Cranston, Rhode Island and chairman of the Rhode Island Committee to Re-Elect the President, reminded Nixon that during the 1972 election the national Republican campaign committee had taken out newspaper advertisements in Rhode Island promising "vote for George McGovern and the Rhode Island Navy bases will close. Vote for Richard Nixon and they will not." If the President defaulted on that promise, Taft proclaimed, it could "result in up to 20 percent unemployment and the loss of over 10 percent personal income in the state." He talked of economic "disaster" and destruction of the people's trust in "our political process." But there was not one word in the advertisement about needing the shipyards for national defense—probably because it had been years since anybody in Rhode Island had actually thought of the bases in those terms.

more acute. The defense industry recession of 1969–71, as the war in Southeast Asia wound down, proved that clearly enough. At a midway point in the recession, Sanford Rose reported:

> The layoffs have hit with shattering force—in West Coast aircraft factories, in ammunition plants across the South, in electronics firms outside Boston. From the beginning of 1969 to mid-1970 about 500,000 defense-related jobs disappeared. From June, 1970, to June, 1971, another half million are scheduled to vanish. Dozens of communities are realizing to their dismay how deeply they are involved in the mammoth business of defense. The occupational dependency is also far greater than one would expect. For example, close to 40 percent of all physicists and one-fifth of all engineers in the country depend on defense work.[8]

When Congress closed out the summer of 1971 brawling over whether or not to guarantee a $250 million loan to keep the Lockheed aircraft company afloat, the proponents of the loan did not pretend it should be approved for security reasons. Indeed, Deputy Defense Secretary David Packard admitted in testimony before congressional committees that the company wasn't needed for that purpose. The only issue was jobs.

Charls E. Walker, then Undersecretary of the Treasury, welcomed the Lockheed loan on the grounds that by saving Lockheed from its own bad management "competition in the air frame industry will be enhanced and our trade balance will be strengthened." No mention of needing Lockheed for national defense, just for business and budgetary interests.

In an exchange with Senator William Proxmire, Treasury Secretary John Connally made the point with even more candor:

> Proxmire: Lockheed's bailout is not a subsidy, it is different from a subsidy; it is the beginning of a welfare program for large corporations. I would remind you that in a subsidy program there is a *quid pro quo*. You make a payment to an airline and they provide a certain amount of services for it. In welfare you make a payment and there is no return. In this case the government gives a guarantee and there is no requirement on the part of Lockheed to perform under that guarantee. A guarantee of $250 million and no benefit, no *quid* for the *quo*.
> Connally: What do you mean no benefit?
> Proxmire: Well, they don't have to perform.
> Connally: What do we care whether they perform? We are guaranteeing them basically a $250 million loan. What for? Basically so they can hopefully minimize their losses, so they can provide

employment for 31,000 people throughout the country at a time when we desperately need that type of employment. That is basically the rationale and justification.[9]

What do we care whether they perform? This has been the commonly accepted attitude in government for at least a generation, of course, but not many officials have been brazen enough to come right out with it.

Building a defense budget on the basis of defense needs—rather than economic needs—is a radical proposal. Indeed, when McGovern made that proposal a central plank in his Democratic presidential platform (with the additional conclusion that about $20 billion could be lopped from the existing defense budget without any reduction in real defense), he was denounced by not only the Republican opposition but also by many Democrats as a treacherous madman out to destroy the economy. None of his opponents denied McGovern's basic premise—that both the United States and Russia had enough nuclear warheads and delivery equipment to destroy each other several times over—but they denied that this was any good reason not to continue building more weapons.

Take the new B-1 bomber, for example, which the Air Force wants to spend $11 billion on and have in the air by the 1980s. There is a very good reason not to build it. In Russia today there are 1000 cities and towns of over 20,000 people. Military experts assume that an average of two nuclear weapons would be required to destroy each of these cities and kill 47 percent of the total population. This would require about 2000 nuclear weapons. Without the B-1 bomber, the United States would have more than 13,000 weapons in position to hit Russia, or six times the number needed to destroy the urban/industrial portion of that nation and wipe out nearly half the people. With the B-1 bomber, the United States would have over 18,000 nuclear weapons in strike position, or nine times the number needed. No sane person suggests that having nine times more nuclear weapons than we need makes us safer than having six times more than we need. And what if China were considered a threat also? The experts say that without the B-1, we would have three times the number of nuclear weapons needed to destroy both China and Russia simultaneously. With the B-1, we would have four times more than we need.

But building it would offer jobs to thousands of engineers, so the Pentagon will continue to press for it, just as it will continue to demand more money for, as the Federation of American Scientists describes, "the Trident Submarine (a premature effort to defend against anti-submarine warfare threats we cannot define), more MIRVed missiles (to penetrate a massive ABM the Soviets have agreed by treaty not to build), and R&D [research and development] for an ABM which we have committed ourselves by treaty not to build."[10]

These scientists and engineers are riding a tiger that they neither know how, nor want, to get off of. They are gripped by a paralysis of both training and will power. They are part of the enormous problem that would confront the nation if it ever took the notion that it would like to return to a peacetime economy.

This continuing crisis comes as no surprise to manpower specialists in the Office of Emergency Preparedness. For years they had been warning that the government should look carefully at the problem of manpower displacement before canceling any defense contracts, because the skills of defense engineers are so specialized that it would be hard to match the workers with job opportunities in civilian industry.

It is partly this forced dependency to which Dr. George Wald referred in his now-famous speech at the Massachusetts Institute of Technology in March 1969:

> I don't think we can live with the present military establishment and its 80-to-100-billion-dollar-a-year budget and keep America anything like we have known it in the past. It is corrupting the life of the whole country. It is buying up everything in sight: industries, banks, investors, universities, and lately it seems also to have bought up the labor unions.

The military establishment's purchase of the universities is best seen in the number of faculty engineers and scientists (25,000) who earn all or part of their income from the Pentagon. Seventy-five percent of all university research is supported by the federal government, and most of this support comes from the Department of Defense. Some of the younger scientists have attempted to break away, but the influence is so deep that Pentagon figures show its contracts with universities are still increasing, and MIT, where Dr. Wald voiced his criticism, leads the pack.

The Pentagon also purchases state government, and communities, in a manner of speaking. When Army nerve gas killed 6000 sheep in Utah, state officials voiced no great protest because the state earns $35 from defense activities for every dollar earned in sheep ranching. One of every three manufacturing employees in Utah looks to the Pentagon for his paycheck. Seventeen members of the National Association for the Advancement of Colored People (NAACP), including Louisiana Field Director Harvey Britton, were arrested and held for twenty-four hours without bond by city officials in Leesville, Louisiana, which depends on Fort Polk trade, for no crime except that, in the words of Leesville Mayor R. J. Fertitta, "Anyone who is not welcome at Fort Polk is not welcome at Leesville." The NAACP delegation, investigating reports of racial discrimination, had been turned away from the military base.

Increasingly, civilian authorities at all levels of government have come to tolerate and sometimes even welcome the military in setting the moral tone of the community and nation. Taking advantage of this, the Pentagon has assumed the right to enforce laws normally left to civilian courts (military tribunals have prosecuted servicemen for income-tax evasion) and has tried to preempt surveillance normally left to the FBI and state and local police. The United States Army Intelligence Command keeps a close watch on nonconformists in civilian life, and in this group it includes congressmen who vote liberal.*

Former Defense Secretary Clark Clifford was right: "Not too many years ago, the War and Navy Departments were concerned almost exclusively with men and simple machines. Defense industries were regarded as mere munitions makers. How remote that era seems!"[11] Today, the arms manufacturers and the military constitute an elite, and they have taken advantage of their new status by intruding into every important element of civilian life.

Pentagon Public Relations

If the military threatens us today, it is not in its cruel aspects (after all, it is safe to assume that cruelty will repel most Americans) but in its benevolent ones. The military is in a position to argue very persuasively that it does not take half the national budget to do evil but to do good. It can show that without the

---

* See the 1971 hearings of the Senate Judiciary Subcommittee on Constitutional Rights relating to Army surveillance of civilians. Also see Arthur Miller, *The Assault on Privacy* (Ann Arbor: University of Michigan Press, 1971).

Pentagon's continuing ambitions, the nation would be thrown into a deep depression. It can cast itself in a father image, pointing out that the benefits and services of the Veterans Administration are potentially available to 47 percent of the total population, and that it is the comforting mainstay to 4,900,000 veterans and survivors, who receive more than $6 billion a year in pensions and compensations.

The military can claim that a hitch in the service has given more people a college education or on-the-job training than all the civilian school-aid programs ever invented (8,420,000 Second World War vets, 2,391,000 Korean vets, and 3,500,000 post-Korean vets). It can even argue that the reason it permits 100,000 illiterates in the armed forces today is not to use them for battle but simply to educate them. It can point to the fact that the military alumni system has built the largest hospital chain in the world, which treats 900,000 veterans each year in its beds and receives 9.5 million outpatient visits. The military can also justify its system by saying that without a hitch in the armed services, the more than 7 million veterans who have bought homes since the Second World War on GI loans would have had to borrow money at higher interest rates elsewhere and might not have qualified. Indeed, so successful has the Pentagon been in altering its image that it is sometimes looked to as the model for running civilian social-reform programs. When Sargent Shriver was director of the Office of Economic Opportunity, he recruited many of his top people from the Pentagon and set out to copy what he considered the Pentagon's efficiency methods.

As extensive as the military's reach into foreign relations and domestic welfare is, perhaps the most damaging result of the ascendancy of the military-industrial complex is that we have, by not admitting the takeover, been forced into a series of national shams and into a distortion of our traditional concepts of honesty. At the least harmful level, the sham takes the form of describing our belligerent efforts as peaceful efforts. The Pentagon calls tear gas a "benevolent incapacitator." Massive bombing raids against North Vietnam, a nation without an air force, were called "protective reaction." When Melvin Laird was Defense Secretary he touted the ABM as "a building block to peace," and in his address to the West Point graduating class of 1971 he said, "Your mission, in a word, is peace." In his first Armed Forces Day address, President Nixon defended the military-industrial machinery as "the apparatus for peace." But this is such an old gambit that it is almost forgivable; it follows a precedent set by such venerable patriots as Andrew Carnegie, who contributed some of his war profits to the Carnegie Endowment for International Peace, which, in turn, was used to lobby for treaties that benefited his railroad. American politicians and capitalists have always had a hard time distinguishing between peace-making and war-making.

On a very dangerous level are the false alarms that are propagated to justify military-industrial activities. Those who desire to increase the defense budget apparently feel obliged to supply a new peril. Every presidential campaign and every new administration since Eisenhower's has been marked by variations of the same budget-induced bogey. The "bomber gap" of the Eisenhower years was followed by the "missile gap" of the Kennedy years, which was followed by the "megatonnage gap" of the Goldwater campaign, which was displaced by the "security gap" of Nixon's 1968 campaign. Secretary Laird was not in office two months before he noticed what his predecessor had failed to notice—that we were confronted by a new missile gap. Then in 1971 he began warning of what cynics called "the big hole gap," this being a reference to sixty silo holes detected by our intelligence agents in the Soviet Union and interpreted by Laird as "confirming that the Soviet Union is going forward with the construction of a large missile system."

This, of course, is merely a continuation of the scare strategy that was used to give the military budget momentum after the Second World War. The strategy is now so threadbare and embarrassing that even members of the defense establishment sometimes blush at its use. In this instance, after Laird's warning, Dr. Herbert Scoville, Jr., former Deputy Director for Research of the CIA, told the Senate Appropriations Committee in May 1971 that reality was perhaps not so dire as Laird pictured it, and in any event "we must ask ourselves how many times are we going to allow the 'weaponeers' to come before Congress, shouting 'missile gap' and 'technology gap,' when in reality they are only creating another 'credibility gap,' through selective disclosure of partially analyzed intelligence, in order to panic the country into expensive weapons programs."

Undeterred by such criticism, Laird cranked up a new gap in 1972—the "free world security gap," which was nicely vague enough to mean just about anything, and he topped it with a fierce warning that we were losing "momentum" in the arms race to Russia.[12]

This sounds all very somber and threatening, but actually it boils down to the old game of keeping up with the Joneses. Congressman Les Aspin, who was an aide to Robert McNamara when he was Secretary of Defense and who is now the most outspokenly critical member of the House Armed Services Committee, puts it this way:

> To avoid talking about how much is enough, the Pentagon talks about how much the Russians have or what the Russians are doing. If they have more, we have to have more. If they are building more, to keep our lead we have to build more. Never mind that we already have many times the amount needed for assured destruction. . . .
>   Sometimes this comparison game is difficult to play, because about 85 percent of the comparisons between the Soviet Union and the U.S. forces show us out ahead. It won't help the Pentagon to compare number of warheads, for example—the United States has 5,900 and the Soviet Union has only 2,500. Nor would it do to compare accuracy of weapons; our weapons are more accurate. Nor would it do to compare reliability; U.S. missiles are more reliable. So it is necessary to compare things in which we are behind. Megatons per warhead are one possibility because the Soviet Union is ahead. Thus, even though megatons are not very important (doubling the megatonnage will increase a missile's destructive capacity by only about a third), the Pentagon compares megatons. The Pentagon also compares missile launchers—the Russians have more. The Pentagon likes to have Congress play these comparison games, even though such comparisons are usually irrelevant.[13]

If it is any comfort, the leaders of the supposedly "enemy" nations go through the same absurd ritual. When Eisenhower was President, he was host to Communist party boss Nikita Khrushchev. One afternoon they took a stroll, and a conversation took place that Khrushchev recounted in his memoirs.

Eisenhower opened by asking, "Tell me, Mr. Khrushchev, how do you decide the question of funds for military expenses? Perhaps first I should tell you how it is with us. It's like this: My military leaders say, 'Mr. President, we need such and such a sum for such and such a program.' I say, 'Sorry, we don't have the funds.' They say, 'We have reliable information that the Soviet Union has already allocated funds for their own such program.' So I give in. That's how they wring the money out of me. Now tell me, how is it with you?"

"It's just the same," said crusty old Khrushchev. "They say, 'Comrade Khrushchev, look at this! The Americans are developing such and such a system.' I tell them there's no money. So we discuss it some more, and I end up giving them the money they asked for."[14]

When the secret Gaither Report of 1957 was declassified recently, it showed that the so-called defense experts on the panel headed by H. Rowan Gaither, Jr., chairman of the board of the Ford Foundation, had urged President Eisenhower to set in motion defense and civil defense programs that would have cost between $19 billion and $25 billion over the succeeding five years. The panelists warned that the Russians were way ahead in weapons technology and that all evidence "clearly indicates an increasing threat which may become critical in 1959 or early 1960." (It was this secret study that Kennedy used to clobber Nixon in the 1960 election, claiming that Nixon and Ike had allowed the development of a "missile gap"—a gap that was later revealed not to exist.) Fortunately, Eisenhower did not panic, brushed the study aside, and thereby prevented our plunging into an even more irresponsible arms race with Russia.[15]

The Pentagon has thoroughly intimidated most of those who would, or should, probe its books. The General Accounting Office, popularly supposed to be "Congress' watchdog," on one occasion refused to act on Senator Proxmire's demands that it study defense profits. The job, said the GAO, was too difficult. On a later occasion the GAO, discovering that the Pentagon had encouraged inefficiency and high profits by defense contractors, first submitted its findings to the Defense Department and to five contractor trade associations for their approval and editing suggestions, after which it drastically modified and softened the report sent to Congress. Nor does the GAO mind being lied to. The GAO sought information from 111 selected defense contractors, only to be told by 46 of these firms that they did not *know* what profits they were making—and the GAO let them get by with that explanation.

The GAO's lethargy is of mixed origins. The best description comes from Richard Kaufman, lawyer-economist on the Joint Economic Committee. The GAO, he says, suffers from "an advanced case of bureaucratic sleeping sickness, complicated by the fact that Congress has often not wanted a very energetic watchdog."[16]

For that matter, the Pentagon is just as arrogant when approached directly by Congress. From 1965, when the big build-up began in Vietnam, to 1970, the United States spent $150 billion on prime contracts, but Pentagon officials—when queried by congressional investigating committees—claimed that they had not kept a record of who made what profits. When pressed for answers to questions about profiteering industries, they replied vaguely that somewhere within the bowels of the massive Pentagon building, scattered here and there, were the figures that could supply the answers, but nobody has compiled them. This sort of reply quite effectively keeps investigators away.

The House Banking and Currency Committee learned in 1968 that it is quite customary for defense contractors to lie to the government about their profits. One company that said it earned only 4.5 percent profits had actually earned 10 percent; another reported 12.5 percent profits but actually had earned 19.5 percent; and another reported a 2 percent *loss* when it had earned a 15 percent profit. The government levies no penalties for this kind of misinformation.

Waste has become so abundant in the military that it is becoming difficult to tell the difference between waste that is due to stupidities and waste that is due to crookedness; both kinds add up to a grotesquery that would almost be funny if it were not so dangerous. Greed has set the defense industry on its head: a standard fighter in the late 1940s cost $400,000; today it costs $9 million. A standard tank in the early 1940s cost $125,000; today it costs $900,000. Even the most hawkish of congressmen, ordinarily willing to go along with any defense expenditures, have begun to worry about whether, at the rate prices are going up, we will be able to afford defense in a few years. As one expressed his fears to the *Wall Street Journal* (December 27, 1971): "We're pricing ourselves out of our strategies. We could wind up having an Army with one tank, a Navy with one ship and an Air Force with one plane."

Meanwhile, however, such fears have not restored sanity. In 1973 Senator Proxmire released a list of defense contractors who had distinguished themselves by profiteering; some profits ranged up to 1902.7 percent return on the company's net worth. On a more modest scale, there were outfits like Norris Industries Inc. of Los Angeles, which makes rockets, rocket launchers, high explosive artillery projectiles, mine systems, and demolition bombs; it was caught gouging the government and was forced to give back $2 million.

Even so it came out of its defense work for the year with a 71 percent profit. Of the 131 defense firms on the list, 94 walked away, with profits exceeding 50 percent of their net worth; 49 made over 100 percent profits; 22 made over 200 percent; and 4 of the defense contractors made over 500 percent profit on net worth.[17]

Much of the waste could be removed by the simple technique of opening defense work to competition. Most defense contracts are awarded by "negotiation"—a euphemism meaning that the Defense Department works out a deal with cronies in the industry— rather than by competitive bidding. What this means to the economy was shown in a 1973 study made by the Center for Defense Information. It found that under a negotiated contract with the Defense Department, General Dynamics Corporation was paid $128,005 for each Standard missile it built in 1966. But the next year General Dynamics had to face competitive bidding to get the contract, and the price fell to $53,921 per unit.

We tend not to see ourselves and our economy as corrupt, however, because as Bert Cochran has written in *The War System:*

> The war economy has a diabolical comfortableness about it that slowly submerges almost every part of the population in a euphoric stupor. Where the strong brews of patriotism and national honor keep the man in the street reconciled to high taxes and enormous financial outlays for military spending, he would resist, with all the righteous indignation bred of years of mass-media conditioning, comparable government spending for "bleeding heart causes" and "egghead welfare boondoggling." Missiles, planes and bombs mean jobs; schoolhouses, scholarships and hospitals mean only more taxes and bureaucracy. . . . The beauty of the military system is that it is the kind of sheer waste which dovetails perfectly with the rest of the economy; the hardware and gadgets that come out of the laboratories and plants compete with no civilian products, do not interfere with the private corporation's patent rights and do not accumulate the kind of inventories that retard continued production. When the munitions do not get used in war, they quickly become obsolete and are junked or sold at knock-down prices or given away to our clients. There are no surpluses, and the demand is inexhaustible.[18]

The Machinery of Cold War

While the nation was busy corrupting itself with the fruits of military industrialization, it was in no mood to object to—much less to challenge—the international machinery of the Cold War that was being established at the same time. The machinery was set up with the approval of Congress, but by and large it was under the control of the executive branch—to the extent that *anyone* in government controlled it.

As early as 1945 the purpose of the machinery was being openly stated by top officials in the executive branch. Navy Secretary James Forrestal urged the "immediate integration" of the War, Navy, and State departments to enable the nation "to act as a unit in terms of its diplomacy, its military policy, its use of scientific knowledge, and finally, of course in its moral and political leadership of the world." If the words—especially the pious last phrase—sounded uncomfortably similar to the cant that had marked the German Third Reich, which the United States was in the process of dismantling, at least Forrestal's statement had the virtue of candor.

With the passage of the National Security Act of 1947, the Army, Navy, and Air Force were brought under a National Military Establishment, which was converted into the Department of Defense two years later. The same act brought into being those cloudy agencies—the Central Intelligence Agency, the National Security Council, the National Security Agency—that bridged both military and diplomatic services and created a force entirely new to the American experience. In the words of the 1947 act, the National Security Council was to "advise the President with respect to the integration of domestic, foreign, and military policies relating to the national security." Thus the military was wedded permanently to civilian diplomacy and, in fact, made preeminent. With the National Security Act the government gave its heart to the spooks, the spies, the underhanded wheelers and dealers in foreign affairs, to the CIA, the Army Intelligence, the Navy Intelligence, the Air Force Intelligence, the State Department's Bureau of Intelligence and Research—agencies that David Wise and Thomas Ross called the Invisible Government and described in a book by that name.[19]

"An informed citizen might come to suspect," they pointed out, "that the foreign policy of the United States often works publicly in one direction and secretly through the Invisible Government in just the opposite direction." And one reason for the efficiency of the secret maneuvering is, in the words of former CIA director Allen W. Dulles, that "the National Security Act of

1947 has given Intelligence a more influential position in our government than Intelligence enjoys in any other government in the world."

Intelligence in this context cannot be limited to spies and undercover agents; whatever names its members go by, the intelligence network must include most international policy-makers, lobbyists, and manipulators who work beyond the control of Congress and, sometimes it seems, beyond the control even of the President. Occasionally they operate through the more standard agencies, such as the Agency for International Development (AID), or through the orthodox military services. Their identifiable characteristic is that they are political outlaws, not in the romantic sense but in the extremely dangerous sense that they are not accountable to the American electorate.

Books have been written about the CIA, but not much is actually known of its activities. It has successfully fought off every effort by Congress to oversee its work seriously. Its costs are scattered throughout the budgets of other agencies and disguised in that way. Nobody knows how many people are employed by the CIA. Secrecy begets wild guesses; a reporter for the British Broadcasting Corporation estimated that the CIA employs 100,000 persons to gather and interpret data about the Soviet Union alone—an exaggeration, no doubt, yet who can say for sure. As for the CIA's budget, the best-informed guessers place it at somewhere between $750 million and $1 billion. In 1973, Senator Proxmire pulled together from a number of expert sources an estimate of the entire cost and size of the U.S. intelligence community: more than 148,000 persons spending approximately $6.2 billion each year. This would include, by his guess, $750 million for 15,000 personnel in the CIA; 20,000 persons and $1 billion for the National Security Agency; 5016 persons and $110 million for the Defense Intelligence Agency; 38,500 persons and $775 million for Army Intelligence; 10,000 persons and $775 million for Navy Intelligence; 60,000 persons and $2.8 billion for Air Force Intelligence; and 335 persons and $8 million for State Department Intelligence.[20]

Does the United States need quite so many people in the spying game? The activities of the CIA lead one to doubt, perhaps because the CIA is given such an undemocratically free hand in how it spends its money. Its overzealousness has included bribing foreign officials as well as subsidizing foreign armies, assassins, and revolutionaries. Not even the President can be sure how the CIA is spending its time and money—until something embarrassing comes to light. The Watergate scandals showed the ultimate in the CIA's irresponsibility: helping to train and equip burglars for political espionage within the United States. That activity not only violates local laws against the specific crimes but also violates federal statutes that prohibit the CIA from practicing its dirty tricks on the domestic scene.

The kind of ghostly guessing game that surrounds the CIA is well illustrated by Vice President Agnew's remark, in an interview on Metromedia News, that he was sure Cambodia's Prince Sihanouk had not been ousted with the help of the United States. "I'm positive that that did not happen," he said, "and the reason I'm so sure is that we didn't have any CIA people in the country."[21] He wasn't trying to be funny. History has shown what the presence of the CIA in a country can mean. The Congressional Quarterly's *Congress and the Nation* recounts:

> The CIA was credited with a hand in supplying Chinese Nationalist troops in Burma in 1950–54; in bringing down Iran's Premier Mossadegh in 1953 and the Arbenz regime in Guatemala in 1954; and in supporting the right-wing Nosavan regime in Laos in 1960. CIA's most spectacular success came to light as the result of a sensational failure: the shooting down of Francis Gary Powers in mid-Russia in May 1960 put an end to four years of aerial reconnaissance over the USSR by high-flying U-2s. CIA's most publicized failure came in April 1961 when Fidel Castro crushed an Agency-organized invasion of Cuba by rebel forces at the Bay of Pigs.[22]

Others have reported CIA activities—armed intervention, disruption of labor unions, propaganda attacks, kidnapping, sabotage, spying, planned invasions, support for one regime, opposition to another—in British Guiana, France, Italy, Brazil, the Dominican Republic, Bolivia, the Congo, Nigeria, and on and on. All over the globe. But to what extent, and by whose order, and to what end— who can be sure? Although it had been an open secret for years, not until 1971, when it was disclosed by Senator Clifford Case, did the nation find out it had spent "hundreds of millions of dollars" through the CIA to support two major propaganda outlets, Radio Free Europe and Radio Liberty, over the past twenty years. In 1970, John A. Hanna, administrator of the Agency for International

Development, publicly admitted that at least since 1962 CIA agents had used AID as a cover for their operations in Southeast Asia. Millions of dollars allegedly spent on "refugee aid—medical supplies, hospitals, resettlement" were actually paid to guerrilla forces directed by the CIA.

Some of the CIA's paid involvement in wars exceeds normal imagination. In the messy withdrawal of the United States from Southeast Asia, the CIA paid Laotian pilots *not* to fly combat missions and paid the salaries of nonexistent Cambodian soldiers—all in the name of "winding down" the war—while at the same time acceding to blackmail demands from local warlords who might, if allowed to follow their instincts, somehow trigger a conflict that would drag us back in. Screwball though it might seem, in this instance the CIA's money was actually working for peace.[23]

In 1966 and 1967 *The Nation* and *Ramparts* disclosed that the CIA had for years been secretly channeling money for its work through the National Students Association, the AFL–CIO, the Newspaper Guild, and a host of other seemingly "innocent" outlets. Most of this activity has been aimed at creating the CIA's own "foreign policy"—whatever the CIA interprets that to mean. In its work with the AFL–CIO overseas, and especially in Latin America, this means suppressing liberal labor unions. In some countries it means creating a "friendlier" atmosphere for United States corporations with investments there. "After the CIA-sponsored overthrow of Jacob Arbenz in Guatemala," writes Sidney Lens, "U.S. private investment spurted sensationally. But a recent report—15 years later—of social conditions shows that three-quarters of the people live on what the U.N. considers a 'below starvation level,' three-quarters are illiterate, four-fifths lack adequate drinking water facilities or toilets, one-fifth of the children die before they reach the age of five."[24]

Arms Peddling

At a White House press conference on March 15, 1973, an exchange took place between President Nixon and correspondent Sarah McClendon that rather accurately conveys the disturbing callousness that the government has shown for a generation in its distribution of weapons around the world:

McClendon: Mr. President, I want to ask you about peace. You have concentrated on peace in your Administration. Don't you find an inconsistency there with continuing to give arms to India and Pakistan and perhaps a hundred other countries around the world?

Nixon: First, we are not giving them, we are selling them.

McClendon: Isn't that worse? That is even worse.

Nixon: I just wanted to be sure that we understood the difference, because of all the concern about aid. . . . All we are trying to do is to seek good relations with both, and we trust in the future that our aid to both can be ones that will turn them towards peace rather than war. . . .[25]

The rationale of seeking friendship and peace by distributing weapons may be a bit difficult to follow, but it is the kind of reasoning the government has been following for a long time. The program promotes a considerable amount of distorted and underhanded militarism passed off as "economic assistance." In 1971 the General Accounting Office discovered that during the previous five years about $700 million ostensibly spent in the Food for Peace Program for what the name implies—food—was actually spent on military arms in a dozen countries, primarily South Vietnam and Korea. Did that disclosure stop the practice? Not at all. The next year it was discovered that of $919.8 million supposedly to be spent on U.S. farm commodities by South Vietnam under Food for Peace, $742.7 million was kicked back to the Saigon government to use for "common defense" purposes; Korea was playing the same game with $20 million in food money, and Cambodia with $7.4 million. In fiscal year 1973 a total of $124 million in "food" money was going to arm our supposedly underprivileged allies around the world.[26]

The people who write up the federal budget try to keep our military aid program as disguised and hidden as possible. As the Center for Defense Information has pointed out:

We spend about $9.5 billion on military aid each year but nowhere in the budget do you find that dollar figure; it is spread around under 17 separate programs administered by several agencies and financed by various appropriations acts. About $2 billion is tucked away under the Foreign Assistance bill, and another $3 billion is buried in the Defense Budget; as for the other $4 billion-plus, it does not require Congressional authorization and is therefore virtually invisible. . . . The Pentagon runs these programs with little oversight by Congress or by any other Executive Agency, including the State Department.[27]

On those few occasions when Congress, in a timid fashion, tries to restrict the distribution of weapons to other countries, the Pentagon simply ignores the effort and distributes the arms anyway. The General Accounting Office found that much of the $38.3 billion in arms aid to sixty-five foreign countries between 1965 and 1973 had flowed "through pipelines outside the regular funded programs."[28] Congress simply did not know what was happening.

One of the odd channels for arms peddling is the Export-Import Bank, which in 1968 was discovered to be up to its cash register in this market. The impact of this discovery was about what would be felt if the Women's Christian Temperance Union was caught selling bootleg whiskey. For a generation the ExIm Bank had had the reputation of an organization devoted entirely to financing international projects of a civil kind—steam plants, commercial airlines, auto manufacturing plants, and the like. But arms? *Never.*

Or so we thought, until 1968. The corruption of the ExIm Bank came about like this:

As the global arms race gathered a critical momentum, and United States equipment was being found on both sides of flare-ups in every sector of the world, opposition to arms sales and gifts stiffened in Congress.* This opposition became especially acute about 1965, when it became apparent that the United States was imbedded in a war in Vietnam from which it would not soon be extricated. Not only the doves in Congress but also some hawks—including the likes of Senators Stuart Symington and Richard Russell—warned against the United States taking on the role of "policeman to the world" and of peddling arms so indiscriminately as to encourage flare-ups that might demand our policing them.

The efforts of these congressional critics went beyond mere complaining; some effective reduction of military assistance was

---

* Another constant irritant with some members of Congress has been the favoring of right-wing dictatorships: Greece, Spain, Portugal, Brazil, Haiti, and so on. If oppressive ideologies do not repel our federal arms distributors, neither does the most grotesque cruelty. After the government of Pakistan had killed an estimated 200,000 "rebellious" citizens of East Pakistan in 1971 and had driven another 6 million or so into exile, our government continued shipments of weapons to the Pakistani army.

Of the sixty-four countries receiving U.S. military aid in 1973, twenty-seven were run by governments that permitted no political opposition. In short, they are dictatorships. When then-Secretary of Defense Laird was criticized by some congressmen for giving aid to a number of South American dictators who suppressed leftist opposition, Laird gave this excuse: "I think it is important for us to bear in mind that the military is the only cohesive group in accomplished in 1965 and 1966, and there were a number of signs at that time to indicate that the antiarms cadre within Congress would be increasingly successful with each coming session. (As it turned out, however, this was a mistaken expectation.)

Against this background, the militarists within the government went to work. Just to make sure that there would be an alternate way in case they ran into a roadblock using the old method of dispensing arms around the world, a method that cut a rather direct route through visible congressional authorization, they decided to arrange a sly, secret route around the congressional troublemakers. They went via the Export-Import Bank, and, as noted, the militarists could not have chosen a less suspicious machinery for continuing their arms traffic.

By the time the ExIm Bank was caught participating in this mischief, it had helped peddle more than $1 billion in arms to major nations and more than $600 million to "developing" nations.* The ExIm's part in the arms race began in 1962 with the financing of arms for both Austria and Italy at a time when those two countries were arguing over the South Tyrol. It was like selling gasoline and matches to two pyromaniacs; at least the State Department seemed to think so, for it was confidentially advising congressmen not to travel in that part of the world at that time. But the ExIm's real plunge came in 1965, and before the bankers were through spreading their credit, they had financed arms for Israel, Jordan, Saudi Arabia, Morocco, Iran, Pakistan, India, Malaysia, Formosa, Argentina, Brazil, Chile, Peru, Venezuela, Australia, Britain, and New Zealand.

There are some strange combinations in that group. Pakistan and India are enemies; we sold to both. And while the State Department publicly favored the cause of Israel, the Department of Defense (through the ExIm Bank) was doing what it could to help the Arab side, too. Either the two departments were working

---

many of the countries of Latin America and that they are very important." (*Washington Post*, April 7, 1971.)

The most notorious example of U.S. military aid is, of course, in South Vietnam, where the government not only refuses to permit a free press and free speech but also tortures political prisoners and engages in drug traffic on the international market. Our explanation for continuing aid to South Vietnam is that the government is "anticommunist."

* The Pentagon "vouched" for the credit of the latter nations, since they were too poor to get arms otherwise.

at cross purposes, or "foreign policy" was being subverted for the cause of the dollar.

It might be the latter. The emphasis on profit is quite open. In defending the ExIm arms financing, Deputy Defense Secretary Paul Nitze testified at a House Banking Committee hearing, "We have found that such sales [not just those through ExIm, but all arms sales] provided about 1.4 million man-years of employment in the U.S. over the past five years and over $1 billion in profits to industry over the same five-year period of time."

The end of the ExIm saga is that the bankers promised Congress that they would stop helping the Pentagon to peddle its arms. Of course, one must always be willing to assume that this promise has since been voided. Indeed, there is so much duplicity and lying in the government's arms aid that it is difficult for the managers to keep from tripping on their own devices. In January 1971, the Defense Department announced a figure for arms aid that was about *eight times* the amount formally listed in the President's budget for military aid. There was a note of black humor at the congressional hearing that received this confession (or mistake, or both; nobody knows). Senator William Proxmire asked the Defense Department witnesses for the total spent on military assistance. One Pentagon lobbyist grabbed a pencil and began working furiously. "Seven billion, three-hundred-thirty-nine million. . . ." Oops. He didn't get to finish the sentence. His boss, Armistead Selden, Deputy Assistant Secretary of Defense for International Security Affairs, cut him off with a "that's not right, that's not correct." So for two and a half hours the Pentagon officials sat there figuring and arguing, and they never did come up with a figure that everyone could agree on.

Our arms are scattered around the globe in such a loose arrangement that officials concede they have no accurate inventory of where they are. Having extended our military assistance so broadly, and for so many years, the idea of withdrawing all such aid is not even contemplated by federal officials. Quite the contrary. They do not talk in terms of reducing the quantity of military assistance, but only in terms of juggling the kinds of assistance—reducing manpower commitment (which drains money out of the country) and increasing arms distribution, especially arms sales (which brings dollars back into the country). Thus in 1970, Deputy Defense Secretary David Packard spoke of putting the gift and sales of arms "in a special position in our foreign policy."

I believe that the best hope of reducing our overseas involvements and expenditures lies in getting allied and friendly nations to do even more than they are now doing in their own defense. To realize that hope, however, requires that we must continue, if requested, to give or sell them the tools they need for the bigger load we are urging them to assume.[29]

In mid-1973 the Nixon Administration decided to start selling more arms to Latin American countries; officials said they were tired of seeing France, Russia, and Britain walk off with that lucrative market (since 1966 there had been a U.S. embargo on arms sales to "developing" countries in Latin America). Also in 1973 the U.S. government's arms peddlers began selling to both sides in the Middle East conflict in an even bigger and more open fashion. Israel already had a half-billion dollar line of credit with the U.S. for the purchase of arms; now it was the Arabs' turn, with Saudi Arabia and Kuwait first in line to buy a fleet of Phantom jets. Explained Secretary of State William Rogers: "We feel it is essential to provide nations in the area with the equipment and help needed for their self-defense and internal security." Government officials also admitted that the sale of arms to the Arab countries would be one way to get some of our money back and help our balance of payments; we were already buying billions of dollars of oil from them, and the price was going up.*

If prolongation and intensification of the Cold War is reasonable, and if spreading the military spirit among developing nations is reasonable, then the argument pushed by Packard and Rogers cannot be improved on. But behind the seeming reasonableness of such men, and of the President whom they represent, one sees that cool phrases like "balance of payments" and "tools they need" can really be equated with the same old dangerous Cold War diplomacy of John Foster Dulles, but now made worse by an economic rationalization. The major nations are worried about protecting not only their ideologies but also their wallets. There is as much business as patriotism involved. *U.S. News & World Report* (January 22, 1973) did not exaggerate in this description:

---

* Of course, the government does not explain these touchy arms sales until forced to do so. The American public did not learn that the government intended to sell more arms and planes to the Persian Gulf countries until U.S. newsmen happened to notice a story about it in *Agence France-Presse* and made the State Department confess.

It is a fiercely competitive business, with the U.S., the Soviet Union, France and Great Britain the principal suppliers.

"International anarchy" is the way one authority describes the [arms peddling] competition, with each nation setting its own rules, offering equipment on generous credit terms, moving in quickly when another seller pulls out of the market for diplomatic or other reasons. . . .

In 1971, according to the U.S. Arms Control and Disarmament Agency, 120 nations spent 216 billion dollars on defense, an increase of 82 percent since 1960. Over the same span, the number of men under arms worldwide increased from 19 million to 23 million.

It is the developing nations that are the main purchasers of weapons from the industrialized countries. . . .

And the United States, packaging its goods with just the right amount of piety, intends to get its share of the market.

The Pentagon
versus the State Department

One of the strange twists that brought about the troublesome militarism of recent years is that at the same time that admirals and generals began superimposing their policies on what should have been strictly civilian programs, some of our civilian leaders began to take over programs that should have been left to the military.

The most harmful innovations of this kind came to the Pentagon under Robert McNamara, Defense Secretary during the Kennedy years and for most of the Johnson years. McNamara enjoyed his reputation for efficiency, and Washington's press corps bored millions of readers by constantly writing about it. Liberals (for a while) thought that McNamara was the greatest thing that had ever happened to the Pentagon because he, more than any previous Defense Secretary, subordinated the military brass to the civilian leadership. But for this "civilianizing" of the military establishment and for the McNamara style of efficiency, a tragic price was paid and is still being paid. Under his civilian hand, the military machine reached such enormous proportions, and its management became so complex, that many (including such Kennedy people as Richard Goodwin, John Kenneth Galbraith, and Marcus Raskin, all of whom once admired McNamara) feel he did more to take this nation down the path of permanent militarism than any number or combination of combat-ready career brass.*

In the name of efficiency and better management, responsibilities that normally (and logically) had rested with the military were brought into the office of the secretariat. Unification was the keynote. No more were the various services allowed to go their separate ways and to have a degree of independent dealings with the press and the Congress. No more were the various services allowed to fight over shares of the budget and to take their arguments to the public for support. McNamara held the channels of communication and public information tightly under his control. Neither military leaders nor civilian officials in the Pentagon were permitted even to talk to reporters unless the conversation was monitored by an official "McNamara monitor." The easygoing days when reporters could wander from office to office were over; now they had to be accompanied by an official escort. Under McNamara the defense budget doubled; the staff working directly under McNamara was 11,800 percent larger than the staff that reported to the first Secretary of Defense in 1947.

It was all very impressive, but what it added up to, in the view of both moderate and hard-line career militarists, as well as in the view of many unhysterical civilians, was (as Colonel James Donovan put it) "a powerful organized war machinery which defies effective democratic and Congressional controls."[30] Ironically, although the traditional fear is of a military coup, McNamara's organization stirred real concern among some military men that democracy might be lost under a supercivilian. General Twining noted in 1966:

> United States law quite plainly declares that this nation will not have a single military Chief of Staff commanding the armed forces. . . . America's citizenry should candidly recognize that, while this nation has no military "man on horseback," and no Prussian-type armed force General Staff, a system has evolved in which the nation now has *a single civilian Chief of Staff* in the Secretary of Defense. This single civilian today exercises the total power which our

---

* McNamara is also credited with being largely responsible for what financial writer Edwin L. Dale, Jr., of the *New York Times* calls "the greatest blunder in government economic policy since World War II"—misjudging the cost of the Vietnam war in 1967 by just about 100 percent. Largely because of the resulting deficit, the economy was swept up into an inflationary whirlwind that was still ripping us apart well into Nixon's second term.

democracy has historically been so reluctant to see fall under one individual's control.[31]

He was referring to the powers held in the office of McNamara at that time. Those powers still reside in the Defense Secretary's office.

Still, the growth of the Pentagon in size and in influence cannot be blamed altogether on ambition or misplaced efficiency. To some extent it was in response to a vacuum made by the shrinking of the State Department's influence.

In an unprecedented public examination of its own defects, the State Department in late 1970 admitted that for two decades its leadership in foreign affairs had been marked by "intellectual atrophy" and a hardening of the "creative arteries." The critical introspective report acknowledged that "with the exception of an active period at the end of the '40s, the Department and the Foreign Service have languished as creative organs, busily and even happily chewing on the cud of daily routine, while other departments, Defense, CIA, the White House staff, made more important innovative contributions to foreign policy."

For one thing, the State Department and its Foreign Service had never recovered from the probing of Senator Joseph McCarthy in the early 1950s, but the moribundity of the department could also be traced to the fact that in matters where the dollar counts— and it counts very heavily in making policy overseas—the State Department had few dollars to deal with. In fact, as the report noted, the State Department controls only about 7 percent of all resources expended abroad in support of our foreign policy.

This was a singular outburst of honesty. Few government leaders have been able to admit that the military sets foreign policy.* To save face in a nation operating on the theory that the civilian element in government is preeminent, these leaders go on

---

* The most dramatic example of how the military can determine foreign policy came with the discovery in late 1972 that General John D. Lavelle had, between November 1971 and April 1972, been ordering air strikes over North Vietnam in violation of the President's orders. To cover what he was doing, Lavelle falsely reported the circumstances of the strikes. Was he punished? Hardly. Although demoted to the rank of major general, he was allowed to retire on a full general's pension. Also, despite the fact that he had been drawing flight pay until shortly before leaving active duty, he was allowed to retire on 70 percent "disability"—which provided him with an annual pension of $27,000, most of it tax free.

pretending that the State Department runs the show, strongly counseled by the Senate Foreign Relations Committee. But occasionally the rumble of caissons and the scream of jets and the firing of arms become so noisy that even members of Congress are jarred into candor.

One such occasion came in a session of the Senate Foreign Relations Subcommittee on Disarmament in early 1967 when Eugene McCarthy, then a member, commented:

> What I am concerned about is the manipulations in the Defense Department. We sit around here trying to be foreign policy experts, and all this is going on. Everybody in Europe is a tank watcher. You cannot ship 150 tanks across Europe, through the Mediterranean, or anyplace else without somebody asking, "Whose tanks are they? What kind of tanks are they? Where are they going?" The whole thing becomes a military determination of foreign policy, and we catch on as the train goes by and say, "OK, let us get up there and try to put on the brakes." I do not know where the policy is made for this kind of thing.

But he really knew, of course, as did every member of the committee: the policy is made in the Pentagon and the National Security Council and similar recesses of militarism in government. And the State Department's main duty is to adjust to it with a pleasant face.

On a later occasion the admission was made quite clearly. Stung by the invasion of Cambodia by United States troops—an invasion that was accomplished apparently without the foreknowledge of the State Department and certainly without the foreknowledge of Congress—Senator William Fulbright said on "Face the Nation" (November 29, 1970) that he believed Defense Secretary Melvin Laird and Henry Kissinger, the President's special adviser on national security, had far more power in the formulation of United States foreign policy than did Secretary of State William P. Rogers.

A reporter then asked if Fulbright thought that perhaps the difference in the strength of Defense and State might not be traced to a matter of style. Said Fulbright sourly, and with the best of logic: "I don't think $80 billion a year [the defense budget] is a matter of style. In our kind of economy this is muscle, this is influence, this is power. It controls everything that goes in our government to a great extent. It's the primary control." He added that to counterbalance that kind of power, developed over a quarter of a century of militarism, a Secretary of State would have to be a "genius."

He would have to be more than a genius; he would have to be a god. And no Secretary of State within memory has come close to divinity—although Marshall and Acheson and Dulles and Rusk sometimes acted to the contrary. Indeed, such secretaries got their great powers—and this is even truer of Secretary of State Kissinger —*because* they did not try to counterbalance the Pentagon, but instead operated within the context of an international militarism, on behalf of Presidents who held the State Department to be merely an extension of the Pentagon.

Presidency II:
The Helpless Giant

By the nature of their ambition, they are compromised men.
They let themselves be handled by advertising agents.
They wear cosmetics. They use other men's thoughts and
other men's words without acknowledging that these are not
their own. They are alien to poetry, have little interest in love
and abase themselves by smiling constantly when there is nothing
to smile about. In short, when you have admired one President,
you have admired them all, as well as all who want to be President.

Russell Baker, New York Times

Whether or not a President has enough power
in domestic affairs, or too much, almost always boils down to an
ideological judgment. If the President is attempting to initiate
some domestic programs that you want to see initiated, you will
probably argue that he does not have enough power and that Congress has become a muscular fiend out to destroy even the feeble
powers he is endowed with. If you don't like what the President is
trying to do, you will doubtless complain that he is trying to

become a dictator and that Congress has become lifeless and supine as a countercheck to his ambitions.

Having just come through eight years of Democratic government, during which he saw Presidents Kennedy and Johnson trying to launch progressive programs that were crippled or blocked by Congress, the liberal historian Arthur Schlesinger, Jr., wrote: "Where a parliamentary Prime Minister can be reasonably sure that anything he suggests will become law in short order, the President of the United States cannot even be sure that *his* proposals will get to the floor of Congress for debate and vote. And no executive in any other democratic state has so little control over national economic policy as the American President."[1]

Schlesinger wrote that in 1969, just after Nixon had come to power. He was thinking, no doubt, of the great Presidents who had attempted to control the economy, and the budget, for positive programs—what critics call "social welfare." Being the biographer of Franklin Roosevelt and the personal adviser to John Kennedy and to a lesser extent to Lyndon Johnson, Schlesinger thought of economy control only in positive terms. And to that extent he was correct in saying the President, by comparison with the chief executive of other democracies, has little control over federal expenditures and other elements of the economy.

But the remainder of Nixon's term in office, especially Nixon's conduct of the Presidency during and after 1972, presented quite a different situation. By coordinating all the varied powers at his command and by exercising them in a *negative* fashion, Nixon proved to have far more control over money matters than most observers had supposed possible. By impounding billions of dollars appropriated by Congress,* by vetoing dozens of spending measures, by slowing down and diverting and burying federal grants, by juggling departmental budgets behind a screen of executive secrecy, by encouraging rising prices without an accompanying rise in income, Nixon managed to "cool" national growth at the consumer level while allowing corporate profits to reach an all-time high. At the same time he went a long way toward reversing the social welfare programs begun forty years earlier under Franklin Roosevelt and perpetuated by every President with varying degrees of enthusiasm down to the second half of Nixon's first term.

---

* Nixon impounded an average of $11 billion a year. And he impounded for keeps, as opposed to previous Presidents, who usually impounded only to defer spending.

Whatever else Nixon's two terms in office may prove, they most assuredly have shown that the *negative* influence of presidential power over the federal government's budget and the nation's economy had previously been highly underrated. The President is weak only if he wants to move forward in domestic affairs. If he wants to reverse the forward movement and if he knows how to coordinate his negativism, he has striking powers.

These powers come to him not through a crisis of excitement but through a crisis of skepticism and depression of spirit, at a time when people have "had enough," when they are momentarily tired of aspiring, when, as Walter Lippmann put it in a 1973 interview, there is widespread repudiation of the Rousseauean "belief that man is essentially good and can be made perfect by making the environment perfect, and that the environment can be made perfect by taxing the mass of people to spend money for improving it. Modern society won't accept that philosophy and it is usually repudiated. Sometimes the repudiation takes the form of fascism, but this rejection [the election of 1972] is morally and intellectually the equivalent of it, without some of the ugly features of fascism."[2] Other activist Presidents have needed other kinds of crises for their powers.

Nixon showed himself to be a tough, adroit reshaper of the federal machinery, especially in the all-important budget office. What had started out in Franklin Roosevelt's day as a small office whose only function was to help the President prepare a budget became under Nixon (with some intermediary growth in intervening years, of course) a superdepartment, the Office of Management and Budget, whose initials OMB struck fear into the hearts of both congressmen and bureaucrats. That may be exaggerating a bit, but not much. Nixon's OMB had critical powers over the expenditure of funds, over the development of programs, over the management of government.

This agency's powers would have been applauded by liberals in the days of Kennedy and Johnson. But, apparently because Nixon was in charge, they were describing the agency as a hydra-headed monster almost beyond the powers of Congress to cope with. Such innovations as the flowering of OMB; plus Nixon's statement through one of his attorney generals, Richard Kleindienst, that the President had the power to forbid federal employees from testifying before Congress under any circumstances—including impeachment; plus Nixon's claim that executive privilege gave him the power to refuse Congress a look at his papers; plus his use of "national security" as an excuse for burglary and wiretapping; plus Nixon's numerous vetoes—all these things changed the critical chorus. Now Democrats who used to argue that the President did not have enough power complained that he had too much, even in economic affairs.

"I am convinced that the United States is closer to one-man rule than at any time in our history," said Senator George McGovern, who had just been defeated by the man he was calling a tyrant, "and this paradoxically by a President who is not popular. ... Today only the presidency is activist and strong while other traditional centers of power are timid and depleted."[3] Another liberal senator, Alan Cranston of California, added:

> Those who tried to warn us back at the beginnings of the New Deal of the dangers of one-man rule that lay ahead on the path we were taking toward strong, centralized government may not have been so wrong. . . . The Presidency—by nature remote from the people, monolithic in structure and with a huge bureaucracy at its command—is the one branch most in danger of degenerating into dictatorship. Especially in these days of vast governmental controls over and interference in the lives of our citizens.[4]

What the senators said may or may not be correct, but it is interesting that they did not have these fears until an activist, negativist Republican President moved into the White House. When a Democrat is in the White House, Democrats quote with approval President Wilson's statement: "His [any President's] office is anything he has the sagacity and force to make it. . . . The President is at liberty, both in law and conscience, to be as big a man as he can."[5] John Kennedy gave fair warning of what he would try to do in the office, telling the National Press Club in 1960, "He [the President] must be prepared to exercise the fullest powers of his office—all that are specified and some that are not";[6] liberals cheered and conservatives gnashed their teeth. When Nixon got his hands on some of those unspecified powers, the cheering and gnashing were reversed.

Checks on the President

Before taking any of these black warnings too seriously, one should remember two things. First, no President can overcome the constitutional powers invested in Congress, especially the House of Representatives, to dominate the budgetary process. No President can avoid Congress' power to override his veto by a two-thirds vote. No President can conjure up magical powers to overcome the Senate's right to reject presidential appointments. And if Congress feels that the Constitution gives the President too much power, it can pass by a two-thirds vote a constitutional amendment that whips right past the White House on its way to ratification by the states. Congress need worry much less about a presidential dictatorship than about its own default.

Second, to achieve enough power to unnerve Congress, a President must erect a most intricate and delicate tower from which to launch his assault. The tower will be constructed of public relations, imagery, reputation, congressional relations, bureaucratic relations, trickery, horsetrading, solid achievements, and everything else that goes into making an all-American pop hero. Furthermore, one solid blow to the structure can bring it all down in a heap. What appears to be the most awesomely sturdy assemblage of power one day may, after a turn of luck, be reduced to a puddle of sufferance the next day.

And so it was with much of Nixon's domestic strength.

After his landslide reelection victory, Nixon was riding high. He opened 1973 with a showing of 68 percent support from the American people. But then came the great outpouring of evidence in the Watergate scandal. By June the Gallup poll showed Nixon's popularity had shrunk to 40 percent—the sharpest six-month drop in presidential popularity recorded by Gallup in forty years. By August it had dropped even further—to 31 percent. And on November 7, 1973, the first anniversary of his reelection, public trust in his administration had sunk so low (27 percent support) and the outcry against Nixon personally had become so great, even from members of his own party, that Nixon felt obliged to go on national television to explain why he would not resign. But it did little to counter his enemies or pacify his party (elections in the fall of 1973 showed that the GOP was in trouble). Senator Barry Goldwater, the guru of Republican conservatives, said that if it could be proved that Nixon was lying about his role in Watergate he should be impeached. Suddenly the talk was not of Nixon's overweening power but of his becoming so powerless as to be a useless President. Scholars like Nelson W. Polsby were asking, "Can a President govern effectively or at all if he systemically alienates himself from most of the rest of official Washington?"[7] It became commonplace to find such pundits as Stewart Alsop writing of the "paraplegic Presidency."

Congress rushed in to take advantage of the cripple. During the first seven months of 1973, it opposed Nixon on 57 percent of 209 recorded votes, the first time in this generation that a President has lost more often than he won. (In 1969 Nixon had been supported by Congress on 74 percent of recorded votes, 77 percent in 1970, 75 percent in 1971, and 66 percent in 1972.) The Senate passed two resolutions within five weeks ordering the White House to adhere to congressional directions on governmental spending. Although the House was not quite so willing to shed its pocketbook conservatism, it also gave clear evidence that it would immediately expect more consideration from the White House in the handling of Congressional programs.

It had happened again. A high-riding President was brought low by circumstances and the desires of Congress, underscoring once more the irony of Richard Neustadt's observation that in foreign affairs where one bungle can blow up the world, any bungler in the Presidency is free to follow his whim, but in internal matters, which could withstand any number of blunders and still be salvaged in the next election, not even the wisest and most imaginative President, much less a reclusive and unpopular one, is ever given more than temporary carte blanche.

The most massive military crisis in the nation's life, the Civil War, gave President Lincoln war powers, national emergency powers that stayed with him until his death and were passed on to every succeeding President to use when needed. However, the most massive economic crisis in the nation's life, the Great Depression of the 1930s, gave President Roosevelt equally inclusive economic powers but only for the first year (in his second year, still in the midst of the Depression, he was complaining to his adviser, Thomas G. Corcoran, "You know, in this business, you remember Ty Cobb. If you bat .400, you're a champion"). These progressive, creative powers certainly were not passed on, except for a few shreds, to succeeding Presidents.

Neither Roosevelt nor any other President was able to ramrod most of his major domestic proposals through Congress until 1965 and 1966. That robust two-year period in Lyndon Johnson's term was the first time since Roosevelt's day that a Democratic President had an overwhelming number of "program Democrats," Democrats willing to back the President's program, rather than the deceptively labeled and often disloyal "party Democrats," such as those Southerners who wear the party label for convenience but vote against Democratic programs as often as Republicans vote nay. Also assisting Johnson in his first year was the sense of mourning that clung to Washington after the assassination of Kennedy. Johnson, recognizing the leverage he had with that hangover emotionalism, pushed several of the key pieces of legislation as "Kennedy programs."

But granting the obstinacy of Congress and the heavy torpor of the bureaucracy, the White House's dismal record for getting things done on the home front cannot be blamed entirely on those burdens. It has also been the fault of the men who lived in the White House. They didn't accomplish more because they didn't try to. There has been a general failure of presidential energy in domestic affairs; the derring-do that marks Presidents in foreign affairs is usually absent when they confront the old bulls of Congress. Even Johnson and Kennedy can be faulted on this. After operating for two years as a daemonic power broker, LBJ began to retrench and fudge on his domestic promises in the second half of his term so that he could try to find an answer to the question he posed one day to reporters in the White House Rose Garden, "How the f— do I get out of Vietnam?"

Kennedy's attitude was often one of gentlemanly passiveness; if he ran into stiff opposition from Congress, he was likely to pass it off with a wry, "Well, it looks like this one will be a 12-month baby."

The White House has a fine movie theater and bowling alley (and, until the end of Johnson's regime, a swell swimming pool), and just about any country club will manage to find a locker for a transient President of the United States. If a President doesn't want to do much, if he doesn't want to take hold of the mildewed elements of the government and drag them into the sunlight, if he is more interested in shooting quail with rich friends in Georgia or in watching Western movies than he is in wrestling with Congress and the bureaucracy, then he won't suffer many disappointments. Calvin Coolidge, whose typical twenty-four hours in the White House included a long nap in the afternoon and eleven hours of sleep at night, seemed quite content with the country's slowly decaying status quo. Eisenhower never expressed keen disappointment in the unfulfilled ambitions he had for the country, perhaps because his ambitions were so modest and his interest in the presidential job so slight. Even with the clarity of hindsight, it is impossible to reconstruct anything resembling an "Eisenhower domestic program" and nearly as difficult to fit together the pieces of his foreign policy. He was, as James David Barber has written, a noble void.

> Should he engage in personal summitry on the international front? "This idea of the President of the United States going personally abroad to negotiate—it's just damn stupid." With the new Cabinet, wouldn't it make sense to oversee them rather carefully? To George Humphrey [Treasury Secretary], the President said, " I guess you know about as much about the job as I do." And his friend Arthur Larson writes that the President found patronage "nauseating" and "partisan political effect was not only at the bottom of the list —indeed, it did not exist as a motive at all." In 1958 the President said, "Frankly, I don't care too much about the congressional elections." . . . His heart attack in September 1955 was triggered, Eisenhower said, when he was repeatedly interrupted on the golf links by unnecessary phone calls from the State Department. . . .
> In early 1957 Eisenhower presented his administration's budget —and promptly invited Congress, much to the amazement of his supporters there, to suggest "sensible reductions" in it. He submitted a civil rights bill and then told the press he did not himself agree with all aspects of it. *Life* magazine commented that "the fiasco of his program is in some part due to his own indecision and seeming unsureness in support of it." With painful honesty, Eisenhower would admit in press conferences that he had "never heard of" significant Administration activities. Sam Lubell found increased speculation among voters as to who was actually running the country.[8]

Into a vacuum so tempting, strong congressional leaders—if such there be at that moment—will inevitably move. Thus Eisenhower's lethargy was a godsend for Senator Lyndon Johnson, Democratic Majority Leader, for it gave him, rather than the President, the opportunity to seem the initiator of a domestic program. From that national exposure Johnson moved on to the White House. Johnson gave Ike a great deal of cooperation, but he was motivated to a great extent by his own ambitions. If a President does not lean heavily on Congress, that mulish animal will normally not move for him voluntarily. Congress watches for every weakness in the Presidency with the intent of taking advantage of it. Do not for a moment doubt that one of Congress' principal preoccupations is to strut its power and, if possible, humble the Chief Executive. Presidents come, Presidents go, but the congressional wheelhorses go on, seemingly, forever.

Most Presidents, confronted with that kind of obstinacy on Capitol Hill, give up easily, especially if they have no driving enthusiasm for domestic affairs. "I've always thought this country could run itself domestically, without a President," Nixon told Theodore H. White in 1968. "All you need is a competent Cabinet to run the country at home. You need a President for foreign policy; no Secretary of State is really important; the President makes foreign policy."[9] Once he became President, Nixon's attitude changed radically on one point; he relied much less on a competent Cabinet than on what he hoped was a competent White House staff. But the thrust of his enthusiasms was as he predicted it would be, illustrated during the first one hundred days of his administration when he had fifteen meetings with the National Security Council and three meetings with the joint congressional leadership.

Even when he had a domestic bill worth fighting for and that he personally believed in, Nixon's mind wandered and his energies flagged when he ran into opposition. On August 11, 1969, he proposed for the first time in American history legislation to establish a floor under the income of every family with children. It was called the Family Assistance Plan, and Nixon himself thought it was "the most important piece of social legislation in our nation's history." It easily passed the House, but it got bogged down in the Senate Finance Committee, where liberals said it offered too little and conservatives said it offered too much. Nixon, fascinated by Vietnam and China and Russia and their more exotic challenges, quickly lost interest in the fight. By 1973 he announced that although he recognized the fact that the country's welfare system was a "crazy quilt of injustice and contradiction," he was junking his plan because he did not think Congress was in a mood to make "overall structural reform."[10]

Thereafter Nixon sought to exert presidential power in domestic affairs not by leading Congress but by obstructing, by slowing things down or dismembering them. In Nixon, Congress was confronted by a new type of adversary. When a President wants to pass a program, Congress can flaunt its negative power. When a President simply wants to maintain the status quo, Congress can have a field day with its own whims. But when a President wants to turn back the clock, then Congress is confronted with the new problem of having to translate the status quo into progress. If it was baffled by Nixon, Congress had brought the problem on itself by failing to deal honestly with the few progressive programs—especially the Family Assistance Program—offered by Nixon in the early days of his first term.

As one member of the White House staff put the matter to Robert B. Semple of the *New York Times* (November 27, 1971): "The President has never said this to me in so many words, but I think he simply gave up on Congress fairly early in the game, when he saw he simply didn't have the horses to create and bring into being a major domestic agenda that he could call his own." So he retreated into foreign affairs. "If you look at the last three years, you will find that the Administration has pulled out all the stops only on those issues—and most of them are foreign policy issues—that affect the President's image of what he thinks a President ought to be and do."

Presidential Image-Making

This preoccupation on Nixon's part should not be belittled. The President's image of himself and the public's image of him combine as his most important tool. If a President is to have any significant influence with Congress, he must have the strength of public popularity.* Public approval is not enough. Nixon won an overwhelming reelection in 1972 because the public approved of the way he was then running the country and because they especially approved of his foreign policy, which already had reopened relations with Communist China and improved relations with Russia. Nixon did not win the election on his popularity because he is not a popular man, not an appealing person, as he is wise enough to know. "I'm an introvert in an extrovert profession," he has said. When CBS reporter Dan Rather asked him why many people thought he "failed to inspire confidence and faith and lacked personal warmth and compassion," Nixon responded in such a way as to equate those characteristics with trivial political fluff. "My strong point," he replied, "is not rhetoric; it isn't showmanship;

---

* Often he begins his term at a disadvantage caused by the democratic process; in fourteen presidential elections—including Truman's in 1948, Kennedy's in 1960, and Nixon's in 1968—the nation wound up being led by a man whom less than a majority of the voters had endorsed. This does not escape the notice of Congress, which prefers to view its opponent at the other end of Pennsylvania Avenue as something less than the embodiment of the people.

it isn't big promises—those things that create the glamour and excitement that people call charisma and warmth."[11]

Charisma, secondary virtue though it may be, offers an extra quantum of power. When a President is very popular, congressmen (except those from safe districts, who don't worry about such matters) may reason that giving support to his programs will make them popular too. Of course, simply because a President gets top ratings with the public does not necessarily mean that his tax program is equally popular or that he can make it popular by "going to the people." But politicians can never be sure about that, and in the House, where members must confront the public so frequently, the barometer of the President's popularity is watched with especially keen regard.

In many respects it is a silly concern. To be sure, the incumbent President has led the Gallup Poll's list of Ten Most Admired Men for twelve of the past fourteen years (Ike nosed out LBJ those two years). But it is a pretty hokey list,* apparently concocted with the votes of people who would put their mother at the top of the Ten Most Admired Women list while secretly opting for socko feminists like Gloria Steinem or Bella Abzug. In short, if Nixon was truly as popular as the people indicated to Gallup in 1971, why was it that when he took prime time in March of that year to be interviewed by ABC's Howard K. Smith—the first presidential TV interview by a single reporter on one network in prime time—ABC estimated that only 9 to 10 million people tuned in, while an estimated 17 million homes tuned to NBC's movie, and 14 million watched the "Doris Day Show" and the first half of the "Carol Burnett Show" on CBS?

Next to being overwhelmingly popular, the best thing is to appear to be; and for the purpose of concocting that appearance, every President since Kennedy has had a crowd-fixing expert on the White House staff.

Sometimes fixing a crowd can be a physically rough affair. To make sure that the people attending a Richard Nixon/Billy Graham rally in 1971 in Charlotte, North Carolina, were "sanitized," White House aides H. R. Haldeman, John W. Dean III, and William Henkel devised this plan: 32,600 tickets were distributed for 12,000 seats. Thus the White House's crowd managers could be selective.

* It's always got people like the Reverend Billy Graham and Howard Baker and Pope Paul and Hubert Humphrey on it, and hardly ever people like Joe Namath or Paul Newman or Russell Baker.

Bouncers were stationed at the door, and anyone who had long hair or "mod" attire—which the bouncers equated with dissenters—was turned away.* Then, just to make sure, the bouncers went through the crowd that had been admitted and threw out a couple dozen other "suspects." A federal judge later called it "a wholesale assault upon the civil rights and liberties of numerous citizens," but President Nixon personally thanked the chief bouncer "and the men you recruited."[12]

To develop a crowd in Washington (the most cynical city and therefore the most difficult place to build a crowd for a President) the common technique is to turn out the government workers and *order* them to show up for the ceremony. Martin E. Underwood, who made a profession of inflating the appearance of popularity for Kennedy and Johnson, says that one technique is to send presidential motorcades down narrow streets and have the crowd bunch up; if the objective is to fill a stadium for a presidential speech, then inundate the state with free tickets. Underwood was proudest of the way he built the crowd in Houston for Johnson:

> There are some tricks to this business. Let's take Houston and the university presidents. What you do, you see, is put them on the reception line. This is your green stamp place. This is where you pay off your debts or make them obligated.
>
> Two days later, I come back and say, "President so and so, would you mind doing me a favor? Would you mind letting your students out? This is a great day and the President's coming."
>
> "Oh no, I'd be glad to," the President says.
>
> "Do you suppose that I could have the 100-piece band you've got?"
>
> "Be a great honor."
>
> Well, Christ we had five universities and we got every damn one of them to let off their students with the understanding they would go out and crowd the highways. We had bands all over town.[13]

The attention to imagery—which is to say, the awareness that the medium is part of the message—has been around for some time. Franklin D. Roosevelt was limited to the radio, but he used it to its fullest in his frequent "fireside chats." Thomas Corcoran says the details for these chats were worked out so carefully that "before the President would go on the air, a pharmacist's mate [Navy

---

* Dictators often have a morbid concern for the way people look. The military junta in Greece forbids the wearing of miniskirts, and the military junta that seized control of Chile in September 1973 immediately ordered everyone with long hair to go to the barber.

corpsman] would, for instance, carefully clean out his sinus passages to make his lovely tenor voice resonant."[14]

Nixon's first lesson in the importance of such details came in 1960, when a serious attack of staphylococcus and an inhumanly rigorous schedule left him looking haggard and mean in the early TV debates that were the focal point of his presidential contest with John Kennedy. This was reinforced by the black imbedded stubble of his beard—wretchedly disguised by his make-up crew—and contrasted in such a way with the fresh, boyish Kennedy that this alone is thought by some to have cost him that close election.

Since then Nixon has always appeared on television well prepared with expert grooming; a cosmetician-hairdresser applies what he calls "just a little beard cover and dusting powder." Nixon will even wear this facial covering in public if the TV crews are around. (Americans, accustomed to such theatrical tricks from their politicians, think nothing about it, but when Nixon visited China the residents would ask, "Why is he orange?") Nixon also uses a rinse to keep down the gray at his temples. White House correspondent John Osborne observed on one occasion that the rain falling on Nixon's head resulted in brown-colored water dripping down the Chief Executive's neck. Johnson was even more vain about his looks; he used hair dye lavishly and sometimes had his hairdresser give him a subtle marcel. He also occasionally padded his hairline with "wings" on either side of his head. Once, as he stepped out of a helicopter, a gust of air from the whirring blades blew his hair-padding away. Secret Service agents went into a panic, thinking something violent had happened to Johnson's head.

To Eisenhower, an appearance on television was painful because he had a normal person's perspective of himself. "I keep telling you fellows," he once complained to his staff, "I don't like to do this sort of thing. I can think of nothing more boring, for the American public, than to have to sit in their living rooms for a whole half-hour looking at my face on their television screens."[15] To Nixon, the pain comes from the tedious but necessary cosmetic preparations and from knowing that the hot television lights give his face a sweaty, "guilty" look.

No President has been more adept than Nixon at surrounding himself with the proper television atmosphere. When he made his first TV appearance after the Watergate exposure, a speech that he hoped would convey his purity to the American people, he was flanked by the American flag, the presidential flag, a large bust of Abraham Lincoln, and a picture of his family.

For the political clout that comes with effective TV appearances, Nixon has doggedly submitted himself to this kind of self-exploitation on a scale unequaled by any other President. In the first eighteen months of his term, Nixon appeared on television fourteen times—more than the *combined* TV appearances of Eisenhower, Kennedy, and Johnson in their first eighteen-month period. On his trip to China he took along seventy TV technicians and forty TV newscasters—more people than in his diplomatic group. He knew exactly how much propaganda punch he was getting. In both Peking toasts he mentioned that he was appearing "before more people than have ever been in one audience before in the history of the world." It was, like jogging up the pyramids on a pogo stick, another first. Firsts are good p.r.

Presidential Styles of Domestic Politics

Success in a President's foreign adventures may depend to a large degree on secrecy, but the best way to win ground for a domestic program is with an aggressive openness—a willingness to mix it up with Congress, to harangue industry leaders and the public, to gamble by spelling out one's ideas for approval or opposition. White House correspondent Don Oberdorfer puts it this way:

> Despite the trappings of royalty, presidents are not monarchs. They cannot legislate in private, wave a wand and will it so. In the end, they must persuade. And to persuade they must inform. . . . Mr. Nixon's massive 1971 legislative program—the "New American Revolution"—was discounted in Congress because no one had been consulted in advance, and discounted in the country because it sounded too big to be true. In a government of checks and balances, of divided powers and divided opinion, the President sooner or later will have to tell the country more.[16]

By the end of 1971, every one of Nixon's six major legislative proposals had been defeated, postponed, or forgotten, because he was incapable of employing even on a modest scale the working philosophy espoused by LBJ: "In every town there's some guy on top of the hill in a big white house who can get things done. I want to get that man on my side."[17]

Lyndon Johnson relished huddles with Cabinet members and

congressional and union and business leaders; he loved to bump knees and whisper in ears and fondle the other man's arm and hands, and tell his earthy jokes. Nixon—a loner, a recluse (as politicians go), a brooder—avoided that sort of thing with great deliberation. Kennedy and Johnson made frequent use of the lunch and dinner routine for consulting with outside advisers from labor and industry and universities. Nixon preferred to lunch alone from a tray in his office.

In 1968 Johnson called together thirty corporate executives to recruit them for the National Alliance of Businessmen, a group that, he hoped, would train and employ the hard-core unemployed. LBJ fed his would-be allies a luscious steak luncheon at the White House; then he began to tell them what commitment he wanted from them. With his rolling style, half sentimental and half bitchy, he constructed an emotional atmosphere in which the executives began to see themselves as white knights. Finally the chief executive of a major aircraft company had been whipped to such a pitch of enthusiasm that he leaped to his feet and shouted, "I commit, Mr. President! I commit! I commit to your program!"

Always the master of such gatherings, right down to the last whimper, Johnson paused, jabbed a finger at the executive, smiled in a teasing way, and said, "Mister, you committed when you took the first bite of my steak."[18]

One cannot imagine that coming from the mouth of an Eisenhower or a Nixon.

To prepare for the final round of decision-making, a President can readily draw on the best minds in the country if he wishes.* The activist Presidents, like Kennedy and Johnson, go in every direction for advice.

Nixon, however, did not like traffic through the White House and did not enjoy personal consultations. Early in 1973 Nixon announced that he was abolishing the White House Office of

---

* To be sure, there is always the question of how much of this calling together of the best minds for advice is sincere and how much of it is a pretense of being open-minded. The White House has appointed so many study commissions in the past twenty years that the Library of Congress concedes it has no accurate record of the number; in the Nixon Administration alone, more than forty special study commissions—composed primarily of private citizens—were set up for a variety of problems, such as racism and violence. Without exception, the findings and recommendations of these commissions have been ignored. Some were even denounced because they dared criticize administration policy.

Science and Technology and the post of science adviser to the President—from whom he had received too much advice he did not like. He ordered even agency heads to submit their problems in the form of "option papers," with the situation reduced in writing to its essentials and the options spelled out. These papers he took into the Oval Room, or the Lincoln sitting room in the family section, or more likely into his hideaway in the Executive Office Building across from the White House, and there he communed with himself and made his choices. One Nixon aide explained, "We can't have a lot of Cabinet guys running in to the President or he'd never have a question refined to where it's worth his making a decision."

Nixon would sit in a conference with advisers and hear them debate a problem, without revealing his own feelings; he would take notes on the yellow legal-size tablet that he was never without; he would ask questions and draw out his subordinates with undirected comments. And then again he would retire for lone deliberation. Thorough. Introspective. Single-minded. And arbitrary. Often his closest advisers hadn't the slightest notion of which direction he would jump. Not until he announced the appointment did White House intimates know he had settled on Warren Burger as Chief Justice. The *New York Times* reported that when the time came for Nixon to decide whether or not to change the 10 percent surtax, "aides were so unsure of Mr. Nixon's mind after a 90-minute meeting that they prepared one announcement justifying changes in the surtax, and another announcement justifying no changes at all."

The result of this hyperprivacy and secrecy was sometimes a mixture of mini-chaos and maxi-confusion. Lacking access to the President, department heads got their signals crossed—if they even heard the signals at all.

On September 4, 1969, after clearing his statement with Nixon, Treasury Secretary David Kennedy announced that the administration would go along with a cut in the oil depletion allowance. Exactly fifty days later the White House announced it did not favor the cut. Nixon ordered the massive increase in bombing of North Vietnam in December 1972 without even consulting his military chiefs. In the summer of 1971, then-Secretary of the Treasury John Connally, Nixon's chief economic adviser, called a special press conference to assure the nation that the President would not impose wage-and-price controls, create a wage-price review board, initiate any tax cuts, or increase government spending. Within one month Nixon had ordered all these things to be done.

What's done can be undone in the same way: in January 1973 Nixon dismantled mandatory price controls—a very intricate matter, involving the foreign as well as the domestic market and money balances—without telling either the head of his Price Commission or his Pay Board what he was going to do. He did it within a few days after Arthur Burns, chairman of the Federal Reserve Board and an intimate adviser to Nixon on economic affairs, had publicly served notice that the administration had "no alternative but to pursue [price controls] for a while longer." Shortly thereafter, presidential assistant John Ehrlichman indicated that Nixon also intended to abandon wage controls, but apparently Ehrlichman had read the smoke signals wrong, for Nixon announced through his press office that Ehrlichman had "misspoke" himself. A few weeks later Agriculture Secretary Earl Butz was asked by newsmen if the administration intended to reimpose a ceiling on meat prices to stop their sharp climb; Butz dismissed the suggestion as "the talk of damn fools." Within hours, Nixon suddenly ordered a ceiling on meat prices.

The strengths and weaknesses of a White House staff are much more observable in domestic affairs than in foreign. It is on the home front that a White House staff can (as they did to Truman and Eisenhower) tarnish the President's image by making him seem to condone kickbacks and conflicts of interest. It is in domestic affairs that the President's staff advisers can (as they did to Kennedy) so easily dilute idealism with wardheel politics. Of JFK's circle of advisers, Richard Rovere wrote, "There was not a reformer among them . . . pragmatism—often the grubbiest kind— was rampant." Under their influence, Kennedy made many pretty speeches, but he seldom gambled his political chips on a good but risky cause.*

But of course the supreme example in our political history of how the conduct of presidential advisers can almost destroy a President came as the Nixon Administration ended its first term. Indeed, as things turned out, Nixon would have done himself a great service if before taking occupancy of the White House he had memorized this advice of the famous sixteenth-century political

---

* Like Johnson did in 1964, when he informed his Senate leaders that he was prepared to lose all other legislation if necessary to wear down and break the filibuster against his civil rights bill.

guru, Niccolò Machiavelli: "The first opinion that is formed of a ruler's intelligence is based on the quality of the men he has around him." Although there was some evidence that Nixon himself carelessly said and did things that helped establish the atmosphere in which gross misconduct could occur, much of the evidence seemed to indicate that it was the President's closest advisers, acting on their own initiative, who made a shambles of the Presidency through "the Watergate affair"—the generic name for an almost endless catalog of political corruption, dirty work, and downright criminal conduct.

Beginning in 1971, when national polls showed that Nixon might have a difficult time being reelected, a coterie of fanatical aides to Nixon began an operation aimed at winning his reelection at any cost in money or morality. Their basic objective was nothing less than to rig the election of 1972, and they continued their scheme even after polls showed Nixon would be a sure winner.

By the late spring of 1973, Nixon's closest White House aides, H. R. Haldeman and John Ehrlichman, along with the White House counsel, John Dean III, resigned their posts, and Nixon's former law partner and Attorney General, John Mitchell, and his former Commerce Secretary, Maurice Stans, were indicted for perjury and violation of election laws. The office of the Presidency had been so badly tainted that there was wide speculation in the press and in Congress as to whether (1) the trail of wrongdoing might eventually lead right into the Oval Office and result in Nixon's impeachment, or (2) the weight of the scandal might at least undercut Nixon's effectiveness to such an extent that he would resign. And these possibilities were being spoken of even before all the sordid story had unrolled either before federal grand juries or before the Senate select committee on the Watergate scandal.

Not since President Harding's corrupt pals broke his heart had a President been so poorly treated by those in whom he had invested most of his management powers. What had made the poison of the Nixon Administration so deadly was that it had been concentrated in a small circle nearest the head of state. The public was left with an unpleasant choice: either Nixon had known about or perhaps even had participated in the corruption, and must be unethical, or he had not known about it and must be an inefficient manager of his own household. So harmful was the choice to the President's image that no amount of special barbering and pancake make-up could repair the damage.

Speaking of Haldeman and Ehrlichman, sometimes known as "Hans" and "Fritz" to those who despised them, Richard J. Whalen (who was also a White House adviser until he got fed up and left) wrote: "No potential danger is more ominous in a free society than the secret leaching away of presidential authority from the man the people choose to the men he chooses. To whom are they responsible? To him and their own consciences, of course, which is the essence of the danger when a President is protected even from the knowledge of what is said and done in his name."[19] Coming before the great scandal broke, this was a prescient comment.

The smaller the circle of his advisers, the less chance a President has to act wisely. Cut off from the public by concentric walls of flunkies, aides, advisers, and whatnot, a President eventually arrives at the delusionary position of believing his aides actually represent the public and speak to him with the voice and heart of the public. As this madness increases, the President comes to think that if many aides speak for the public, fewer aides will speak with the purer, distilled voice of the public—so on important decisions he seeks the advice of fewer and fewer people.

The result is, of course, the kind of ignorance that is perhaps the President's closest link (although it is doubtful he interprets it that way) to the ignorance of the masses. The point was made accidentally by J. Fred Buzhardt, a special presidential counsel, in late 1973, when newsmen seemed skeptical about Nixon's claim to lack inside information about the Watergate cover-up. Said Buzhardt: "I'm sure the President doesn't know a lot about this. Most people are confused to the deuce. What makes anyone think he's in a different position?"[20] It was a chord of modesty seldom heard in the modern White House.

Nixon was held in splendid isolation by his staff.* Although it is probably true, as John Gardner said, that "people in power usually have deep complicity in their own isolation," and although it has already been seen how Nixon leaned in that direction, there is also ample evidence that an elite circle of advisers encouraged

---

* And since he never read the newspapers, Nixon probably didn't know when his staff gave him erroneous information. For example, in mid-1970 Nixon said he had sent Congress an emergency housing bill months before and had asked speedy attention. Congress had ignored his plan, he said, showing its heartlessness. Somebody on Nixon's staff had goofed. No such legislation had ever been sent to Congress. In 1971 Nixon vetoed a child care bill, denouncing it as "the most radical piece of legislation" of the year. His staff apparently had forgotten to tell him that his wife was the honorary chairwoman of a group that had fought for two years to get the bill through Congress.

this characteristic, shutting him off from the rest of the White House staff and most of the Cabinet and leaving him to rely on a narrow conduit through half a dozen of his most trusted intimates for contact with the outside world.

In the Haldeman era, which lasted for four years, the corridor was guarded jealously even against some of Nixon's most important counselors. Haldeman once insisted, "Every President needs an S.O.B. and I'm Nixon's." If that was his job as he saw it, he filled it splendidly. Whalen wrote:

> Within the first hundred days, Haldeman drew a virtual siege line —soon called "the Berlin Wall"—at the threshold of the President's office. One morning in the spring of 1969, Arthur Burns emerged after an appointment with the President. As he did, he remembered something the Postmaster General had asked him to mention to Nixon and he turned to re-enter the room. Haldeman blocked the way. "Your appointment is over," he said. Burns explained that he wanted only a moment—he must keep his promise to the Postmaster that he would deliver the message personally. That didn't mean anything, Haldeman said curtly. Loyalty to the President overrode every other consideration. He told Burns to submit a memorandum, which he would place in the President's reading folder. Amazed and at a loss for words, the Counselor to the President walked away.[21]

Other loyal aides received similar treatment. Cabinet members (except for Mitchell) often had to cool their heels in the waiting room. Senior congressmen had a difficult time getting Haldeman to return their calls, much less inducing him to set up an appointment for them to see the President.

When Haldeman departed under a cloud and was replaced by General Alexander Haig as the President's appointments secretary, many outsiders believed that at last Nixon's iron cocoon would be shattered and that the White House would become looser and more relaxed and more penetrable. It didn't work out that way at all. Nixon continued in isolation. Even when Nixon decided on Gerald Ford as his substitute Vice President, he did not convey that information to Ford personally. He sent General Haig. Admittedly, this seclusion had its perverse advantages. When a group of senators talked of going to Nixon to urge him to resign, their ardor for the mission was dampened, according to *New York Times* columnist Tom Wicker, by the thought that they probably wouldn't even get to see the President and would have to settle for a chat in a side room with Haig.

If a President enjoys this way of handling other politicians, he will just naturally make remoteness his primary technique for handling the press also.

Although Kennedy and Johnson doted on the press, reading everything they could get their hands on pertinent to their jobs, devouring even the froth of television (LBJ kept three sets on constantly in his office), Nixon isolated himself from the press, read little, and reportedly did not look at television news at crisis moments (such as riots) for fear of being influenced by the excitability of the screen. Nixon's idea of keeping on top of the news was to have five monitors on the White House staff digest the *Washington Post*, the *New York Times*, the *Chicago Tribune*, the wire services, and columns and editorials from fifty other newspapers, as well as TV news, and deliver a thirty- to fifty-page summation to his desk at eight o'clock every morning.*

The President and Congress

The first major attempt to deal with Congress on a totally structured basis was made by Kennedy. He required every department and agency in the bureaucracy to deliver a written report to the White House by Monday noon each week, telling what congressional lobbying they had done in the previous week and what they intended to do in the upcoming week. Then Kennedy's aides boiled these down and gave a report to the President, which permitted him to coordinate the White House's congressional lobbying with that of the rest of the executive branch.

White House staff liaison with Congress continues, of course, but on a less dynamic basis; after being brought to a hyperstage of activity under LBJ, it fell into a rickety condition under Nixon.

---

* Almost as though he anticipated the coming of President Nixon, Clinton Rossiter in 1956 advised:

> The modern President must be on guard lest he be made a prisoner in his own house. He needs badly to know what people are thinking about events and about his handling of them. If he values his independence, he must have clear channels to the outside, and there is no substitute—certainly not a one-page digest of news and opinion prepared by his own secretaries—for a front page of the *New York Times* or the *Chicago Tribune*, an editorial in the *St. Louis Post-Dispatch* or the *New York Daily News*, a cartoon by Herblock or Fitzpatrick, a column by the Alsops or Pearson, or a magisterial lecture on the Constitution by Lippmann or Krock. An occasional half-hour in the appendix of the *Congressional Record* is an experience no President should miss. (*The American Presidency* [N.Y.: Harcourt Brace Jovanovich, 1956].)

For example, five Republican and twelve Democratic senators sent a letter to Nixon begging his assistance in a labor dispute; they never received a reply. Even though Senator Edmund Muskie had incorporated several Nixon proposals into the air-pollution control bill, he was pointedly *not* invited to attend the signing of the bill into law. New Republican members of Congress sometimes found that after they had been in office six months the White House's congressional liaison office still did not have their names. Routine bipartisan courtesies were ignored: Thomas Eagleton, a Democrat elected in 1968 who would gain some notoriety as McGovern's first running mate, had been in Washington nearly three years before he got a call from the White House—and the silence was then broken only because the White House wanted a favor.

Ordinarily, for the sake of protocol and smoother relations with Congress (if nothing else), a President will give advance notice to senior members of the Senate Foreign Relations Committee of the ambassadorial appointees that the Senate will be asked to confirm. In 1973 the committee first learned of Nixon's ambassadorial choices by reading about them in the newspaper. Partisan courtesies were equally scarce. The ranking Republican on the Senate Agriculture Committee did not know Nixon was going to nominate Earl Butz for the office of Secretary of Agriculture until a few hours before the nomination was sent to Capitol Hill.

Early in 1973, Nixon summoned thirteen Democratic and eighteen Republican congressional leaders to the White House for breakfast and promised that he would consult with them more often. They should not feel that they were being left out of things, he told them. Then he spoke for about ten minutes on the problems in Vietnam—but refused to take any questions from the congressmen.

The difference such things can make was best explained by Senator Hubert Humphrey:

> That's what got most of these fellows mad around here. Nixon robs you without any courtesy. Now, Johnson used to rob the Senate, but when he wanted to take something from you, he'd invite you to lunch. He'd put his arm around you and talk to you while he picked your pocket. You'd got away thinking you'd contributed something, and you'd at least feel consulted. But Nixon sticks you up in the night. You don't even see him. It's like rape without any personal contact. I mean, the Senators are used to being had, but not being ignored. That drives them mad. Under Nixon, you find out about

program cuts on cheap departmental press releases. You don't get advance notice from the President, and the Senators miss that White House stationery.[22]

Aside from learning how to unbend courteously with the federal legislators and aside from assembling a Congress-oriented staff that knows how to scratch the itches of the old legislative bulls, a President does have certain weapons he can use in his effort to push his domestic programs through, although even in victory it is difficult for a President to come out of an encounter with Congress looking like a statesman. This is because the weapons at his disposal are rather base ones for the most part: camouflage, deals, favors, threats, vetoes, and propaganda.

Camouflage. That is, hiding one's ultimate intent. Many conservative members of Congress were angered by the fact that young people working in the VISTA program would organize poor neighborhoods in such a way that the residents could have more political influence at the local level—organize to force the city council, for example, to give them better garbage pickup service. The critical congressmen felt that federal funds should be "neutral" in local politics. Joseph A. Califano, Jr., a White House aide in the Johnson period, recalls, "One night when we were in the middle of a tough fight for VISTA funds, he [LBJ] said to me: 'Keep those damn kids out of politics'—and added with a shrewd twinkle, 'At least until we get the appropriations through Congress.' "[23]

Walter Hickel tells of a piece of camouflage thrown over some legislative maneuverings when he was Nixon's Interior Secretary:

> In the midst of our fight for tough new legislation [for mine safety], I began receiving widely publicized pressure from the White House and Capitol Hill to remove [Bureau of Mines Director John F.] O'Leary, a Democrat. It bothered me because I had not yet had time to evaluate the quality of his work. However, my instructions were clear: Remove O'Leary. Following my orders from the White House, I took steps to let O'Leary go. But before I could make the official announcement, I received a call from Bryce Harlow telling me to hold off for a while.
>
> He said this would mean two more votes on the Administration side of the ABM [anti-ballistic missile] question. I thought to myself, "Okay, so I'll be a team player." But I wondered: "What about the miners? How in hell do all these political games help solve *their* problems?"[24]

Deals. Many liberals have the notion that their heroes are above making dirty deals and that they grudgingly consent to deals of any sort. This is a quaint pipe dream. Harold Ickes tells of one of the many instances when Franklin Roosevelt had to choke down a pill for the sake of a healthy administration:

> A short time ago the President sent in the name of Dr. Tugwell for Under Secretary of Agriculture. The nomination was referred to Senator Smith's committee. But Senator Smith proceeded to pigeon-hole it and let word go out to the wide world that he wouldn't report it favorably. It happens that Senator Smith has wanted a certain man appointed United States Marshal. This man is said to have a homicide record, but aside from that seems to have a very good reputation. So the President sent for Smith and told him he would give him his United States Marshal if he would report Tugwell's name favorably.[25]

On September 26, 1961, President Kennedy nominated Thurgood Marshall, counsel for the NAACP, to become a judge of the Second Court of Appeals as a stopover on his way to the Supreme Court. For fifty weeks his nomination remained bottled in the Judiciary Committee, ruled by Senator James O. Eastland, a Democrat from Sunflower County, Mississippi. Then one day Attorney General Robert Kennedy met Eastland in a Senate corridor, and Eastland remarked, "Tell your brother that if he will give me Harold Cox I will give him the nigger" (meaning Marshall).[26] Marshall was thereupon cleared, and Cox, who had roomed with Eastland in college and was the senator's protégé, was appointed a federal judge in the circuit that handles most of the Deep South's civil rights cases; he subsequently made something of a name for himself on that bench by such tricks as calling black defendants "chimpanzees." Many would say that Kennedy had made a disastrous bargain.

Favors. On the surface, favors seem like deals. But they differ from deals in that there is no firm *quid pro quo* agreement. The President simply tosses favors out and hopes they will pay off. Sometimes they don't. Sam Houston Johnson, President Johnson's brother, tells of hearing LBJ complain on one occasion: "That damned fool, Senator ———. I got him two defense plants last year, and now he's giving me nothing but trouble."[27]

Favors can range all the way from a free ride home with the President aboard Air Force One (the kind of prestige trip that doesn't exactly hurt a congressman's image with the home folks) to sparing a congressman from federal indictment by the merciful intervention of the Justice Department (a favor that is believed to have been granted more than once in the Nixon Administration). One of the most potent types of favor is the high-echelon appointment. In an effort to woo Charles Halleck, then leader of the House GOP, Johnson appointed Halleck's intimate pal Hamer Budge to the Securities and Exchange Commission. Budge was a poorly qualified, right-wing Republican.

Sometimes a President will ignore party labels to throw his endorsement to somebody in another party he thinks can do him more good. Thus in New York's 1970 Senate race, the White House successfully backed the Conservative party nominee James Buckley over Republican Charles Goodell because Goodell had been bucking the Nixon war policy. In 1972 Nixon made many GOP stalwarts angry by ordering party campaign funds and endorsements withheld from several dozen Republicans running for Congress. Moreover, he went out of his way to assist such Democrats as Mississippi's James O. Eastland. Cabinet officers Richard Kleindienst and Earl Butz gave their attention to Eastland, obviously on instructions from Nixon; at the White House, Nixon's press aide stated that the President had "great respect" for Eastland. What was Eastland's Republican opponent getting? He was not even allowed to sit on the speakers' platform during an appearance in Mississippi by Vice President Spiro T. Agnew. Nixon knew all too well that the conservative Democrat chairman of the Senate Judiciary Committee could do him much more good than a freshman Republican.

More commonly a President will do favors for a region of politicians rather than for an individual. He may establish a more generous grazing program on federal lands for Western ranchers or push a loan for Lockheed to help California aircraft workers or order the Department of Agriculture to buy an extra supply of orange juice for the federal school-lunch program from Florida citrus growers swamped in an overflow crop.

Threats. Threats are probably the President's least effective way of dealing with Congress, but at the same time few Presidents would be quite so reluctant to use them as Calvin Coolidge, who said, "I have never felt that it is my duty to attempt to coerce Senators or Representatives or to take reprisals."

The most effective kind of informal presidential threat is thrown like a boomerang; it isn't aimed directly at the "enemy" but is tossed in such a way as to curve out and around and hit the opposition from behind. Johnson was a master at this. When Senator Frank Church of Idaho was giving LBJ a great deal of trouble, the

White House leaked this story, which became one of the favorite anecdotes of that administration: Supposedly, when Senator Church came to the White House one day, he was tongue-lashed by Johnson for making an antiwar speech. Church allegedly replied, "I didn't go any further than Walter Lippmann," to which Johnson allegedly responded, "Well, Frank, the next time you need money to build a dam in your state, you better go to Mr. Lippmann." According to Church, whose word is good, no such conversation ever took place. The first account he had seen of it, he said, was in a New York newspaper. But the moral behind the leak seemed plain enough to Church: Johnson "was trying to threaten the dissenters, trying to suggest the kind of punishment that *could* be taken against us."[28]

The President can go far beyond a mere threat in his battle to influence Congress if he is willing to use the power of criminal investigation to disturb political campaigns. White House aide Charles Colson was reported to have helped develop a *Life* magazine article (from confidential government records) showing that Senator Joseph Tydings of Maryland had aided a company in which he held stock to get a profitable contract with a division of the State Department. This alleged conflict of interest became a major issue in his reelection campaign in 1970. After Tydings' defeat by a Republican, the State Department disclosed that its investigation of him had turned up nothing to suggest that he had done anything illegal. More important, however, is the fact that reporters learned the administration had come to this conclusion *before* the day of the election but had withheld the clearance for obvious reasons.

And then there is the common threat to embarrass a powerful legislator in a test of strength. Representative Wilbur Mills, chairman of the Ways and Means Committee, wanted to add to Nixon's tax bill an amendment that would allow voters to check off part of their taxes as a subsidy to the political party of their choice. The Democrats, in debt, would have benefited more than the Republicans in the 1972 election. Nixon threatened Mills with defeat on the floor of the House by defection of a large group of Southern Democrats, who Nixon knew would much rather have him than a liberal of their own party in the White House. Mills felt that he would lose too much face if members from his own section of the country voted against him, so he backed down.

Vetoes. The presidential veto is a perfectly legal and useful device to make Congress pause and think twice about whether it really wants a particular piece of legislation. If a President says no to a bill, Congress must drown him out with a two-thirds vote. Given the ideological and sectional schisms among the 535 members, that overriding vote is not always easy to muster. When Nixon's popularity plummeted in 1973, in the wake of the Watergate scandals, it was at first presumed that one result would be his inability to sustain a veto. But even his 1973 vetoes of social legislation—the kind of bread-and-butter issues that Congress would normally fight for to win favor with the electorate: emergency medical services, minimum wage increase, vocational rehabilitation, disaster loans, water/sewer funds—were upheld by a one-third-plus coalition of Republican and Democratic conservatives.

For a President whose policy is to dismantle and obstruct, or for one who is simply thrifty, the veto is a most convenient weapon, especially when it is fired like a blunderbuss, with a half dozen or so pellets hitting Congress at once. One day in 1972 Nixon vetoed nine social bills. From 1970 to 1973 he was averaging about ten vetoes a year, including seven education, nine health, four economic development, three veteran, and four aid for the elderly bills. It is difficult for Congress to do more than stay on its feet, much less move forward, in the face of such gusty opposition from the Chief Executive.

Propaganda.   John Adams once said enviously of George Washington, "If he was not the greatest President he was the best Actor of the Presidency we ever had." Herbert Hoover said of himself: "I have never liked the clamor of crowds. . . . The crowd is credulous, it destroys, it hates and it dreams—but it never builds." Comparing these two statements, Emmet John Hughes commented: "It appears never to have crossed his [Hoover's] mind to wonder how a President could govern the 'crowd' of the American Republic if they stayed *in*credulous toward him. Obviously, he had never heard the first President described as 'the best Actor' in the role. Nor could he have remembered the pointed sense of Washington's own aphorism: 'The truth is the people must *feel* before they will *see*.' "[29]

Of necessity, the President is in the strictest sense a rabble-rouser. And to arouse the rabble to support him and give him the strength he must have to deal effectively with Congress, a President will use every propaganda device, even pamphleteering. When columnist Joseph Alsop wrote in 1971 that many of the doves in Congress "are eager to be proved right by an American defeat in

South Vietnam," the White House sent out thousands of reprints of this column to the people in the country who were considered to be at the "opinion-shaping" level.

The President can also turn the bureaucracy into a propaganda machine. In 1973 the Nixon Administration issued propaganda kits called "The Battle of the Budget, 1973" to top officials in the bureaucracy and ordered them to start making speeches denouncing the "wasteful" Democratic-controlled Congress. Specifically, the officials were told to denounce fifteen programs up for legislative approval. The kits supplied "sample epithets to call Congress," explained how "Horror Stories Might be Used" in the speeches, and gave sample editorials to plant with newspapers and television stations ("Each day the Congress persists in its efforts to foist on the American public a gaggle of runaway spending schemes," etc., etc.). It is illegal to use taxpayers' money to lobby for or against legislation, and the General Accounting Office ruled that the White House probably broke the law in its campaign against the fifteen bills. Nevertheless, Nixon's crowd was not doing anything that Kennedy had not done to push his anti-poverty programs or that Johnson had not done to build public support for the Vietnam war.

One of the corniest but least dangerous propaganda devices is hyperbole. Of his trip to China, Nixon said, "This was the week we changed the world." When he signed a revenue-sharing bill, he hailed it as the beginning of "a new American revolution." He called the astronauts' moon-landing the greatest event since the birth of Christ. At the conclusion of the Smithsonian Agreement in December 1971, devaluing the U.S. dollar, Nixon said it was the "greatest monetary agreement" that had ever been made—an evaluation that sounded a bit hollow only fourteen months later when the "greatest monetary agreement" fell apart, and the dollar was devalued again. But, of course, as an ol' politico like Nixon knows, and as he admitted in an interview with *Time* magazine, "Where you need a lot of rhetoric, a lot of jazz, a lot of flamboyance, is when you don't have much to sell." In the passage of time, neither Nixon's actual physical presence in China, nor the revenue-sharing bill, nor the NASA adventures proved to have all that much to do with changing the life of man. History showed why he felt the need for the hard sell.

One of the most obvious propaganda weapons is the White House press conference, which is seldom held for the purpose of conveying information to the public but virtually always to peddle a "line," to sway the public and to marshal its opinion on the side of the President—often on behalf of what he is trying to achieve with Congress. Commonly, the questions asked of the President are ones that were planted with friendly newsmen by the White House staff.

The striking thing about Nixon as a propagandist is that, compared with other recent Presidents, he has made so little use of the press conference. At one point he went fourteen months without a televised press conference; it was not unusual for him to go four or five months without meeting the press at all. But there were good reasons. For one thing, during the heyday of the Watergate scandal he undoubtedly knew that the normally docile White House press corps would hit him with nothing but questions about a topic he preferred to discuss only in a proscribed way and on his own terms. Second, he had no well-formed legislative program that he wanted to swing public opinion behind. And third, he consciously made as his major targets those things best achieved not by public debate but through secret diplomacy and secret militarism.

Confidence. This positive technique is not least on the list. The people seemingly want, almost desperately, to believe in the President. Members of Congress are often as softhearted on this point as the general populace. Perhaps it is because in such a disparate, splintered, sprawling, geographically inchoate nation it is comforting to have one peg at the top to hang one's political hopes on. In any event, the President who can inspire confidence and moral leadership is equipped with a special armament in his political wars with Congress. Naturally, it can be obtained only if the President's aims are fairly obvious. His values must be, accurately or not, out in the open. The so-called do-good programs of the Kennedy and Johnson years conveyed this sense of values quite clearly. Eisenhower's hands-off paternalism, although more shapeless, also conveyed a strong feeling of values. Nixon has had more trouble in this respect. In his 1968 campaign he ran on what was basically a conservative platform, and promptly repudiated most of it once he was in office.

On this point Emmet John Hughes, once an assistant to Dwight Eisenhower, wrote:

> After the thirty-seventh President, Richard Nixon, had been in office more than a year, I asked a man who had known and worked with him intimately for almost a quarter of a century if he could

assuredly state any of this President's immutable convictions. "Yes, I think there are clearly two," he replied. "He really is a fiscal conservative who believes in balanced budgets. And he has built his political life on a kind of anti-Communism he will never temper." After three years in office, of course, Mr. Nixon was on his way to Peking to reestablish serious dialogue with Communist China, and the programmed deficit of his Presidency was on its way toward $90 billion.[30]

In his 1972 campaign, Nixon maintained such a low profile that very little, if any, message came through to the people. This left him enormous room for flexibility, to be sure; it left him free to pull the kinds of surprises that had often worked so well (although occasionally, too, not so well) in his first term. But politicians are not expected to be magicians; the public does not expect them to pull things out of a hat. Rabbit tricks, although often applauded, do not inspire confidence.

It was this handicap that Robert B. Semple, White House correspondent for the *New York Times*, wrote about at the time of the second Inaugural:

> In the eyes of his critics, and indeed even in his own, the President's style may have complicated the task of fulfilling his agenda. He came to office as a man without a fixed political address, his values, goals—that is, his conscience as he saw it—essentially unknown. He still has no fixed political address (the White House? Key Biscayne? San Clemente? Camp David?), while his vision of the future—that is, what he wants the country to be and what he is prepared to fight for—remains as ambiguous as ever.[31]

Nevertheless, Nixon might easily have gone on to steer a plain and inspiring course, arousing the wide popular confidence that he had often missed in the past, had it not been for Watergate. As the confrontation between the White House and the Senate investigators reached its climax, Senator Sam Ervin, chairman of the investigating committee, declared: "I think that high moral leadership demands that the President make available to this committee any information in the form of tapes or records which will shed some light on that crucial question: how did it happen that burglars were caught in the headquarters of the opposition party with the President's campaign funds in their pockets and in their hotel bedrooms at the time?"[32]

But President Nixon continued to resist making the disclosures, preferred winning a point on "executive privilege" rather than seizing what Ervin called "high moral leadership," and his potential claim on popular and congressional confidence slipped away, at least "at that point in time." Indeed, it may have slipped away forever when he claimed he could turn over only seven of the nine court-ordered tapes because two apparently were "missing" from his files.

In ticking off the devices and stratagems that are available to the President, one will eventually reach that melancholy point where one realizes that if the President had a hundred times as many devices and stratagems, victory for him would still be a random thing, an accidental development, and as rare as a program actually aimed at the public welfare.

Congress: The Most Deliberative Body, and a Swamp

*Since the foundation of the Republic, Congress has rarely
initiated anything, rarely faced up to current problems, even
more rarely resolved them. . . . The bonds which hold
the Congressional Establishment together are: White supremacy;
a stronger devotion to property than to human rights; support
of the military establishment; belligerence in foreign affairs;
and a determination to prevent Congressional reform.*

Senator Joseph Clark, Congress: The Sapless Branch

The best thing that can be said about Congress
is that it is so easily buffeted by ribald criticism and heavy-handed
jokes that it cannot possibly escape democracy, no matter how
hard the numerous stuffed shirts among its 535 members may try.
When Edward Everett Hale was chaplain of the Senate he was
once asked if he prayed for the senators. "No," he reportedly replied, "I look at the senators and pray for the country." Such
humor is seemingly endless. And the worst thing that can be said
about Congress is that most of the ridicule and criticism is merited.

Few lofty and shining moments have ever broken through the career of Congress as a body. In the face of the most pressing social demands, it almost always acts sluggishly, grudgingly, suspiciously, if it acts at all. The periods of congressional dominance in federal life, Stewart Alsop has remarked, "as after the Civil War, or in the nineteen-twenties, or in the early McCarthy period, have not been proud chapters in American political history."[1] He left out at least one important period in this shabby series—the era, following Jackson, when Congress moved into the vacuum resulting from the loss of a strong President and permitted its proslavery element to take control (then, as now) and ride the nation into the Civil War.

By its inaction, or grotesque actions, Congress has driven people to desperate thoughts. It has even made some of its own leading members admit that rigor mortis is seldom associated with life. Having diddled and dawdled its way through all but the last twelve days of the 1972 session, the House then shoveled its way through eighty bills, with virtually no deliberation or thought. Speaker Carl Albert conceded that it was a "nightmare." But had the House learned a lesson? Neither House nor Senate ever learns a lesson. During the first three months of 1973, the House met on forty-three days—but for a total of only eighty-eight hours, or an average of just barely two hours a day. And during those forty-three days it passed only fifteen minor bills. The dawdling had begun all over again.

Things are no better in the Senate. Senator Sam Ervin, Jr., the old North Carolinian with the acrobatic eyebrows that became famous during the months he chaired the Watergate investigation, put it best: "A lot of Congressmen and Senators like to draw their breath and their salaries and not do much else."

Problems sometimes drag on to intolerable lengths while the days pass in limp salutes to protocol, tradition, and ancient egos. Even the appearance of bustle is transparent to all but the most innocent. One of the questions frequently asked of a politician campaigning for reelection is, "How many roll calls did you attend?" Ah, sweet naiveté. Senator William Saxbe, being a reasonably honest politician, answered with the proper scorn: "Well, we have a dozen roll calls a day, and most of them don't amount to a damn in the Senate. The votes are 75 to nothing. We had 400 and some roll calls last session. That's a ridiculous number of roll calls. If you answer most of them, most people think that indicates that you are right on the ball, you are sitting there listening—well, what it really means is that you are sleeping in the cloak room until the bell rings, and then you run out there like a fireman and vote."[2]

Another wise view of the much vaunted roll call vote is given by *Washington Star-News* writer Tom Dowling:

> At length, there was a roll call and most of the Senate, fresh from deliberations elsewhere, arrived to do their duty. The Senate has been described as a men's club of elderly dodderers in stuffed chairs, snoozing over their papers. But that ignores the youthful quality of the place, the boy's prep school atmosphere of physical camaraderie.
>
> Even the most elderly senators bounded spryly into the chamber to shake a hand, squeeze an arm, slap a back, deliver a mock frat house punch to a shoulder.
>
> To see Mike Mansfield lean against a desk in the Senate well—his arms folded across his chest, his mouth primly puckered in resignation, his eyes fixed on the ceiling—is to be reminded of a weary headmaster waiting for his high-spirited charges to calm down for class. To see Bayh of Indiana bustle around the room giving the old glad hand is to be reminded of the perpetual candidate for president of the High School Student Council. To see Tunney of California lope along in the tracks of Kennedy of Massachusetts is to be reminded of the captain of the high school football team and his loyal sidekick, whatsisname.
>
> The Senate is no doubt a boring enough spectacle. But like baseball or the floral profusion of spring, it gives off a satisfying sense of life's continuity and pattern. It takes you back to simpler, friendlier days—to that 10-minute bell between classes in high school when you horsed around and exchanged greetings with the same buddies you'd talked to an hour before: Hey, Teddy. How's it going, Scoop! What's up, Strom? Can you get your old man's wheels tonight, Barry? . . .
>
> Still, all play and no work didn't make for much of a school. So the Senators were at length forced to disentangle themselves and cast a vote on the pressing matter at hand—the so-called constitutional crisis over presidential impoundment of funds. That done, they ambled off, either for lunch or further deliberation in the privacy of their offices.[3]

As Dowling says, one of the most striking characteristics of the Senate is the continuity of all this horsing around. Every time mortality or the voters shake a few of the old faces out of the picture, newsmen rush to write about the "new" Congress. Let a Richard Russell die, and the press is immediately full of predictions that the South is losing its powerful grip. The South has been reportedly losing its grip for at least two decades; the old knuckles may be a bit whiter, but the grip is still firm. As for the prevailing philosophy, that, too, is still lashed to the tiller. At the end of the 1972 congressional year, more senior members of the House of Representatives departed Washington forever, either through retirement or defeat, than ever before in the memory of living man— six committee chairmen, seventeen subcommittee chairmen, and the senior Republicans on nine of the twenty-one standing committees. But the old hands who moved up to fill their shoes made it ever so clear that nothing would change.

One of the old clichés around Washington describes Congress only in negative terms: "The House kills the good bills, and the Senate kills the bad." Although this is not altogether accurate, it does underscore the quality of Congress that accounts for the decades that sometimes elapse between the public's awareness of needs and congressional response to those needs. When Harry Truman went around the country in 1948 winning public support for his candidacy by denouncing "that do-nothing Eightieth Congress," he was, in fact, committing something of a fraud because the Eightieth Congress was no more of a do-nothing Congress than most Congresses.

In the intervening time the public has come to realize this and admit it. After Congress refused to touch President Kennedy's major proposals in 1963, Walter Lippmann echoed a prevailing anger among the egghead electorate when he asked, "What kind of legislative body is it that will not or cannot legislate?" No answers were forthcoming. Two years later, such was the concern among scholars at the decay and atrophy of Congress that a group of eminent political scientists met at the Harriman estate in New York to decide what, if any, hope remained for revitalizing Congress. The report issued at the conclusion of that meeting sounded rather pessimistic. It saw Congress as continuing to operate in a nineteenth-century fashion, "insulated from the new America . . . losing its ability to act quickly and decisively," and warned that unless it somehow reforms itself, "Congress may cease to be a legislative body in the traditional sense."

The realization that Congress may be incompetent to cope with the problems and needs of more than 200 million people has even penetrated the mind of Congress itself. Richard Bolling, an outstanding moderate from Missouri, whose two decades in the House have left him limp with cynicism, acknowledges that the House is "ineffective in its role as a coordinate branch of the federal government, negative in its approach to national tasks, generally unresponsive to any but parochial economic interests"[4]—in other words, virtually worthless as a federal legislature.

After his first term in Congress had ended in 1970, Representative Abner Mikva, who came to Washington after crusading service in the Illinois state legislature, commented on his new surroundings and his new colleagues:

> It's my impression that you can live your whole life in Congress being only nominally exposed to the real outside world. Even the real world in Washington. You park in the underground garage of the House office building, you walk from your office to the Capitol in the underground walkway. You drive back to your better-than-average apartment or house without having to pass through the areas that reflect the real Washington. I think there are guys who have been here 15 or 20 years who have forgotten what the real world looks like.

Then he recalled a parade that he was in the previous Labor Day in Chicago: "There we were, the bands and the banners and all the hoopla. I was in the second car. And there were the people on the curbs—their arms folded. You would have thought we were leading a funeral procession. They don't trust politicians, any politicians. And who can blame them?"[5]

The political battle cry "Power to the people" was first used widely by the Black Panthers in the late 1960s. It quickly became so popular that Richard Nixon, never before known to take a fashion from the Panthers, began regularly using the phrase, as in his Budget Message of 1970. He declared that a central purpose of the budget was "to return power to the people." And in campaigning for the election of Republican congressional candidates that fall, he would sometimes appraise one of his programs as "meaning more power to the people" and raise his hand high in saying so, although, as one political writer remarked, "stopping well short of clenching his fist."

It was inevitable that the heartfelt cry of the people would be turned into a political sales pitch, but that does not make it any less real. The people want their government back, or at least a piece of it. Disenchantment with professional politics, and especially with Washington's variety, can no longer be considered merely the grumpiness of the sophisticates. In just one brief period has the public stated its confidence in the conduct of Congress,

1964 to 1966, the only really productive years since Franklin D. Roosevelt's first term. Before and since that unique 1964–66 blossoming, only about one-third of the public has consistently said it thinks Congress is doing a good job.

A Congress of the People?

In recent years the population majority, and with it the major problems of the nation, has swung from rural areas to urban centers. But, in general, Congress does not address itself to this urban majority. Of the twenty-one chairmen of standing committees in the House of Representatives, only six come from urban centers of more than 100,000 population, and one of these six—George Mahon of Lubbock, Texas, chairman of the House Appropriations Committee—grew up on a farm. Four of the chairmen come from towns so small that they are not listed in the *World Almanac*, which lists any center of more than 2500. Such men have as little interest in familiarizing themselves with the needs of the central city as urban congressmen have in learning how to milk a goat.

The two most powerful men in the House (aside from Speaker Carl Albert, who hails from Bug Tussle, Oklahoma) are Wilbur Mills, chairman of the Ways and Means Committee, who comes from Kensett, Arkansas, a place of less than 100 population; and Mahon of Lubbock, which is not so much a city as it is a big general store for the vast farming and ranching area of which it is the hub. These two men, who represent both legislatively and spiritually the most stagnant backwaters of America, have much to say about the pace and style of our national life because they are empowered to answer these most basic questions: Who and what is Congress going to tax, and who and what will it allow to escape taxation? How and where and when is the money going to be spent?

The House is close to Norman Rockwell's America. Its leaders are a languid fraternity of uncomplicated men who are guided by the principle that the simplest things are best. The man who presides over the Education Committee (Carl D. Perkins) hails from a Kentucky town of 793 and never graduated from college; Wright Patman, the octogenarian gentleman (Texas hometown population: 30,000) who guides the Banking and Currency Committee, is so caught up in antiquated economic feuds that he periodically makes a speech denouncing John D. Rockefeller, Sr., who has been dead for more than three decades, and thinks that the pinnacle of his career was reached in 1932 when he proposed the impeachment of Treasury Secretary Andrew Mellon.

The House Armed Services Committee is presided over by F. Edward Hébert. Although a son of sophisticated New Orleans, Hébert adheres to the viewpoint of small town nineteenth-century (or seventeenth-century) America: that black is black and white is white (he vetoed Louisiana's integrated Junior ROTC program because "we couldn't have that"), that young people should be seen and not heard (during student demonstrations in the late 1960s he proposed, "Let's forget the First Amendment"), and that anyone meriting the name enemy during time of war should simply be wiped off the face of the globe (of the Vietnamese, "We should move and destroy everything—everything that is in the hands of the enemy"). Harley O. Staggers presides over the Interstate and Foreign Commerce Committee; he is an ex-coach and ex-sheriff who lives where he was born, in Keyser, West Virginia, population 7000. His committee has a profound influence on one of the most complicated problems of urban America—the federal transportation policy—and yet his home district has virtually no four-lane highways, much less an expressway system. He treats the federally subsidized train system as though it were a toy; for months he forced the Department of Transportation to run one of its crack Amtrak trains (at the time, it had only two) into his home district on a daily basis, just to show off to the home folks. It cost the U.S. taxpayers $69,500 a month.

In the Senate there are many cosmopolitan, sophisticated members; twenty-seven of the one hundred senators are millionaires. But the tone is still set by the less populated areas of the country, and especially by the South. Of the seventeen standing committees, only one, Labor and Public Welfare, is chaired by a member from the Northeastern states (Harrison Williams of New Jersey), and that did not take place until 1971, when the Southern chairman was defeated, and the West Virginia senator who was next in line stepped aside so that he could remain chairman of a more important committee. The Ninety-third Congress (1973–74) had these men chairing its most important committees: Aeronautics and Space, Frank Moss of Salt Lake City, Utah, population 175,885; Agriculture and Forestry, Herman Talmadge of Lovejoy, Georgia, population 191; Appropriations, John McClellan of Little Rock, Arkansas, population 132,483; Armed Services, John Stennis of De Kalb, Mississippi, population 880; Banking, Housing, and

Urban Affairs, John Sparkman of Huntsville, Alabama, population 137,802; Commerce, Warren G. Magnuson of Seattle, Washington, population 530,831; Finance, Russell B. Long of Shreveport, Louisiana, population 182,064; Foreign Relations, J. W. Fulbright of Fayetteville, Arkansas, population 30,729; Government Operations, Sam J. Ervin, Jr., of Morganton, North Carolina, population 14,000; Interior, Henry Jackson of Everett, Washington, population 53,622; Judiciary, James Eastland of Doddsville, Mississippi, population 190; Labor and Public Welfare, Harrison A. Williams, Jr., of Westfield, New Jersey, population 33,720; Post Office and Civil Service, Gale W. McGee, of Laramie, Wyoming, population 23,143; Public Works, Jennings Randolph of Elkins, West Virginia, population 8287. (This list does not include the committees on the District of Columbia, Rules and Administration, Veterans' Affairs, and Select Small Business, which are of second- or third-rung importance.)

Of course, it would be absurd to suggest that men of rustic or nonmetropolitan background would be unable to show the necessary flexibility to cope with the problems of city folks. It would be especially absurd to suggest that even the most homespun of these chairmen has not lived in Washington so long, and probably traveled the world so widely, that what he lists officially as "home" is anything more than a stake to keep him in good with his electorate. But the fact remains that at the level of the committee chairs, there is a grotesque imbalance of representation for the small town, the wide open spaces, and the South. Eight of the fourteen committee chairmen listed above hail from Dixie. If you totaled the population of these home towns you would have less than half a million people, or about the population of Louisville, Kentucky. It is not likely that among those eight chairmen you could whip up more than a thimbleful of sympathy or understanding for the ghetto resident of Bedford Stuyvesant or Watts or for the person who commutes daily through the Los Angeles smog belt.

The Seniority System

The leadership of Congress has been determined not on the basis of talent or wisdom or imagination (although these have not been considered demerits) but on the basis of political longevity. Seniority has been the key to power, the key to chairmanships and all that goes with them.

There is nothing inherently wonderful about youth and nothing inherently awful about old age. If the ancient fools of Congress were weeded out there is no assurance that they would be replaced by young whizbangs, nor any assurance that some of the wise old men wouldn't be replaced by young asses. The Senate was hardly improved in quality in 1970 when Tennessee replaced Albert Gore (then sixty-three) with William Brock III (then forty), who ran a poorly disguised campaign against Gore as a "nigger-lover." And it was critically shortchanged when Illinois replaced the great Paul Douglas (then seventy-four) with the genteel, mediocre Charles Percy (then forty-seven). There is no inevitable conclusion that one can reach about the mentality of the congressional leadership today if that conclusion is based solely on the fact that the average committee chairman was in his forties a century ago, and today he is over sixty-seven.

But one thing can be concluded from the seniority system: it cripples ambition and enthusiasm. The typical congressman elected in 1972—according to a scholar-fed computer—would have to wait forty-one years before he would have the opportunity to move into the House Appropriations Committee chair, thirty-nine years before the House Armed Services chair would be vacant, thirty-seven years at Public Works, and thirty-eight years at Ways and Means.

Pitiful things can happen during the long wait. In his book *Both Your Houses*, Warren Weaver, Jr., cites Congressman Chet Holifield as an example of the kind of victimizing that occurs. When Holifield came to the House from California in 1942 he was thirty-eight years old and a man of strong liberal instincts and humane motivations. By the time he finally became a chairman, in 1971, he had been sapped not only of his physical vitality but also of his humanitarian juices. He was pinched and crabbed, a strict establishmentarian, a crafty and sometimes deceitful protector of his own turf—and to heck with the social consequences. When his own committee, writes Weaver, "finally produced a consumer protection bill in 1971, he collaborated secretly with the Nixon Administration and Republican committee members to emasculate the final product. Challenged by reporters, he would respond with an emotional, incoherent defense of his entire career. Holifield had been forced by the system to wait too long, and it was too bad."[6]

The seniority system is not statutory; it is not run by regulations. It is a tradition, a policy, and not very old. There are two kinds of seniority: one kind is a member's seniority in the branch in which he serves, and the other kind is his seniority on his committee. The broader seniority is sometimes ignored in the assignment of members to committees. But a member's seniority on a committee is almost sacred. Almost, but not quite. In the House, Adam Clayton Powell, the Harlem cut-up, was removed as chairman of the Education and Labor Committee in 1967. As for subcommittee chairmanships, they are more fluid. Several times in recent years powerful Southern committee chairmen have taken away the subcommittee chairs of moderates who, to their mind, were getting out of line.

Former Senator Fred Harris has summarized several of the more unsavory features of seniority:

> Once a man is assigned to a committee as a freshman . . . he has only to remain alive and get re-elected in order to ensure that he will one day chair that committee (assuming his party remains in the majority). Chairmen can decide what legislation their committees will consider, and indeed, *whether* a given piece of legislation will be given any consideration at all. On many committees, chairmen alone exercise the power to hire and fire most committee staff members, and to establish subcommittees.[7]

Equally critical, seniority prevails on the House-Senate conference committees. Far too little attention is given by the public to the machinations of these dictatorial cabals. With the clear-headed perspective of a deposed politician, former Senator Albert Gore provided this description of a typical conference committee:

> It is here, in secret meetings often not even announced until the last minute, that a few men can sit down and undo in one hour the most painstaking work of months of effort by several standing committees and the full membership of both houses. It is here, after the tumult and shouting and public debate have faded from the House and Senate and after the headlines have shifted to a new subject, that appropriations measures, tax bills and other substantive legislation can suffer remarkable mutation.
>
> After the conference committee's "report," or agreed action, is taken, the two houses must then vote on it up or down, in toto, without amendment. There is usually scant explanation or debate before the vote to accept or reject. The conference deliberations are not published and the reports are often all but unintelligible to the public and Congress alike—sometimes legislators are not aware of what they have voted for.[8]

As an example of what goes on there, he told of "a cold December night in 1969" when the conference committee met secretly to dispose of the so-called Tax Reform Act of 1969. By 2:30 A.M., he said, the committee had agreed to increase the tax exemption for the wage earner by $150 a year but at the same time to create other special deductions that would give "the head of General Motors, and others with like earned incomes . . . as much as $90,000 per year" of added tax relief. This provision, he explained, had been slipped into the House's tax legislation "at a midnight session of the House Ways and Means Committee just before the bill was approved and reported to the full House. It represented an extra $200-million loss to the government, or gain to the highly paid, and the ordinary taxpayer would have to make up the deficit."

Gore fought it in the conference committee, but he was greatly outnumbered on the final vote. The conference bill was then approved by both houses, which received it just three days before the Christmas vacation and didn't want to get into an argument that would interfere with the holidays. And so the nation was strapped with a costly piece of special interest legislation that was not debated in the full committee of either house or debated on the floor of either house, and, as Gore said, "the general public never really became aware of it."

Those who have benefited most from the seniority system—or, as cynics call it, the senility system—have been those politicians who come from safe districts or safe states, where the Establishment sees to it that as long as they follow tradition and protect the status quo no serious challengers will arise to endanger their place in Congress. And, since the safest no-contest areas are in the South, that area has benefited most in Congress. Southerners chair most of the important committees in both houses.

All Southern chairmen are nominally Democrats. But only a couple of them cast their votes more than 50 percent of the time with the national Democratic party platform, and some cast their votes as much as 80 percent of the time with the conservative Republican opposition. The House Democratic Study Group's analyses show that

one of three Democratic committee and subcommittee chairmen vote against Democratic programs and against the majority of their Democratic colleagues more frequently than does the average

120

Republican. In fact, opposition by Democratic chairmen was responsible for half of the major defeats suffered by the Democatic majority during the 90th Congress [1967-68]. Similarly, rigid Democratic adherence to the seniority system has, in the past 15 years, resulted in giving committee and subcommittee chairmanships to 59 members who in 1956 signed the "Southern Manifesto" pledging that they would employ "every available legal and parliamentary weapon" at their disposal to reverse the Supreme Court's school desegregation decision and defeat all civil rights legislation coming before Congress.[9]

The presence of so many "party" Democrats from the South is the main reason that the Democratic programs so often fail. Since 1938, the House did not again have a majority of "program" Democrats until after the 1964 Democratic landslide, and that majority ended in the 1966 election.

Seniority is treated with far more hallowed respect as a "custom" than it deserves. Although the rule of seniority has been almost ironclad since the Second World War, before then it was violated a great deal. Studies show that in the House, from 1880 to 1910, of the 750 chairman appointed by the Speaker (who at that time had the power to appoint committee members and chairmen), 429 were indeed senior committee members, but 321 were not. Between 1910 and the Second World War, there was a slight tightening of the seniority system; in those years chairmen were the senior committeemen in 676 appointments but were not in 224 appointments. In other words, there is a deep tradition for ignoring seniority if Congress should choose to do so. It appears to have no such changes in mind; its attempts at change only prove how uninterested the members really are.

Boodle and Pork Barrel

Congress is distracted by its political venality, by the fact that it is usually motivated by mundane rewards. The more candid members of Congress, such as Representative Bolling, admit—without startling anybody—that "the mortar that binds the system consists largely of what has been called inelegantly but properly 'boodle.' "

Boodle includes the location of a military installation, with a construction payroll followed by a steady payroll of civilian and military employees who live and spend and pay taxes in a member's district. It also includes a wide variety of public works—dams, rivers, and harbor projects, federal post office and office buildings, conservation and reclamation projects. The boodle in itself is legitimate and productive. The hitch is in the way it is distributed. Generally, the stay-in-line orthodox members will come away with the fuller plate.[10]

The other phrase for this is, of course, pork barrel; and Bolling is incorrect when he says it is legitimate and productive. Often it is not. In a $200-billion budget the barrel may not be bottomless, but there is quite enough pork to go around. Representative Jamie L. Whitten of Mississippi, in asking speedy approval of a $3-billion public works (dams, post offices, and so on) appropriations bill, asserted, "Since the works provided reach into every nook and corner of the country, the report has had the attention of practically all the membership of the House."

In a typical year, 1968, the House rejected proposed financing of bilingual education, funds for a larger Teacher Corps for slums, funds for rehabilitating the handicapped, but it *added* $138 million to the education package for the antiquated "impacted area" program, which pumps federal money into areas where federal employees live, whether or not the areas need the money. For example, Montgomery County, Maryland, one of the richest counties in the nation, gets "impacted" money because it is home to many of Washington's government workers.

Why would Congress turn down money for the crippled and increase funds for well-to-do children with no handicaps? Because there are more voting parents of the latter than of the former. In 1969, when President Nixon vetoed the education bill partly because it contained such a generous allotment for the impacted areas, Speaker John McCormack harangued the House in an honest manner. "Do you want to wipe that program out?" he asked. "You are not going to do it. That affects about 300 congressional districts in the country and 300 members are interested—and I do not blame them. In his veto message the President said, 'My veto of both of these bills is painful.' If he was coming up for re-election this year, it would be so painful he would sign the bills."

This appeal for support of legislation because it touches so many lives and therefore fits quite logically into representative government is misleading; that has never been a consistently effective way to evoke congressional support. Medical care for the aged was proposed in every session of Congress for a generation before it was finally, reluctantly, passed; yet there were certainly old people

who needed this protection in every district.* When President
Nixon sent a mild industrial safety bill to Congress in 1970, he
acknowledged that the legislation had been needed for three decades or more. Indeed, legislation of that sort had been proposed for
that long, yet Congress had previously turned it aside and did not
rush to deal with Nixon's proposed answer to the industrial dangers that every year kill more than 14,000, injure 260,000, and
lay up 390,000 with occupational illnesses. Every district would
have been helped by its passage, so why didn't Congress act?

In 1950 President Truman established a special Commission
on Migratory Labor, which made recommendations for helping the
transient farm hands with federal laws regulating housing and
health and work conditions. Nothing was done. In 1960 there was
a flurry in Congress following Edward R. Murrow's famous television documentary about migrant laborers, "Harvest of Shame."
Since then there have been several more flurries, a kind of fibrilla-
tion of the congressional heart. And yet in 1973 witnesses were
still trooping to Washington to tell about migrant children whose
average life span is twenty years shorter than other Americans'
life expectancy; some 400,000 of these migrant youngsters pick up
pieces of education at 8000 schools while passing to and from the
harvest fields, most of them never graduating from grade school.[11]
Nearly a quarter century after Truman's commission, why had
Congress managed to accomplish so little for them?

Since the early 1950s there have been periodic efforts to get
Congress to establish programs guaranteeing that nobody in America will go hungry. Since the early 1960s these efforts have been
increased. But today millions of people, including hundreds of thousands of school children, haven't enough to eat, and Congress still
refuses to take the final steps that would correct the situation.
Why? Stiff controls on the sale of guns have been advocated for
years by the FBI, the associations of police chiefs, and most scholars of crime (in addition to the public, which polls regularly find to
be in favor of controls). After the assassination of John Kennedy
fresh efforts were made in Congress to pass a gun control act;

---

* The American Medical Association thought that it would lose money through
a nationalized health program, which is why the AMA fought it so bitterly for
so many years; as it turned out, doctors are getting rich from the program,
and one no longer hears the faintest whisper of a suggestion from the AMA
that the program be done away with. The Senate Finance Committee found
that in 1968 4300 doctors each got $25,000 or more from Medicare; 68 collected
$100,000 or more each. By 1973, the doctors were really hitting their stride,
with one obstetrician in Washington, D.C., collecting $205,000 in Medicaid
payments.

after the assassinations of Martin Luther King, Jr., and Robert Kennedy the campaigns were renewed. Yet with the exception of a clamp-down on mail order sales, the gun traffic is heavier today than ever before.

It isn't that Congress cannot work swiftly if it chooses to. Sometimes, in fact, it moves so swiftly that one may justifiably suspect it is traveling without the weighty burden of thought.

It is quite common for either house to appropriate billions of dollars for military hardware with less than ten minutes of debate. Members sometimes act with precipitous speed on tax legislation favoring special interests, as the Senate did in the closing hours of the 1966 tax debate; many millions of dollars of exemptions were voted on the floor to help, among others, aluminum companies, oil companies, tobacco companies, hearse manufacturing companies, investment funds, and persons earning more than $25,000 a year. It was called, for good reason, "The Christmas Tree Bill."

It has always been that way; whether in the 1930s or the 1960s or the 1970s, Congress manages to show the most speed when the demands on it are made by powerful, moneyed groups.

Or just plain money itself, of the public payroll variety. In mid-1973 the Senate voted itself a 25 percent pay boost in a matter of seconds, without a word of explanation, discussion, or a record vote. When the bill died in the House, an effort was made to revive it again in the Senate, but this time it ran into major opposition and finally was killed by a broadside of sarcasm from Senator James Allen of Alabama, who pointed out: "The other day, when the war powers bill was being considered, there were exactly three senators on the floor discussing this extremely important matter. I recall that on many of the end-the-war amendments an attendance of four to six senators was a pretty good turnout. We have passed multi-billion-dollar appropriation bills with only four or five senators on the floor. But this afternoon we have around 75 senators in attendance...."[12] Personal money really gets the old blood to churning.

Partisan emergencies can also inspire haste. In the last half of his term President Johnson was running into more debt than he wanted his budget to reflect. So he called on his old Texas friend Wright Patman to hustle through a piece of legislation that would permit Johnson to sell bonds of a type that would not show up in the budget. Patman obliged, strong-arming that bill through a thirty-minute session of the Banking and Currency Committee that excluded witnesses opposing the move.

The pattern is clear. When the action benefits friends in the party or indulges special interests to whom the lawmakers are indebted (or hope to become indebted) or helps somebody make money on a grand scale—speed is not out of the question. But there is not much money to be made from giving food stamps to the poor or building clean housing for migrant laborers or doing many of the other things mentioned above that Congress was slow to act on.

Overlapping—and Conflicting—Interests

It is not surprising to see Congress most energetic in those matters that mean profits, because to a great many men in Congress making legislation and making profits mean the same thing.* According to records filed with the House Ethics Committee, 117 of the 363 members reelected to the Ninety-second Congress (1973–

---

* To avoid apoplexy at every turn in this tour through the federal government, one must keep steadily in mind that the foremost purpose of Congress as well as of the bureaucracy (with the President and the courts, this is more of a variable) is to serve business. The gap between patriotic myth and reality could not be wider on this point. V. O. Key, Jr., once observed that businessmen actually would have us believe that "all solutions are contained within the magic phrase 'free enterprise,' " and yet it is surely true, as Key went on to say:

If by some miracle we should overnight establish a free enterprise system by wiping from the statute books all interferences with economic liberty, it would be regarded tomorrow as a catastrophe. The pressures on Congress to restore the status quo ante would be formidable. On hand to assert that they wanted none of free enterprise would be the lobbyists for the airlines, the steamship conferences, the investment trusts, the chambers of commerce, the banks, the truckers, the petroleum industry, the real estate developers, the cosmetologists, and the Nevada gamblers. ("Public Opinion and the Decay of Democracy," *The Virginia Quarterly Review*, Autumn 1961.)

A team of special assignment reporters for the Associated Press dug up information in August 1971 that gives weight to Key's prediction. The AP found that "private enterprise in America collects roughly $30 billion a year in government subsidies and subsidy-like aid, much of it hidden or disguised." The AP conceded that it could not be certain of its figures, but it was convinced that the subsidies would total "at least" $28 billion and "may run as high as $38 billion" a year. Tax breaks, incentives, and exemptions may run as high as $15 billion annually; farm subsidies total between $6 billion and $9 billion; loans to business (direct, guaranteed, and insured) come to $250 billion, "six times the outstanding credit advanced by all commercial banks"; the maritime industry gets $450 million a year, the airlines $63 million (including $10.5 million to multi-millionare Howard Hughes' Air West Airlines), and the railroads $172 million over a five-year period; defense contractors get to use $14.6 billion worth of government property for profit-making purposes; United States companies doing business overseas receive over $6 billion in loans and insurance.

74) held outside professional and/or business interests. This does not count the freshmen legislators, who had not had time to cut their outside ties—if they wanted to. Of those 117 House members earning money from outside activities to augment the $42,500 they are paid by the taxpayers, 41 are associated with law firms; these include House Judiciary Committee Chairman Peter W. Rodino, Jr. (D., N.Y.), and House Crime Committee Chairman Claude Pepper (D., Fla.). Pepper was also listed as a director and vice president of a savings and loan institution. The possibility of conflicts of interest for such men is enormous.

Forty-four House members acknowledged being officers of financial institutions. Melvin Price (D., Ill.) is a bank director—he is also chairman of the House Ethics Committee. Among others who acknowledged holding offices in banks or savings and loan institutions are Wayne Hays (D., Ohio), chairman of the House Administration Committee; Thomas Morgan (D., Pa.), chairman of the House Foreign Affairs Committee; Chet Holifield (D., Calif.), chairman of the House Government Operations Committee. House Majority Leader Thomas P. O'Neill, Jr. (D., Mass.) is owner of a real estate and insurance agency and director of a hospital stock corporation. Majority Whip John J. McFall (D., Calif.) is associated with a law firm. Aside from the lawyers and bankers, fifty-three other congressmen admitted income from business ventures ranging from oil to funeral homes.

It is highly unlikely that these 117 are the only House members making cash on the side. There are many ways to fudge on the report. As for outside income on the Senate side, those aristocratic fellows do not even make the rudimentary gesture offered on the House side toward disclosure, so there is no way to know.

The question behind these activities, of course, is: How much do they affect the legislators' votes? Are bankers likely to vote for a tax on banks? Are lawyers likely to vote for some legislation that might cut into their clients' profits? Is not the secret promise to deposit a large amount in a bank, and ask no interest or reduced interest, perhaps enough to buy a banker-congressman's vote? If General Motors becomes a client of lawyer-Congressman Hamhock of Georgia, would Hamhock be likely to vote for stiffer auto safety standards? An 1863 law forbids lawyer-congressmen from taking clients who do business with the government, but there are easy ways to get around it. When ex-Congressman Emanuel Celler was chairman of the House Judiciary Committee, he used a clever "two-door" system at his law firm. Clients doing business with the federal government went in one door, and Celler claims he never talked to them; *his* door, he said, only welcomed the other kind of clients.

It is commonplace for congressmen owning oil and gas stock to vote in favor of that industry on tax legislation, and for congressmen owning stock in the broadcasting industry to vote for bills that would protect its income (such as the legislation aimed at salvaging cigarette commercials for TV). Senator Russell Long of Louisiana, chairman of the Senate Finance Committee, which has been a citadel guarding the oil depletion allowance, is a millionaire from his oil holdings and admits to being "the darling of the oil industry."

Except for defense industrialists, no group of businessmen is so protected by the American taxpayers as those big-big farmers who prefer to call themselves "agribusinessmen." It is for them that the Department of Agriculture is funded by Congress. While about 150,000 noncompetitive small farmers are forced to sell out each year, the agribusinessmen who are taking over grow wealthier from federal price supports and from subsidies for not planting certain crops (the euphemism is "acreage diversion").* The biggest windfall payments go to the cotton growers. The second biggest to wheat growers. Of the thirty-six members of the House Agriculture Committee, twenty-one are from cotton states and nineteen from wheat states (the overlapping is from states big in both, like Texas). On the Senate Agriculture Committee, six of the thirteen members are from cotton states and six from wheat states. W. R. Poage, who owns two farms in Texas, is chairman of the House group; Texas gets the largest handout of all—nearly one-third the total paid to the nation's cotton farmers. Texas also gets the fifth

---

* There are less than half as many farms today as there were in 1940, but the Department of Agriculture's budget has quadrupled, largely as a result of the fatter subsidies. Little of this is shared by the 14 million rural poor; it goes to outfits like the James G. Boswell farm corporation in California, which has received as much as $4.4 million in a single year from the federal government. In 1970, nine such corporate farmers were paid more than $1 million; twenty-three got subsidies of $500,000 or more. That was the year Congress passed a law that was supposed to limit each individual farmer to no more than $55,000 in subsidies; but some of our leading Americans, like Senator James Eastland and actor John Wayne, simply split up their farm holdings among family and friends, and the new law saved the government not a penny. One of the more interesting free enterprisers standing in line for a handout was Kenneth Frick, the very man who administered the Agriculture Department's farm subsidy program; he and his brother stood to earn $110,000. In 1973 Congress further lowered the subsidy ceiling to $20,000 per farmer, which means that more splitting of farms will have to be done to achieve the same booty.

largest handout for feed grains; Poage raises feed grains. James O. Eastland, the second-ranking member of the Senate Agriculture Committee, owns a 5000-acre cotton plantation in Mississippi.

Senator John McClellan, chairman of the Permanent Investigating Subcommittee, once held a brief—very brief—investigation into an oil lobbying scandal, but he cut it off before involving such clients of his Little Rock law firm as Standard Oil, Seaboard Oil, Carter Oil, and Tidewater Oil companies. McClellan has, with a great deal of fanfare, investigated bank scandals; he has been quieter about the fact that his law firm opposed the chartering of banks that would compete with two that he holds stock in.

With overlapping interests, if not conflicts of interest, so common in Congress, it is probably to be expected that members see nothing wrong in taking favors from these moneyed allies.* Congressmen on committees handling bills that could affect airlines often receive free trips to exotic places from those same airlines; congressmen who have control of legislation that will affect the profits of trucking firms, steamship lines, banking houses, agribusiness firms, the giant dairies, and all the other big and little blocks in the U.S. business playpen, unfailingly receive generous contributions at election time—whether or not they have opposition—as well as receiving generous favors between campaigns. To suggest that the relationship might be otherwise often brings an incredulous response from our politicians. When Edward Garmatz was in

---

* Being tolerant of their own conduct, congressmen are also tolerant of others in government who own a piece of the action. After reading more than two hundred confirmation hearings held by thirteen Senate committees since the Nixon Administration took over in 1969, the Associated Press reported (April 13, 1971) that there was "scant mention of the federal laws which prohibit officials from having certain investments. And nowhere in the 2,619 pages of testimony was reference made to a broad 1966 presidential order stating that federal officials 'may not have direct or indirect financial interests that conflict substantially, or appear to conflict substantially, with their responsibilities. . . .' " Congress interprets that rather loosely, the AP concluded, seeing as how Interstate Commerce Commissioner W. Donald Brewer acknowledged his ownership of $185,000 in stock of oil companies whose pipeline subsidiaries are regulated by the ICC; Federal Aviation Administrator John H. Shaffer acknowledged his ownership of nearly $350,000 in stock of an electronics and aeronautical firm; Deputy Defense Secretary David Packard acknowledged his ownership of $300 million of stock in a company that relies on the Defense Department for 20 percent of its sales; and Export-Import Bank President Henry Kearns acknowledged that he owns 8 percent of a company that has a "very large" loan from his bank—but in every case these men, and dozens of their peers in similar profitable situations, were confirmed by Congress to their posts. Sometimes, of course, they were asked to put their stock in "blind trusts" until they left office, as though this would end their interest in it.

Congress he was chairman of the House Merchant Marine Committee and had a singularly cozy relationship with the big shipping lines. Asked why he received most of his election money from the maritime industry, he snorted: "Who in the hell did you expect me to get it from—the post office people, the bankers? You get it from the people you work with, who you helped in some way or another. It's only natural."[13]

Does this sort of thing matter in the conduct of congressional business? It matters in many ways. Perhaps it matters least in tangible, measurable corruption of the members. Under the Federal Corrupt Practices Act lobbyists list expenditures of about $5 million in an average year (knowledgeable observers say that the correct figure is probably three or four times that high), but it is unlikely that many members of Congress actually receive payoffs. Nor is there a lobbyist-supported atmosphere of wine, women, and song in Washington. Nor is it likely that enormous profits go to the members whose own financial interests overlap those corporations whom they are supposedly regulating—or at least not enormous profits as a direct result of legislation they pass.

The primary effect of the friendships and overlapping interests among members and industry is that nothing is done. Most industries do not send their lobbyists to Washington to seek profitable legislation; they send them to Washington to block legislation that might control or cost them more in taxes. The major goal of the Washington lobby is not to pass legislation but to maintain the status quo. And from all appearances they are quite successful.

The Mechanics of Congress

Another reason for Congress' sluggishness is the mechanics of the place. President Kennedy, in a television interview in 1962, summarized the various booby traps:

> The Constitution and the development of the Constitution give all advantage to delay. It is very easy to defeat a bill in the Congress. It is much more difficult to pass one. To go through a committee, say the Ways and Means Committee of the House—to go through one of its subcommittees and get a majority vote, and then the full committee and get a majority vote; then go to the Rules Committee and get a rule; then go to the floor of the House and get a majority; then start over again in the Senate—subcommittee and full committee—and then go to the Senate floor, where there is unlimited debate (so you can never bring a matter to a vote if there

is enough determination on the part of the opponents, even if they are a minority); and then unanimously get a conference between the House and Senate to adjust the bill, or, if one member objects, to have it go back through the Rules Committee, back through the Congress, and have this done on a controversial piece of legislation where powerful groups are opposing it—that is an extremely difficult task. So that the struggle of a President who has a program to move through the Congress, particularly when the seniority system may place particular individuals in key positions who may be wholly unsympathetic to your program and may be, even though they are members of your own party, in political opposition to the President, this is a struggle which every President who has tried to get a program through has had to deal with. After all, Franklin Roosevelt was elected by the largest majority in history in 1936, and he got his worst defeat a few months afterward in the Supreme Court bill.

In some respects Congress can claim to be the most deliberative body in the world. But it is not always clear whether this means thoughtful or plodding. In 1969, for example, while legislation for electoral reform, equitable taxation, crime control, and appropriations piled up awaiting action, the Senate spent twenty-nine days—the sixth longest debate in a quarter century—discussing the merits and demerits of the Sentinel anti-ballistic missile complex (ABM). When the Senate wishes to ponder and talk, it ponders and talks; and no force in the world seems capable of rushing it. The House, even without the protracting influence of the filibuster (it was outlawed in the House in 1841), sometimes talks through the night.

About 90 percent of Congress' work is done in committee. Congress hires many experts—lawyers, economists, field specialists —among its 10,000 office and committee employees to help figure out just what is going on in the country and what should be done. Nevertheless, what at first appears to be careful attention to the problems of the nation on second glance begins to look very much like payroll-padding, wardheeling, and jockeying for publicity. There are thirty-eight standing committees in the Senate and the House, and these are supported by more than three hundred sub-committees.* This gives everyone a better chance for a title or for a seat on an important, or important-sounding, committee. Four-fifths of the Democrats in the Senate are chairmen of committees or subcommittees, although some must settle for such fiefs as the Judiciary Committee's Subcommittee on Federal Charters, Holidays, and Celebrations (with a membership of two).

* At last count. They split like amoebae, and the count keeps going up.

Some committee assignments—the House and Senate money committees (Finance, Appropriations, Ways and Means) especially —are sought because of their enormous prestige. Some committee assignments are prized because they give a good excuse for visiting overseas holiday spots at the taxpayers' expense. At the end of the 1972 session, Senator Abraham A. Ribicoff (D., Conn.), traveling as chairman of a Senate Finance subcommittee on international trade, took his wife and a staff assistant to London, Paris, Rome, and Tel Aviv to study "balance of trade problems." He was just one of dozens of senators and more than two hundred House members who, accompanied by relatives and favorite staffers, spent $700,000 that season on junkets. Among the vacationers were sixteen congressmen who had retired or had been defeated and thereby could not excuse spending the public's money for the trips; but they spent it nonetheless.

Some committee assignments are prized as an inside track to more pork barrel. Smithville, Tennessee (population 2400), the sleepy home town of Representative Joe L. Evins, was given a $1.4-million "model cities" grant (nearly one-fifth the amount given to Atlanta) by the Department of Housing and Urban Development. Evins is chairman of the subcommittee that oversees HUD's budget. Other committees are prized because they are good platforms for publicity. Congressman Otis Pike of New York puts it candidly: "These subcommittee assignments are important to us because that's how a political animal gets his exposure. If he gets on a good subcommittee, he gets his name in the newspapers."

Senators appointed to the special Watergate investigating committee struck the real mother lode of politically rich exposure. Joseph Montoya (D., New Mexico) and Edward Gurney (R., Florida): two of the most invisible and lightly regarded men in the Senate; Lowell Weicker, Jr. (R., Connecticut): a bright and gutsy fellow, but with virtually no seniority and no important committee assignments and therefore very little stature; Herman Talmadge (D., Georgia): a lightweight rustic who was known to the general public, if at all, as the son of one of the South's most notorious demagogues; Howard Baker, Jr. (R., Tennessee): a genial gentleman with little seniority and less clout, best known as the son-in-law of the late Republican powerhouse Everett Dirksen; and Sam Ervin, Jr. (D., North Carolina): a dignified and stouthearted champion of civil liberties and ardent foe of overbearing bureaucrats, but hardly a politician of national repute—and yet here they were suddenly famous. Suddenly their faces were among the most widely recognized in the nation, thanks to weeks of exposure on television.

Two publishing houses rushed into print with "wit and wisdom" collections of Ervin sayings, and overnight Baker became a "possible" Republican presidential candidate. All because they lucked into the right appointment.

Some assignments are prized because they give a good excuse to make fence-mending trips home, at taxpayers' expense. In 1970, his reelection year, Senator Henry M. Jackson of Washington took four trips home for "inquiries and investigations" on behalf of the Senate Interior Committee, of which he is chairman. The work of that committee is just as important in other Western states, but for some reason Jackson did not need to expand his inquiries and investigations beyond Washington's borders. Senator Ted Stevens of Alaska, up for reelection, went home to Alaska for the Interior Committee and nine days later went back for the Post Office and Civil Service Committee. It's commonplace.

About 30,000 pieces of legislation are introduced in each Congress. Hundreds of these are duplicates, and hundreds more are so trivial or so parochial as to not warrant the attention of the full Congress. Still there remain several thousand bills that are of such substance that Congress could well consider their passage. It is inconceivable that a member could give even a hundred bills, much less a few thousand, the consideration they deserve.

So the committee system is supposed to give the members at least a fighting chance. The bills are parceled out, with the bulk going to the seventeen permanent committees in the Senate and the twenty-one in the House, according to broad fields of specialization—banking, military affairs, appropriations, taxation, public works, education, and so on.

But the committee system, logical as far as it goes, falls woefully short of a solution to the work load of Congress. A senator from a major state may find himself assigned to half a dozen committees and more than a dozen subcommittees; he may face a morning in which six of these groups are holding hearings. He cannot possibly give personal attention to all that is going on. He may spend half an hour in each of the hearings, flitting from one to the other to make a *pro forma* appearance, and leave the actual studying of the bills to his aides. This transference and fuzzing of power is especially acute on the Senate side, where many aides are known to hold so much influence with their employers as to dominate them. The aides write the legislation, meet most of the lobbyists, write the speeches that go into the *Congressional Record*, make the compromises that go into the rewriting of legislation, and in every other way operate as surrogate lawmakers. Many of these aides are brilliant and well motivated—but in effect they are running the Senate without having to face the electorate and answer for their mistakes.

Most senators would not be as candid on this point as ex-Senator Saxbe, Ohio Republican: "On the Appropriations Committee they tell me you have to be a member for at least four years before you can see the curve on the ball, because it is all handled by the staff. Frankly, the lobbyists in Washington never talk to the Senators or Representatives. People think that we are carried around on a chit all the time, and that they are wining and dining and influencing us. But they are talking to our staffs. They are talking to the staffs of these committees. This is where the work is done."[14]

House members also depend on aides, especially on committee staffs. But because most House members hold membership on only one important committee, they have more time to at least read the legislation that comes to their committee and to make their own legislative compromises. But that isn't saying much. The day that a bill comes to the floor in either house is usually the first time that the members have seen it, much less studied it. That may seem, as former Representative Richard L. Ottinger once declared, "absolutely incredible," but that's the way Congress has been operating for years. And there are no signs that it has any plans to develop the kind of nonpartisan legislative research bureau that could summarize and analyze all major legislation for members long before they have to cope with it.

Thus the fate of legislation within the committee is of vital importance to its reception on the floor. If a bill receive a committee's unanimous approval, it is virtually guaranteed approval by that side of Congress. A study of thirty-five bills in the Eighty-fourth Congress showed that if they received more than 80 percent of the votes within the committee, they passed their floor vote test every time; if they received 60 to 79 percent of the committee votes, they passed on the floor 90 percent of the time. But legislation that got a negligible majority—51 to 60 percent of the committee vote—passed only 56 percent of the time.[15] The meaning is simply that the rest of the chamber looks to the committee for guidance. The committee vote is a weather vane that congressmen not familiar with the legislation can use for a quick reading of a bill's value.

The major defect in this follow-the-committee system is that many of the most important committees do not reflect a cross-sectional viewpoint. Membership on the money committees, for example, is largely conservative, and the cues they give are based more often on ledger balances than on human needs. Many of the pork barrel committees—such as the farm committees, already mentioned—are stacked in favor of the industries they deal with. Notorious in this regard are the armed services committees in both houses. Congressman Robert Leggett of California shows an unusual objectivity toward the House Armed Services Committee, of which he is a member:

> The forty guys on the committee should come from all walks of life. But they don't. Practically all of them have conflicts of interest. Not that any member is getting a piece of the cash or owns stock in a company that will benefit. Such as myself. We have the Mare Island Navy Shipyard in my district and the only nuclear naval shipyard. I like to build lots of those nuclear subs. I've done some personal emissary work to get some of the contracts. In my district is the Travis Air Force Base, the Beale AFB, the Mather AFB, the McClelland AFB, the Sacramento Army Depot and Aerojet General Corp. When it comes to the defense budget, my thinking is jaded. The basic problem with the committee is that it is made up of people who are postured that way because of commitments within their district and region.[16]

The membership of the important committees in both houses has remained largely conservative and unbending over the years because conservatives dominate the procedure for appointing members to the committees. In the Senate, Southerners make up one-third of the steering committee, which names Democratic senators to committees. In the House only veteran congressmen—who have shown their ability to go along with the system—are ever appointed to the Ways and Means Committee, whose Democratic members also serve as the Committee on Committees for the assignment of Democrats.*

---

* Only one freshman since 1913 has been appointed to the Ways and Means Committee. No black has served there since Reconstruction. Only one of its twenty-five members is a woman, Representative Martha Griffiths of Michigan. Sixteen are lawyers, and most of the others are businessmen. The average age in 1974 was fifty-six. Virtually all are from safe districts; most win regularly by more than 60 percent of the vote. Six of the fifteen Democrats are Southerners. In his book *The Politics of Finance* (Boston: Little, Brown, 1970), John F. Manley summarizes the above clues: "Extremely controversial men who fight what their colleagues believe are lost causes, or who are unshakably committed to objectives alien to the interests of other members, who demonstrate they cannot be relied on to engage in reasonable compromise . . . have little chance of becoming members of Ways and Means."

The scramble for power and jurisdiction by the committees has resulted in another kind of chaos. As explained by Representative Bolling:

> Committee jurisdiction is now a maze that confounds even veteran members. For example, as many as eighteen committees have jurisdiction over one or more programs of aid to education. In any one Congress, only one-third to one-half of the education bills are referred to the Education and Labor Committee itself. Interstate and Foreign Commerce, for an obscure historical reason, has jurisdiction over education bills affecting physicians and dentists; Veterans Affairs over education programs for veterans; Armed Services over programs for servicemen and women; Ways and Means over legislation to give tax credits to parents with children in college; Banking and Currency has had bills relating to college classroom construction; and Science and Astronautics over science scholarships.[17]

In 1973 there was a sluggish lurch toward reforming the committee system, for even Congress was alert enough to recognize that since the last major committee reforms of twenty-five years ago the national issues have changed somewhat. Major problems such as the energy crisis, pollution, and urban decay have emerged, but no single committee deals with any of these; instead the problems are chopped into pieces and scattered. At least four committees in the House, for example, claim some jurisdiction over the energy crisis.

But the select House committee studying reform of the committee system discovered at once that its first task would be to overcome the jealousies of powerful chairmen; once they get their hands on a field, they don't want to let go. In fact, they want to expand their jurisdiction. When Agriculture Committee Chairman W. R. Poage showed up to testify, he voiced typical aggression: "I certainly don't want to be accused of being out to grab some other committee's jurisdiction. However, I have long felt that there are many items of legislation which are presently assigned to other committees which could more logically fall within the jurisdictional scope of the Agriculture Committee." And before he was through, he had proposed raiding nine other committees for issues.

This jealousy of jurisdiction, plus the lust for publicity, cannot be reformed by legislation, and yet it is perhaps the biggest hang-up of all. Often the chairmen of matching committees in the two houses are not on speaking terms. Chairmen within the same house often engage in a sly underhanded feud. Senator Edmund

Muskie, Maine Democrat, has often been called "Mr. Environment" by the newspapers, and he cherishes the title; so when Senator Henry Jackson, Washington Democrat, introduced an environmental quality bill, Muskie quickly introduced one too. Jackson's went to the Interior Committee, of which he is chairman, Muskie's to the Public Works Committee's Air and Water Pollution Subcommittee, which he chairs—although the bills were virtually the same. Thereupon ensued a long, nasty, and totally unproductive fight to see who could sneak his bill through first and get credit. Jackson brought up his bill on a Thursday afternoon, when most of the senators had already left town for one of their typical four-day weekends and only seven were on hand to vote, so he got the jump on Muskie. That's one reason little reform is accomplished in Congress: the reformers are usually at one another's throats in a contest of piety.

Secrecy and ignorance also take their toll. Until 1971, all sessions of the House Appropriations Committee were held in secret (in 1971, with the advent of some mild reforms, the door opened, but rarely). In addition to being secret from the public, these sessions were also in practice off limits to congressmen who were not members of the particular appropriations subcommittees involved.

Secrecy still predominates. The $270-billion budget is cut up and parceled out to the thirteen appropriations subcommittees, isolated from everyone else inside and outside of Congress. (Somehow, powerful special interest lobbies manage to keep well informed on what is happening behind the closed doors and exert their influence where it will do them the most good before the legislation emerges again.) These thirteen subcommittee chairmen share the almost total power of full committee Chairman Mahon in deciding how much money will be spent, and where.* (By custom, all appropriation bills originate in the House. If the Senate tries to launch one, the House won't accept it.)

Each subcommittee chairman is czar of the money over which his group has jurisdiction. When Orville Freeman was Secretary of Agriculture he often said, "I have two bosses—Lyndon Johnson and Jamie Whitten." Congressman Whitten has been chairman of the Agriculture Appropriations Subcommittee since 1949. He throws just as much fright into Republican administrations. Newsmen in 1971 demanded that Russell Train, chairman of the Council on

---

* And, incidentally, eight of the thirteen House appropriations subcommittee chairmen are from the South or border states.

Environmental Quality, make public his plans for combating agricultural pollution, which—because of such things as pesticides runoff—is one of the most serious sources of water contamination. Said Train: "I can't make any commitment. I've got my own problems. I've got to get my money from the Agriculture Appropriations Subcommittee." When Ramsey Clark was attorney general, he admitted that Representative John Rooney of New York, chairman of the subcommittee handling Justice Department funds, "had us so cowed that if we needed 100 lawyers, we'd ask for 20 and hope to get five."[18]

It was men like these that Representative Michael J. Harrington had in mind when he complained, on behalf of the new wave (or ripple) of young dissidents in the House, that the rot of the old establishment goes "down into the bowels of Congress where insulated subcommittee chairmen make national policy in almost total obscurity. These men, 42 percent of whom come from rural districts despite the fact that 80 percent of the nation's population lives in urban areas, are named without contest, are not beholden to other members of Congress, nor to party, nor to a national constituency."[19] And when Harrington says they make national policy he is not exaggerating, for Mahon, who chairs the defense funds subcommittee as well as the full committee, "has reviewed and passed upon military budgets brought up to the Hill by ten different Secretaries of Defense." In the same vein, Richard L. Lyons, the *Washington Post*'s reporter of House affairs, estimates that "to State Department bureaucrats, their subcommittee chairman, Representative Rooney, is more to be reckoned with than a Secretary of State."[20]

The transcript of the hearings compiled by each subcommittee will commonly run to several thousand pages. Even the report summarizing the hearings of a subcommittee will be from forty to two hundred pages, and this report is not released to members of the House until two days before a bill goes to the floor for a vote. It is impossible for members to know what they are voting on. It is also virtually impossible to amend the appropriations bills on the floor because under the debate rules a member would have less than a minute—and sometimes only thirty to forty-five seconds—to explain his amendment. In a study made in 1970 by the House Democratic Study Group, it was discovered that in the previous five years, of sixty-three appropriations bills considered by the House, forty-six passed without one cent being changed as the result of floor debate.

In the Senate, three-quarters of the Appropriations Committee hearings are open to the public, but again the massiveness of the legislation makes it almost impossible for members to know what they are voting on when the money bills come to the floor. William Welsh, who has served a dozen years on Capitol Hill as aide to several senators, summarizes the typical aide's dilemma:

> We are least prepared in the area of most importance—the budget. The only place to get information is from the appropriations subcommittees that handle the various sections of the budget, and each chairman holds everything in his fist. Have you ever seen an appropriations bill? Well, it's a monstrous riddle, and two days after it comes out of committee it's up for a floor vote. You're flying by the seat of your pants. You hope that whoever is handling it knows what he's doing, is protecting the party and the people. But God help you as to finding a way to brief your Senator on it.[21]

The biggest hunk of the appropriations budget is, of course, earmarked for defense, and it is analyzed by Congress in only the most rudimentary fashion. When Saxbe was a member of the Armed Services Committee, he confessed ignorance:

> It is the job of our committee to approve the budget for the Department of Defense. . . . It takes more money simply to put together the budget in the Department of Defense, and more manpower and people, than the whole cost of running the Congress of the U.S. We have only 15 people on our committee staff and we are supposed to take that budget apart and analyze it. I might add that most of these people are patronage people of members of the Committee, and they also have to spend a lot of their time campaigning for those members. They fetch and carry, run their offices, haul their wives around. Thus, they are not available to me as a member of that Committee. . . .*
> We have this tremendous giant, the Department of Defense, spending $87 billion, coming back to the Congress where we have 15 staff members and 17 Senators, and we are supposed to pick this budget apart. It's like trying to pick out a rate-increase request for the Bell Telephone Company. It's in there but you can't find it.[22]

As a result of these procedures, "what really happens," says the Democratic Study Group, "is to concentrate the 'power of the purse' in the hands of a few men while relegating most other members to the role of rubber-stamping their decisions. It also prevents

---

* He is right; there are actually only two members of that staff who analyze the budget.

proper consideration of appropriations bills, denies the taxpaying public an opportunity to effectively influence national priorities, and makes a farce of the principle of representative government."[23]

Putting aside for a moment the question of whether the public has a right to sit in on the committee sessions where Congress decides how to spend the public's money, there remains the question of whether Congress can effectively do its job of representing the people when its own members are so ignorant of what is going on.

It is in the armed services committees of both houses that one finds the most intense secrecy (and accompanying ignorance) and the most dictatorial manner of doing business. One member of the House Armed Services Committee, Congressman Otis Pike of New York, claims that the first time he learned about a defect in the wing of the cost-plagued C–5A cargo plane was when he was drinking with a test pilot in California. "I didn't learn about this in the committee, from the chairman, or from the Pentagon," said Pike, "no, I learned about it talking to a guy in a bar. That's how we're treated in the Armed Services Committee."[24] The C–5A had been underway for six years and had already cost $2 billion before the committee was given a briefing on it.

Since the members of Congress are often handicapped by the trickery of their own colleagues, they naturally think nothing of imposing the same upon the public. Students of Congress like to think that the *Congressional Record* is an actual record of congressional debate; courts look to the *Record* for clues as to the "intent" of legislation, so that they can construe the laws in accord with Congress' wishes. Both students and courts are deceived. The *Record* is not a verbatim account. In fact, it often comes closer to fiction than fact. Members have five days in which they may "correct" the record of the day's proceedings. This gives members a chance to insert long speeches that they never gave, sometimes even to reconstruct bogus "debates." Often they were hundreds of miles from Washington when the actual debate took place. It also gives them time to delete thoughtless and inaccurate remarks and to knock out insults.

When Senator Abraham Ribicoff of Connecticut and Senator Jacob Javits of New York got to quarreling over school desegregation in 1971, Ribicoff accused Javits of "hypocrisy"; of being "unwilling to accept desegregation for his state, but ... willing to shove it down the throats of the senators from Mississippi." The

Record does not show these hot words ever to have been spoken. Nor does it show Ribicoff's remark to Javits: "I don't think you have the guts to face your liberal constituents who have moved to the suburbs to avoid sending their children to school with blacks." Instead, it was depersonalized into "The question is whether northern Senators have the guts. . . ." Thus history is rewritten in the embryonic stage.

On the Senate floor, July 14, 1970, Senator Barry Goldwater referred to military devices that are "helping our men in Laos especially—our airmen and our ground forces." Oops. Officially the United States had no ground forces in Laos, so to jibe with the Pentagon and State Department lines, Goldwater edited out the phrase "ground forces."

An extreme example of *Congressional Record* "ghosting": On July 2, 1970, the *Record* ran to 112 pages. Yet on that date the Senate met for only eight seconds, the House not at all. The *Record* was done by remote control—by adding, by revising, by expanding from the comfort of the members' offices—and often done not by the members themselves but by their staffs.

To observe an individual tour de force, turn to the *Congressional Record* of March 24, 1971. There it is recorded that eight times that day Senator Birch Bayh of Indiana rose to make statesmanlike utterances: urging strategic arms limitations; expressing his regret at the deaths of Whitney Young and deputy Democratic party chairman Ira Kapenstein; praising a health care plan; regretting a low voter turnout; urging group action lawsuits in consumer cases; and denouncing the supersonic transport, funds for which were up for a vote that day. There was only one defect in Bayh's performance: he wasn't there. Part of the day he was in Colorado skiing, and the rest of the day he was in the air returning to Washington. He missed everything, including the vote on the SST, but one could never tell from the *Record*.*

* Not only does the *Congressional Record* severely lose in candor as a result of long-distance insertions and after-the-fact editings; it is also a costly plaything in another sense. Just plain money. It cost an estimated $150 a page, at early 1973 prices, to print the *Record*. When Representative Bella Abzug, the wild woman from New York, stuck 136 pages into the *Record* on the subject of abortion, her little fling at propaganda cost the taxpayers about $20,000. When Representative Charles J. Carney, an Ohio Democrat, stuck into the *Record* the history and membership lists of the Saint James Catholic Church in Youngstown, Ohio, those five and a half pages doubtless allowed Carney to make point with his constituents, but it cost the taxpayers $770. By the end of 1973, the cost had risen to $209 a page.

Attempts at Reform

Congress is not devoid of self-criticism. Many members would agree with Representative Henry S. Reuss of Wisconsin that the institution should not be, but often is, run on "seniority, senility, secrecy and satrapy." Many members would sympathize with California Congressman Thomas Rees's complaints: "Everything is screwed up here. I finally moved half my staff to Los Angeles because I can't get anything done here. Scheduling is erratic. Nobody knows when bills will come up. There is no flow chart of work. You can't look ahead even a week. I really don't see how things can go on like they are."[25]

Congress is exceedingly reluctant to act on such criticisms. It does so about once every generation. In 1956 there was some bland reorganization of the place. Then in 1965 a Joint Committee on the Organization of the Congress was created; its recommendations, overwhelmingly approved by the Senate in 1967, got lost for the next three years in the House Rules Committee. But finally, in 1970, the House, too, approved some changes. No longer would the House, as it had done since the founding of the country, cast non-record votes on most of the legislation created while it was sitting as a "committee of the whole." From then on, if as many as twenty members asked for a record vote, they would get it. (When the issue is important, even the House can always supply twenty candid fellows.) Before the new rule, members could take one position publicly and then vote the opposite way without their duplicity being discovered, because most important votes—on the ABM, on the fight against hunger, on the war, on crime legislation—were taken on a nonrecord basis.

The first test of the new rule proved its virtue. For the previous decade the House had approved one money bill after another to support research for the SST; by 1971 the total had reached $864 million—all approved by nonrecord votes. Then in March of that year the House was asked to approve $134 million more for the highly controversial supersonic plane. This time the vote would be recorded. Knowing that they could not lie to their constituencies about where they were when the vote was taken and how they cast their vote, House members turned out in almost unparalleled numbers: 420 were there (in the unrecorded vote on this issue in 1970, only 188 took part), and they rejected the appropriation (and the multitude of aerospace lobbyists). As a result of such actions, some reform-minded members have taken heart. Says Representative

Morris K. Udall of Arizona, "I really can't say any longer that the House is rooted in concrete."

But it is still rooted in something. The reforms of 1970 left the all-important seniority system virtually untouched. Efforts to put an age ceiling on the committee chairman (even an age ceiling of seventy) and to limit the number of terms a member could serve as chairman (even allowing for an eight-year tenure) were beaten down. Democrats agreed that if ten party members challenged a chairman, that challenge would be submitted to a vote of the Democratic caucus. Optimists called that an achievement. But practically speaking, it was not. When it comes to a showdown, few members have the courage to oppose the reelection of a powerful chairman, even with the best of reasons for doing so.

This was proved at the Democratic caucus in 1971, when Congressman John Conyers of Michigan challenged the seniority of the five members from Mississippi, all of whom had been re-elected on a ticket that was not recognized by the national Democratic party. Since this constitutes disloyalty to the party, there was ample precedence for stripping them of their Democratic seniority. Or, if they were considered third-party members, being neither full-fledged Democrats nor Republicans, there was ample precedence for putting them at the bottom of the seniority list.

Conyers did not have much hope of winning the challenge, but he thought he might get 100 votes out of a possible 242. He got 55. So for those who want to know how many Democrats in the House believe in truly reforming the seniority system, or, to put it another way, how many will stand up to throw off the Southern yoke, there's the answer: 55. Less than one-quarter of the Democrats in that body.

What about the secrecy that has hung for generations over some of the key committees—was it lifted by the reformers of 1970? No. Committees that previously preferred to do their work openly continued to do so, and committees that preferred privacy continued to do most of their work privately. But the Legislative Reorganization Act of 1970 did encourage a voluntary lifting of some of the secrecy. The Appropriations Committee, which had always conducted its business in private, was not *required* to open its doors. But on very rare occasions it does so, with great fanfare and much talk of its "democracy." At the first of these new public shows the committee even allowed the television cameras to come in, with Chairman Mahon proclaiming heroically, "This committee has been in existence for 105 years and we thought a little experimentation would not be out of order." Later in the hearing, when a committee member complained about the hot TV lights, Mahon said: "They are hot, but that's what these hearings are all about. We want to shine the bright light of truth on this fiscal situation." Ah, if only that proved to be the prevailing philosophy of the future.

During the first year the new law was in effect, 1971, the public was barred from attending House committee hearings 41 percent of the time—a decrease from the 48 percent of 1970, but about the same as the 42 percent secrecy recorded in 1969. And in 1972 the House had moved back to a 44 percent secrecy level. The Appropriations Committee, whose chairman, Mahon, had made such a big production of "opening" his committee, actually was open to the public only 8 percent of the time in both 1971 and 1972.

On the Senate side, there was slightly more candor. Its committees met in secret 30 percent of the time in 1971, a bit better than the 33 percent secrecy of the year before but even worse than 1969, before the "reform" Legislative Reorganization Act, when they met secretly only 28 percent of the time. And by 1972 the Senate committees were setting a new record for secrecy, barring the public 37 percent of the time. As for the Senate committee meetings designated as "business sessions"—those in which they organized, marked up the legislation, voted on it, or held briefings —these were closed 97 percent of the time in 1972; in the House, the business sessions were closed to the public 79 percent of the time. Reform may have opened the doors briefly, but certainly not long enough to cause a draft.

As a result of the reformation the House of Representatives did loosen the hold of the ancients among its membership when it was agreed that no one could hold more than one chairmanship of a legislating subcommittee (that is, a subcommittee that processes bills; investigating subcommittees did not come under this provision). Previously, any one old fellow might hold not only the chairmanship of a full committee but also four or five subcommittee chairmanships; in this way, about forty senior members literally controlled the show.

Most aspects of the reformation were unimpressive because, perhaps, efficiency is not the highest goal of government anyway. Senator Hubert Humphrey, who sometimes sounds more like a preacher than a politician, made a strong point when he told his colleagues who were worrying because Congress was such a seemingly antiquated machine:

> I am not so worried about efficiency. You can read the Old and New Testaments, verse by verse and chapter by chapter, and the word "efficiency" never appears. Not once. But love, justice, liberty, God, people, brothers, sisters appear. You can read the Magna Carta and the word "efficiency" is not to be found there, yet it is a great document of representative government.
>
> You can read the Declaration of Independence and all of the grievances therein listed and not once did our founding fathers talk about the inefficiency or the efficiency of government. They had grievances about the injustice and the inequities that were imposed upon them.
>
> You can read the Constitution of the U.S. from the Preamble to the last word and not once find the word "efficiency" or in the Emancipation Proclamation. . . .
>
> Hitler was efficient and so was Bismarck. That did not give them justice and I think that what the American people want is justice.
> . . . I think that what they want out of the Congress and the Executive is not a fight over procedure, but what you are going to do about your cities before they blow up.
>
> I think what they [Americans] want from the Congress of the U.S. is response to human problems, and while we sit here fighting the battle of procedure, the American people become more disgusted with our government; not with our country, but with our government because what they see is government locked in quicksand, so to speak, spinning its wheels on debates between Presidents and Congress over procedures and forms.[26]

And between committee chairmen in Congress, and between regional blocs, and between population blocs, and between party and ideological blocs. Nag, nag, feud, feud: nagging and feuding about how the machine should run as often as about what it should process. Humphrey is quite right: efficiency is not the highest goal. But he also might have added that what the people want out of their government is honesty, and they have been disappointed in that with rare consistency.

Perhaps the key to the biggest quantum jump in honesty would be the establishment of a new method for financing elections. Congress has studiously avoided coming to grips with the inherent corruption of campaign funds.

Congress passed the Corrupt Practices Act in 1925. The act was, as President Lyndon Johnson later observed, "more loophole than law." From 1925 to 1972, no federal politician was prosecuted under that act. On rare occasions indictments were sought against donors, such as Tony Boyle, then president of the United Mine Workers; but Senator Humphrey, the gentleman of the pious tongue, who received $30,000 of the $45,000 illegally distributed by the UMW, was not indicted.[27]

The defects of the law were often highlighted by hypocrisy. In February 1971 it was disclosed that House Minority Leader Gerald R. Ford did not report $11,500 in campaign contributions the previous year from stockbrokers, an oilman, bankers, doctors, and a union group. Congress apparently failed to see the embarrassing irony of this situation, for it was not brought up at his vice-presidential confirmation hearings. And yet here was Ford—who had led the attempt to have Supreme Court Justice William Douglas impeached for receiving outside income from a foundation—pulling rank monkeyshines with his own campaign money. The Corrupt Practices Act requires full public disclosure of all campaign contributions received with a candidate's knowledge or consent. When Ford's campaign fund reached the legal limit allowed by Michigan law, he signed the other contributions over to the national Republican party headquarters, which then fed the money back to several cover committees, such as "Latvians for Ford" and "Veterans for Ford."[28]

The Justice Department did not take any action against Ford under the Corrupt Practices Act. Nor did Congress take any action against Ford as performing in an unethical way. Indeed, it would have been amazing if such action had been taken, since he had done nothing that a great many other congressmen had not done. Senator James L. Buckley of New York received nearly half a million dollars in 1970 through phony committees set up in Washington, D.C., to hide the true names of his donors. District of Columbia law did not require the listing of the names of campaign contributors, so fifty false-front committees—with such names as "Committee to Keep a Cop on the Beat" and "Scientists for Sensible Solutions to Pollution"—were set up in Washington to collect the money, and they in turn sent the money back to one hundred other Buckley committees in New York. Result: the chief law-and-order candidate in the New York senatorial race slipped neatly through the loophole in the law, and the public will never know who paid for his campaign.[29]

The Corrupt Practices Act required a House or Senate candidate to swear out "a correct and itemized account of each contribution received by him or by any person for him with his knowledge and consent, from any source, in aid or support of his candidacy." Yet every campaign year there were highly respectable federal politicians who filed reports in which they solemnly swore that they had not received a dime (their committees might have, but they pretended not to know about that). Zero-contribution reports have been filed, for example, by Senator George McGovern, Senator Edward Kennedy, Senator Edmund Muskie, Senator Lloyd Bentsen, Senator William Brock, and Congressman Carl Albert. To hear them tell it, politics is a free ride.

Addressing itself to a variation of the same problem, the Corrupt Practices Act required that "any committee, association or organization" giving to federal campaigns in *two or more states* must submit to Congress a list itemizing all donations. Digging around in the 1970 campaigns, the Associated Press discovered that the executives of four major defense contractors (McDonnell Douglas, Northrup, Ling-Temco-Vought, and Olin Corporation) and an oil company (Union Oil Company) and an aerospace contractor (TRW Inc.) had set up ad hoc groups and contributed an estimated total of more than $400,000 to dozens of campaigns in as many as thirty-one states, but did not file a report.[30]

Apparently the executives were also fudging on another provision of the Corrupt Practices Act that prohibted corporations from putting their money into political races. Pretending that it wasn't corporate money but was instead the personal money of corporate executives was a charade that took place every election. In presidential years it got pretty thick. The Citizens Research Foundation of Princeton, New Jersey, found that in 1968 this regulation was side-stepped by the officials of forty-nine companies, all of which were among the top beneficiaries of federal contract spending: their gifts totaled more than $1.2 million. No indictments followed, nor did Congress conduct an investigation.

A new law went into effect on April 7, 1972, which was supposed to plug most of the campaign funding loopholes and force honesty not only on all who run for Congress but also on presidential candidates. How well did the Federal Election Campaign Act of 1971 work?

Of the more than $60 million raised by Nixon for his 1972 campaign (twice what he raised in 1968), much—exactly how much will probably not be known for several years, but already $19.9 million has been traced—was collected by President Nixon's campaign fund-raisers before the deadline of April 7. Thus the law was not violated, except in spirit, for the names of many of these contributors were never revealed. Records of the sources for at least $2 million were destroyed. Some of this money was used to pay the Watergate burglars and other political saboteurs in 1972.

The farce so common under the old Corrupt Practices Act—corporations funneling money into politics via the "personal" gifts of their officers—was as rampant as ever. And purchased favors hung over the 1972 election in the same old thick clouds. Oilmen, for example, who must be regulated by Nixon-appointees on the Federal Power Commission, gave hundreds of thousands of dollars to the Nixon campaign. Robert L. Vesco, facing charges by the Securities and Exchange Commission for looting four mutual funds of $224 million, sent a $100,000 contribution in cash. The courier who brought the cash, in a suitcase, told Nixon's chief fund-raiser that Vesco expected some help.

From all indications, ambassadorships were, if not purchased outright, at least coincidental to great generosity. Walter Annenberg, ambassador to England, gave $254,000. Ruth Farkas, wife of a department store owner, gave $300,000; she became ambassador to Luxembourg. Henry Catto gave Nixon $25,000; his ambassadorship was in El Salvador. John N. Irwin II, appointed ambassador to France, gave at least $50,000 and is the brother-in-law of Arthur Watson, who gave $300,000. And so it went around the globe.

Between October 26, 1972, the deadline for preelection campaign fund reporting, and November 7, election day, the Nixon camp took in more than $1 million. The new law said they should report this money within forty-eight hours; they did not report it until January 31, 1973.

Much attention was later given to contributions by the big dairy organizations. Some people thought there just might be some connection between the fact that the dairymen gave $2 million to Nixon and friendly congressional candidates, and the fact that the administration gave the dairymen a price increase worth about $500 million a year. Some of the dairymen's contributions were never reported, in violation of the new law. Some of the contributions were made to members of Congress after their election (if the dairymen backed the wrong man, they were willing to pay off the other fellow after the race). The dairymen contributed generously to all nine members of the House Agriculture Dairy Subcommittee, to at least twenty-six of the thirty-one members of the full Agriculture Committee, and to at least eight of the eleven members of the House Agriculture Appropriations Subcommittee.

Wright Patman, chairman of the House Banking Committee,

was unopposed in 1972, but the savings and loan industry gave him $2000 anyway. House Majority Whip Thomas O'Neill, Jr., who had been found to have used a hidden committee to collect $12,000 for his unopposed campaign in 1970, was still collecting money in 1972 (well over $30,000 this time), although once again he was running unopposed. He was just one of a dozen congressmen who had neither primary nor general election opposition in 1972 but who, together, collected more than $145,000 even before the new law went into effect on April 7.

This is apart from the gross inequities of campaign financing, a problem Congress has largely ignored. Incumbents are always able to get big contributions more easily than challengers, and congressmen all feel that, whatever other label they wear, they all belong to the Incumbency party. Some critics believe that is the only party that exists. "Money flows to incumbents because it is an incumbent who has the power to provide help and assistance," says Fred Wertheimer, legislative director of Common Cause, stating the obvious. "The result is that in Congress today we have neither a Democratic nor Republican party. Rather, we have an Incumbency Party which operates as a monopoly." To bolster his argument he points out that the average total contribution to a House incumbent in 1972 was $525,809, while the average challenger was totaling only $243,070.[31]

Indeed, the outpouring of money to some incumbents is so grossly generous as to raise questions about what their backers want with it. In Texas, for example, Senator John Tower, a Republican, reported collecting and spending $2,303,355—$3.65 for every $1 spent by his Democratic opponent—to win reelection to a job that pays him only $42,500 a year. Who else benefits, and how, from his being in the Senate?

The new campaign disclosure provisions of the law were intended to hold down huge contributions by embarrassing the donors with exposure. It was not exactly a great success as a restraint. Of the $66.4 million spent by House and Senate candidates in 1972, less than $1 out of every $3 came from small givers ($100 or less). Nixon's top ten donors gave more than $4 million; his top one hundred backers gave $14 million.[32]

In short, the law that Congress passed and the President signed with great claims of having finally "reformed" the bottomless corruption of campaign financing turned out to be big enough to drive a Watergate through, plus dozens of smaller scandals. The Justice Department did not seem very excited, however. Common

Cause alone discovered and reported more than three hundred campaign violations, but as of mid-1973, nine months after the election, only one campaign fund violation had stirred the Justice Department to action—against a committee set up to impeach the President.

Neither Congress nor the White House seemed very enthusiastic about further improving the ethics of campaign financing. After the Senate in 1973 passed a bill to put ceilings on campaign contributions and expenditures, and to create an independent commission with enforcement powers, the Nixon Administration sent a cool message to Capitol Hill that it was not prepared to take a "final position" on the reform legislation. The White House also refused to take a public position on the proposal to finance campaigns out of tax dollars and thereby eliminate the buying and selling of candidates on the private money market. The House of Representatives was also consumed, as usual, with lethargy; Representative Wayne L. Hays, Ohio Democrat, through whose House Administration Committee the reform legislation would probably have to pass, said in late 1973 that he could not "see anything pressing this year."

One should not presume from this, however, that Congress does not now and then have faint twinges of guilt and misgivings about its misconduct in and between elections. Ethics committees were set up in each house in the 1960s. To be sure, they have been singularly inactive, but at least they exist. And there is even a kind of logic for their inaction. John Swanner, staff director of the House Ethics Committee, explains:

> Everybody tries to relate the House of Representatives to organizations that have a disciplinary structure, where the worker can be disciplined by the supervisor and the supervisor disciplined by the plant manager and the plant manager by the third vice president, et cetera. But there is no boss in the House of Representatives. A fellow can come up here and pick his nose, and so long as his constituents like nose-picking they can send him back, and there's not much anybody else can do about it so long as he doesn't bugger up everything else.[33]

A Congress by the People?

The faces of Congress may be changed by the electorate, but once the members get to Washington, they operate aloof from the electorate. Of course, they cannot entirely insulate themselves from the public, nor is that their desire. But they are aloof. They view themselves as specially ordained to conduct the public's business with a wisdom that they see descending upon themselves as they cross the Potomac. The longer they stay in Washington, the less modest and the more coated in certitude they become.

Are their decisions wiser than the people would make? Or is a representative form of government necessary simply because a true democracy would be too unwieldy? General James Gavin (taking his cue from General Charles de Gaulle, who put one of France's periodic crisis questions to a public referendum) once suggested that it might be a good idea to rig up a permanent apparatus to permit referendum guidance for the government in this country, perhaps laying the issues before the people via television and equipping their sets with yes-or-no response buttons linked to a central computer. "It would," mused Gavin, "have the important function of bringing the people into government."

Indeed it would. But while the people might enjoy the sport of it, that system would grate on the nerves of most politicians and offend the theories of most scientists. Generally speaking, they agree that a process by which government was run by direct popular decision would be fatal.

Recently this question was put to several members of Congress:

> If we were able to establish a system by which the entire electorate could mandate Congress—that is, if the electorate had a way of ordering Congress on a daily basis, "We want you to bring such-and-such a program into being, but we will leave the details to you"—and if that mandate carried the weight of law, would you favor it? There would still be a Congress, but the people could require action from you.[34]

Wright Patman, the old populist from East Texas, said he would not think of taking orders directly from the electorate. "That system doesn't contemplate intelligent consideration of the facts. Intelligent thought requires a body where all the facts can be presented. I don't object to town hall meetings, but when a judgment is required based on facts, that requires a contemplative body like Congress. I've had to vote against some things that the public's for. But when you explain your vote, they are usually for it."

The same kind of response came from congressmen known for their liberalism: Henry Reuss, whose attitude and record in Congress is often faithful to the radical socialist traditions of his native Milwaukee; Robert William Kastenmeier, one of the creators of the "Liberal Papers" of the late 1950s; Phil Burton, one of the liberal dissenters California sent to Washington; Claude Pepper, who was chased out of the Senate by the Florida electorate for his liberalism in 1950 and wangled his way back into the House by moving to a liberal district; and Don Edwards, an ex-president of the Americans for Democratic Action but in fact much more progressive than the mass of that organization. Here is a group of men who have pitched their careers to fighting that vague bogey, "the establishment," and championing what Henry Wallace used to call, just as vaguely, "the common man." But one and all they shuddered at the thought of the public dominating the machinery of government.

Burton made no pretense of respecting his constituents' depth of understanding: "The best votes I cast are those for bills that, at first blush, my constituents would be against." Kastenmeier implied the same thing, "It's not that I don't have confidence in the electorate; I just like to think they have confidence in me." Further conversation indicated that he meant he had confidence the electorate would send a good man to Congress who then would have the strength to disregard the people who supported him.

Each year Kastenmeier faithfully polls his constituents as to their ideas on this or that subject—and then, just as faithfully, disregards their wishes. His reasoning is the same as Reuss's: "The procedure has even broken down in the New England town meetings because the questions have become so very complex. We aren't just dealing with problems; we are dealing with the problem of stating the problems. A lot of static would come through the electronics gear."

Pepper says it too: "If you were to ask the people, 'Do you want to clean up the slums?' most people would say yes. But if you asked them, 'Do you want to pay $30 billion more over a certain period to clean up the slums?' you'd get a different response. It's a very difficult thing to establish priorities. Congress in its bungling way is in a better position to see the whole picture and to make the decisions." Of them all, Edwards—although he flatly states, "The worst thing you could have is simply a reflection of what the people think"—is perhaps a shade more trusting than the others. He sees Congress less in the role of a father than in the role of a teacher. He calls it "an educational institution" that is necessary "for the evolvement of modern and higher-level thinking."

Laying aside the inevitable quantum of vanity that leads congressmen to such a conclusion, their arguments do seem to have some validity. If Congress is often stolid and inflexible, when compared with the mercurial and flighty quality of public opinion (as reflected in polls) those congressional characteristics almost seem to be virtues. Public response to President Johnson was symptomatic. In May 1967, the Harris poll found Johnson failed by three points to have a majority support; but the next month the Johnson balloon was flying again, and a six-point majority said they would favor Johnson in an election. The reason for the electorate's shift? Simply that he had stayed out of the Middle East crisis—making this perhaps the sharpest reversal of public sentiment recorded in recent years as the result of *no* action. Four months later the polls showed Johnson again would lose to Romney, Rockefeller, Nixon, or Reagan, if an election were held right then; but two months later the public had reversed itself once more and said it would favor Johnson over any of the GOP contenders. Nothing better expresses the public's quality and degree of stability than the quote the *U.S. News & World Report* carried in May 1968 from a man-in-the-street, Juan Cruz, a human-relations coordinator from the Chicago Board of Education: "If the election were held tomorrow, I would have to vote for Nixon, the man with the most experience. I might change my mind later and go for Kennedy. But I think the country should draft Johnson. I don't think we should change horses in midstream." Semper fidelis.

If the passions of the public are fickle and fluctuating over the colorful personality of a President, might they not also be so, dangerously, on questions of war and peace? (Not that the public could do much worse than Congress has done in that regard.)

And how much assurance would there be that the public knew something about the topic it was voting on? "If people are asked whether they approve of the reciprocal trade program, for example, many of them will cheerfully confess that they never heard of it," V. O. Key, Jr., wrote. "That is the fate even of issues that have been as well ventilated as the Taft-Hartley Act or the Bricker Amendment. Senator Bricker's proposal received extended attention from the press and the electronic media and set off a debate that reached a high temperature. Of Mr. Gallup's sample of the population, though, 81 percent said that they had neither heard nor read of the Senator's scheme to clip the wings of the President in foreign affairs."[35]

Periodically and never failingly, public opinion polls show that more than half of the American voters can't name their congressman, and sometimes their ignorance of who represents their state in the Senate goes as high as 65 percent. A poll in 1970 showed that 86 percent could not identify anything their congressman has done, and 96 percent could not identify anything their congressman stood for. (Instead of reflecting ignorance, the inability to name these things may have been an indirectly accurate observation of what the congressman was doing.)

And what reason is there to suppose that public opinion, brought to bear on Congress through electronic referenda, would be a power for positive rethinking? What indication has the public given that it really wants to change things? Although the public hoots and jeers and complains of Congress' incompetence, of its pork-barreling and boondoggling, of its lack of sensitivity, of its backwardness and irrelevance, the public has used few of the utensils available to reform Congress. Few, if any, members of Congress have been thrown out of office because they voted for useless military hardware. A few, but only a few, have been defeated because they took favors from lobbyists. Few, if any, have been dumped by the electorate because they failed to vote funds to support education for the handicapped, housing for migrants, health insurance for the old.

So run some of the arguments of those who feel that the public is best kept at arm's length. There is much logic in what they say. Still, one cannot help but wonder.

It might indeed be impossible to arouse the national electorate to an informed vote on something as drearily complex as the D.C. Area Transit Compact (to which the House Judiciary Committee, in however slipshod a style, devoted several hundred pages of hearings), but one suspects—and one suspects that Congress also suspects it—that the national electorate might make some rather sensible decisions on such questions as whether to subsidize corporations at the taxpayer's expense or whether to permit railroads to give up passenger service or whether to make wealthy agribusinessmen wealthier for doing nothing.

In any event, the mystique that has developed around the "special competence" of Congress to speak for the people has gone at least a bit too far. It now occasionally creeps over the line of absurdity. In April 1971, a federal judge granted a postponement for the bribery-conspiracy trial of Representative John Dowdy of Texas. This action was taken after Bethesda Naval Hospital doctors issued a report declaring Dowdy "neither physically nor mentally capable of standing trial at this time." The doctors judged him to be "unable to consult rationally" with his attorneys. In short, he was not believed to be all there.

But Dowdy continued to serve in Congress, continued to cast votes on national legislation, continued even for a time to chair his subcommittee. To some it might appear strange that a man who was mentally incompetent to answer questions in court considered himself nevertheless mentally competent to speak for his congressional district and for the nation. But apparently Congress didn't think it strange. As one of Dowdy's colleagues explained, with a straight face, "It's possible for a person to be competent for one thing and incompetent for another."[36]

It would be grossly misleading to end this chapter with the implication that Congress represents only the residue of electoral indifference and institutional deterioration. Nor should it be presumed that members of Congress never rise above their lowest common denominator. Anyone who thinks so will be in for some surprises, as on that day in July 1973 when the House took the rare step of reversing an Appropriations Committee cut. The reversal was not achieved to please some money-heavy special interest, but it was done for—hang on—the National Foundation on the Arts and Humanities, which is seldom suspected of having a heavyweight lobby. And who came to the rescue of the cultural budget? Some very nonegghead congressmen like Thaddeus J. Dulski of Buffalo and Mario Biaggi of New York. The brightest moment of all was when Representative Al Quie quoted Aleksandr Solzhenitsyn in an eloquent appeal to give the Foundation the money it needed to spread enlightenment in the boondocks. The sight of an ex-farmer from Minnesota quoting a Russian novelist was enough to give some observers a timorous hope for Congress' future.

The fact is that, although they are too rare to exert a prevailing influence on Congress, there are at any given time in history a significant minority of members whose courage and integrity and brilliance could rival the models of any age. The two earliest and most consistent critics of our involvement in the Vietnam war, Senators Wayne Morse of Oregon and Ernest Gruening of Alaska, pursued that course without wavering, although it was evident that by doing so they would risk defeat in the next election; and they were defeated. Senators Ralph Yarborough of Texas and Albert Gore of Tennessee supported antisegregation laws, advocated a moderate course in the Southeast Asian war, voted against the two Southern nominees to the Supreme Court, Haynsworth and Carswell, and opposed favoritism for oil companies and other powerful interests that carried considerable weight in their home states. They took positions that went strictly counter to the general feelings in the South, and they knew it was risky to do so; and they were both defeated in 1970.

Aside from that kind of gutsy fellow, Congress also produces some spectacular one-man crusades. In the Senate, William Proxmire of Wisconsin, as chairman of the Joint Economic Committee, has almost singlehandedly forced his colleagues to reorganize the waste and corruption of the Pentagon budget. He has a long way to go before he makes it a popular target for reform, but at least he has pushed his investigations so far that other members can no longer ignore what is going on in military spending. His most dramatic victory in recent years was stalemating the development of the SST with the threat of a one-man filibuster.

To hound the auto industry into turning out a better product, even if the process were much more costly, would not seem to be the safest way for a Michigan politician to operate—but that is exactly what Senator Philip Hart has been doing for years, working hand in hand with Ralph Nader on some of his most punitive crusades. Hart has taken the same uncompromising attitude toward other industries that are abusing the consumer, and he is apparently unfazed by the fact that some of these industrialists have indicated their willingness to spend any amount to unseat him.

Congressman Robert Eckhardt of Houston, Texas—a city as Southern in its biases and passions as any in the Old Confederacy —has ignored political safety to support black colleagues in unpopular causes. He spoke in favor of seating Harlem's bad boy, Adam Clayton Powell; he was the only member of the House to second Conyers' motion that the Mississippi delegation not be seated. The petrochemical industry is the most important one in Eckhardt's corner of Texas, but he has gone out of his way to hold hearings to embarrass those industrialists for making the Houston ship channel one of the most polluted bodies of water in the world. He was, moreover, the only member of the Texas delegation to vote against the oil industry's biggest coup of 1973—an unregulated hand in building the trans-Alaska pipeline.

Senator Sam Ervin, Jr., of North Carolina has been one of the most obstinate foes of civil rights laws, but he has at the same time proved to be the Senate's most adamant defender of civil liberties, which gave him special credibility as chairman of the special committee set up to investigate the Watergate affair. Although super-patriotism is part of the dominant philosophy of the South, it is at that point that Ervin parts company with his native region. He stood virtually alone among Southerners in opposing the Pentagon's program of sending military agents to spy on left-wing politicians and left-wing professors and students. In 1971, when the Senate was considering whether to expand the witch-hunting powers of the Subversive Activities Control Board, old Ervin, once a small-town judge in the foothills of North Carolina, stood up and with his eyebrows jumping and his judicial jowls shaking for emphasis, told the Senate why he could not vote yes:

> I hate the thoughts of the Black Panthers. I hate the thoughts of the Weathermen's faction of the Students for a Democratic Society. I hate the thoughts of fascists. I hate the thoughts of totalitarians. I hate the thoughts of people who adopt violence as a policy. But those people have the same right to freedom of speech, subject to a very slight qualification, that I have. I love the Constitution so much that I am willing to stand on the floor of the Senate and fight for their right to think the thoughts and speak the words that I hate. If we ever reach the condition in this country that we attempt to have free speech for everybody except those whose ideas we hate, not only free speech but freedom itself are out in our society.

His side lost that day, as the right side usually does in Congress; but as long as that body can produce such moments as when a Southern conservative makes an impassioned plea for society to quit harassing its pariahs, perhaps it isn't yet hopeless.

The Supreme Court: Fortunate Imbalance of Power

If anyone showed that book to my daughters,
I'd have strangled him with my own hands.

Chief Justice Earl Warren,
commenting out of court on a pornographic book

Although it may not seem so from a distance, the men who sit on the Supreme Court—who swaddle themselves in black, seldom give interviews, and hand down their judgments with all the pomp and stuffiness of tribal gods—are susceptible to the same rage, fright, envy, and pique that rock the breasts of us mere taxpayers. Chief Justice Warren was a hot-tempered man, and he may not have been exaggerating when he said that he would have gone for the throat of a porn-purveyor. The Present Chief Justice, Warren Burger, also has something of a temper, as tele-

vision reporters discovered when he chased them out of a hall where he was about to deliver a speech, and as two newspaper reporters discovered one night when they knocked on Burger's door and were greeted by the august jurist with a gun in his hand.

But the men who have made up the Supreme Court down through the years have, seemingly at least, managed to keep from translating personal emotions directly and swiftly into law. They may have made the translation indirectly, and after prolonged consideration, but for the most part they have been fairly level-headed in times of stress.

They are much less prone to be carried away by passions than is the President or Congress, pressured by volatile public opinion, or especially the public itself, whose ad hoc opinions often seem to operate in accordance with the physical principle of a Duncan yo-yo.

This is especially true in regard to basic constitutional rights. If the voters, running Washington by pushing buttons, made disastrous decisions on bread-and-butter issues, the Republic would survive; bureaucracy would somehow keep the planes flying, the butter warehoused. The *big* worry is whether the electorate, given its head, would maintain anything resembling our traditional constitutional democracy for longer than forty-eight hours. For the truth is that a dangerously large slice of the American public is willing to settle for totalitarian solutions. "It is in protecting our civil liberties," says Representative Don Edwards, "that Congressmen run into the most serious opposition from their constituents. We have had poll after poll that shows the people would not re-enact the First Amendment to the Constitution [freedom of religion, speech, press, and assembly] if the question were put to them today."[1]

One of the fundamental boasts of the American people is that their press is, and should be, free of restraint from the government. Yet in April 1970, the Columbia Broadcasting System took a poll that showed 55 percent of the people in its sample believed that newspapers, magazines, and television should *not* have the right "to report any story . . . if the government feels it's harmful to our national interest."[2]

The adherence to the principles of free speech and the rights of the minority are, theoretically, just as hallowed in this country. Of lip service to the principle, there is an abundance. In practice, other emotions grip the electorate. Seymour Martin Lipset wrote about this in 1964, in terms that have been underscored by all subsequent developments in the ailing civil rights evolution:

> Recently we have seen that the general principle of support for civil-rights legislation is endorsed in polls by close to two-thirds of the non-Southern electorate, yet when specific civil-rights measures have been subjected to referenda in various Northern cities, a large majority of the whites have voted against them. The relationship between opinion on a general principle such as civil rights and a specific issue such as fair-housing ordinances may be quite unstable, as in the cases concerning "right-to-work" or anti-Communist party legislation. Knowing the electorate's *general* position on the principles involved may result in serious errors concerning how they will vote on a specific *real* measure.[3]

Among political scientists, it is an old truth. Four years prior to the appearance of Lipset's article, James W. Prothro and Charles M. Grigg had taken a poll from which they concluded:

> The discovery that consensus on democratic principles is restricted to a few general and vague formulations might come as a surprise to a person whose only acquaintance with democracy was through the literature of political theory; it will hardly surprise those who have lived in a democracy. Every village cynic knows that the local church-goer who sings the creed with greatest fervor often abandons the same ideas when they are put in less lyrical form.[4]

Their immediate reason for joining the village cynic in his sentiments was that their poll (using Tallahassee, Florida, and Ann Arbor, Michigan, as sample areas) showed that more than half the electorate would be in favor of refusing to allow a Communist to speak publicly, that more than half the electorate would bar a Communist from taking office even if he were elected fairly, and that 58 percent would even bar Communists from political candidacy in this country. Seventy-nine percent felt that only taxpayers should be allowed to vote.

The results of a survey conducted by University of California professors showed that on a "totalitarian" scale, 33.8 percent of the general electorate sounded happily fascistic. The method of the survey was to present to the sampled voters a series of statements and ask if they agreed. Here are some of the results:

"The majority has the right to abolish minorities if it wants to." 28.5 percent agreed.

"We might as well make up our minds that in order to make

the world better, a lot of innocent people will have to suffer." 41.6 percent agreement.

"I don't mind a politician's methods if he manages to get the right things done." 42.4 percent agreement.

"The true American way of life is disappearing so fast that we may have to use force to save it." 34.6 percent approval.

"Almost any unfairness or brutality may have to be justified when some great purpose is being carried out." 32.8 percent agreement.

"If Congressional committees stuck strictly to the rules and gave every witness his rights, they would never succeed in exposing the many dangerous subversives they have turned up." 47.4 percent agreed.

When the question is a high-flying cliché of democracy, the general electorate can really wring its heart, but it responds with much less enthusiasm when the principle of fair play and constitutional law are applied in the particular case. To the statement, "No matter what a person's political beliefs are, he is entitled to the same legal rights and protections as anyone else," 94.3 percent of the sampled "general electorate" agreed, yet three-quarters of these same people turned around and agreed with the statements, "Any person who hides behind the laws when he is questioned about his activities doesn't deserve much consideration," and "If someone is suspected of treason or other serious crimes, he shouldn't be entitled to be let out on bail." While 81 percent of the sample agreed with the broad concept of freedom of the press ("Nobody has a right to tell another person what he should and should not read"), more than half of these same people changed their minds when the principle was given a particular application ("A book that contains wrong political views cannot be a good book and does not deserve to be published").

Herbert McClosky, who put the study together, was being more realistic than pessimistic when he concluded, "The findings furnish little comfort for those who wish to believe that a passion for freedom, tolerance, justice, and other democratic values springs spontaneously from the lower depths of the society, and that the plain, homespun, uninitiated yeoman, worker and farmer are the natural hosts of democratic ideology . . . ."[5]

It is not difficult to imagine the sort of clobbering the electorate would deliver to the Bill of Rights if the voting button were pushed according to their transient sentiments.

Many in Congress, of course, would like to oblige the electorate in such matters. Lawrence Speiser, former head of the Washington office of the American Civil Liberties Union and a Senate committee counsel, says that "hundreds of bills" are introduced every session of Congress to undo the civil libertarian decisions of the Supreme Court. (Fortunately, most of these bills contract a fatal dose of congressional torpor.) Senator James Eastland, chairman of the Senate Judiciary Committee, and some of his colleagues have promoted legislation that would overturn every Supreme Court decision relating to internal securities; others have proposed legislation that would crush freedom of the press in the name of an antipornography crusade. Speiser, who speaks the fears of many ACLU officials, is convinced that if the issues were left to the general electorate, Eastland and his like-minded associates would have their way at once.

And that's where the United States Supreme Court comes in, if it wants to—as a restraint on the hasty passions of the public and Congress, and as an antidote to the national disinterest and lassitude in the face of pressing social needs. But lest the Supreme Court seem too much to fill the hero's role, let it be hurriedly added that the efficacy of the Court as a restraint and antidote varies with its composition and with the public's willingness to heed the Court. And even at its best the Court is often much too slow or too clumsy or too obtuse to do the job the people need to have done.

One well-known example of tardiness out of the past: In 1862 President Lincoln suspended the writ of habeas corpus for all people arrested for disloyalty to the Union. Their trials, he ordered, should be before military commissions, even in areas where the regular civilian courts were open. He had not a shred of statutory authority for acting in this fashion, and not even the most tortured argument could make his actions seem just or reasonable within the context of the Bill of Rights. Lambdin P. Milligan, a pro-Confederate resident of Indiana, was convicted by a military commission and sentenced to hang. The Supreme Court finally got around to scolding Lincoln and overturning that conviction with a lofty edict—"The Constitution of the United States is a law for rulers and people, equally in war and peace, and covers with the shield of its protection all classes of men, at all times, and under all circumstances. . . ."—but by that time the war was over and Lincoln had been dead eighteen months.

Indeed, the Court has a long record of flinching from the question of Bill of Rights versus war powers. From the time of the

Japanese attack on Pearl Harbor until late in 1944, the governor of Hawaii suspended the writ of habeas corpus and declared martial law, even though during that period the civilian courts were available. Not until six months after the end of hostilities did the Supreme Court get around to ruling that the governor had overstepped his power in subjecting civilians to military trials. When thousands of loyal Japanese-American citizens were scooped up and herded into concentration camps, the Supreme Court remained silent. Then, nearly three years later, on December 18, 1944, with the momentary fear of a Japanese invasion long past and the concentration camps already being dismantled, the Supreme Court stuck its head out from under the covers long enough to deliver on the same day two opinions that proved its ability to weasel: one opinion held that Mitsuye Endo, an American citizen of Japanese ancestry whose loyalty to this country was acknowledged by the government, had been unlawfully detained. But having ruled that the detentions were wrong, the Court then fudged the other direction in a separate case (*Korematsu v. United States*), with the double negative excuse, "We cannot—by availing ourselves of the calm perspective of hindsight—now say that at that time these actions were unjustified."

That the Court is capable of blundering even in its finest moments is nowhere better illustrated than in its order to implement the 1954 school desegregation decision "with all deliberate speed." (Why didn't it just say "now," as Justice Black, in hindsight, said it should have done?) The lower courts floundered in the backwash of imprecise directions, and every evil school board in the South experimented for the next sixteen years or so in ways to beat the Court's ruling.

Nevertheless, although the Court sometimes falls short where and when it is needed most, the ideal of the Court is often of a sufficient validity to restrain the nation's worst impulses.

The Court's Role

The Constitution is a simple document. It is a short document; it can be read in half an hour. Its wording is highly generalized. Yet it remains, in our extremely complex age, as useful and alive as it was when written; it is as potent in dealing with the millions of specific problems of the second half of the twentieth century as it was in dealing with the broad problems arising with the founding of the nation. The explanation for this is quite obvious. "We are under a Constitution," said Charles Evans Hughes in 1907, "but the Constitution is what the judges say it is," and the Supreme Court says various things about it depending upon the era.

Setting aside for the moment such influences as political and mental and physical considerations (the last two simply refer to the influence that headaches and pique and biliousness must have on Court decisions), we see that each new generation becomes a different prism for catching the light by which the Court must read the Constitution. Try as it may, the Court would find it impossible to maintain a historical consistency. "Throughout its entire history . . . the Supreme Court has been in search of the Constitution," writes Carl Brent Swisher, "as the judges sitting were able to see and define the Constitution, and throughout its entire history the Court has been seeking to determine the character and dimensions of its own role in the government."[6]

The search is perpetual because the Constitution is elusive. It seems to be only words, but it is much more than words; words alone are never enough, and they are never certain. Conservative lawyers would violently disagree with that statement. Senator Sam J. Ervin, Jr., is preeminent in arguing the conservative side. The words of the Constitution never change for him, or so he imagines.

> We are told that the words of the Constitution automatically change their meaning from time to time without any change in phraseology being authorized by Congress and the states in the manner prescribed by Article V, and that a majority of the Supreme Court justices possess the omnipotent power to declare when these automatic changes occur, and their scope and effect. This notion is the stuff of which a judicial oligarchy is made. . . . Everyone will concede that the Constitution is written in words. If these words have no fixed meaning, they make the Constitution conform to Mark Twain's description of the dictionary. He said the dictionary has a wonderful vocabulary, but no plot.[7]

Unfortunately for Senator Ervin's position, it is supported by neither the history of the Court nor the more candid statements of those who have sat on it.

The Fifth Amendment guarantees that the government cannot take life, liberty, or property "without due process of law." That language could not be vaguer; in fact, its imprecision has driven some justices—Frankfurter and Brandeis, for example—to suggest that it be repealed. It has meant something different to every new line-up on the Supreme Court. The same is true for such guarantees as the Sixth Amendment's right to a "speedy and public" trial. The First Amendment says, "Congress shall make no law respecting an establishment of religion." Does that mean Congress cannot permit prayers in the schools? The national debate on that issue for the past decade indicates there is no simple answer. The First Amendment goes on to guarantee "no law . . . abridging the freedom . . . of the press." Does this clear the way for the press to advocate an overthrow of the government? The Fourth Amendment prohibits "unreasonable" searches. It is rather unlikely that the framers of the Constitution had in mind the seizing of evidence through electronic eavesdropping, yet the amendment must somehow be made to apply to this modern instrument.

And so it goes throughout the Constitution. It is a marvelous piece of elastic reasoning that must be stretched into new shapes with every generation. The best men who have sat on the Supreme Court are quick to acknowledge that this is true.

In 1968 Richard Nixon promised that if elected to the Presidency he would appoint to the Supreme Court only men who were "strict constructionists," meaning men who would interpret the laws of the land in the light of the exact meaning of the words of the Constitution, without stretching the words in any direction or "modernizing" the intent of the Constitution in any way.*

On other occasions he said that he would appoint men to the highest court in the land who believed that their duty would be to interpret the Constitution rather than to "make new law" from the bench. This was just another way of saying that they would be strict constructionists and not creative constructionists.

Nixon's concept of the duties of the Supreme Court is popular with many people, especially residents of the South. If the Constitution were an extremely detailed document, touching every conceivable action that might take place in commerce and in the lower courts and in the schools and in religion and in the press and in Congress, then there might be some justification for hoping that a strict construction of the Constitution would actually meet the needs of life in twentieth-century America. But the Constitu-

* And yet the liberal Justices Douglas and Black were a great team of strict constructionists of the First Amendment. When the Constitution says, "Congress shall make no laws . . . abridging the freedom of speech, or of the press," they judged it to mean just that—*no law*, and that includes no laws against pornography, for example. Is this what Nixon meant, too?

tion is not that kind of instrument, and to suggest that a strict construction of it will do the job is, at best, gross deception.

When they speak of being "strict constructionists," conservative judges usually do not just mean that they want to do only what the Constitution says they can do and no more; they mean also that they do not want to do anything that can be done by Congress or the President. They believe the Court should keep its hands off social problems, as long as there are still channels for change open elsewhere. For the most part this attitude leaves reform and progress up to the legislative branch, to the political process, or, in other words, this attitude believes wholeheartedly in the principle of majority rule. This is a pretty principle, but it simply does not take care of all our problems.

It was this attitude that permitted segregation to hang on so long without federal interference. These conservatives reasoned that if the blacks living in the South did not like the Jim Crow laws, they could always elect state legislators who would change them, couldn't they? Well, theoretically. And if they were blocked from making change in that way because state laws prevented them from voting in the state elections, the blacks could always send men to Congress who would institute safeguards, couldn't they? Yes, *if* they could get the white folks to let them vote in a federal election.

The theory of democratic reform hung like limp bunting over the stage of American politics for many years, and when the Supreme Court was asked to come to the aid of the black man, the men sitting on the highest tribunal pointed proudly to this bunting and said that no Supreme Court assistance was needed.* That's the way it was until 1954.

---

* Almost every emotional issue raised by a minority refutes the logic of the political-process argument. The Flag Salute Cases were brought to the Supreme Court by a relatively small group of religious fundamentalists who felt they owed only God their allegiance. In these cases, Samuel Krislov noted:

[Justice Felix] Frankfurter took the position that, so long as the channels of change were open, the Court had no right to intervene. [Justice Robert] Jackson rejected this position emphatically, suggesting some rights are not subject to the majority rule. (One is reminded of Godfrey Cambridge's nightmare: A telephone rings and a voice announces, "We've had a referendum on slavery in California and you lost. Report to the auction block in four hours.") But Frankfurter's argument itself pinpoints its own refutation: Most restrictions on liberty are not overtly handicaps to seeking remedies to that specific legislation. To take another instance, the Communists were free to seek repeal of the Smith Act. (*The Supreme Court and Political Freedom* [N.Y.: Free Press, 1968].)

It was a very foolish theory, of course. In 1950 Congress passed a law that made it a felony for a "Communist" even to apply for a passport, much less obtain one. The Supreme Court killed that unconstitutional law in 1964. How much longer would we have had to wait, if the restoration of sanity had depended on Congress or the general public?

On this point Samuel Krislov argues sensibly that any significant group in our society that is cut off from the political process should get the Court's help for at least two reasons:

> If migratory workers are normally unable to convey their point of view, not because of lack of numbers, but because of the nature of their lives, their pattern of residence and leisure time, the Court might assume some greater protectiveness toward them not merely as an expression of . . . "infracanineophilism" (or, a love of the underdog), but as a healthy expression of the need for society to properly correct some of the inequities that are inherent in any institutionalization of the political process.[8]

The key word here is *institutionalization*. Most politicians operate according to concepts of institutionalized freedoms, institutionalized patriotism, institutionalized free enterprise. This is not altogether their fault—or at least it is not unnatural—for politicians do not operate from the abstract to the particular. They operate according to a practical catalog of values, a catalog that fits the needs of the majority of their constituents.

The "strict constructionists" belong to a simpler age. And so do those many people who feel that the Supreme Court's main job is testing the constitutionality of the work of Congress, holding up each new law to the supposedly "fixed" criteria of the Constitution. If this were the case, the Supreme Court could be considered the most inactive and most tolerant arm of government, for in its first sixty years of existence the Court nullified only two acts of Congress; in its first one hundred years the Court nullified only twenty acts. Even in the period of the sharpest clashes between the Supreme Court and the Congress—when President Franklin Roosevelt was pushing his reform programs through Congress at a record clip between 1933 and 1935—the Supreme Court nullified only seven acts of Congress. The truth is, the Court allows Congress enormous leeway in the writing of laws.

The main function of the Supreme Court in recent years has not been to hold back Congress and the Chief Executive, operating as a kind of brake or negative "balance," but to throw its weight wherever needed to create a fortunate imbalance, to revive old concepts of justice and fair play, and to encourage Congress—to the extent that that antiquated body can be encouraged—to take progressive action. The main function of the Supreme Court in recent years has been to serve as the federal conscience when Congress seemed incapable of serving in that way.

In 1950, when the Court was presented with one of its periodic debates over civil rights, Justice Robert Jackson asked, "Isn't the one thing that is perfectly clear under the 14th Amendment that Congress is given the power and the duty to enforce the 14th Amendment by legislation?" and then he answered himself, "I suppose that realistically the reason this case is here is that action couldn't be obtained from Congress." That has often been the answer.

The "Revolutionary" Warren Court

Earl Warren, former governor of California, was appointed to the Chief Justice's chair in 1953, succeeding Fred M. Vinson. Within a few months the Court had decided the great *Brown v. Board of Education* school desegregation case, and because of that landmark decision the entire period from his appointment to his retirement in 1969 is thought of as the Warren era. Actually, Warren was not really in command of the Court, in the sense that he could usually feel confident of mustering a majority on important issues, until the retirement of Justice Felix Frankfurter, a persuasive conservative, in 1962.

Never in its entire history has the Court served its function as the nation's conscience more forcefully than it did under Warren, which is not to say that the Warren Court was always responsive to social needs but that it was more responsive than any other Court had been for a century—a responsiveness that brought from Justice William Brennan the happy comment that "law is again coming alive as a living process responsive to changing human needs. The shift is to justice and away from finespun technicalities and abstract rules."[9]

Conservatives felt that the Warren Court went far too far as a social reformer; liberals, in retrospect, condemn it for falling short of their ideal. They thought that, considering the needs of the time, simply being better than previous Courts was not enough. In December 1968, the last year of the Warren Court, Erwin Knoll wrote in *The Progressive* magazine:

> The record of the Warren Court is by no means uniform. The Court came late and half-heartedly to the issue of McCarthyism in the 1950s. Even today, it has made little headway against the abuses of Congressional investigating committees. Its decisions on censorship are confusing and obscure. Its record in the area of its greatest achievement, civil rights, is uneven. "Only where racial barriers were overtly obnoxious—and, therefore, openly contradictory to the American creed of equality—has the court deigned to move," Lewis M. Steel, associate counsel of the National Association for the Advancement of Colored People, wrote in *The New York Times* this fall. "In recent years, a cautious Supreme Court has waltzed in time to the music of the white majority—one step forward, one step backward and sidestep, sidestep." (For his act of *lèse-majesté*, Steel was fired by the NAACP national board.)

The Warren era saw the Court most dramatically influential in three areas: the equalizing of political representation, the equalizing of the machinery of justice for the poor as well as the wealthy, and the equalizing of the civil rights protection of the Constitution.

Of course, the Warren Court was operating against the background of such a drab Court history that it was not difficult to appear "dramatic." For example, it wasn't until 1936 that the Supreme Court set aside a state criminal conviction because the defendants had been abused (to be exact, in this instance they had been whipped and choked into signing confessions) and thereby, ruled the Court, had not received the protection of the Fourteenth Amendment. When one considers that the nation was nearly 150 years old before the Supreme Court decided to invade such provinces—that is, decided that a state's "right" to run its own system of justice did not take precedence over an individual's right to call on the Constitution for protection even in state trials—it is not difficult to see why the Court's conduct in the last two decades has seemed so revolutionary to some observers. The "revolution" was that the Court had come alive.

In 1956 the Supreme Court again passed a milestone in criminal justice, ruling that a person who has been convicted of a crime and wants to appeal his conviction to a higher court cannot be denied a transcript of the trial proceedings (necessary in the filing of appeals) simply because he is too poor to pay for it. In

1963 a significantly higher plateau of criminal justice was reached when the Court ruled that no one accused of a felony can be deprived of the services of a lawyer just because he is a pauper. In 1964 the Court ruled that a defendant must be notified of his right to an attorney at the very beginning of the procedure of justice—at the time of arrest and booking—and that confessions made prior to his obtaining legal defense cannot be accepted by a court. In 1966 it ruled that a suspect must be advised of his constitutional rights before questioning.

James E. Clayton, author of *The Making of Justice: The Supreme Court in Action*, summarized the Court's influence in this area:

> Put simply, the situation 15 years ago was that most of the guarantees of individual freedom set out in the Bill of Rights did not protect a citizen from the activities of his state and local governments.
>
> Unless his state had seen fit to grant similar protections in its own constitution, a citizen had no real guarantee against being tried without a jury and without a lawyer to defend him, against having his home searched without cause or, even, of being tried two or three times for the same offense.
>
> During the last decade, the Supreme Court has ruled that most of the provisions of the Bill of Rights do restrict state and local governments, as well as the government in Washington. It has compelled a nationalization of the process through which justice is administered and has forced every state to provide at least the same basic protections for its citizens that the federal government grants on a national level.
>
> Since no one else . . . was attempting to police the police and to ensure that the process of justice was basically fair, the burden of correcting what was really an intolerable situation fell on the Court.[10]

In any discussion of the Warren Court, sooner or later the word *revolutionary* will be used, but not everyone uses it in the same temper. Former Associate Justice Abe Fortas once remarked "It is fascinating, although disconcerting to some, that the first and fundamental breakthrough in various categories of *revolutionary progress* has been made by the courts—and specifically the Supreme Court of the United States."[11] Disconcerting to some it certainly has been.

Senator Ervin, considered by some to be the Senate's foremost constitutional scholar, has repeatedly spoken of the Warren Court's "revolutionary decisions," by which he meant that the

Court had seized "discretionary power to fashion policies based on such considerations as expediency or prudence to guide the course of action of the government of our country," even though "there is not a syllable" in the Constitution that gives the Court policy-making powers "even to accomplish ends which may be desirable." To men like Senator Ervin, the Supreme Court was intended to be simply an adjudicator, nothing more.

In a debate with former Attorney General Ramsey Clark, Ervin had explained what is a general feeling among conservatives:*

> A policymaker is an agency of government which bases its decisions upon what it considers to be expedient or what it considers to be prudent or what it considers to be wise. It is the duty of the Supreme Court to apply the Constitution and the laws in accordance with their true meaning regardless of whether the justices consider them to be expedient or prudent or wise. The right to base actions upon considerations of expediency, prudence, or wisdom is a legislative and not a judicial power.[12]

Adolf Berle, noted as a presidential adviser for three decades, went so far as to see this revolution as having given the Supreme Court the "ultimate legislative power." If this is true, it is indeed a revolution. For the Court to make laws, as Warren conceded it must, is one thing; to give it the *ultimate* legislative power is something else. How did Berle see it taking place? It all began, he said, when the "equal protection" clause of the Fourteenth Amendment was brought into full play. The first step was for the Court to decide that unequal protection did not come solely from improper *action* on the part of the states; it came also from improper *inaction*. For example, even if a state took no discriminatory actions to prevent blacks from obtaining their share of social largesse, it might still be held as operating in an unconstitutional way because it took no positive steps to assure the blacks of getting what was theirs.

That having been decided, said Berle, the next step in the revolution was for the Court, faced with state inaction, to assume "the task of filling the vacuum, remedying the failure. In plain

---

* For the record, Ramsey Clark's position was: "The Court is neither merely a policymaker nor an adjudicator. Life isn't that simple. The law isn't that simple. And to frame it so starkly misses the hard experience of our existence. . . . What [the Court] does is it extends the policy of the Constitution of the United States to our daily lives by the process of adjudication. That's what it does. And you can't do that merely by reading words."

English, this meant undertaking by decree to enact the rules which state legislation has failed to provide. This second phase was the really revolutionary development—and incidentally, set up the Supreme Court as a revolutionary committee."[13]

This second phase was seen perhaps most clearly on March 26, 1962, one of the truly historic days in the life of the Supreme Court, when it handed down its decision (*Baker v. Carr*) that state legislatures must be apportioned in such a way that the members of both houses reflect the principle of one-man, one-vote. The same principle, it decreed, must determine the boundaries of the districts for the United States Congress. Warren said he believed this to be the most important ruling of his years on the bench. It opened the way to legal attacks on the apportionment of state and national legislative seats. The ruling forced reform in some states where the legislative district lines had not been redrawn in forty to sixty years. Instead of one lawmaker representing three or seven or even ten times as many voters as another lawmaker, all districts were to be made more or less equal through reapportionment.*

* The irony of the *Baker v. Carr* ruling was that, in effect, it found Warren retroactively chastising himself. He did not see it that way, of course; being as vain as the next man, he interpreted the ruling as a demonstration of his "growth" from politician to high court judge. His feeling on this point was revealed the year he stepped down from the Court in an interview with Anthony Lewis of the *New York Times.* Lewis reminded Warren that when he was governor of California, there had been grossly unequal representation within that state. Los Angeles County, with 6 million people, had one state senator in the legislature—the same as a California mountain district with between 50,000 and 100,000 people. Why hadn't Warren tried to correct that when he was governor? Because, he said, "our system was getting along. We were doing pretty well and I went along with the thought that we would leave well enough alone." So what changed his mind when he reached the court? "I saw it in a different light," he recalls.

Politics has been said to be the art of the possible, and in it we accomplish by compromise and by getting agreement with people. We look at a problem from that standpoint, not perhaps from a standpoint of exact principle, because politics is not an exact science. But when we come to the Court and we face a similar problem where the question of constitutionality is raised, we then test it by constitutional principles; if it violates the constitutional principles, we no longer can compromise, we no longer can change to bring people into agreement, we have to decide the matter according to the principle as we see it.

Now, when I got to the Court, I found what was happening in some of these other states—Tennessee, for instance, where the matter first arose under *Baker v. Carr*, and other states where they had a constitutional provision that the representation must be equal. They had terribly malapportioned legislatures for over 60 years, and those who were in office and had sole control of whether there should be a reapportionment absolutely

172

Many argued that the reapportionment decision violated the constitutionally guaranteed separation of powers between the state and federal levels of government; they argued that the states had the right—without interference from the federal government—to set their own arena for elections. Quite true, said the Supreme Court, *but* (the Supreme Court can always find a *but* if it wants to), as Berle put it, "where state power is an instrument for circumventing a federally protected right, the federal courts may move in."

In other words, a state can run its own business as long as it does so without violating constitutional guarantees. That is a loose enough concept to give the Supreme Court all the preeminence over the states that it could possibly care to have, even in its most liberal moments.

The startling thing is not that the Supreme Court now serves in this way but that it took so long to assume its proper duties. In fact, for many years the Supreme Court was a hindrance to the best impulses of the legislators. For the first five-sixths of its existence the Court supported property rights and had little interest in human rights.

Before the late 1930s the Court usually ruled on behalf of the business establishment (notwithstanding its support of antitrust regulations). Ultraconservatives were very social about wanting to impeach Earl Warren for presiding over a Court that "legislated" protection of individual rights, but their ultraconservative forebears raised not a sound of protest when the Supreme Court in 1916 declared invalid (by a vote of 5 to 4) a law passed by Congress to keep out of interstate commerce any goods produced by child labor. A clearer case of judicial legislating has seldom been seen, and that ruling prohibited the protection of child laborers until 1941, when a different Court overturned the previous ruling.

To reverse its character, the Court had to reverse a number of previous decisions. There was nothing sacrilegious about this. In its first 180 years, the Supreme Court reversed itself 135 times.

refused to permit any change of any kind because it would affect their possibilities for election. (Quoted in Anthony Lewis, "A Talk with Warren on Crime, the Court, the Country," *New York Times Magazine*, October 19, 1969.)

In short, it is easier for a federal judge to be noble about such matters than it is for a politician because it is much easier to see the unfairness of a situation in Tennessee when one is Chief Justice than it is to see the unfairness of it in California when one is governor of that state.

The Warren Court was unusual only in that it was less timid about upsetting tradition; about one-third of the reversals (45) in the Court's history have been made in the past two decades. The Warren Court simply remade law more generously. And Chief Justice Warren was unusual only in his candor. On leaving the Court he was asked about the criticism that his Court had made laws instead of interpreting the Constitution, and he replied: "Well, I think that no one could honestly say that the Court makes no law. It doesn't make it consciously, but because of the very nature of our job we make law."[14]

It was not the process of "making" laws that irritated critics of the Warren Court (President Eisenhower, for example, said that appointing Warren Chief Justice was the "biggest damfool mistake I ever made"), it was the results of the process that irritated them —and pleased the Court's fans (President Johnson called Warren "the greatest Chief Justice of them all"). Judgments of the Court's work, like the Court's work itself, are subjective to a large extent and thereby subject to distortion.

When the Supreme Court outlawed Bible-reading and prayer in the public schools as being in conflict with the constitutional separation of church and state, it was widely misinterpreted (a misinterpretation that was encouraged by the subsequent rulings of some lower courts) to mean that "God was outlawed." As a matter of fact, the Court specifically said at the time that the Bible could be read and studied as freely and thoroughly as anyone might desire in the public schools—as long as it was done as part of the curriculum, "as part of a secular program of education," presented as a piece of literature or history (*Abingdon School District v. Schempp*, 1963). The Court merely outlawed Bible-reading as a ritual.

Politics and Justice

One reason the Warren Court seemed "revolutionary" was that it followed the Vinson Court, which was much more interested in supporting the powers of the government than it was in supporting the rights of the individual. That was the period in which J. Edgar Hoover and Cardinal Spellman and Joseph McCarthy and like-minded patriots thought it quite a bargain to sacrifice constitutional liberties in the struggle with what they identified, somewhat hysterically, as the monolithic worldwide communist conspiracy. The Supreme Court went along with them, at least part way, but with Justices Black and Douglas giving notable dissent.

As the legal scholar Alexander M. Bickel has pointed out: "It was more characteristic of the Vinson Court that all too often it supported, in a tone of avuncular patriotism, the loyalty-security mania and the xenophobia of the day. In *Dennis v. United States* it upheld, rather con brio, the power of the government to punish seditious speech and association. In criminal cases, it could speak with the one-sided zeal of the prosecutor. Far from entering new claims to judicial supremacy, it seemed at times to forget even its independence."[15]

With the Court seeming to encourage, rather than restrain, their super-patriotism, the Un-American Activities fanatics of Congress went baying down the corridors in search of "subversives"; and President Truman and his crowd, not to be outdone, demanded improved oaths of loyalty and rigorous investigations for clearance of even the most humble government workers. These were days that led directly, and probably inevitably, to McCarthyism.

But with Justice Vinson gone, a new mood of moderation and balance eventually settled over the Court. By the mid-1950s, the Court had begun to free citizens from the need to shout their undying loyalty to fatherland. In 1956 the Court threw out state laws punishing "sedition" against the federal government (*Pennsylvania v. Nelson*). The same year it made it a little less easy for the witch-hunters to have their way by ruling that only federal employees in "sensitive" jobs could be fired as security risks (*Cole v. Young*). The infamous Smith Act of 1940 had made it a crime to "advocate," either orally or in writing, even the "desirability" of overthrowing the government. In 1957 the Court somewhat eased the threat to free speech and free press by ruling that simple advocacy as an abstract doctrine was not enough to sustain guilt; to be guilty, a person had to actually get out and recruit and incite others to take *action* to overthrow the government (*Yates v. United States*). In 1958 the Court ruled that the Secretary of State (the State Department was paranoiac about "subversion from within") could no longer deny passports on the grounds that somebody "believed" the wrong thing or "associated" with the wrong people (*Kent v. Dulles*). And in 1959 the Court said the government had to stop using secret informers in the industrial security program (*Greene v. McElroy*).

These refreshing actions were taken at a time when the House Un-American Activities Committee, the Senate Internal

Security Subcommittee, the Subversive Activities Control Board, a number of loud if not always powerful individual members of the House and Senate (Joseph McCarthy, Richard Nixon, Karl Mundt, William Jenner, to name but a few), the State Department, the Department of Justice, the FBI, and a great portion of the daily press were thumping the anticommunist drum in ragtime.

Those who approved of the Warren Court's new direction talked grandly of its returning to the true constitutional path; those who opposed it talked darkly of its "playing politics." This is the usual division of opinion over any Court's action in a controversial field. The constitutionality of a Court's action can be sensibly, if never definitively, argued; but it is really quite futile to argue how much of what it does is a political action or reaction. At that high level, law and politics are sometimes almost indistinguishable, and at that level, law, like politics, is so easily rationalized. Arthur Schlesinger, Jr., was quite correct in saying that a Court can defend itself, whatever its actions, because "the resources of legal artifice, the ambiguity of precedents, the range of applicable doctrine, are all so extensive that in most cases in which there is a reasonable difference of opinion a judge can come out on either side without straining the fabric of legal logic."

Is this law or politics? "A naive judge," Schlesinger continued, "does this unconsciously and conceives himself to be an objective interpreter of the law. A wise judge knows that political choice is inevitable; he makes no false pretense of objectivity and consciously exercises the judicial power with an eye to social results."[16]

The distinction between the quality of politics and the quality of justice is blurred by the court concept *stare decisis*, which, roughly translated, means "stick with tradition." Just as politicians tend to hug the system and its traditions, Supreme Court justices —even the most progressive ones, even those who seem to be enemies of the status quo—hug the traditions of their own system. From the way Warren talked about "principles" directing the Court, one would suppose that each case stands or falls according to the way each justice measures it against the immutable principles of the Constitution.

Sometimes that's not quite the way things work out. Shortly after Warren came to the Court, he was confronted with a case in which a gambler had been convicted with the use of eavesdropping evidence (*Irvine v. California*). In later years the Warren Court made nothing plainer than that it would overturn any case that was developed with bugs and wiretapping. But in his first case of this sort Warren voted to *uphold conviction.* Why? Two reasons. First of all, "I being a new Justice on the Court still groping around in the field of due process, I went along with that opinion, shocked as I was at the conduct of the police." A pretty weak reason: permitting justice to be created by one's insecurity. The other reason Warren gave for going back on principles in this case was that there had been a very recent case in which illegally obtained information had been upheld by the Court (*Wolf v. Colorado*)—and the justices didn't want to admit they were wrong this soon afterward.

The rationalization: *stare decisis,* stick by the old decisions. With many former Supreme Courts, it was a sacred philosophy. With the Warren Court it was much less so, and this is another reason the Warren Court appeared to be so revolutionary; in fact it was only running the show according to basic principles—tempered by politics—rather than by previous interpretations of basic principles.

The Court Decides—
But Who Enforces?

No matter how much politics and public opinion actually shape, or fail to shape, the Court's edicts, they certainly determine the effectiveness of the edicts. When public opinion and politicians fail to respond to a Court's decisions, it makes the whole concept of justice look sick. Justice Frankfurter, fearing, with good cause, that the public was not ready for a desegregation ruling from the Supreme Court, warned in 1952, "Nothing could be worse from my point of view than for this Court to make an abstract declaration that segregation is bad and then have it evaded by tricks."

Burke Marshall, Assistant Attorney General for Civil Rights under Kennedy and Johnson, spoke on this point:

> Since 1870, there has not been any doubt of the constitutional rights of Negroes to vote, and that right has been theoretically enforceable by private suit since 1871. Yet virtually no suits were brought, and no progress was made on the problem at all in some areas, until the Justice Department was authorized to bring suit itself in 1957. . . . The system has been protected thus far, since the mid-1870s, by nonrecognition of federally guaranteed rights. This has not necessarily meant massive resistance in the sense of outright defiance of federal authority, although we have had that, but it does mean an open failure to comply with unquestioned standards of federal law until forced to do so. There is no parallel

to be found in law enforcement. It is as if no taxpayer sent in a return until he personally was sued by the federal government, or no corporation respected the Sherman Act until an injunction was issued against it.[17]

If conditions are contrary to the enforcement of its judgments, the Court can be the most helpless branch. It is a natural helplessness; the Court can decree, but Congress and the President have to back it up, or the decree is so much air.

President Andrew Jackson, infuriated when the Supreme Court invalidated a Georgia law that in effect permitted the state to steal land from the Indians, said "[Chief Justice] John Marshall has made his decision, now let him enforce it."

It was a petty but effective remark, and Southern foes of the Supreme Court have enjoyed repeating it or paraphrasing it on appropriate occasions. In 1956, when Governor Allan Shivers of Texas refused to send state police to protect black students trying to integrate the high school in Mansfield, Texas, he also said, "The Supreme Court passed the law, so let the Supreme Court enforce it." The same philosophy was applied to congressional action after passage of the Civil Rights Act of 1964, when Alabama Governor George Wallace announced, with his usual rococo embellishments: "The liberal left-wingers have passed it. Now let them employ some pinknik social engineers in Washington to figure out what to do with it."

The efficiency of law in a democracy, as Justice Frankfurter once pointed out, depends almost entirely on "the habit of popular respect for law." Laws and court decrees have no intrinsic power. If the people don't obey, then some method must be contrived to make them obey. And if the executive branch makes only a half-hearted effort, or no effort at all, to enforce the Court's rulings, and if public disobedience is widespread enough, it is likely that the people's recalcitrance will prevail.

This commonsense mechanism operates in every area. The indifference of the executive branch in enforcing desegregation edicts made the *Brown* decision appear to be just so much rhetoric for more than fifteen years. The executive branch's indifference to enforcing the 1899 Refuse Act that forbade polluting of navigable waters had visible results for the next seventy-two years.

Total success could not be claimed for any of the three reform areas marked out by the Warren Court, to say the least. When Chief Justice Warren stepped down from the bench in 1969, nine states still had not reapportioned their political districts in accordance with the one-man, one-vote edict. And in 1969 only 20 percent of the black students in the Old Confederate states were actually attending integrated schools, often under conditions of persecution and harassment. As for the protection of defendants in criminal cases, the Court decisions were often ignored in practice by police and the lower courts. In *Crime in America*, former Attorney General Ramsey Clark writes:

> Nor do the rights of the individual under many vital and controversial Supreme Court decisions mean anything if the police do not implement them. And many important rights do go unenforced. The *Miranda* decision, widely blamed as a major cause of crime, requires police at the time of arrest to warn suspects that they need not make a statement, that if they do, it can be used against them, that they are entitled to a lawyer and that one will be provided if requested. These requirements are generally ignored in many jurisdictions, sometimes ignored in others and misapplied elsewhere.[18]

Nevertheless, there was more success than failure in these three reforms, no matter how unpopular they were. More citizens of the United States live in urban areas than in rural ones, and their representatives rushed to the support of the reapportionment edict. Although there was continued resistance in the South to the desegregation edicts and a resistance in the North and West to the idea of attacking de facto segregation, by and large the nation seemed to have accepted the idea that the desegregation laws were here to stay and that there would have to be at least a modest adjustment toward obedience. And although there was widespread criticism of the Court for "coddling criminals" by extending constitutional protection to all criminal suspects, no matter what their income, there was even more general support for the new rules of fair play in criminal justice.

That's what made the Warren Court outstanding—it got some support from the public and from Congress. Not an overwhelming amount, but some. And public support makes all the difference. Consider these largely unpopular or ignored rulings in the decades that preceded the great 1954 *Brown* decision:

In 1935, *Norris v. Alabama*, against systematic exclusion of blacks from juries.

In 1938, *Gaines v. Canada*, for provision of equal advantages in higher education.

In 1941, *Mitchell v. United States*, against unlawful and unjust discrimination (not against "lawful" and "just" discrimination) in transportation and common carriers.

In 1944, *Smith v. Allwright*, against denying blacks the opportunity to vote in primary elections.

In 1946, *Morgan v. Virginia*, against segregation in interstate travel.

In 1948, *Shelly v. Kraemer* and *Hurd v. Hodge*, against restrictive covenants that prescribed residential areas.

In 1950, *Sweatt v. Painter*, for admission of blacks to the school with superior advantage when unequal provisions are made for higher education (in other words, ordering white law schools to open their doors to blacks).

In 1950, *Brotherhood of Railroad Trainmen v. Howard*, constraining labor organizations barring black membership.

The Court had failed to prod the public in the slightest with all these rulings. Segregation was as firmly entrenched in American life at the time of the *Brown* decision as it had ever been. And indeed, it remained so until Congress, buoyed along by public opinion, passed the strong Civil Rights Act of 1964, opening public accommodations to blacks, and the Voting Rights Act of 1965, which at last made it possible for blacks in the South to overcome the manipulations of local elections boards to keep them off the voting rolls and out of the voting booths. With these statements from Congress, and at least lukewarm attention to the matter of civil rights on the part of the Department of Justice, the racial walls at last began to crack, if not crumble, but it did not begin until a decade after the Supreme Court had spoken in the *Brown* case.

The Burger Court:
Mirror of a President?

When the Court moves too far ahead of the crowd, it inspires widespread suspicions and even hatred. Many see it as a subversive body, "foreign" to the temper of the general populace. In the twilight of the Warren Court era, Robert H. Bork of the Yale Law School charged that the Court had created an atmosphere in which "political retaliation [aimed at the Court] is increasingly regarded as proper. This raises the question of the degree to which the Warren Court has provoked the attacks."* Conceding that the War-

---

* Before reading Bork's opinions further, one should bear in mind that he is a very conservative gentleman who does not believe in rocking the Establishment boat. When Attorney General Richardson and Deputy Attorney General Ruckleshaus were forced out of government by Nixon in 1973 because they

ren Court operated with the best of will, Bork still felt that "in its eagerness to reform wide areas of national life, it has made its own job impossibly difficult. It has assumed an omnicompetence in problems of political philosophy, economics, race relations, and criminology, to name but some of its areas of activity, that no small group of men, particularly no group with very limited investigatory facilities, could conceivably possess."[19]

The same irritation was felt by Professor Philip Kurland: "It behooves any critic of the Court's performance to close on a note reminiscent of the wall plaque of frontier times: 'Don't shoot the piano player. He's doing his best.' It is still possible, however, to wish that he would stick to the piano and not try to be a one-man band. It is too much to ask that he take piano lessons."[20]

The joke is a good one only if you agree with Kurland that the Supreme Court is *not* duty-bound to be a one-man band. The fact is, the Supreme Court is obliged to be available to rule on all areas under the umbrella of the Constitution, which, in these regulatory times, covers an enormous ground indeed. And this duty, always pressed on the Court, was not accepted until the Warren era.

Catching the widespread mood of disenchantment with the Warren Court's progressive activities, Nixon in 1968 made his campaign promise to appoint such men to the Court that the Warrenesque influences could be reversed.

With an opportunity that rarely comes to a President, Nixon was able to appoint four justices during his first term (by contrast, FDR had to wait until well into his second term before appointing the first of "his" justices). He had selected them so accurately for their conservatism that by the time Nixon was up for reelection he could honestly claim to have made a strong beginning toward fulfilling his 1968 promise.

In the months before the voters went to the polls in 1972, the Committee for the Re-Election of the President—which was, ironically, the organization later revealed to have financed the Watergate burglary and other political espionage that year—sent out campaign brochures boasting: "The courts are once more concerned about the rights of law-abiding citizens as well as accused lawbreakers. President Nixon has appointed four members to the Supreme Court—Chief Justice Warren Burger, Justice Harry Blackmun, Justice Lewis Powell, Jr., and Justice William Rehnquist—

refused to fire the special prosecutor in the Watergate investigation, President Nixon measured Bork as the kind of chap who would go along with his orders, and he made him acting attorney general.

who can be expected to give a strict interpretation of the Constitution and protect the interests of the average law-abiding American."

Here, of course, the code phrase "strict interpretation" meant simply "conservative." And in this sense the appraisal was correct. The Burger Court had shifted directions. Although the old Warren Court was not being reversed in a wholesale fashion, the bold thrust of the Warren days had been stopped. There was a tempering, a shading, a caution about the Court's action that pointed to a new generation of justice.

Tampering with the Court in this fashion is nothing new. No doubt every President selects justices who he thinks will reflect his own ideology. But critical dangers can accompany the fashioning of a Supreme Court to the shape of campaign oratory. Justice Frankfurter, a conservative himself, warned in 1950 (*United States v. Rabinowitz*): "Especially ought the Court not reinforce needlessly the instabilities of our day by giving fair ground for the belief that law is the expression of chance—for instance, of unexpected changes in the Court's composition and the contingencies in the choice of successors."

Yet there is little doubt that these very contingencies are now at work in President Nixon's appointments to the Supreme Court and especially in the temper and philosophy of Chief Justice Warren Burger. The year before Burger became Chief Justice he told the Ohio Judicial Conference:

> We must constantly recognize that the Constitutional concepts "tacked on" in these dozen years or so [of the Warren Court] may not be as permanent as they appear when they are consistently arrived at by the margin of one vote with four Justices sharply suggesting that the cake which the Court was baking did not have all the essential ingredients for a good cake and that it has not been in the oven long enough. To paraphrase one of the felicitous lines of Elizabeth Barrett Browning, consequences "so wrought may be unwrought so." Thus, the constitutional result so wrought against the protest of four may be "unwrought" by so simple a happening as the advent of one or two new Justices.[21]

It is safe to say that if Burger had not held that political truism, President Nixon would never have considered him a worthy appointee.

Burger was well known in Republican circles as a political manipulator before he was well known as a jurist. He served as campaign manager for Harold Stassen in 1938, when Stassen won the governorship of Minnesota, and in 1952 served as one of the key negotiators in seating the pro-Eisenhower Texas delegation to the Republican National Convention. It was mainly for this work that Ike appointed him assistant to Attorney General Herbert Brownell and then appointed him to the United States Court of Appeals in the District of Columbia.

Burger did not sever all his political ties when he took the Chief Justice's job; he was still approachable, and he still knew how to approach others for favors. A private letter to him from then-Attorney General Richard G. Kleindienst, for example, apparently helped the Nixon Administration obtain favorable changes in the new rules of evidence for federal courts. (The rules helped protect the identity of the Justice Department's stool pigeons.) This does not mean that Burger overruled his own intelligence to do a favor for the Attorney General, but it is interesting to note that the Judicial Conference Committee, the advisory group to the Supreme Court, had originally rejected these rules; it changed its mind and accepted them after Kleindienst wrote Burger.

Burger also has lost none of his own zest for lobbying, either for professional or personal causes. He sent his top aide to House Speaker Carl Albert to lobby against the passage of a new set of consumer protection laws. (Burger felt that the laws would increase Supreme Court work too much.) Perhaps only by coincidence, Burger's aide was accompanied by superlawyer-lobbyist Thomas G. (Tommy the Cork) Corcoran, whose law firm has a number of corporate clients who would have been hurt by the consumer laws.

But it would be a mistake to conclude that Burger is as much a politician as a judge. Indeed, Burger may have left politics with too few of the techniques under his command, rather than too many. For the Chief Justice, having only one vote of his own, must rely on a considerable amount of intrabench politics to carry a majority of the Court with him.

It was Warren's deeply ingrained political skills that made the difference in this regard. One widely circulated account of the making of the school desegregation ruling is that in 1953 the justices were split 5 to 4 in favor of continuing segregation. Then Chief Justice Vinson died, and Warren took his place and began campaigning among his colleagues. He gave this campaign the personal touch in every way, writing out in longhand his opinion against segregation and personally taking it around to each member for a long conversation and then subsequent conversations as needed to keep the pressure on; Justice Jackson was in the hospital, where Warren visited him with good cheer—and a copy of his argument. When the ruling was announced in 1954, it was, to the nation's surprise, unanimous.

By contrast to the relative smoothness by which Warren's Court operated, the Burger Court has been marked by bitter factionalism and sometimes even by an exchange of personal insults. Burger has been unable to win any significant support from the justices who remained from the Warren era. Rarely have all nine justices agreed even on which cases should be heard, much less on the judgments that should be handed down in the most important cases. Among the Nixon appointees, however, there has been great cohesion; Burger and Blackmun and Rehnquist and Powell operate like the conservative team Nixon had dreamed of. During their first term together as a team, the "Nixon four" voted together in fifty-four of sixty-six cases. Although Nixon was still one vote short of having appointed a majority, his four could usually count on either Justice Byron White or Justice Potter Stewart to give them the swing vote they needed.

On June 22, 1972, for the first time in eighteen years, the Supreme Court broke ranks in a school desegregation case. The Court ruled that Emporia, Virginia, had violated the Constitution by carving out its own school district to frustrate a county-wide mandate to desegrate; but the ruling came as a result of the unanimity of five hangovers from the Warren Court. All four Nixon appointees dissented.

The Burger Court reversed the evolutionary liberalism of the Warren Court on "obscenity," which is routinely the stickiest and most difficult question that confronts every new Supreme Court. The difficulty, of course, comes from definition. What *is* obscene? Every generation has a new definition, and every judge does too. Justice Stewart measured the problem properly when he said that he didn't really know how to describe hard-core pornography, but "I know it when I see it."

The first of the Warren Court decisions on obscenity came in 1957 when it ruled—with Justices Douglas and Black dissenting—that the freedom of speech guaranteed by the First Amendment does not protect obscenity; at that time it defined obscenity as material whose dominant theme "appeals to a prurient interest," as judged by "the average person applying contemporary community standards." But then in 1966 the ruling was liberalized greatly when the Court added that before something could be judged obscene it must be totally devoid of redeeming social value. Thus material could be judged obscene only if it met all three tests: (1) it had to offend the whole community—and the Warren

Court really meant *national* tastes, not village tastes; (2) its basic theme had to appeal to lewd instincts; and (3) the work had to be utterly useless.

This ruling was so loose that a multibillion-dollar smut industry grew up around X-rated movies and "adult bookstores." The question became not only one of quality but one of quantity. And it became one of place and time. If it was legally okay for a man to look at dirty movies in his home, should he also have the opportunity to watch movies of fornication on New York's 42nd Street? And if on 42nd Street, why not on the screen of the suburban drive-in theater?

These were questions that the Warren Court had not had to deal with, but that had arisen from its earlier decisions. They had to be faced by the Burger Court, and the outcome, as Louis M. Kohlmeier wrote in the *Wall Street Journal* (November 9, 1970), would have a much broader meaning than related simply to smut:

> If the President or Congress or probably even a majority of voters were answering these questions, they would quite likely opt for censorship in the name of public morality.
>
> The Supreme Court may well join the crowd. But if it becomes too much a part of the crowd it will diminish the role that distinguishes it from the two elective branches in our Constitutional system.
>
> For the Court is the delicate branch that, if it cannot be isolated from the crowd, also cannot merely mirror the popular will. In the finest sense it exists to preserve the Constitution, by containing the exercise of power by the Executive and Legislative branches and protecting the rights of individuals and minorities from excessive exercises of governmental power.
>
> In this sense, the issue for the Burger Court isn't really obscenity. The real issue is whether the Court now or in the years ahead will stand sufficiently above politics and beyond the crowd to preserve its delicate role in balancing majoritarian power against private rights in all areas, including obscenity, crime, student disorder and racial injustice.

On June 21, 1973, the Burger Court (split 5 to 4) gave broad new powers to local authorities to crack down on what the Chief Justice called "the crass commercial exploitation of sex" by defining obscenity as that which offends local, not national, tastes. Replacing the Warren Court allowance that obscenity was material "utterly without redeeming social value" was the Burger majority's stricter definition of it as material that, taken as a whole, "does not have serious literary, artistic, political or scientific value."

As expected, the Burger Court began to take a much sterner law-and-order posture. (It was a speech by Burger in 1967 criticizing Warren Court decisions expanding the rights of defendants in criminal trials that first prompted Nixon to regard Burger in a favorable way.)

New powers of intrusion and prosecution were given to governments when the Burger Court ruled that state juries could convict with less than a unanimous vote; that only defendants who have been indicted are entitled to lawyers at line-ups; that a state may demand that a defendant disclose his alibi in advance of trial; that even if a defendant were brought to trial in a state court under a law that is probably unconstitutional, the federal courts should not interfere except in the most flagrant cases of abuse (a critical retreat from the Warren years); that police and FBI do not need a warrant to let an informer carry an electronic bug on his person to record conversations.

The Burger Court ruled that a grand jury might require newsmen to disclose their confidential sources to grand juries; that a shopping center could be closed to peaceful pamphleteers; that a member of the U.S. Congress was not immune from a grand jury summons to tell how he acquired classified documents (in reference to Senator Gravel's publishing of the Pentagon Papers); that the Attorney General had the proper power to prohibit a Marxist journalist from coming to this country to participate in academic conferences and discussions; that civilians who are targets of surveillance by military spies cannot take the Army to court unless they can show that the spying suppressed their activities.

Among this lush tangle of decisions, some thought they could see the sproutings of a suppression of dissent. The *Washington Post* complained that the Court's failure to protect a reporter's sources and its weakening of a congressman's immunity, for example, "indicate that the new majority on the Court is remarkably insensitive to the First Amendment to the Constitution and to what we had always thought were two fundamental principles of a republican form of government—the need of the public to know what is going on in and out of government and the need of the public's representatives to communicate freely with it."[22]

Tom Wicker of the *New York Times* likewise interpreted the Court's "decision holding that reporters have no First Amendment right to protect their confidential sources" to "significantly limit freedom of the press," and he felt that the deimmunizing of congressmen who release classified documents would mean "that members of Congress now will think twice before releasing classified information to the public—which members have frequently done, usually with the result that the public finds out something the government has been trying to hide through the classification system. If a grand jury can haul in a Senator to question him about his sources of information, both those sources and the Senator's willingness to use them will soon disappear."[23]

As for the Warren Court's great reapportionment ruling, the Burger Court even managed to modify that: it held that community of interest, not merely a head count, must be considered when drawing the lines for political representation, that cities and counties and districts should not be chopped up merely to meet the rigid balancing of one-man, one-vote constituent numbers.

With the coming of the Nixon appointees, there became evident on the Court a friendlier attitude toward big business (the Court narrowed the grounds on which states and individuals could launch antitrust suits) and a tougher attitude toward welfare recipients (it upheld state requirements that welfare people work on public jobs).

Such rulings as these did not kill the Warren Court's principles but withheld nourishment from them. By giving limited and narrow interpretations to the precedents set during the Warren era, without necessarily overruling them directly, the Burger Court achieved a subtle change. As a long-time writer on court affairs, John P. MacKenzie, put it, "In a field of law where principles either grow or wither, some legal precedents may be left for dead."[24]

Although President Nixon could claim victory in changing the philosophy of the Court, he could not—if he had wanted to—claim to have made it obedient, or politically loyal. Through the history of the Court it has been impossible to predict what kind of rulings a justice will hand down on the basis of the political philosophy of the President who appointed him. As John P. Frank points out:

> Wilson chose McReynolds, who proved to be the total antithesis of everything Wilson stood for and became the most fanatic and hard-bitten conservative extremist ever to grace the Court. Coolidge chose his own attorney general, Harlan Stone, and Stone is commonly regarded as one of the great liberal justices. Anti-Federalist Presidents sent justice after justice to the Court only to see them captivated by Marshall; among the more amusing stretches of American legal history are the papers flowing between Justice William Johnson, a Jeffersonian appointee, and Jefferson as Johnson attempted to account for his deviations from good Jeffersonian

faith. Chief Justice Chase, Secretary of the Treasury during the Civil War, handed down an opinion invalidating the very financial system that as Secretary he had administered; and Holmes, who had been the choice of Theodore Roosevelt, bitterly disappointed T.R. by going against him on the heart of his anti-trust program, the *Northern Securities* case.[25]

Two of the moderate liberal justices, Warren and William Brennan, were appointed by Eisenhower, whose later opinion of Warren has already been recorded. One of the most conservative men on the present Court, Justice Byron White, was appointed by President Kennedy.

The Burger Court's ruling on obscenity had fulfilled one of President Nixon's campaign promises, and its tougher law-and-order stance fulfilled another. But just as often, the very men he had appointed to the Court made judgments that went against his administration, for the Burger Court's mood and philosophy were much more complex than gloomy journalistic appraisals of its work would indicate.

The Court unanimously ruled that the executive branch of federal government could not wiretap suspected "domestic" radicals without a court warrant, thus dealing a stunning legal setback to the claims of former Attorney General John Mitchell, one of Nixon's closest advisers, that the President and his aides could wiretap at whim. The Court also ruled unanimously that the extreme radical group Students for a Democratic Society could not be prohibited from organizing on campus even if they advocated violence—as long as they behaved themselves while on campus. And the Court killed a ninety-year-old law banning all unauthorized demonstrations on the grounds of the U.S. Capitol—a law often used in the past to justify arresting antiwar and other protestors who had brought their messages to Congress. So the Burger Court was clearly not as insensitive to First Amendment guarantees as some of its critics feared.

And if the Burger Court seemed eager to put new tools in the hands of the prosecution and police, it was also willing to help the accused. In a historic extension of the Sixth Amendment, the Court ruled for the first time that defendants must have a lawyer even in misdemeanor trials, if conviction could carry a jail term of any length.

The Burger Court ruled unanimously that people could not be jailed simply because they are too poor to pay fines—a ruling that, as Fred Graham of the *New York Times* noted, "outdid the Warren Court's best egalitarian efforts by creating a right that exists only for the poor. An affluent person can be put in jail forthwith for failing to pay his fine, but some other method of collecting fines from the poor (installment payments, perhaps) must be tried first."[26]

Not content with that magnanimity, the Court went on to rule that people who want to obtain divorces but are too poor to pay filing fees and court costs must be given cost-free divorces by the states. Chiding Burger on that one, Justice Hugo Black, the only dissenter, commented: "Is this strict construction? If ever there has been a looser construction of the Constitution in this Court's history, I fail to think what it is."

For years President Nixon had been promising tax relief for parents who sent their children to private schools, but on June 25, 1973, the Burger Court ruled that such favoritism violated the constitutional separation of church and state (it was a 6 to 3 decision, with Blackmun and Powell joining Warren-era holdovers to make a majority).

One of the most remarkably nonstrict interpretations of the Burger Court—and one that flew in the face of President Nixon's expressed political position—came on January 22, 1973, when by a vote of 7 to 2 (Rehnquist and White dissenting) the Court overruled all state laws that prohibit abortions during the first three months of a woman's pregnancy, and liberalized abortion laws during the remainder of the pregnancy period except for the last ten weeks, during which time a state may prohibit the killing of the fetus. Not only was the rejection of the President's position supported by three of the justices he had appointed—Burger, Powell, and Blackmun—but the majority opinion was written by Blackmun.

Moreover, the decision was written with all the flights of introspection and sociological guesswork that might have accompanied even the most imaginative rulings of the Warren Court. Uneasily propping up his opinion with references to the implied "right of privacy," which he nevertheless admitted is not recognized except between the lines of the Fourteenth Amendment, Blackmun at the same time rejected on behalf of the fetus the "right to life" explicitly guaranteed by the Fourteenth Amendment, on the grounds that the right to life is vouchsafed only to "persons" and, except perhaps in the last ten weeks of its prenatal existence, the fetus is not a person. During most of the 1950s and 1960s, a ruling constructed so loosely as that would have brought forth another several dozen billboards urging "Impeach Earl Warren." Indeed, where in this opinion was that stiff, cold logic that Nixon had promised from his appointees? Almost apologizing for the fact that justices cannot escape their human-ness, Blackmun wrote, "One's philosophy, one's experiences, one's exposure to the raw edges of human existence, one's religious train-ing, one's attitude toward life and family . . . are all likely to influ-ence and to color one's thinking and conclusions about abortion."[27] And, for that matter, about almost any other topic that would come before the Court.

But the Burger Court has seldom felt compelled to make such apologies for pushing back disputed social frontiers. One of the most momentous rulings of the Burger years came in mid-1972—the abolition of the death penalty on the grounds that it was "cruel and inhuman" punishment—lifting, at one stroke, that pall from the lives of the 598 men and 2 women then on death row. The decision was made without the assistance of a single Nixon appointee to the Court; they all dissented.

The new era is not one of adventurous strides but of cautious steps. More significant than any other change from the Warren days is the Burger Court's tempo and its different sense of mis-sion. Gone is the rush to reform. Gone is a rush of any kind. Gone—whether for good or ill, it is too early to say—the broad sweep of the Court. More than by anything else, perhaps, the Court's new direction seemed to be pointed by Burger's pleading with Congress, publicly, not to burden the federal courts by passing laws that would encourage the public to seek its rights at court. In August 1970, in a "State of the Judiciary" address to the American Bar Association in St. Louis, Burger complained that "not a week passes without speeches in Congress and elsewhere and editorials de-manding new laws—to control pollution, for example, and new laws allowing class actions by consumers to protect the public from greedy and unscrupulous producers and sellers."

All very worthy, no doubt, he said, but "I can do no more than emphasize that the federal court system is for a limited pur-pose and lawyers, the Congress and the Public must examine carefully each demand they make on that system."

His moral was that Congress should think twice about pass-ing a pro-public law if by doing so it might give the courts more work. If that attitude prevails at the Supreme Court level, then the initiative for reform that was begun in the Warren era will have been completely canceled, and all hope for social progress will once again, as it did a generation ago, rest solely in the rheumatic hands of the politicians.

Bureaucracy:
Our Prolific Drones

*Every once in a while one gets the view down here
in Washington that the respective departments
are members of the United Nations, and that each
has a separate sovereignty.*

Senator Hubert Humphrey,
quoted in Emmet John Hughes, The Living Presidency

In just over a decade (1958–71), the number of managers, engineers, and other high-salaried employees in the top five ranks of the federal bureaucracy grew 300 percent. And unlike gold, whose weight carries it to the bottom of any pile of material, bureaucratic gold rises to the top. For example, the minimum salary for a bureaucrat at the GS–14 level rose from a minimum of $11,355 in 1958 to a minimum of $20,815 in 1971, and it bounced upward again to a minimum of $23,088 in 1973. Moreover, if the worker manages to keep from being fired for extraordinary incom-

petence during the next ten years, he will be eligible for a salary of $30,018 at the end of that time.

Mind you, a GS–14 is not even considered a superstar in the bureaucracy. There are four more pay levels above him. In fact, there are 73,000 persons in the federal bureaucracy earning salaries at the GS–14 level and higher. What are all those faceless functionaries doing up there to earn that kind of salary? What kind of leadership are they giving to the hirelings below, and what does their cumulative labor mean to the average taxpayer? The federal budget is eighty times larger today than it was in 1930— what are they doing with all that money?

There are no signs that the bureaucracy will stop growing. As the following table shows, the number of government workers as a percentage of the total number of civilian workers increased more than two and a half times between 1929 and 1970 and will have almost tripled by 1980.*

	All civilian workers	Government workers	Government percentage of total
	(Figures are in thousands)		
1929	47,630	3,065	6.4%
1950	58,920	6,026	10.2
1960	65,778	8,353	12.7
1970	78,424	12,647	16.1
1980*	95,100	16,800	17.7

* Projected
Source: U.S. Department of Labor, "Occupational Outlook Handbook" (Washington, D.C., 1970).

* And, incidentally, people in government tend to watch out for themselves. Labor statistics show that in periods of recession since the Second World War, while the total labor force declined, government employment continued to climb; and so did government salaries. The Tax Foundation reports that the average annual pay for a government worker is 9.3 percent higher than that of a worker in private industry. In 1955 they were about even. Between 1962 and 1974 there were thirteen federal salary increases; the federal payroll, including military, more than doubled in that time, from $25 billion to nearly $60 billion.

The problem of trying to cut bureaucratic costs while the federal workers thrust their hands steadily deeper into the treasury is underscored by the fact that although the number of civilian workers on the federal payroll was reduced by 231,295 between 1968 and 1973, the payroll for those remaining increased $11 billion. Reason? Clerks and janitors and blue-collar workers were lopped off at the bottom of the payroll, while the number of white-collar workers in the top pay grades (up to $36,000 a year) increased in number. ("The Federal Diary" in the *Washington Post*, September 17, 1973.)

That, needless to say, is a lot of bureaucrats. Together they easily outnumber all the workers on all the payrolls of manufacturers of durable goods—trains, planes, autos, appliances, furniture, defense materials.

But do not lay all this growth at the door of the federal government, for eight out of ten of those bureaucrats work for state, county, or city governments, and the growth rate of the federal bureaucracy is not nearly as rapid as is the rate at other levels. Consider the following table:

	1960	1970	Percent gain
(Figures are in thousands)			
Federal government	2,270	2,649	19%
State and local governments	6,083	9,998	64
Durable manufacturing	9,459	11,146	18
Trade	11,391	14,947	31
All civilian jobs	65,778	78,424	19

Source: U.S. Department of Labor, "Occupational Outlook Handbook" (Washington, D.C., 1970).

Federalism, Old and New

From the 1930s to the end of the 1960s, taking those only as rough boundary periods, most liberals were convinced that progress lay with the federal government and that since the federal government got most of the tax dollars and had the best apparatus for enforcing its will on the people, the government could also be utilized most easily for doing good. The building of highways, dams, utility plants, post offices, docks; the subsidizing of farms, airlines, banks, railroads, school programs, publishing houses; the protection of bank deposits and labor unions; the policing of the stock market; the regulation of transportation fees and schedules; the underwriting of housing loans—activities of this sort, multiplied endlessly, were seen as the natural benevolence of big federal government.

Many of the programs were successful; most of them received wide and permanent popular support. After the programs had been well established, even conservative politicians supported them, or at least were silent in their opposition; in some cases they even pushed to expand the programs. Under Eisenhower, the only

Republican President to serve out his term during this period, federal statism grew and so did some FDR-launched programs, such as social security benefits, which once were held anathema by the conservative establishment. Under the Nixon Administration statism was refined further to offer such corporate assistance as underwriting the insurance for commercial airplanes that private insurance companies refused to handle and guaranteeing loans to aircraft companies that banks considered a poor risk.

But with these benefits came a sharp decline in direct electoral control of the government. Each of the beneficent programs created its own bureaucracy. Congress could not administer the burgeoning programs. Neither could the President and his executive department, nor did Congress desire that the President have enough supervisory power to do the job. So the bureaucracy of the welfare state swelled both in size and in independence, until, as archconservative Barry Goldwater correctly appraised it: "It is so massive that it literally feeds on itself. It is so large that no one in or out of government can accurately define its power or scope. It is so intricate that it lends itself to a large range of abuses, some criminal and deliberate, others unwitting and inept. The government is so large that institutions doing business with it or attempting to do business with it are forced to hire trained experts just to show them around through the labyrinthine maze made up of hundreds of departments, bureaus, commissions, offices and agencies." And he went on to point out, with equal accuracy, that "it would be downright laughable if it were not so serious to consider how many of our people actually believe that a national administration firmly controls the Federal Government. It is true that broad overall policy is determined at the White House level or at the cabinet level in the government bureaucracy. But its implementation is too often left to the tender mercies of a long-entrenched bureaucracy."[1] Presidents come and Presidents go, and so do congressmen, but the faceless bureaucrat lives forever, and so (seemingly) do his often outdated and irrelevant policies.*

* Before going further we had better give a working definition of bureaucracy. By that we mean the Cabinet departments and the commissions, agencies, and boards that have been erected as governmental needs have arisen. The earliest administrations had War, Navy, State, and Treasury departments. A young country needs only the basics: some way to protect itself, deal with other countries, and handle its finances. There was also an Attorney General, but the Department of Justice that is now thought of as his domain came almost a century later, in 1870. Interior was added in 1849. The Commissioner of Agriculture, added in 1862, was promoted to Cabinet rank in 1899. The

These days many liberals, no longer certain that the best way to do things is through the federal superstructure, would agree with Mr. Goldwater's tone as well as with his meaning. Although most liberals disagreed with President Nixon's methods for achieving his objective, most agreed with his position, stated just before his reelection, that "after 40 years of unprecedented expansion of the federal government, the time has come to redress the balance—to shift more responsibility and power back to the states and localities and, most important, to the people all across America."[2]

To that end, he lobbied for what he called "New Federalism" —a restructuring of government and a greater sharing of revenue by the federal government with the state and municipal governments. The theory was that instead of social programs always having to be channeled through Washington to be adequately funded, the federal government would simply dole out baskets of cash to the state and local governments, which then could independently fund whatever social programs they believed best fit the needs of their areas.

This was the theory, and it was an intelligent one. But like all theories that must survive the stranglehold of the status quo, this

---

Office of Postmaster General, created in 1789, was made a Cabinet department in 1872 (and in 1971 was made an independent agency). Commerce and Labor came into existence in 1913, Defense (unifying in a clumsy way the various military services) in 1947, Health, Education, and Welfare in 1953, Housing and Urban Development in 1965, and Transportation in 1966.

As business and industry began to abuse their powers under the laissez-faire philosophy that dominated our nation's life in the second half of the nineteenth century, Congress began creating regulatory and administrative commissions. Because the railroads mistreated the farmers in the way of rates and service, the Interstate Commerce Commission was established in 1887. In an effort to end the boom-and-bust cycles by stabilizing the dollar (and by regulating the banks) the Federal Reserve Board was established in 1913. Unfair trade practices and monopolistic activities of the period gave birth to the Federal Trade Commission in 1914. The utility robber barons and the buccaneers of the natural gas fields helped create the Federal Power Commission in 1920. The chaos of the airwaves industry resulted in the Federal Communications Commission in 1934. The disastrous stock market crash brought about the creation of the Securities and Exchange Commission in 1934, and the brutal labor-management wars of the early 1930s were responsible for the establishment of the National Labor Relations Board in 1935. The Civil Aeronautics Board (1940), the Atomic Energy Commission (1946), and the National Aeronautics and Space Administration (1958) were responses to the need for controls and policy guidance in the new industries of aviation, atomic energy, and space— all of which are just as subject to exploitation in these sophisticated times as railroads, banks, and stock markets were subject to exploiters in those more rugged eras.

one didn't fare too well. For one thing, state and city governments simply do not think as "loftily" as the federal politicians. For all their many faults, it was the federal legislators—not state legislators—who established the great social reform programs of the last forty years. And although some of these programs are too well established now to be destroyed by the indifference of state and local politicians, it is also true that these officials do not always feel obliged to be very generous in supporting "national priority" programs that had their origin in Washington. As a result, programs for deprived minorities will undoubtedly decline when administered by the lower governments.

An auxiliary step taken by President Nixon to decentralize the government was to set up regional offices for a number of the bureaucratic departments and give these offices a major share in decision-making. But, as happens so often with the bureaucratic amoeba, splitting it up only compounded the problem. New York Governor Nelson Rockefeller has found the regional offices a "waste of time" because "it takes us six months to get a grant application through a regional office, and then the thing goes to Washington, and it's another six months and then you find out they didn't have the money anyhow."[3]

In any event, the New Federalism seems no different from the old federalism in size and complexity, except that it is larger and more involved, which is not exactly the result that those (including Nixon, no doubt) grown weary of the federal bureaucracy's mistakes had in mind.

The "Mindless" Bureaucracy

The most notable characteristic of mammoth bureaucracy is its seeming chaos and mindlessness.* The Department of Defense, which hires one-third of all employees of the federal government, was appraised by a special presidential task force in 1970 and found to be "an impossible organization." The chairman of the

---

* The labyrinth of government being what it is, one can hardly be surprised that workers in one part don't know what is going on in other parts. And so we have situations, as reported by the Library of Congress, in which "the federal government spends nearly 4 billion dollars annually on research and development in its own laboratories, but it does not know exactly how many laboratories it has, where they are, what kinds of people work in them, or what they are doing."

group, Gilbert W. Fitzhugh, who is also chairman of Metropolitan Life Insurance Co., said they had found: "Everybody is somewhat responsible for everything, and nobody is completely responsible for anything. They spend their time coordinating with each other and shuffling paper back and forth,* and that's what causes all the red tape and big staffs in the department. Nobody can do anything without checking with seven other people."[4]

Actually, that isn't a bad description for most portions of the bureaucracy.

Over the years the bureaucracy's mindlessness has become almost comically legendary: there was the $375,000 that the Navy spent to test the flight characteristics of frisbees; there was the $6 million spent by the Department of the Interior to study American recreation habits, after which the study was thrown away, and the Department started over with another study of the same subject; there were the twelve films produced by the Defense Department, all on the same subject: "How to Brush Your Teeth"; there were the houses, built by HUD for low-income families, none of which sold for less than $76,000; there was the directive issued by the Veterans Administration that only employees earning from $4.07 to $4.50 an hour would be allowed to change fluorescent light fixtures, while the regular light bulbs would be changed by workers making $2.80 to $3.11; there were the 371,875 letters sent out to postal employees warning them not to stick pencils in their ears or let their toenails grow to excessive lengths; there was the

---

* Another symbol of the federal leviathan is the paperwork required of and by the bureaucracy. There is a legend that the federal administrator who signed the order to destroy the original War Department files of the War of 1812 did so only with the proviso that copies be made of everything. Apocryphal it may be, but the spirit of it is exceedingly true. The thickness of the paperwork jungle is staggering. It is estimated that government employees use more than one *trillion* pieces of writing paper each year in carrying out their duties.

An appraisal of just one part of the paper mess was given by the Senate Select Committee on Small Business in 1973, when it estimated that the cost to business for compliance with the federal reporting requirements, entailing 6000 different federal government forms, is $18 billion a year and that the cost to the government "to print, shuffle and sort out all these forms" is another $18 billion. The subcommittee estimates that the yearly flow of paper to the federal government from business adds up to 2 billion forms, which fill about 4½ million cubic feet of storage. The cost of storage costs another $8 billion.

But those are small-business forms only. The total number of federal forms was estimated by the subcommittee to be 650,000, but some expert outside observers say that figure is much too low. The Internal Revenue Service alone has an estimated 14,000 forms with which to give the public writer's cramp.

$19,300 spent by HEW for a study of why children fall off tricycles (findings: "unstable performance, particularly rollover while turning"); there was the $15,000 spent by the Forest Service to study public attitudes toward Smokey the Bear; there is the $59,000 paid yearly to store 127,118 pounds of feathers "stockpiled" by the Office of Emergency Planning.

Any group of nearly 3 million persons spending so many billions of dollars can, of course, be allowed some dim-wittedness and a few quaint slip-ups. But in fact these are more than quaint slip-ups; they are symptoms of deeper problems that have to do with perspective and priorities.

The psychology of the bureaucracy is not balanced; its profile is not pretty. Ralph Nader has described the bureaucracy as a sometimes timid, sometimes arrogantly vicious institution operating under an intentionally dull, drab cover. It is neither dull nor drab, nor is it harmless. It has immense power, as Nader points out, because it sets the rules and working conditions for those officials who decide pesticide levels, give out food stamps, handle subsidies to business, and determine what chemicals go into water, how sanitary food will be before it goes on the market, whether unsafe cars will be allowed to keep rolling.[5]

How well does the federal bureaucracy do its job? Not well at all. Largely because it takes so little interest in protecting the consumer, we spend about $200 billion a year (these are Senate figures) on products that are worthless or unsafe; or we go to work in unsafe places; or we breathe deadly air on the street; or we pay black-market prices for homes or do without; or we go to schools where we are treated as unwelcome aliens. Its sins, as Goldwater says, are due to the fact that bureaucracy is sometimes corrupt and always unfeeling and archaic. One way or another, the bureaucracy cheats us every day.

In an era that is beginning to recognize how unfairly women are treated in the work market, the federal bureaucracy is slowest to make reforms: as of mid-1973, women accounted for only 5.6 percent of the government's 322,243 top civil servants who earn between $16,600 and $36,000 a year. In the very top ranks—the supergrades where the starting salary is $31,000—there were only 148 women compared with 8710 men.

The Equal Employment Opportunity Commission, the agency whose mission is to eradicate discrimination, was found in 1973 to be guilty of some of the worst discrimination in government; most blacks and Spanish-surnamed individuals on the EEOC payroll were stuck away in low-paying clerical or maintenance positions.

Although the 1964 Civil Rights Act obliged the Health, Education, and Welfare Department to desegregate predominantly black and predominantly white colleges as well as grade schools and high schools, HEW ducked this responsibility. This fits into a large picture of bureaucratic lawlessness in regard to civil rights, as thoroughly documented in 1970 by the U.S. Civil Rights Commission in a huge report the size of the Manhattan telephone directory.

Bureaucracy is a vast kingdom cut into dozens of fiefdoms, ruled over by cocky, well-fed, and wealthy dukes. At the Defense Department alone, fifty bureaucratic bigwigs rate private chauffeurs. Even such a nobody as the administrator of the National Credit Union Administration holds court in an office equipped with a wide-screen television, a hi-fidelity stereo system, deep pile rugs and overstuffed chairs, a custom-made stand-up signing desk; he, too, gets a limousine that comes with telephone and chauffeur. The director of the Law Enforcement Assistance Administration had his office papered with silver foil at a cost of $4362. Commerce Secretary Frederick Dent, deciding his private elevator showed signs of age, took over the public elevator and put up a wall so that the public could not share it with him. Newspaper photographers who tried to take a picture of it were chased away by government cops.

The top bureaucrats take great care, at great expense, to present themselves in the best light for the press. Aside from the hundreds of public relations workers on their staffs (which law forbids them to have, so they are called "information officers"), the larger departments of the bureaucracy hire outside advertising agencies to improve their images. An incomplete tally for the years 1970–72 shows at least $80 million spent by the bureaucracy on Madison Avenue puffery. However, sometimes their p.r. eagerness comes a cropper; in 1972 the p.r. office at the Department of Justice cranked out a press release to tell the world that then-Attorney General Richard G. Kleindienst had been elected to the Hall of Heroes. Later it was discovered that he was the only person in the Hall and that he had been tricked into taking part in a promotional stunt cooked up by a comic book publisher. Interior Department's top officials hired a $121-a-day consultant to tell them how to make the public love them more, and he dutifully advised them to let Interior Secretary Rogers Morton have his picture taken as often as possible by the press because "Secretary Morton is not only the most photogenic member of the administration—but he's also able to participate physically in all kinds of outdoor situations and look natural." When Congress caught Interior's officials in this intramural beauty contest, they asked to see the consultant's entire report, but the blushing bureaucrats refused to let it out of their hands on the grounds that "it could result in personal embarrassment."[6]

The priorities of the bureaucracy are sometimes difficult to figure out. It spends millions of dollars building roads through parks and forests that other federal agencies are spending millions allegedly to preserve. When the Indians rebelled at Wounded Knee in 1973, more than four hundred federal officials showed up at that tiny village to mediate and consult with, and sometimes to shoot at, the Indians. But when it was discovered that traders licensed by the Interior Department's Bureau of Indian Affairs were cheating and defrauding the 130,000 reservation Navajos in Arizona and New Mexico with prices as much as 100 percent higher and interest rates 60 percent higher than in the outside world, not one bureaucrat could tear himself away from Washington to look into the matter.

For forty years the U.S. Public Health Service used 430 black men—without their permission—as guinea pigs in a study of syphilis. They were given no treatment because the USPHS wanted to see what effect the venereal disease had on the human body. At least two dozen of the men were allowed to die from neglect. When this marathon abuse was revealed in 1972 by Associated Press writer Jean Heller, the U.S. Public Health Service's response was to give the survivors a certificate of appreciation. The victims had all been buried free of charge. In a similar show of conscience lag, the Pentagon admitted in 1972—sixty-six years after the event— that the Army had been wrong to dishonorably discharge 168 black soldiers in Brownsville in 1906 for a shooting spree in which none of them participated; the two survivors received a framed honorable discharge and were assured that when they died they would be buried free of charge—but otherwise were cut off from any back pay or veterans' rights.

These episodes, which spanned many Democratic and Republican administrations, indicate correctly that this arrogant view of the public is nonpartisan. It exists because in every administration the ruling philosophy is a hard one. When Robert Mardian (later implicated in the Watergate scandal) was assistant attorney general he expressed the worry that "we're getting more people in government who feel they should be ruled by a sense of conscience" rather than by what the bureaucracy expects of them.[7] That clearly would not do, so the Nixon Administration tightened its screening procedure to make sure that the bureaucracy would be filled only with people who are "reliable."

Reliability is measured by how little the boat rocks. Leslie H. Gelb, the former Pentagon bureaucrat who was director of Policy Planning and Arms Control and who headed the agency's Vietnam war study (popularly known as the Pentagon Papers), says: "There's a premium on getting along. If you're the Korean desk officer in the State Department your universe is about half a dozen people—two or three under you, an Assistant Secretary of State, an admiral on the Joint Staff. It's silly to shrink your universe by offending any of these bodies. . . . 'Soft' is never a favorable adjective in government. 'Hard' is good. But you don't talk about soft-hearted or hard-hearted. You don't talk about the heart at all."[8]

When this attitude exists at the top, it seeps all the way down to the clerks. After dozens of phone calls to a variety of bureaucratic offices where the underlings treated him rudely, Representative John Rousselot, a California Republican, declared furiously that if a congressman was so treated—moreover, a congressman who sat on the committee overseeing the Civil Service Commission—"God help the average citizen trying to get help!"

Divine assistance has doubtless been invoked by many Presidents as well. An old story around Washington is about the White House visitor who suggested a management innovation to President Kennedy. "That's a first rate idea," Kennedy replied. "Now let's see if we can get the government to accept it."

Bureaucratic Autonomy

Since the passing of the spoils system, no President has been able to lay his ideological or methodological imprint very deeply on the bureaucracy. How can he hope to herd along in the direction of his choice the nearly 3 million people on the federal payroll, since he has as his "sheep dogs" only about 2500 appointive officials?

One of the larger departments, Interior, has more than 60,000 employees; fewer than 100 are there by presidential appointment and removable by him. And some appointees, for political reasons, are not safe to remove. Of a particular Assistant Secretary of the Interior who displeased President Nixon, the *New York Times* observed, "He is now so entrenched in the bureaucracy that the Administration finds it easier to move around him than to force him out." Even if it were possible for the President to appoint ten times the one hundred jobs open to appointments, it is not likely that a feeling of cohesive efficiency would develop within the Interior Department because its domain and functions are too sprawling to permit such a feeling. The public land under the jurisdiction of Interior totals more than three times the area of Texas, and Interior officials are quite candid about the fact that they do not know exactly how many parcels of land they manage or where all of them are.

The Department of Health, Education, and Welfare is another Cabinet slice of the bureaucracy that allegedly is under the jurisdiction of the President. But this can hardly be the case when it is not even under the jurisdiction of his Cabinet Secretary, except theoretically. HEW—with its 108,000 employees, its largely inflexible budget of nearly $98 billion, its more than 250 programs covering everything from family planning to Social Security, its 40 agencies—sometimes squabbling for funds and priority status like "feudal kingdoms" (to use former HEW Secretary Robert Finch's simile)—is such a chaos of emotional issues and often-quixotic bureaucrats that even the best of administrators (a description that fits few of HEW's secretaries over the years) could easily find himself cracking up physically, as Finch himself did after only a year in the job.

The attitudes of the bureaucracy run deep through many layers and become locked in by time. No part of the bureaucracy underscores this unfortunate truism more precisely than the Department of Agriculture, which for more than a generation has been operated primarily for the benefit of agribusiness corporations, not for the family farmer or the food consumer. The USDA makes no bones about that. Indeed, in 1972 it flatly opposed, and lobbied against, legislation that would have helped protect the family farmer against the overbearing competition of farm corporations, such as Southern Pacific Railroad and Tenneco, which own hundreds of thousands of acres of the best farmland in the country and which dominate the market.

The USDA is supposed to administer the buying and distribution of farm surplus foods to poor people and to school lunch programs, but it has worked hard to cripple all such programs. In 1972, for example, the USDA told the Senate that only 1100 additional schools wanted to participate in the school breakfast program when, in fact, 4900 more schools wanted in.[9] The USDA happily spends public money to assist wealthy commercial interests; in 1973 it admitted that it was giving Cotton Inc.—a promotional organization used by the cotton industry to help sell its products—$10 million a year. This grant permitted Cotton Inc. to simply bank the $12 million to $15 million it collected annually from its members for promotional purposes.[10]

A President, whether he wants to or not, inherits all these old attitudes of the bureaucracy. In the case of the State Department, for example, he inherits policy papers and rationalizations that were created long before he sought the office of President. Senate Foreign Relations Committee hearings have shown that the same group of men within the State Department have handled Laotian matters through four administrations, and the changing of administrations seems to have had no discernible effect on the policies.

Charles Frankel, an Assistant Secretary of State from 1965 to 1967, explains the problem: "A new policy dispossesses people; it takes their property away. The point of what they know how to do, of what they have always done, is lost. The old outfit, the old group, loses its rationale, its importance, its internal pecking order."[11] Resistance, therefore, is massive.

Some portions of the bureaucracy are eminently loyal and responsive to the President's wishes, primarily that part of the bureaucracy operating under the title of the Executive Office. Beyond that sphere the President's role as "chief administrator" becomes progressively weaker.

Perhaps the best-known quote to illustrate this lack of control came from President Franklin D. Roosevelt. Roosevelt reportedly had this exchange with one of his aides:

> When I woke up this morning, the first thing I saw was a headline in the *New York Times* to the effect that our Navy was going to spend two billion dollars on a shipbuilding program. Here I am, the Commander in Chief of the Navy having to read about that for the first time in the press. Do you know what I said to that?
> No, Mr. President.
> I said: "Jesus Chr-rist!"[12]

Presidents, like the public, have learned that there can be times when cursing is one of the few comforts available to those who attempt to deal with a wayward and obstinate bureaucracy. The sad story is echoed by their henchmen. Frank Carlucci, No. 2 man in Nixon's Office of Management and Budget and the President's chief assistant in bureaucratic reorganization, claims that it takes "from six to eight months for a presidential directive to be translated into agency guidelines and reach the action level," and in some extreme cases, he says, the decision-to-action translation takes two or three years.[13]

The President
and His Bureaucracy

Granting all that as true enough, our Presidents have to some extent overstated their helplessness. Until the early 1960s, he had a great deal of power over bureaucratic structure. He could create new departments without approval of Congress; all he had to beware of was congressional veto. Eisenhower set up the Department of Health, Education, and Welfare by executive edict, and when Congress didn't object, the order went into effect automatically.

But when Kennedy tried to establish the Department of Housing and Urban Development in 1961 he made the impolitic announcement that he intended to head the department with a black. At once Southern Democrats, assisted by Republican allies, teamed up to change the reorganization law in such a way that from then on the President had to have the approval—not merely the absence of disapproval—of Congress before he could create or abolish an executive department. Thus when Nixon tried in 1971 to reorganize the Cabinet along broader categories—departments of natural resources, human resources, community development, and economic affairs, to replace seven existing departments—he had to take his plan to Congress, and Congress turned it down.

The President is left with considerable leeway, nevertheless, to transfer functions from existing department to department (as long as Congress does not veto such shifts within sixty days). And he has great power to make changes within his own personal fiefdom, that special portion of the bureaucracy known as the Executive Office of the President, including more than 2200 officials in sixteen agencies. Within the Executive Office are such increasingly potent sources of policy determination as the Office of Management and Budget, which has broad powers ranging from making up the federal budget to approving environmental enforcement policy, the National Security Council, which has more immediate clout than the Defense Department and the State Department put together, and the Office on Telecommunications Policy, which increasingly has been usurping powers once vested in the Federal Communications Commission.

A President has his best chance for clout through the so-called independent regulatory agencies. The terms of members are staggered to prevent any one President from appointing his own men in wholesale numbers at the beginning of his term, but it doesn't take long—thanks to deaths and pressured resignations—before he can claim a majority of appointees on every agency.

Of thirty-eight positions on six major regulatory bodies—the Civil Aeronautics Board, the Federal Communications Commission, the Federal Power Commission, the Federal Trade Commission, the Interstate Commerce Commission, and the Securities and Exchange Commission—Nixon had appointed twenty-eight after less than five years in office. The chairmen of all six agencies had been named by him.

Furthermore, only the most naive citizens fail to understand the attitude of the White House toward these appointees, an attitude best illustrated by a memo that surfaced in mid-1973. When Charles W. Colson, formerly one of Nixon's top aides, left the White House, he went into the practice of law in Washington with Charles H. Morin. Morin had a favorite lawyer in mind whom he wanted G. Bradford Cook, then SEC chairman, to name to the SEC's top legal post. The memo that came to light was from Morin to Colson, and it read: "We have to lean on Brad. He ought to be reminded of how he got the job."[14]

Stated baldly in that way, the spirit of *quid pro quo* sounds pretty crass; but it is the standard spirit of presidential politics. Furthermore, in packing the regulatory agencies with men of his own stripe as swiftly as possible, Nixon was performing in an old tradition. The only thing about it that is somewhat surprising is that Congress takes it so docilely. Although Congress is supposedly jealous of its ties with the regulatory agencies and considers them creatures of Congress (as they are) and properly more responsive to it than to the Presidency, this is not really the way things work.* Presidents can and usually do appoint members who reflect their own economic and political philosophies, and the Senate almost always confirms their nominees.

* One reason Congress exercises such sloppy control over the bureaucracy is that so many of Congress' leaders are willing to let it get by with just about anything as long as they are permitted, through their friends, to participate in the goodies. One of the biggest rackets of our era is government consulting. The bureaucracy hands out $50 billion a year to consultants, and many of them are handpicked by bureaucracy's chums in Congress. In 1972 the voters of Colorado finally decided to dump Senator Gordon Allott, long-time friend of lumbering, mining, and railroad moguls; but he was taken care of the next year for all his good services when the Interstate Commerce Commission awarded him a $650,000 consulting contract that provided him with a $60,000 annual salary (on top of his posh senatorial pension). Ironically, during his time in the Senate, Allott served on the Joint Committee on Reduction of Non-essential Federal Expenditures.

When the Senate in June 1973 rejected Nixon's nomination of Robert H. Morris, a lawyer who did work for Standard Oil, for a position on the Federal Power Commission, it was the first time in memory that the Senate had done such a thing. In this instance it did so only because the FPC, which regulates the interstate oil and gas industry, already had four pro-industry members, and Morris would have made it five. The Senate thought it best, for appearances' sake, if at least one member was pro-consumer. But this gesture did nothing to prevent the FPC from granting natural gas price increases that would cost the consumer an estimated $750 billion over the life of the gas reserves.

A subtle means that a President has to color the thinking of the bureaucracy is through the appointment of advisory commissions. Whenever a problem comes up that makes headlines —housing scandals, consumer dissatisfaction, heroin addiction, transportation snarls—he can appoint an advisory commission, which in turn can issue a report that puts pressure on Congress and the bureaucracy to get something done. (That is, he can use it in that way if he approves of its findings; if he doesn't, he can squelch its report.)*

As of May 1973, Nixon had put together the amazing total of 1439 such commissions, which were busy dispensing advice on everything from how to curb cholera to how to make agribusinessmen richer. Although their work was unofficial and often useless, they cost the taxpayer $25.2 million annually.

If it sounds like we are talking about ways to circumvent bureaucracy's natural obesity, you're right. But none of these efforts matches the brilliance of Nixon's having conducted his international affairs without carrying the burden of the State Department lard wherever he and his negotiators went. The high-level, supergrade, and "executive" positions in the State Department add up to 3718, a force seventy-eight times the size of the White

---

* Another use the President can make of these commissions is to appeal to the egos of rich men, whom he can later call on for campaign donations. In 1971 then-Secretary of Commerce Maurice Stans named eighty businessmen to the Nixon-created National Business Council for Consumer Affairs, which was supposed to work on "current and potential consumer problems." Some people thought it odd that a number of the men named by Stans (and approved by Nixon) were top executives with corporations that had in the past been in trouble with the government over such things as false and misleading advertising. But later a possible explanation came to light when Stans became chairman of the President's reelection finance committee, and a number of the men on this board made heavy contributions to his campaign.

House staff that actually conducted state affairs well into 1973 under Nixon's advisor, Henry Kissinger. Of the forty-seven professionals on his staff, only eight were his "intimates."

As he rounded out his first four years with Nixon, Kissinger was still talking belligerently in these terms: "This Presidency has been a transition period, which needed a strong unifying concept, an integrating idea. But first . . . first of all, you have to weaken the bureaucracy! There are 20,000 people in the State Department and 50,000 in Defense. They all need each other's clearances in order to move . . . and they all want to do what I'm doing! So the problem becomes: how do you get them to push papers around, spin their wheels, so that you can get your work done?"[15] The task of giving them wheel-spinning assignments while he alone did the important stuff became easier when, in 1973, he became the official as well as the de facto Secretary of State.

Information Gathering, Dispensing, and Withholding

While it is the mass and complexity of the bureaucracy that beats down Presidents, it is its store of information that allows the bureaucracy to dominate Congress. The bureaucracy gathers data about everything from weather trends to how to grow onions; data about the inner workings of the latest ballistics missile and how much the tax-exempt foundations didn't give away last year and how much marijuana is sold at what prices in Abilene, Kansas —there is no aspect of life in America that the bureaucracy does not know something about or does not have ways of investigating.

Indeed, its multiplicity of tools (bugs, wiretaps, computers, data banks) and legal excuses (tax reports, census reports, job applications, grant applications) has spread an atmosphere of psychotic snooping over the bureaucracy, with the FBI, the CIA, and the various military intelligence units trying to outdo one another in prying into the private lives of civilians. Occasionally the intrusions provide scandalous headlines, as when the personnel office grilled a female government worker for six hours about every aspect of her sex life, and when several congressmen and senators discovered they were snooped on by Army dicks, and when the FBI admitted it had bugged a congressman's office.

But the bureaucracy does not draw its power from this kind of exotic information; rather it comes from the kind of basic data around which an industrial nation revolves. Bureaucracy has kept pace with the revolution in analytical technology, while Congress has not. Congress has less than half a dozen computers, and for the most part it uses these for nothing more profound than to keep its payroll and personnel affairs in order. By contrast, the bureaucracy of the executive branch has more than 4000 computers churning out data on substantive policy issues. Computer analysts and programmers are everywhere in the bureaucracy.

This is not data for the sake of data. It is data that can be cashed in for big bureaucratic budgets and for the kind of legislation that can be enormously profitable for the bureaucracy's allies in the business and corporate world. With its data, the bureaucracy can shade and weight legislation to suit itself and its friends, manipulating the information to show why a particular piece of legislation should or should not be passed. And it can withhold information that would help "the other side," sometimes by simply refusing to supply it but usually by delaying tactics or by pretending it does not know what Congress really wants.

Two-thirds of the bills passed by Congress were not written by Congress nor were they written by those portions of the executive branch specifically responsive to the President; they were written, usually with the assistance of private pressure groups, by agencies within the independent or quasi-independent bureaucracy.

It's good when Congress can get the information it needs out of the agencies, but it's bad when that is the only place Congress can get the information. The executive assistant of one Midwest senator summarized Capitol Hill's complaints:

> We're in their hands. We rely too much on the executive's bureaucracy downtown. I can't tell you if we need a bill for V.A. benefits until I check with the Veterans Administration. We make hundreds of calls a day to the agencies. All these bills are so complex we can't understand them without help from the bureaucrats. At the conference-committee hearing on an education bill, say, somebody is constantly running out in the hall to ask one of the H.E.W. flunkies hanging around the door to call down and find out what a particular formula means. Sometimes I get to feeling there is only one branch of the government—the executive and its bureaucracy.[16]

What the federal legislators are most ignorant about happens also to be the most important issue that confronts them: the budget. On this they get little assistance from the agencies, which are of course always intent on putting the best face on their requests. Without an extensive staff of specialists of their own to comb the entire federal budget and discover just what kind of subterranean activities are going on in the bureaucracy, Congress is helpless. Therefore, for better or worse, it will usually settle for the word of the agencies.

And it is clear that the bureaucracy loves to cultivate this dependency by overwhelming Congress with a "liaison" staff, which stays around Capitol Hill partly to be of assistance to the legislators but mainly to serve as lobbyists for their agencies. These are no trivial efforts. The Defense Department keeps more than 300 top- and middle-pay-grade civilian and military men on congressional liaison duty all the time. (Top-level liaison men earn $42,000 a year, which is as much as the congressmen are paid.) Even the relatively dinky Securities and Exchange Commission, which has fewer than 1500 workers, keeps 35 liaison people on the Hill.

Altogether the bureaucracy hires more than 500 liaison people, which means that the ratio is nearly one agency lobbyist per legislator.

But, to repeat, just because the bureaucracy possesses the information does not mean it will turn loose of it, unless turning loose of it will help the bureaucrats. Robert Shaw, manager of the Minnesota Newspaper Association, heard that the Internal Revenue Service was going to share its confidential information with other agencies of the executive branch. Shaw wrote a Minnesota congressman to find out if this unsettling rumor might indeed be more than a rumor. He received this answer: "We have tried for some time to get information for you with respect to conference which may have taken place between the IRS and other governmental bureaus. There is simply no way, under existing law, to obtain this information, when the agencies of the executive branch do not want members of Congress to have it."

Although the Internal Revenue Service wants to know all about your financial affairs, it feels no obligation to make its own finances public. It spends about $1 billion annually to operate its vast and complex tax-collecting operations, but it refuses to let the General Accounting Office, Congress' bookkeeping sleuths, audit its books to see just how much waste or illegality is involved in these expenditures. So Congress, like the general public, remains in the dark.

In 1969 the Senate Commerce Committee, which supposedly

oversees the Interstate Commerce Commission, requested that the ICC supply it with a copy of a study that was critical of the Commission's merger policies. The ICC refused. And only after prolonged diplomatic negotiations did the ICC (by a one-vote margin) consent to show the House Commerce Committee *some* of the documents relating to *some* key mergers, including the disastrous merger between the Pennsylvania and New York Central railroads (Penn Central), the biggest business merger in the nation's history.

The Civil Aeronautics Board's Advisory Committee on Finance held its 1970 organizational meeting in the New York offices of James P. Mitchell, a vice president of the Chase Manhattan Bank, at which time the committee voted that all its sessions would be closed to the press and the public.* The action of the advisory committee, an unofficial group, was in harmony with the CAB's own regard for an open government.

The previous year, when the CAB granted a $300-million fare increase to the nation's airlines, it allowed industry representatives to be on hand but it refused to permit congressmen to listen to the rate-making process, much less take part in or object to it. When thirty-two congressmen sued the CAB because they were excluded, the United States Court of Appeals ruled wisely that "if congressmen are excluded from these ex parte meetings . . . ordinary rate-paying members of the public . . . would have little chance indeed to be admitted."

The very fact that congressmen have occasionally taken to fighting back in this way is indicative of how far the withholding of information has gone, for Congress seldom acts prior to a crisis condition. Ignorance is crisis, and Congress has plenty of ignorance. Information that could be used by Congress for writing safety or consumer laws is frequently covered up, one prime example being the secrecy imposed by the Federal Aviation Administration on the Boeing 747 jetliner's critical engine failures.

---

* If anyone had been innocent enough to expect objectivity out of the committee, this cozy session should have clarified his thinking, seeing as how Chase Manhattan Bank was identified in 1969 as the biggest stockholder in Northwest Airlines, the second biggest stockholder in Eastern Airlines, trustee for the largest single block of stock in Trans World Airlines, and—according to Senator Lee Metcalf, who for several years has been probing corporate mischief—"the major creditor for five of the nine local service carriers." (*Washington Post*, April 26, 1971.)

The Corruption
of the Bureaucracy

Although its ability to intimidate Congress and the President is indeed impressive, nothing about the bureaucracy is nearly so impressive as its pervasive corruptibility. The special interests that it is supposed to regulate for the general public's welfare almost invariably seem to wind up running the show.

This is not so unusual, given the adopted economy of this country. It is a natural situation in that it is the expected response to what might be called the "physics of politics," or at least one law of that physics, namely, that more pressure can be exerted through a narrow opening than through a broad opening. The narrow opening is at the top of the economic power structure. As Adolf Berle pointed out:

> Agriculture aside, most of the business of the United States, where it is not carried on by the government, is carried on by corporations—to be specific, about 1,200,000 of them, big and small. But four-fifths or more of the total activity is carried on by about 3,500 corporations in all, whose stock is listed respectively on the New York Stock Exchange, the American Stock Exchange, or the over-the-counter markets. Even this is not a fair index. Eight hundred corporations probably account for between 70% and 75% of all American business activity; 250 corporations account for perhaps two-thirds of it. These figures do not take into account the fact that great numbers of smaller concerns are in effect, though not technically, controlled by their large associates. Thousands of gasoline stations and automobile dealers in the United States are nominally independent; practically, most of their decisions are predetermined by supply arrangements, franchise contracts, or agency agreements with the large corporations whose oil or cars or gadgets they sell. Far and away the major part of the American supply-and-exchange system is constituted of a few hundred (at most) clusters of corporate enterprises, each of whose major decisions are determined by a central giant.[17]

Needless to say, it is much easier for a dozen of those central giants to agree on policies to promote their welfare, and to muster the finances for a propaganda campaign to promote those policies, than it is for 50 million or 100 million random citizens to make countermoves. The advantage in pressure politics, therefore, is always at the top. And since these special interest groups maintain an unrelenting pressure on the bureaucracy and especially on the regulatory agencies, it is to be expected that these elements of government eventually give in, to varying degrees, and become subjects rather than masters of industry.

The motor vehicle industry annually turns out about 9 million cars and trucks comprising five hundred different makes and models. The National Highway Traffic Safety Administration, which is supposed to closely police the industry, tests only about fifty-five vehicles each year for compliance with *some* of the safety standards. Most of its money is used to test tires, not autos. U.S. auto makers recall millions of vehicles each year for various safety reasons—but only about 100,000 of the vehicles are recalled because of Safety Administration testing. It's a flop.[18]

Although the Food and Drug Administration has a candid and open relationship with the industries it is supposed to regulate, the FDA has traditionally been very reluctant to let the public know what it was doing. So it came as something of a revolutionary leap forward when, after sixty-one years of silence, the FDA decided in 1972 to disclose how much mold, insect parts, rat manure, rot, worms, hair, fruitfly eggs, and other "natural" filth it allows in the nation's food supply. For those who are interested in such things: it allows one rodent manure pellet in each pint of wheat, insect damage or mold in 10 percent of coffee beans, up to 10 million bacteria per gram of dried eggs, mold from 20 to 40 percent in most tomato products, and so on. The General Accounting Office found that the FDA wasn't cleaning food up even as well as the above careless standards might imply; in fact, the GAO found, in a random sampling, that 40 percent of all food processing plants allow "serious potential or actual food adulteration."[19]

Meat has supposedly been regulated by federal law for a long time—since 1865. Back in the good old days when rotten meat smelled and usually looked rotten, the consumer had a chance to be his own cop. No longer. Nowadays the boys in the backroom of the slaughterhouse know how to use seasoning, preservatives, and coloring agents in such a way as to trick Mom into putting garbage on the table. And she gets very little help from the bureaucracy. In federally controlled plants, inspectors who do their jobs well can anticipate being fired or banished to a less desirable location.

There is a kind of fuzzy legend that hangs over the Justice Department's antitrust office. Many people believe the department keeps the mammoth corporations from joining forces to steal from the public on any grander scale than they already do. As a matter of fact, since the Sherman Antitrust Act was passed in 1890, businessmen have spent a total of less than two years in jail for the billions of dollars of buckaneering they have committed in antitrust crimes. The law is worse than useless because, as enforced by the Justice Department, it falsely leaves the impression of protection. And what about the lowly worker? Isn't he protected by stiff safety law enforcement? For an earthy sample, let us turn to the Bureau of Mines. Its Health and Safety office installed a telephone "hot line" that miners anywhere in the country could call, collect, to report a safety violation. The phone was unmanned, but incoming calls were allegedly taped and played later by Bureau of Mines officials. On December 22, 1971, a young environmentalist reporter discovered that the tape hadn't been checked by Bureau of Mines officials for two months and that, in fact, "somehow" the messages had all been erased.[20] Back to the mines.

The fact is, most of the bureaucracy does not feel it is set up to help the public or to conform to whatever progressive legislation gets through Congress.

When an official tries to resist industry and to do his job on behalf of the general public, he doesn't last long. Dr. Herbert L. Ley, Jr., was Commissioner of the Food and Drug Administration from 1966 to 1969, a period when the FDA began to show a few signs of becoming consumer-oriented (three hundred drugs were taken off the market as ineffective). After his ouster Dr. Ley admitted that he had been under "constant, tremendous, sometimes unmerciful pressure" from the drug industry, which does a $100-billion business each year. "Some days," he says, "I spent as many as six hours fending off representatives of the drug industry."[21] For fending too well, he was fired by HEW Secretary Robert Finch.

When not fired outright, conscientious civil servants may pay through the nose in other ways. A top-level official at the Department of Agriculture who spoke out against what he considered corrupt practices was stuck in a room by himself and given the job of organizing departmental beauty contests. A National Institutes of Health scientist who complained about the safety of certain vaccines lost his secretary and his telephone and was put in a small room by himself. A USDA geneticist, Samuel Scheinberg, had spent thirteen years developing a test group of 450 pigeons and 250 chickens used in blood research. When he protested having to move his research flock to a building he considered unsanitary, he was fired, and the birds were destroyed without Scheinberg's being given notice or a chance to buy them.

Considerable evidence supports Senator Proxmire's claim that "there is little room in the government service for men of character, independence and guts. The government doesn't want the free spirits—the highly intelligent, strong-minded, truthful men—working for it. What it wants instead are time-servers, conformists and 'yes' men."[22]

There is so much shuttling between industry and government that it is sometimes difficult to see the line of demarcation between the regulated and the regulators. William H. Tucker, who ruled in favor of cutbacks in service for the Penn Central when he was ICC chairman, later left the commission to become a vice president of Penn Central. At the same time that his department was trying to help the Penn Central avoid bankruptcy in 1970, Secretary of Commerce Maurice Stans held $300,000 worth of stock in a subsidiary of the railroad.

When Clifford Hardin left the Agriculture Secretaryship in 1971, he became vice chairman of the board of Ralston Purina, one of the biggest agribusiness corporations in the country. He was replaced by Earl L. Butz, a stockholder and director not only of Ralston Purina but also of two other agribusiness corporations, International Minerals and Chemicals Corporation and Stokely-Van Camp Company.

Butz helped swing the sale of $750 million worth of grain to Russia in 1972. It was a disaster for the consumer. U.S. taxpayers laid out $130 million to subsidize this deal, and because of a resulting shortage of wheat in this country they paid an estimated $400 million extra in the price of wheat products. But the big grain exporters, who may have been secretly tipped off that something was up, made windfall profits of more than $100 million. Among the exporters who shared this bounty were Bunge and Continental Corporations. Perhaps coincidentally, one of USDA's top officials, Clifford Pulvermacher, who had helped Butz arrange the wheat deal, shortly thereafter became Continental's vice president, and another key USDA official in the deal, Clarence Palmby, became the Washington representative of Bunge.

In 1971 James J. Needham moved from his $38,000-a-year post as commissioner of the Securities and Exchange Commission to the $150,000-a-year post of chairman of the New York Stock Exchange; the SEC regulates the NYSE. Nicholas Katzenbach quit as Attorney General in 1966, and three years later he joined IBM as vice president and general counsel, and is handling IBM's defense against a Justice Department antitrust suit.

In August 1970, Senator John Tower announced that Federal Power Commission member Carl E. Bagge was helping him draft legislation to exempt the well-head price of natural gas from FPC regulation—hardly the act of an impartial commissioner. Three months later Bagge legitimatized his role by quitting the FPC to become president of the National Coal Association, which, despite its name, is dominated by the oil and gas industry. His place was filled on the FPC by Pinkney C. Walker, who had previously been a paid consultant to three utility companies seeking a rate increase. Bagge defends the practice of regulatory officials taking jobs with the industries they regulate. "You couldn't get people, except elitists, on regulatory bodies if they couldn't utilize the knowledge and insights they've acquired about how a system operates," he says. "If that's a deferred bribe, then so be it."

According to Robert Fellmeth, a "Nader Raider," more than half the commissioners leaving the Federal Communications Commission in recent years moved into high executive positions in the communications industry, and ten of twelve of the commissioners leaving the Interstate Commerce Commission in the past decade have gone, like Tucker, directly into the transportation industry or have become lobbyists and consultants for the industry.

Every regulatory agency, every arm of the bureaucracy, has spun its share of this web of industry-government commonality. And when it isn't jobs they exchange, it's favors. In March 1971, for example, the nation's leading defense contractors hosted a dinner party in Washington in honor of Comptroller General Elmer B. Staats, whose agency, the General Accounting Office, is supposed to audit with a policeman's eye all defense contracts (and does a very poor job of it). Members of the Securities and Exchange Commission, which supposedly police the stock market, allow people in that business to treat them to trips and hotel stays and meals.

It is commonplace to see ICC commissioners at the head table being wined and dined at banquets paid for by truckers or railroad executives and lobbyists. One of the most flagrant examples occurred on Inauguration Day, 1973, when the chief lobbyist for the Chesapeake & Ohio Railway had at least five of the ICC commissioners to lunch at the ritzy International Club; none of the commissioners who attended saw anything wrong with being there, even though a large railroad like the C & O nearly always has cases pending actively before the commission. Was the lobbying direct and blatant? Probably not. A transportation lawyer explained to Stephen Aug of the *Washington Star-News*, who exposed this chummy get-together, "The whole lobbying technique here is to become very friendly without necessarily discussing a particular case or problem, but through indirect communications indirectly convey ideas and concepts."[23]

When Virgil Day, vice president of the General Electric Company, flew Mrs. George H. Boldt to New York on a GE plane and later treated her and her husband to dinner and the opera, the *Wall Street Journal* put an account of the evening on its front page. The reason: Boldt was chairman of the Pay Board, an outfit whose decisions meant a great deal to all industrial pocketbooks, including GE's. Boldt, of course, thought the *Journal* was picking on him and that this was all a tempest in a teapot. "To my mind," he said righteously, "the most you might say is that it was a breach of Washington's concern for appearance rather than substance. It was a trifling incident."[24]

Trifling it was, and no one suggests that the regulators who accept favors and jobs are being bought off, exactly; but the atmosphere does seem somewhat too cozy. When Donald P. Schlick, the Interior Department–Bureau of Mines' deputy director for health and safety, accepted a ride (as did three of his aides) aboard the corporate airplane owned by FMC Corporation, the Interior Department was mildly embarrassed and told him not to do it again. The FMC Corporation, it seems, holds a $7.6-million contract with the Bureau of Mines for mine safety research, and federal law forbids government employees from accepting any favor, gift, entertainment, "or anything of value" from persons or corporations seeking or doing business with the government. Reporters from the *Louisville Courier-Journal* discovered that this wasn't the first time Schlick had accepted favors from organizations doing business with the Bureau of Mines.

There are many, many ways that the bureaucracy can and does return the favors. Aside from permitting special interests to loot the federal lands and treasury (an exercise to be discussed more fully in Chapter 7), the bureaucracy also specializes in being unable to see corporate evil, or, if it is forced to acknowledge the evil, in doing nothing about it or doing it so slowly as to avoid remedy. In other words, it suspends the law for friends.

On December 14, 1967, President Johnson signed the Flammable Fabrics Act, with the promise: "For the first time, fabrics used in blankets, rugs, drapes and upholstery will come under the law's protection. So will hats, gloves and shoes." In mid-1971 an Associated Press investigating team did a survey to find out how well the law had been applied. It discovered that, although in the intervening years 10,000 Americans had been killed in fabric fires and another 525,000 injured, the bureaucracy had not applied the law to any material but large carpets and large rugs.[25]

The 1967 Flammable Fabrics Act was also supposed to apply to the sleeping garments of children, but industry successfully blocked this part of the law from going into effect until July 29, 1973. The enforcement of it was then handed over to the Consumer Products Safety Commission, a wing of the bureaucracy that was so new its employees hardly knew how to find their way to work, much less to ride herd on wayward cotton manufacturers.

The delay was partly due to industry's technological lag, but it was also partly due to an attitude best illustrated on February 24, 1972, when Mrs. Dennis Brehm of Des Moines testified at the Commerce Department that the fireproof requirements should go into effect immediately—in fact, that they should have gone into effect five years earlier. Her evidence was at her side: a three-year-old daughter whose cotton nightgown had caught fire, burning 50 percent of her body. The accident resulted in thirty operations for skin graft at a cost of $25,000. Reporters who were present at the hearing said that the largely male audience of fiber, textile, and garment manufacturers greeted her testimony with restless sighs, sniggers, and sometimes laughter.[26]

The Food and Drug Administration's list of kind actions for the drug industry is endless. Just to mention two: In June 1971, the FDA admitted that for four years or more it had allowed large-scale distribution of an anticancer medicine, Methotrexate, for unauthorized use in the treatment of the skin ailment psoriasis. A four-year delay is nothing to the latitude the FDA has sometimes given. The Relaxaciser—an electrified gadget strapped to the body by those foolish enough to think it would reduce weight—appeared on the market in 1949 and was sold for twenty-one years before the FDA cracked down and forced it off the market; meanwhile, the firm had bilked 400,000 people of $40 million for a device that was not only worthless but so dangerous that it could cause heart failure, kidney failure, epilepsy, and an assortment of other serious ailments. Explaining why the FDA was so slow, an official said: "How much of the taxpayer's money should be spent protecting the gullible? The government says, 'Protect the fools, not the damn fools.'"

The Federal Communications Commission supposedly keeps the nation's television and radio stations in line with the threat of suspending their licenses if they do not service the public adequately. Some threat. Of the more than 7000 broadcasting stations licensed since 1934, only about 50 have lost their licenses, usually for lying on their license applications, not for substantive sins against the public.

One of the most important guidelines in the industry is the "fairness doctrine," which supposedly requires stations to give time for the discussion of both sides of a controversial topic. Hundreds of complaints of violations of this doctrine have been lodged with the FCC, surely some of them with adequate documentation, but only once has the FCC suspended a station's license for this reason.* By law the FCC is obliged to break up (or at least not to encourage) the concentration of media ownership, but only once in its history has the FCC taken away the license of an existing station with the explanation that it wanted to diversify ownership.

The airwaves are in many respects a tightly closed corporate monopoly to which the people have little access, and the FCC sees its primary function as keeping it that way. After the FCC ruled in 1968 that a Jackson, Mississippi, television station should be allowed to renew its license even though it hired announcers who used the word *nigger* and promoted the segregationist line, Commissioners Nicholas Johnson and Kenneth Cox, in a seventy-page dissent, concluded that "the only way in which members of the public can prevent renewal of an unworthy station's license is to steal the document from the wall of the station's studio in the dead of night." The most accurate estimation of the value of the FCC was given by the *Washington Post's* television columnist Lawrence Laurent:

> The highest service that the Congress or the White House can perform for the radio and television audience in the United States

---

* The FCC has a very flexible definition of fairness. In 1967 it ruled that stations had to provide antismoking spots roughly equal to one-fifth the time taken up by tobacco advertisements (a ruling forced on the commission by the U.S. Surgeon General's decree that cigarettes are a potential health hazard). Okay, so how about time to refute all potential health hazards—things like gasoline and automobiles? After all, the President's own Council on Environmental Quality admitted that there is more lung cancer in areas where auto fumes contribute to a high degree of air pollution. The FCC nixed that idea fast, ruling in 1970 that although it was true that many products—including detergents, gasoline, automobiles, and disposable containers—do contribute to pollution, business is business, and if stations were required to give time for the message from antipolluters it would lead to "the undermining of the present system [of American television], based as it is on product commercials." And that would be un-American.

would be to abolish the Federal Communications Commission. The FCC is a non-regulatory agency, staffed mainly with men who live in fear of the broadcasters they license. Worse, it provides a disservice to the American public by its very existence. If no such agency existed the public would not be misled into thinking that a government agency is looking after the public's air waves.[27]

For the most fully realized and corrupt wedding between industry and government, many observers insist that one must go to the Interstate Commerce Commission, the oldest of the regulatory agencies (established 1887). Leonard Ross, a law professor, has given this summation of the ICC: "The ICC, once run by the railroads, has modernized in the last few decades by selling out to the truckers. It is now in the business of keeping truck rates high by excluding new firms, and keeping railroad rates even higher to prevent them from competing. As a sideline, the ICC publishes a tough truck-safety code, which it does not enforce, and a weak household-movers' code, which it also does not enforce."[28]

Its relationship with the railroads has been especially instructive. The perversion of its regulatory purpose became official in the First World War, when the railroads did such a rotten job of serving the nation that the federal government had to step in and help them; this crisis openly began a new relationship—Government the Regulator became Government the Promoter. In the 1930s —when again the railroads, like all industry, were in trouble—the government increased its assistance to such a degree that it could never again pull back. From then on the chief objective of the federal government (including especially the ICC) was not to punish the railroads if they gave shoddy service at inflated rates but to help them make more profits more easily.

The last two steps in this climb toward total corporate favoritism were taken in 1948 when Congress exempted railroad mergers from the antitrust laws and in 1962 when the ICC began encouraging rail mergers in a wholesale fashion, not only permitting but even urging the establishment of monopolies in some regions. Even the conservative *Encyclopaedia Britannica* acknowledges that the ICC's "position has been compared to that of a superboard of directors of the railroad industry."

The results are plain to anyone who travels, or tries to travel, by train. In 1929 there were 20,000 passenger trains in operation. Forty years later there were 450. They did not want to give passenger service; by deceptively juggling their books to charge expenses to the passenger service that rightly should have been charged to their highly profitable freight service, the railroads persuaded Congress to pass the Railroad Reorganization Act of 1970, which reduced the number of passenger lines from 366 in service at the time the law was passed to 125—the very sort of reform the public, through cynical experience, has been taught to expect. The rail network that remains has left broad areas of the nation without any passenger service at all. With few exceptions, that is only quantitatively worse than the passenger service that is given: filthy trains, surly personnel, inadequate schedules, broken or antiquated equipment. Some passengers who have traveled the 2000 miles from New Orleans to Los Angeles by Southern Pacific have been able to obtain food only from a vending machine. When they complained to the ICC that man cannot live comfortably by sandwiches alone, the ICC responded, in effect: "We have no power to tell the railroads what kind of service they give. We can tell them where and when they must supply passenger trains, but we have nothing to say about the quality of service."

The reception given to these complaints was not unusual. Any individual citizen—who does not hold an important position in industry but simply wants to protest the treatment he has received at the hands of one of the regulated industries, either because of price gouging or fraudulent service—who attempts to obtain the ear of the appropriate agency will learn all too quickly that the agencies speak and listen to spokesmen for the industry, but seldom to outsiders, and that the hope for getting a comforting word, much less redress, is virtually nil.

Can the Bureaucracy Be Reformed?

Because so many portions of the bureaucracy are no longer responsive to the needs of the general public, and because they do their narrowly selfish work without fear of reprisal from the public, it may seem useless to talk of reform. But it isn't useless to talk of reform; it is only naive to expect much.

Scandal does not put even a dent in the bureaucracy; if it could, the Small Business Administration, which has supported all sorts of shady activities, including Mafia-linked companies in Florida, New York, Illinois, and Louisiana, would have been scratched from the budget long ago. Nor does notorious uselessness quickly put bureaucrats out of business; the Subversive Activities Control

Board uncovered only one "subversive" organization (the old sitting-duck Communist Party USA) since it was set up in 1950, and yet until Nixon abolished the board in 1972 Congress had cranked out $450,000 every year to keep it going.

Could reorganization do it? Even if it could, all previous efforts to jar loose the rigid structure of the bureaucracy have failed almost totally. Congress, where such reforms must originate, is under the same corporate thumb that pins the bureaucracy. There have been several efforts to reorganize the government in the last twenty-five years. But in the Reorganization Act of 1945, Congress exempted so many agencies (ICC, SEC, FTC, among others) from the reforming hand of the President that no significant change resulted. In 1962 President Kennedy had his own ideas about bringing the regulatory agencies more closely under his dominion and setting up some modernized agencies within the Cabinet departments, but Congress repulsed him. Nixon, too, had some ambitious ideas; he wanted to refashion eleven Cabinet departments into four, but Congress gave his plan an icy reception. Even so, Nixon accomplished more than most Presidents in this regard; he not only got Congress to transform the Post Office Department into a quasi-private corporation, he also set up by Executive Order two new environmental agencies, despite stiff resistance from several Cabinet members whose powers he thereby diminished.

But restructuring the government is only a cosmetic answer. Shuffling the same old drones into new hives is not likely to increase the quality or quantity of the bureaucracy's work.* Operating behind a great wall of secrecy and anonymity, perpetuating

---

* If ever there was proof that merely shifting the bureaucracy around is not enough to make progress, the Postal Service is neon-outlined proof. The main results of the new status of the Postal Service are negative. More waste: early in 1973 the Postal Service announced that it intended to scrap more than $18 million worth of mail processing equipment it had put into service only seven months earlier. More boondoggle: as of February 1973, the Postal Service offered 1846 noncareer jobs paying between $15,000 and $60,000 (while it was still a government agency, the Postal Service had only eighty-four such jobs). These included such strange positions as "manager of creative services" at a top salary of $33,493; "suggestions award administrator" at a salary of $30,280; and "fringe benefit specialist" at $24,783. Less service: an impromptu pony express route was set up between Philadelphia and Washington by irate customers of the Postal Service to prove—and they were right—that horses and riders can deliver the mail twenty-four hours faster between those two cities than can the motorized Postal Service. Senators weren't surprised; one told of having mailed a letter from the Dirksen Senate Office Building to the Russell Senate Office Building, a distance of about twenty yards. It was delivered two weeks later.

itself with a budget that Congress is incapable of understanding, praised and protected by business and industry whom it serves so faithfully—the bureaucracy is not going to be changed simply by changing the title on the door.

As for the regulatory agencies, some critics have suggested that they could be made more responsive to the public if their independence of presidential tenure was taken away. They argue that if each President appointed the men to head the agencies, to serve only as long as he desired, then the President would have to take the responsibility (to be judged in the voting booth) for their actions. One who takes that position is Philip Elman, who left the Federal Trade Commission in 1970 after nine years of service. As it is now, says Elman: "A President knows that after an independent agency member is appointed, he is essentially on his own. And if he proves to be incompetent or unresponsive to the public interest, the President will usually not be held at fault." Consequently, "the independence of the regulatory agency tempts a President to satisfy a political debt to a deserving friend or supporter by appointing him to a comfortable agency berth."[29] If the appointee goes sour thereafter, the President can merely shrug and say there's nothing he can do about it.

Elman's is a persuasive proposal, and comforting to contemplate, except that one is left to wonder where is the President who would appoint men to the FPC willing to make the oil companies toe the line, or men to the FCC willing to offend the networks by forcing them to meet at least minimum standards of intelligent programming, or men to the FDA willing to make the powerful drug and food industries stop lying about their products. In short, where is the President who will chastise the people who paid for his last campaign?

The best chance for improving the departmental bureaucracy and the regulatory agencies would come from a procedure by which the public could confront civil servants who don't do their jobs right. On this point few can quarrel with Elman:

> No reforms in the structure of the regulatory agencies will succeed unless there also are radical changes in the climate of government and the political processes. We must institutionalize the means whereby the public may be aware of, and participate in, political and governmental processes that affect the quality of all our lives. We must open wide the doors and windows of government agencies, so that the public may see for itself what is or is not being done, and demand an accounting from those in charge.[30]

Demand an accounting from those in charge: that could indeed be the answer. As *The Nation* magazine once proposed, and as did Ralph Nader later, bureaucrats whose irresponsibility or indifference or greed causes them to do things that harm the public should be liable to penalties ranging from fines to demotion to dismissal to imprisonment. If, for example, they know that a product is unsafe and they fail to take it off the market and that product harms someone, there should be some procedure by which the public can reach right through the bureaucratic curtain and lay its hands on and punish the offending officials.

Is there a taxpayer anywhere who does not take heart at the possibility of such justice? The establishment of the procedure is not out of the question. It is mainly a matter of the public's getting in the proper frame of mind to demand that Congress establish such a procedure, and refuse to be refused. And getting in that frame of mind is mainly a matter of learning to think and talk more honestly: to call corporate thieves and con-men what they are, thieves and con-men, and to call their bureaucratic frontmen and fences what they are, frontmen and fences. As Nader points out:

> Corporate fraud and other economic crimes escape the normative perception that would be applied, for example, to a pickpocket by most people. The law is much more comfortable sentencing a telephone coin box thief to five years than sentencing a billion-dollar price-fixing executive to six weeks in jail. Corporate economic, product, and environmental crimes dwarf other crimes in damage to health, safety and property, in confiscation or theft of other peoples' monies, and in control of the agencies which are supposed to stop this crime and fraud.[31]

When most Americans speak of organized corporate criminals that accurately, then politicians and civil servants will no longer feel quite so safe in contributing to their delinquencies.

Occasionally there is a propublic gleam in the dinosaur's eye. An *occasional* gleam, and an occasional twinge of what appears to be life in the recumbent body. For instance, for many years the Federal Trade Commission was generally considered to be one of the most useless "regulatory" agencies in Washington; it was timid, inept, lazy, and indifferent. It was totally intimidated by big business. Commonly, prosecution of cases of mislabeling and false advertising and deceitful practices would be dragged out by the FTC for so many years that they just fell apart and died—the witnesses scattered, the evidence misplaced, and often the accused company itself gone into bankruptcy.

But then in 1971 consumer critics of the FTC began noticing something strange: an agency they had thought was not only dead but rotten was, in fact, trying to stand up and walk. It wasn't performing very well, but the fact that it was moving at all was a very big miracle. It was boldly accusing such hallowed outfits as Coca-Cola Company, MacDonald's Hamburgers, Reader's Digest, and Proctor & Gamble of deceptive promotion; it was suggesting that Wonder Bread really wasn't doing anything special to build strong bodies twelve ways; it was committing such heresies as to demand that the manufacturers of automobiles, electric razors, and air conditioners send evidence of the accuracy of their advertisements.

Moreover, the FTC came up with a novel form of proconsumer corrective. Instead of merely hitting manufacturers with a cease-and-desist order to make them withdraw false advertisements—orders that usually were dodged by the manufacturers until long after they had voluntarily quit using the ad because it was outdated—the FTC began ordering false advertisers to place *corrective* ads, in which they acknowledged that their previous ads were false. The FTC also advocated letting consumer groups have free television time to respond to ads they disagreed with.

Industry was outraged, and it began putting pressure on the White House. The FTC had offended some of Nixon's biggest campaign contributors, and they were growing publicly vocal in their anger. The result was predictable: White House spokesmen denounced the FTC's actions, likening its treatment of industry to "a verbal stoning in the public square." Herbert Klein, Nixon's Director of Communications, declared that the FTC had gone "too far" in its protection of the consumer. And then, early in 1973, Miles W. Kirkpatrick, chairman of the FTC, resigned. There was no indication that the President had pressed him to stay.

Why was Kirkpatrick's leaving important? Because he had been largely responsible for the reviving of the agency. In 1969 he had headed an American Bar Association commission that, after studying the FTC, concluded that if it didn't start fulfilling its duties in antitrust and consumer protection, it might as well go out of business. In 1970 he was brought in as chairman of the FTC to put his theories into practice. Apparently he did his job much too well to suit some top politicians and their financial backers. That conclusion does not promise much for general bureaucratic reform, but the very fact that Kirkpatrick lasted a couple of years promises something.

Scratching around for other meager shards of hope, one comes upon the inimitable George Romney. For a bit more than four years he was Secretary of the Department of Housing and Urban Development. He got little support from the White House, for HUD had such out-of-favor duties as providing low-cost housing to low-income people. It was also a period of keen embarrassment for HUD; it was shaken with numerous scandals. It was discovered that much federal housing subsidy that was supposed to go to impoverished home owners wound up in the pockets of the middle-men. Some federal housing officials were implicated in a $200-million housing fraud in New York. HUD officials did such wildly stupid things as to allocate $300,000 for developing a new parking lot in downtown Cheyenne, Wyoming, that in the first six weeks took in 75 cents. Shortly after Nixon's reelection, Romney threw in the trowel.

What's promising about that? Well, at least he was candid, and that is a rare quality in the bureaucracy. He did not try to cover up his department's mistakes, or at least he did not spend all his time covering up. Instead he admitted that his wing of the bureaucracy was replete with "incompetence, conflict of interest, favoritism, graft, bribes, and fraud."[32] He admitted that HUD had bungled subsidized housing so badly that it might just be better to do away with the program and start over because "we can no longer afford $100 billion mistakes." He denounced the urban renewal programs administered by HUD as a waste of taxpayers' money. And as he put on his hat and walked out the door for the last time, he said something about setting up another citizens' reform coalition that would focus attention on the tender areas of government that politicians never mention when they are running for office. If the bureaucracy attracts a fellow like that into its bowels once in a while, it can't be totally unredeemable.

Your Land and Mine, and How It Got Away

As matters currently stand, government does not even deserve
to be called the executive committee of the bourgeosie.
Rather, it is a subsidiary branch of the corporate community.

Andrew Hacker, quoted in Corporate Power in America

By 1980, the bad news will be that we'll be drinking
raw sewage. The good news will be that
there won't be enough to go around.

Harvey Ruvin, Dade County (Miami)
Commissioner, quoted in New York Times, April 22, 1973

One's view of the environment all depends on
one's perspective. A coal company executive suggested recently
that strip mining, a technique that was turning Appalachia into a
sandless desert, might actually be a boon. He proposed that the
area could be promoted as a new "Badlands" and thereby become
a great tourist attraction. Critics of the environmentalist movement
hooted at the idea that containers should be "biodegradable" so
that they would clutter the landscape for a more limited time. Why
worry? Hadn't Dr. Edward L. Owen, a specialist in the corrosion

of metals and a member of the faculty at Pennsylvania State University, proved that the tin can is absorbed by the earth in about one hundred years and the aluminum beer can absorbed in five hundred years? Melvin J. Grayson and Thomas B. Shepard, Jr., former vice president and publisher, respectively, of *Look* magazine, came out with the book *The Disaster Lobby: Prophets of Ecological Doom and Other Absurdities* in 1973, in which they hailed the financial troubles of the Sierra Club and the hang-ups of environmental legislation in state legislatures as "harbingers of a new era of sociopolitical sanity."[1]

Perhaps they are right. Perhaps there is nothing to worry about. Or if we must worry, perhaps we should turn our concern first, as Grayson and Shepard suggest, not to the pollution of steel companies and rubber companies but to that of the *New York Times*, whose Sunday paper alone results in eight-and-one-half million pounds of trash each week, which, when burned, send 87,000 pounds of particulates into the atmosphere.

But that perspective must be judged to be somewhat frivolous and Pollyanish if even half the things the environmentalists and the anticorporation crusaders are saying are true.

By now everyone who can read must be aware that the world is developing a crust of putrefaction from pole to pole. Manipulating statistics to emphasize the devastation has become almost an editorial game—citing the high and low tides of garbage, the tonnage of dead fish, the expected precipitation of soot over a given area and time. Thus we find Colman McCarthy ticking off for the readers of the *Washington Post* the reminder that "50 percent of the nation's drinking water has been discharged only a few hours before from some industrial or municipal sewer. In the last 10 years, 128 known outbreaks of disease or poisoning have been caused by contaminated drinking water; strip mining may soon claim 71,000 square miles of American land, an area the size of Pennsylvania and West Virginia combined; in 1976; we will have the disposal problem of 58 billion non-returnable bottles and cans; 40 million pounds of dog dung are deposited annually on streets by dogs in New York City."[2] That was topped the next year in the *New York Times* when Bill Kovach reported that "cities are annually accumulating a trash heap of 250 million tons" and within five years "46 percent of the cities will run out of places to dump their trash."[3]

Air pollutants, man-made erosion (affecting 180 million acres yearly), and fires kill as many trees as would make up our housing shortage. From sea to oil-slick sea we exhaust into the atmosphere each year 142 million tons of various poisons (including 12 million tons of sulphur, which, with a little rain, can make dandy sulphuric acid). Some scientists estimate that by the end of this century there will be 25 percent more carbon monoxide in the atmosphere—enough perhaps to change the climate. The National Center for Health Statistics reported that the cancer death rate rose in 1972 at the fastest pace in twenty-two years, probably because of increased exposure to cancer-causing chemicals in air, water, soil, and food.

Roving reporters from the *Washington Star*, after learning that "many scientists concerned with environmental pollution fear that the 1970s will be the dawn of Doomsday" went forth to discover the first cracks of that dawn; among other things, they found that in Colorado's Eagle River fishermen "if they still go there, catch toilet paper, not fish. Which is hardly surprising to those already aware that 2600 municipalities in the nation still pour their human excrement into the nearest rivers and streams, following the example of the sewage disposal plant that serves the nation's capital area by depositing 240 million gallons of mostly raw excretion into the Potomac River every day.

How could such a thing happen right under the very nose of Congress? The question has added piquancy when one considers that this has in fact been occurring under Congress' nose since before the turn of the century. Historically the river has been a cesspool in the capital area. From 1881 to 1909 the capital had an average of two hundred typhoid deaths a year. In 1908 Theodore Roosevelt asked, "What are we going to do about our river?" The question has been repeated constantly over the years. And the answer, though unspoken, is obviously, "Nothing." Some portions of the Potomac have a bottom that is fourteen feet or so deep with raw sewage and silty filth. Government laboratory technicians say the water from Georgetown to Mount Vernon has a bacteria count one hundred times too high for safe swimming. The threat from the river is so great that health officials advise against even boating in the river, lest spray be thrown up on the body. Contact of any kind is seen as a health hazard. And this, as Roosevelt indicated, is the one river that Presidents and congressmen may claim as "ours." If they condone its condition, what can we expect them to do about other rivers in the country?

Just about everything, we are told, is dead or dying. Lake Erie is dead, the victim of a daily supply of 51.5 billion gallons of household, industrial, and municipal waste and 3.8 million pounds of oil-well sludge each year. Wading in the lake means stepping on 30,000 sludge worms per square yard. The other Great Lakes are moribund. Lake Michigan is considered by some experts to be in worse condition than Lake Erie. The Illinois Department of Health, pioneering in candor, announced not long ago that no river in the state is safe for swimming. In the South, the Chattahoochee River sings a different song these days—The Song of Sewage and Waste—as it daily carries 40 million gallons of untreated municipal sewage, 40 million gallons of partly treated sewage, and an inaccurately measured amount of industrial filth from Atlanta to the Gulf of Mexico. Up the East Coast things are equally wretched. Swimming in Long Island Sound can be a bit thick, for the Sound receives a steady 196 million gallons of waste from forty-six municipal plants, fifty-nine industrial plants, and seven federal installations every day. Dr. Paul Ehrlich, who believes in telling the patient when his case is terminal, has predicted the possible death of the oceans within a decade.

And some scientists feel that life in the Los Angeles basin— where school children have become accustomed to seeing notes on their bulletin boards that read: "Warning! Do not exercise strenuously or breathe too deeply during heavy smog conditions. APCD" —may be extinct within fifteen years at the rate things are going there. Some ecologists have predicted "mortality incidents" from air pollution in the Los Angeles area by 1975. The earth refuses to cooperate: industrial waste that was chunked down deep shafts a dozen years ago, out of sight and hopefully out of our lives, is now coughing to the surface again, or draining into subterranean water supplies miles away, or—some scientists vouch for it—even causing earthquakes.

Only the cruelest ecologists even refer to New York City any more, for Gotham has slipped into history with Nineveh and Tyre. The Department of the Interior, in its typically optimistic fashion, has tried to cheer New York up by suggesting that it may become the petroleum capital of the world. Interior Department scientists have discovered a way to convert one ton of wet urban refuse— minus bottles and cans, unfortunately—into more than one barrel of crude oil by putting it under 1500 pounds of pressure per square inch while at the same time treating it with carbon monoxide and steam at 250 degrees centigrade.

Many other cities are not far behind New York. Planes taking off and landing at New York's airports dump more than a ton and a half of fuel emissions onto the city every day, but the nation's capital catches more than a ton of aircraft effluent daily. Although the total national air pollution from planes comes to only 1 percent (78 million pounds) of all air pollution annually, in the urban areas beneath the heavily traveled air routes the dumpage is heavy enough to be used for hair oil.

Ecological experts told a Senate subcommittee in mid-1971 that there is already so much industrial mercury on the bottoms of the nation's streams in nearby offshore ocean fields that the mercury concentration in fish may within fifty years make them unfit to eat. Already some women dieting on little else but swordfish and tuna fish have suffered damage to their central nervous systems from mercury poisoning; in New York State, doctors have started advising pregnant women to refrain from eating fish until more is known about the effects of mercury on fetal brains.

The chemical atmosphere in which the public must survive has suddenly become a matter of grave concern among scientists. At meetings in 1971, Environmental Mutagen Society and American Chemical Society scientists listed evidence of the many new perils they had uncovered: genetic changes in chromosomes of wild fruit flies, caused by DDT spraying in the West; the appearance of PCB, an industrial plasticizer and insecticide, in human fatty tissues; findings that indicate that every child in this country "begins life in the womb with chlorinated hydrocarbon insecticides (DDT, DDE, heptachlor, dieldrin, etc.) in its body tissues"; the appearance of selenium, which is more toxic than mercury, in the microscopic animal life in Lake Michigan, possibly as the result of fallout from the fumes of burning oil and coal; the appearance of dangerous amounts of cadmium and arsenic in the water supplies of twelve urban areas.

The list is a long one, and if it included the threats to birds, helpful insects, and wildlife, it would be an interminable list. In 1971, for example, Oregon and Washington fruit growers had to import 2 billion honeybees from California to pollinate their orchards; most of the local hives had been killed by corn farmers spraying the area with the pesticide Sevin.

Like the Indian of old who believed in having his favorite horse and dog buried with him, we are making certain that if we must go, our wildlife will go with us or will have gone ahead. Some we have dispatched to the happy unpolluted hunting ground with poisons and pesticides, some with guns.

Although the word *predator* no longer has a burdensome meaning in this country except in a historical way (because there aren't that many predators left), the Department of the Interior still shells out more than $3 million a year to encourage ranchers and farmers to slaughter coyotes, foxes, bobcats, wolves, and weasels. Predatormania is also resulting in the eradication of the bald eagle, the national symbol, and the golden eagle; the government doesn't exactly encourage the shooting of these grand birds, but neither does it seem too disturbed to hear of helicopter hunts that wipe out hundreds in a season. Long gone are the passenger pigeon, the Carolina parakeet (the country's only member of the parrot family), the Labrador duck, the heath hen, the Great Plains wolf, the great auk, the sea mink, the Stellar's sea cow. Going fast are the Everglades kite, the whooping crane, the golden-cheeked warbler, the California condor, the mountain lion, the timber wolf, the grizzly bear, the polar bear, the osprey, the pelican, and two hundred or so other endangered species. Apparently they just don't fit into the American way of life, and so at any price they go: Minnesota paid $350 for seven bountied timber wolves suspected of killing a goat valued at $15.

Corporate Exploitation of Our Land

America has become the goodbye land. Valedictions are being said to air, water, timber, grass, wildlife, the land itself—and someday very likely, as a result, the words of Woody Guthrie's song will be as unintelligible as "Sumer Is Icumen In." Your land and my land is now their land, and they let us use it grudgingly, if at all.

It's nothing new. When President Harrison set aside the first forest reserves on behalf of the people in 1891, senators favoring the continuation of lumber exploitation by corporations threatened to impeach him. Between 1962 and 1970, the United States Forest Service's projected outlays for timber-sale administration and management (proindustry) were trimmed only 5 percent, while the budget for maintaining roads and trails that might benefit campers and picnickers was cut 26 percent, and the budget for recreation was slashed 55 percent. For more than a decade conservationists in Texas have been begging the federal government to set aside the Big Thicket of East Texas as a national park. As of mid-1971 only 300,000 acres remained of its original 3.5 million acres, and this famous habitat of rare wildlife was being depleted at the rate of

50 acres a day. In California, the Redwood National Park's 58,000 acres of primeval forest is far too small to withstand the onslaught of timber commercialism from every side. From that park in the spring of 1971 Joseph Morgenstern of *Newsweek* reported:

> A few steps beyond the grove and you look out over acres of amputee stumps, an area just outside the federal land that has been worked over by the timber companies' vaunted scientific forestry methods and may be ready for another dose of science in a hundred years or so. Every day but Sunday, commercial logging trucks come roaring through Redwood National Park with timber from adjacent private land chained to their backs. This is all perfectly legal, given the lunatic compromises that Congress made with industry during the long, bitter battle that led to the park's creation. The roads are public, and these immense logging trucks have as much right to use them as any visitor with a VW camper. So intricate were those compromises that in certain areas of the park the federal government now owns the land but the timber companies own whatever trees have fallen on it. . . . From the right angles you see paradise, from the wrong ones you see paradise lost.[4]

Only 8 percent of the land in the national forests and national grasslands is protected against commercial exploitation. Only in the 8 percent is there safety for "wilderness." In the 92 percent, picnickers and hikers must share the landscape with the ranchers' pickups and the loggers' trucks and the miners' bulldozers—for these businessmen are allowed to exploit the national domain at bargain basement prices. Mining companies, operating under an 1897 law, are free to cut roads right through the heart of wilderness areas of our national forests.

A hallmark of the government over the years has been its generosity with our land in its dealing with favored elements of society.

The land users.   No one got more from the government than the railroads. Between 1850 and 1871 they were given public land totaling more than the area of Texas. The generous politicians argued that if the railroads were induced with free land to build their lines across the country, farmers and merchants would follow them, and the general populace would be close behind. It was done in the name of "building" America.

But like most commercial "builders" the railroads took advantage of their favored position. Within a few years it was a railroad system (to use the description of Norman Pollack) "in which discriminatory charges had eaten away all prospects the farmer had for breaking even, a railroad system which gave preferential treatment to favored shippers, dominated state legislatures, blackmailed towns into issuing bonds, held large tracts of land off the market, and refused to assume a proper share of the tax burden."[5] In some cases farmers burned their crops rather than submit to the railroad extortion.

Not content with surrendering veritable kingdoms, Congress at the turn of the century set about to perfect its gift. It passed a law that sounded very noble. The law established "forest reservations" and provided that anyone who owned property within the reservations could exchange it for federal lands outside the reservations. Millions of acres of railroad land—land from which all timber had been cut, land that the railroads owned on top of the Rockies where snow prevailed the year around, land owned by the railroads in the deserts of the West—were included in the "forest reservations," thus giving the railroads the opportunity to exchange this worthless land for equal amounts of the choicest federal lands in the fertile valleys of Washington and Oregon and Idaho and Montana.*

Testimony in the Watergate hearings in 1973 revealed that the railroads are still working some cute swaps. It was disclosed that a White House aide put pressure on the Department of Agriculture and the Forest Service to speed approval of an exchange of national forest lands for land owned by Burlington Northern Railroad. This was to assist in the creation of a resort in Montana known as Big Sky, promoted by former network newscaster Chet Huntley but largely owned and financed by Burlington Northern Railroad, the Montana Power Company, Northwest Airlines, the Continental Oil Company, the Meridian Investing and Development Corporation (a Florida real estate company), and the General Electric Pension Fund. As usual, approval of the land swap just zipped through the bureaucracy.

Who have received the greatest land windfalls, and how are

* Having given away great hunks of the West to the railroads, the government then encouraged hunters to supply them with cargo: they wiped out buffalo herds, leaving the meat to rot on the prairie and shipping the skins East where they were much prized. All hail to the buffalo hunter who was starving the Indians into subjection, said General Phil Sheridan, "Let them kill, skin and sell until the buffalo is exterminated, as it is the only way to bring about lasting peace and allow civilization to advance." So they killed, skinned, and sold at the rate of 1 million animals a year in the 1870s. Other enthusiastic rooters of the slaughter were cattlemen, who didn't want their commercial herds to have to share the grass with buffalo.

they treating their gifts? Peter Barnes and Larry Casalino, writing for The Center for Rural Studies in Berkeley, give a clue or two:

> The biggest of these railroad land barons are in the West. They include the Southern Pacific, which owns 3.8 million acres in California, Nevada, Oregon, Texas and Utah, plus mineral rights to an additional 1.3 million acres; the Burlington Northern, with 2.4 million acres stretching from Lake Superior to Puget Sound, and mineral rights on 6 million additional acres; the Union Pacific, which has mineral rights to 7.9 million acres; and the St. Louis and San Francisco ("The Frisco"), which owns surface or mineral rights to 1.4 million acres in Arizona, New Mexico and Texas, although it doesn't run a railroad there.
>
> Most of this land is seemingly held or exploited in violation of the terms of the original grants. The Southern Pacific, for example, which owns nearly five per cent of all the private land in California, failed to sell land to settlers at $1.25 an acre, as its 1864 grant required. (Back in the old days, in fact, it would kick settlers off at gunpoint: read Frank Norris' *The Octopus.*) Revenues from timber, oil and other minerals are copiously harvested by the railroads from their granted lands, despite the prohibitions of the law. Frank Barnett, chief executive of Union Pacific, stated recently, "We don't even care to guess what (our minerals) are worth. If we did, we'd have tax assessors all over the place." *Forbes* magazine guesses they're worth over $1 billion.
>
> Some of the land owned by railroads, besides being valuable for timber, minerals and commercial development, is suitable for agriculture. Southern Pacific's vast holdings on the west side of the San Joaquin valley are a prime example. These fertile croplands, irrigated by state and federal reclamation projects, would be ideal for family farmers or farm-worker cooperatives. But Southern Pacific holds on to them and leases them to companies such as Russell Giffen, Inc., the second largest farm operator in the United States, and Anderson, Clayton & Co., the largest cotton merchandiser in the world.[6]

Another group at the fore of civilization's advance in the West were the miners who, using hydraulic devices to carve out the sides of hills, spent much of the 1870s and 1880s laying waste to much of the Western countryside, filling the rivers with silt, and destroying huge areas of fertile bottomland. Sometimes whole towns built on the rivers were endangered. But the politicians defended the action as being necessary for the health of what was one of the West's leading industries.

No one has left a mark on the landscape like the coal miners, continuing down to the present. Sometimes, because of careless procedures, their mines caught fire; in Pennsylvania alone it is estimated that more than one hundred mine fires are still burning. They threaten the lives of 700,000 people and half a billion dollars worth of property. Coal companies have not paid a cent toward putting out the fires or paying restitution to the people who have been harmed. Instead, the state and federal governments—without complaint—are paying for it; the cost is expected to come to at least $250 million. Picking up the pieces at the expense of the taxpayer is done quite cheerfully by the federal bureaucracy.

The sinking of land caused by careless mine operations affects more than 2 million acres of land, including about 160,000 acres in urban areas; homes and commercial buildings have collapsed, utility lines have ruptured, some neighborhoods have been abandoned as unsafe.

But the land exploiters really hit their stride with strip mining. No coal-harvesting technique returns such a quick and easy profit, and no process results in such awesome heaps of ugliness. It's said that the slag, mud, and refuse hills left behind by the strip-mining coal companies are of such quantity that they could be spread over a mile-wide trail from New York to San Francisco. Some ecologists estimate that the acid runoff from the disturbed earth has polluted 13,000 miles of streams. Appalachia used to be the center for this kind of destruction, but in recent years The Gem of Egypt, The Silver Spade, The Mountaineer—nicknames for the giant earth-scooping machines that can take two hundred tons in one bite—have done much of their dirty work in Ohio and Illinois and North Dakota and Montana and Arizona and half a dozen other Midwestern and Western states. All indications are that millions of additional acres will be chewed up before this decade is over.

In April 1971 the United States Geological Survey issued the first independent and scholarly study of the effects of strip mining; it was an eleven-year measurement of the changes in the ecology of a twenty-five-square-mile creek basin in McCreary County, Kentucky. Mining operators and their friends in Congress and the Department of the Interior insist that when strip-mined areas are "restored" they are often better than before. But the Geological Survey scientists found that for six years after the cessation of strip mining in the McCreary County area, the streams—fed with acid runoff and clogged with silt—were depopulated of fish.

Even if the coal operators and their federal apologists were correct in saying that restored strip-mined areas were better than ever, one must consider how little reclamation is going on: of the

1.8 million strip-mined acres, only 58,000 have been "reclaimed" in a manner of speaking. Virtually none. Which means that the Geological Survey's findings of critical damage can be assumed to apply to all of the nearly 2 million stripped acres. Seven of the twenty-six states with extensive stripping operations have no reclamation laws at all.

The coal companies are generally responding to the increasing public outrage by trying to hide the destruction or by insisting, in high-priced public relations campaigns, that they are nice people who wouldn't do such things. In West Virginia, for example, former Secretary of State John D. Rockefeller IV—the state's most ardent enemy of strip mining—accused the companies of putting fences around their operations "in an obvious move to keep the public away from their devastation."

The big grazers. The Bureau of Land Management in the Department of the Interior supervises the use of 500 million acres of federal land in eleven Western states and Alaska. Theoretically, this is land that any resident of the country should be allowed to walk over, camp and hunt on, enjoy in any way he wants. Practically speaking, this land is managed by BLM for the commercial benefit of big cattle and sheep raisers.

The livestock businessmen pay about one-quarter as much for their grazing fees as they would if they were renting private lands. Furthermore, most of the cost for fencing the land—that is, fencing the general public *out*—comes from the taxpayer's pocket. The land leased to these stockmen can be passed on by them to whoever buys their other property. That is, if a rancher holds 10,000 acres under his own name and leases another 150,000 acres from BLM, he can sell his 10,000 at a price that includes the value of the other 150,000 acres of public land. Great wealth has been accumulated by parlaying privileges granted by the federal government.

The 1880s saw cattlemen swarming over the public rangeland of the prairies with devastating effects. Grass once waist-high was eaten to the nub; then came the eroding rains, and the prairies were never again the same. Nineteenth-century-style greed and devastation continue today. The Council on Environmental Quality in 1970 reported that the depredations of the commercial livestock herds had "dramatically affected these lands," which are almost totally in the arid West, where "dry years have usually coincided with falling market prices." So, to make up their losses, the ranchers overstock the already overgrazed lands, with the result that they remain today in desperate condition, as wind, rain, and drought have swept over them and eroded their exposed soils. Although the effects of overgrazing in rich pastures and prairie farmland can be quickly corrected, the process is often irreversible in much of the public lands that have limited soils and arid climate.

Ranchers who lease the BLM lands are free to overgraze and thereby ruin the land. Some officials have admitted that 80 percent of the BLM lands have been "used up." In the long run, of course, this perverse misuse of the land may work for the public's benefit. When the ranchers can no longer make money out of the BLM ranges, they will no doubt return them to the federal government, and when that day comes perhaps the general public will again be free to use its own land for recreational purposes.

The timber harvest. The pattern for helping the lumber companies was thoroughly fixed in the nineteenth century. Although the federal government led the Great Giveaway then, the states competed furiously, selling off vast stretches of forest for as little as ten cents an acre. Of the 183 million acres of national forests that remain, 97 million acres supply commercial timber.

Because the private forests have been overcut and underplanted for so long, the lumber industry has increasingly turned to the public supply, and the United States Forest Service has given it free rein, in some areas allowing nearly 20 percent more timber to be taken from the forests than was the legal quota. Under the guise of "meeting the housing shortage," the lumber industry in 1971 was allowed to cut nearly three times more timber than it had been allowed to cut in 1950, even though there was no comparable housing boom. Moreover, the lumber industry ships about 3 billion board feet of American timber each year to other countries, and half of this comes from the national forests. Nearly all the timber cut in Alaska goes to Japan.

After a long investigation, James Risser of the *Des Moines Register and Tribune* concluded in a series of articles in 1971 that the Forest Service operates in collusion with the lumber industry in the pricing of the public trees, sometimes structuring an "auction" to meet the needs of one particular lumber company and often reducing the prices far below what the market would allow. A report by the staff of Senator Gale McGee of Wyoming also showed that even when lumber prices go up on the national market, the Forest Service holds down raw timber prices for the industry's sake. The report points out that "in the first half of 1968, when softwood lumber and plywood prices were skyrocketing, the

Forest Service not only didn't increase its appraised stumpage prices, it decreased them."

The Forest Service has also allowed lumbermen to "clear-cut" —that is, cut *all* the trees in a given area, just scalping the mountainside, rather than selectively cut only the mature trees. Experts testified in 1971, in emergency hearings called by the Senate Interior and Insular Affairs Subcommittee on Public Lands, that "clearcutting" so destroys the ecology of the land, and so encourages erosion, that it is almost impossible to reseed the area. Dr. Robert Curry, a geologist from the University of Montana, testified that "clear-cutting" speeds up bacterial action that renders the soil sterile and that the Forest Service's forest management practices were so ruinous it would take 50,000 years or more to restore the soil to its normal fertility.

The Risser study uncovered the fact that "today the Forest Service is five million acres behind in reforesting previously logged public lands, another 13 million acres behind in badly needed tree-thinning and other timber-stand improvement." If the Forest Service ever got around to taking this action, it would cost the public about $1 billion.

Dissatisfied with the amount of its timber loot, the industry— aided by Forest Service and USDA spokesmen—sought to get a 60 percent increase in the allowed cuttage from public lands in 1970. Congress turned down the request. But three months later President Nixon issued an Executive Order that gave the industry what it wanted and did not require that it reseed the areas it destroyed.

In 1973 Nixon again accelerated the wholesale deforestation of public lands, while at the same time slashing the Forest Service's budget 20 percent (meaning: fewer replantings). That was in the spring. Came autumn, and again Nixon ordered that lumber companies be allowed to increase their logging in national forests. This time he acted, he said, on the advice of a White House Timber Advisory Group—made up mostly of representatives of the lumber industry. The order was given over the objection of such groups as the Sierra Club, whose chief forester in San Francisco said the allowable cut in national forests is already two to three times more than it should be. Nixon excused the action by saying the lumber was needed to build houses in America—but in fact 8 percent of the timber from public forests was being sold on the Japanese market.

Conservationists won some significant, although probably

temporary, support in November 1973, when a federal district judge ruled that the U.S. Forest Service was, and had been for seventy-six years, routinely violating the law (the Organic Act of 1897), which forbade clear-cutting. He ordered the government not to permit private companies any federal forest harvesting except of dead or mature trees. The Nixon Administration's only defense for its part in this perpetual lawlessness was that "Congress has been aware of what is happening on the national forests," and because it hadn't acted to stop the practices it had, in effect, sanctioned them. The administration said it would appeal the ruling, so that industry could continue to scalp the forests.

In 1970 the Council on Environmental Quality warned: "Mismanagement of timber cutting, in addition to being an eyesore, can also damage natural systems far beyond the forests. Debris and erosion of the limited soils of the forested West often choke streambeds far downstream." As the forests disappear, so do the birds, and then come the leaf-eating and bark-eating and pulp-eating bugs. "The greatest loss of timber is not from fire and disease but from insects, which can devastate large forests of single species."[7] It's a deadly circle: widespread application of insecticides often follows, and these poisons further destroy the habitat of wild animals and wild birds.

There is no gainsaying our wretched condition, but using the theme of "corporate irresponsibility" in the environmental crusade is acceptable only if it is calculatingly done for propaganda purposes. None but the most naive persons would seriously suggest that corporations would voluntarily cope with such things as "social responsibilities." Corporations surrender public lands and clean up their messes and operate honestly when forced to do so, and not otherwise. That's the American way of life.

The real villains in the environmental scandal are (1) the government agencies, which have failed to use available laws to keep the corporate invaders and polluters in line, and (2) the general public, which has not been militant in demanding its right to live and play in a clean, comfortable land.

The Government as Despoiler

Throughout the expansionist and industrial periods of our history the federal government has not only abetted the polluters and despoilers, it itself has been among them. This practice continues and is visible on many fronts.

By its great use of strip-mine coal, the Tennessee Valley Authority is the most infamous polluter of streams and mangler of the hills of Appalachia.

In 1972 Congressman Les Aspin of Wisconsin, a member of the House Armed Services Committee, disclosed that the military has been given virtually a blank check to abuse valuable woodlands in twenty-four states. He cited as an example that 26,000 of 117,000 acres of Mississippi forest lands used by the military are "so contaminated with live munitions no human being can set foot on the land ever again," and that 6000 acres in Louisiana are similarly contaminated.

In the late 1960s, United States Forest Rangers, in an effort to increase the water runoff for the big irrigation farmers in the Salt River Valley of Arizona, began spraying a portion of the Pinal Mountains with the kind of defoliant that is used in Vietnam. It may have assisted agribusiness, but it destroyed the orchards owned by small farmers in the foothills, poisoned goats so severely that 60 percent of their offspring were born dead or deformed, poisoned some of the residents so severely that the women suffered internal hemorrhaging and miscarriages and the men suffered chest pains, respiratory ailments, and swollen feet.

The Atomic Energy Commission for years has been licensing nuclear electric-generating plants without considering their potential for thermal pollution. At some of the plants the discharges from the cooling system have raised river temperatures by as much as twenty-eight degrees; many conservationists believe this is a sure way of killing fish. The AEC, which is wholly oriented to the atomic industry, claims that its licensing law confines it to considering only the question of radiological health and safety, despite the fact that the National Environmental Policy Act enjoins all governmental agencies to weigh environmental factors in their decisions.

Foremost among the federal polluters, in a style that can only be described as infamous, is the Army Corps of Engineers. The Corps is a unique blending of most of the worst, and some of the best, impulses in our politics. On the positive side, the Corps symbolizes America the Builder, and on the negative side the Corps represents all the horror that comes from endless political pork barrel. For good reason Justice William Douglas has called it Public Enemy No. 1.

The Corps is nearly as old as the nation. It was set up in the early 1800s and assigned the specific job of removing "snags, sawyers, planters and other impediments" from the Mississippi and

Ohio rivers. In the intervening century and a half, the Corps has widened its job perspective to changing the face of the United States. It has done so with the consent and encouragement of Congress and powerful special interests, and despite some efforts on the part of the executive branch to control it. These efforts were futile, for the Corps is apparently uncontrollable. In 1949 the Hoover Commission Task Force on Water Resources and Power recommended that the Corps be disbanded and its functions transferred to a proposed Department of Natural Resources. The suggestion was never taken seriously. Nor have other suggestions, made by reformers within Congress, to somehow strip the Corps of its might and transfer its duties to agencies more responsive to the control of Congress and the President. Legislation to do this never even gets out of committee.

Theoretically, the Chief of Engineers, who heads the Corps, must answer to the Secretary of Defense and (through the Secretary) to the President. In practice, the men who run the Corps answer to no one. Unlike any other federal agency, the Corps has received carte blanche permission from Congress to spend up to $10 million on any project without clearing the expenditure, as long as the federal legislature has by resolution approved the project itself.

The source of the Corps' clout is no secret: it spends most of its money in the districts of friendly congressmen. At appropriations time, the moral is clear: root for the Corps, and the Corps will come into your district and build a canal or a dam—whether it is needed or not. That will put people to work, and it will put money into the pockets of the building contractors and construction workers, and they will thank you with campaign money and votes.

Every year the Corps has a billion dollars or more to spread around as it wishes. Ninety-eight percent of its work is contracted out to civilian firms. That's a lot of pork.

The results of its spending make many groups happy. The multibillion-dollar inland waterways transportation industry, which is free to use the canals and rivers cleared by the Corps without paying a cent, is very happy. So are the dredging contractors. So are those firms that sell heavy-duty earth-moving machinery. So are those real estate promoters who own land near the artificial lakes built by the Corps. So are the owners of almost worthless boondocks land that is inundated by Corps dams; the federal government is the only buyer that could possibly be interested in their land. And so are the big agribusinessmen who get cheap water through the irrigation waterways dug by the Corps.

Many results of the Corps' enthusiasms, however, defy logic or humanity or aesthetics. Justice Douglas pointed out that dam-building projects in Arkansas were huckstered as being sure-fire ways to bring in the tourists through fishing and boating camps, big motel establishments, the usual Chamber of Commerce whoopee. He said:

> The Corps had introduced Arkansas to at least 14 such river projects that buried free-flowing streams forever under muddy waters. The fishing is good for a few years. Then the silt covers the gravel bars where bass spawn and the gizzard shad—the notorious trash fish—takes over. The people are left with the dead, muddy reservoirs. There is electric power, to be sure; but Arkansas already has many times the power that it can use. So why destroy the rivers—rivers man can float in solitude, fish, camp on sandspits and rid himself of the tensions of this age?[8]

There is hardly any lunacy the Corps of Engineers will not hesitate to perform in the name of "water sports" or commerce. The Dismal Swamp, in Virginia near the North Carolina border, is one of the great wild spots of America; although it has shrunk to only a fraction of its original size, thanks to the encroachments of land hucksters and subdivision developers, it is a miracle that it has survived at all. The Corps of Engineers has absolute control over the water rights of Lake Drummond, which feeds the swamp, and the Corps has done nothing over the years to stop land speculators from draining off the water. One of the worst drains is via the Dismal Swamp Canal, dug by the Corps as part of the Intercoastal Waterway and operated by the Corps. Every time a barge or canoe goes through the canal, the Corps proudly opens the locks—and out goes another precious 3 million gallons of water from Lake Drummond.

All over the nation the Corps proceeds at will, slashing, gouging, damming, locking, filling, bridging, with no regard for the natural development of life. In the last three decades it has spent nearly $10 billion on dams and levees, but flood damage is four times heavier today than it was when it began. The Corps has no overall program, no national strategy for attacking this or any other problem. Everything is based on ad hoc boondoggle.

But in addition to the physical scars that the Corps has left behind, it has also been responsible for a great deal of the putrefaction of the nation's waterways by its own activities and by approving harmful commercial activities. Gutting wild riverbeds on behalf of barge companies is bad enough; fouling the rivers and harbors is the final straw. The Corps became notorious around the Great Lakes for dredging out ship channels and then—oil, feces, the settling of garbage—everything that the Corps scooped up, back into the lakes it would go.

The Government as "Enforcer"

The example of the Corps brings us with a full leap into one explanation of how the country got bunged up: the reluctance to enforce the available environment-protection laws, either with penalties for violators or money for reformers. In fact, the government has indicated it would much rather pass a new law covering the same offense than enforce an old law that would do the job just as well. That way, everyone gets credit for good intentions but nothing gets done.

New laws there are plenty of: the modern granddaddy of them all, the Federal Water Pollution Control Act of 1948, took twelve years from its original introduction to final passage. Seven years later Congress decided it was getting a little difficult to breathe, so it passed the pioneer Air Pollution Act of 1955. Some of the major legislation in recent years includes the Clean Air Act of 1963, the Water Resources Act of 1964, the Water Resources Planning Act of 1965, the Highway Beautification Act of 1965, the Clean Air Act of 1965, the Motor Vehicle Air Pollution Control Act of 1965, the Solid Waste Disposal Act of 1965, the Water Quality Act of 1965, the Clean Water Restoration Act of 1966, the Endangered Species Act of 1966, the Air Quality Act of 1967, the National Wild and Scenic Rivers System Act of 1968, the Estuaries Preservation Act of 1968, the National Environmental Policy Act of 1969, the Water Quality Improvement Act of 1970, the Clean Air Act Amendment of 1970, the Environmental Education Act of 1970, the Water Pollution Act of 1972, the Noise Pollution Control Act of 1972, the Environmental Pesticide Control Act of 1972, the Ocean Dumping Act of 1972—just to mention a few of the fifty or so major bills enacted over the past two and a half decades.

The titles are impressive. But the fascinating career of the Refuse Act of 1899 should remind modern reformers that a law that is found nowhere but in the statute books is a very dead law indeed.

The Refuse Act of 1899 prohibited anyone or any corporation from dumping refuse into navigable waters without the permission of the Army Corps of Engineers. Furthermore, the 1899 law imposed a fine of not more than $2500 nor less than $500 and required that the Justice Department prosecute "vigorously" anyone caught violating the law. One other provision of importance: the person who turned in evidence on the polluter got to split the fine with the government.

For most of the intervening years, this law had been all but forgotten. The Corps and the Justice Department had done virtually nothing to enforce it. Between the passage of the act in 1899 and its "rediscovery" seventy-one years later, the Corps had granted only 415 permits for waste disposal in navigable waters, although it admitted in 1970 that there were at least 40,000 polluters that either should have been forced to get a permit or should have been prosecuted. In twenty-two states—including such industrialized ones as Connecticut, Maryland, Michigan, Rhode Island, Virginia, and West Virginia—no permit had ever been granted. The water pollution was all illegal, but nobody in the bureaucracy had cared very much.

In 1970, however, several congressmen tried to put the law to use. Congressman Henry Reuss, chairman of the House Conservation and Natural Resources Subcommittee, collected evidence on several hundred violators of the 1899 law and submitted the evidence to a United States Attorney. Nothing happened. He wrote the Attorney General asking why, and he got back a letter from Assistant Attorney General Shiro Kashiwa saying, "It would not be in the genuine interest of the government to bring an action under the Refuse Act to secure a criminal sanction against a company which admittedly is discharging refuse into the navigable waters of the United States but which, pursuant to a program being conducted by the Federal Water Quality Administration (FWQA), is spending significant amounts of money to secure the abatement of that pollution."

That's a generous attitude, but it had little to do with the issue, for Reuss had submitted the names of corporations that were not trying to abate pollution. As Reuss pointed out in his rebuttal, some of the companies were three years behind in the schedule they had promised the FWQA they would follow.

Congressman Edward Koch, who prepared a list of ten violators of the Refuse Act, was similarly repulsed by the Justice Department and with a similar absence of bureaucratic logic, for six of the ten industries named in his affidavit had not yet even established a pollution abatement timetable—much less taken action to begin abatement—even though they had been required to do so under their State Health Department's Pure Water Program, which got underway in 1965. In other words, they had flaunted the law for five years, yet the Justice Department said it did not want to prosecute them because they were "trying" to do better.

After public pressure could no longer be withstood, President Nixon ordered the 1899 law to be enforced.* He also ordered that polluting industries inform the government as to what they are dumping in the streams and lakes. This was no more information than the House Conservation and Natural Resources Subcommittee had been requesting the executive branch to obtain ever since 1963, but the request had heretofore been rebuffed because of pressures from (according to Ralph Nader's calculations) the American Petroleum Institute, the Manufacturing Chemists Association, the American Meat Institute, the National Canners Association, the U.S. Chamber of Commerce, the National Association of Manufacturers, and the American Paper Institute.

The Highway Beautification Act of 1966 (passed in 1965), which was supposed to remove thousands of unsightly billboards from along the nation's highways, had not removed a single one until 1971. On a cold day in late April, federal and state officials came together at a spot on Interstate 95, near Freeport, Maine, to celebrate their fragile victory over the billboard lobby and, after many speeches, to take down discard No. 1 with the aid of a boom. But by that time, according to the Federal Highway Administration, there were 20 percent more billboards beckoning to motorists than there had been when the law was passed. This means more than 800,000 billboards lining 235,000 miles of roadway. But of course optimists can point out that although enforcement was five years late in coming, once the government started to enforce it, things really got rolling; well, sort of. In the next two years 50,000 billboards bit the dust—a pace that would require sixteen years to do the whole job, assuming no more were erected.

Only the greatest of luck will find the Motor Vehicle Air

---

* This kind of grudging cooperation is all the more irritating because the success that often follows only goes to show what could have been accomplished long ago if Washington officials had wanted to apply the laws. Industries that have been dumping mercury into lakes and streams claimed they hadn't the facilities and couldn't afford putting in the facilities to stop the outflow of poison. But faced with the threat of a shutdown by the state of New York, one plant within a matter of hours managed to cut its outflow of mercury from a daily twenty-one pounds down to one pound. Federal Water Quality Administration officials say that "many companies" have, with heavy fines in the offing, "quickly cut mercury pollution from pounds down even to ounces."

Pollution Control Act of 1965 having any significant effect on the air we breathe before 1975—one decade after passage. Each day cars emit pollutants weighing more than a string of cars, bumper to bumper, stretching from New York to Chicago; cars account for 50 percent of the air pollution, 75 percent of the carbon monoxide, 50 percent of the hydrocarbons, 50 percent of the nitrogen oxides.

Not only has the government failed to speed the enforcement of laws prohibiting exhaust pollution, it has taken devious steps to protect the auto industry against exposure to greater public contempt and potential lawsuits. Here is the background: According to a number of experts, including Smith Griswold, former air-pollution control chief for Los Angeles County, the auto industry knew how to control exhaust fumes at least as early as 1953. So blatant was the evidence on this point that the Justice Department was forced, in 1969, to file a suit against General Motors, Ford, Chrysler, American Motors, and the Automobile Manufacturers Association, charging antitrust conspiracy. More than a dozen states joined in the suit, charging that for seventeen years the major car builders had united to squeeze out any competition for making and installing motor vehicle pollution-control devices. Before the case came to trial, the Justice Department and the auto manufacturers negotiated a consent decree by which the companies promised not to conspire against antipollution devices, but they did not have to admit they had done so in the past. The important and suspicious part of the episode was that by entering the consent decree with the government, the car makers thereby shut off public revelation of the evidence of conspiracy.

Then, in May 1971, Congressman Phillip Burton of California got his hands on a secret Justice Department memo, circa 1968, that revealed the department was fully aware of the antitrust conspiracy. Evidence was so strong that Justice Department investigators urged their superiors to prosecute selected officials within the industry. Drawing heavily on the findings of a grand jury investigation in Los Angeles held in 1966 and 1967, the memo notes that the auto companies suppressed antipollution technology simply for the sake of higher profits; it cited the various techniques used by the auto industry to avoid complying with government requests to install antipollution devices. The memo quotes, for example, Errol J. Gay, an industry consultant, as saying, "Hell, they could have done it prior to 1938, if necessary." Meaning, the auto companies had the technical know-how for installing devices to control crankcase fumes nearly thirty years before they were installed. Despite this memo and the evidence of criminal conspiracy, Donald F. Turner, then head of the Anti-Trust Division of the Justice Department, let the companies escape prosecution.

One of the greatest threats to the ecology is from the erosion caused by the heavy winds of rhetoric. In his 1970 State of the Union message to Congress, President Nixon declared: "I shall propose to this Congress a $10 billion nationwide clean waters program to put modern municipal waste treatment plants in every place in America where they are needed to make our waters clean again, and do it now. We have the industrial capacity, if we begin now, to build them all within five years. This program will get them built within five years."

There were two massive weaknesses. The $10-billion program was predicated on the basis of $4 billion from the federal government and $6 billion from the states—and many states already operate in the red. For them the program might as well not be proposed at all. Second, many water control authorities believe it will take $40 billion, not $10 billion, to do the job.

In the first five years after the Solid Waste Disposal Act of 1965, Congress appropriated less than half the amount requested at the federal level for grants to build sewage treatment plants. But even that much help was tripped up by the White House. Despite his beautiful rhetoric, quoted above, Nixon impounded $6 billion that Congress had earmarked for building water sewage treatment plants. To free the money, the states affected had to take Nixon to court. In the same five years, Congress appropriated only about 60 percent of the amount requested for air-pollution control. At the rate we are going, we will have passed well into the 1980s before every state has set up the air- and water-pollution standards and enforcement programs that were encouraged in a vague way by legislation passed in the 1960s.

In 1973 the nation was treated to a classic pollution case that showed just how long an industry can drag its violations out. Every day for sixteen years the Reserve Mining Company of Silver Bay, Minnesota, sixty miles from Duluth, had been dumping 67,000 tons of tailings into Lake Superior, supposedly the largest and purest freshwater lake in the world. The tailings were grains of ore from which magnetic particles of iron had been extracted. Reserve Mining had the distinction of being the only major industry dumping anything into Lake Superior. How had it gotten by with this for so long?

Weak enforcement of weak laws. Prior to the advent of the Environmental Protection Agency in 1970, the state and federal agencies that tried to change the industry's way of operating made such feeble efforts they are not even recorded. Then in 1970 the EPA moved in and told Reserve Mining to stop dumping in the lake. The company said that alternate methods of getting rid of the tailings—such as burying them on land—were too costly. EPA kept pressing and finally turned the case over to the Justice Department after issuing a deadline requiring Reserve Mining to meet federal and state water-quality standards by mid-October 1971.

A few days before the deadline, officials of Republic Steel Corporation and Armco Steel Corporation, which jointly own Reserve Mining, met with President Nixon's advisers in Washington. It was a friendly session, for Willis Boyers, chairman of Republic, was also vice chairman of the Ohio Republican Finance Committee, and C. William Verity, head of Armco, was a generous and active Republican fund-raiser.

In January 1972 the EPA asked the Justice Department to take action, but the Justice lawyers didn't even seem to notice the request until after the election in November. And so the case staggered on, no nearer solution than when the EPA arrived on the scene several years earlier. Meanwhile, had the pollution done any harm? Much more than at first thought. In June 1973 the government admitted that cancer-causing asbestos fibers—probably from the taconite tailings—had polluted the drinking water of Duluth and neighboring small towns to such an extent that it was unsafe for children to drink; the EPA said it wouldn't do any good for adults to stop drinking the water because they had been drinking it for so long the damage, if any, was already done.

The EPA is the first and so far only visible hope the people have received from the government that *some* action—however paltry and late it may be—will be taken against industrial spoilers. The EPA, which came into existence in October 1970, is now the major federal agency for the administration and enforcement of environmental legislation. It has about 6000 employees and a budget of something over $2 billion. But whether it has the will and the stubbornness to do its job despite the counterefforts of vested interests in industry is still to be discovered.

Often it has needed goading, or support, from outside conservationist groups before it found the strength or inclination to carry out its duties. Only after the Sierra Club had sued EPA to set stiffer clean air standards, and been upheld by the Supreme Court, did the Environmental Protection Agency take steps to upgrade its air standards.

In 1972, William D. Ruckelshaus, then administrator of

EPA,* refused to give the auto industry a year's delay, as it requested, in meeting emission standards for carbon monoxide and hydrocarbons on 1975 models, as stipulated in the Clean Air Act of 1970. But buried by pressure groups responding to industry's call, Ruckelshaus in 1973 backed down and said the year's delay was okay. When the announcement was made, the *New York Times* recalled that "after a recent visit from Chrysler's chairman, Lynn Townsend, presidential assistant John Ehrlichman told a Detroit news conference that parts of the Clean Air Act did not make sense.' "⁹

A few days later, the Environmental Protection Agency gave the city of Philadelphia and the E. I. Du Pont Company emergency permits to continue dumping millions of gallons of municipal and industrial waste off the Delaware coast—as they had been doing for years. And the next month the EPA asked Congress to give the Los Angeles area an additional two to four years to meet 1977 federal clean air standards.

In the summer of 1973 the EPA granted the aircraft industry an extension of deadlines—from 1976 and 1979, to 1979 and 1981, depending on what poisonous vapors are involved—by which time they must cut back on the tons of carbon monoxide, hydrocarbons, smoke, and nitrogen oxides the airlines are presently dumping on our settled areas.

If it looked like the EPA was caving in, sympathy was called for. Actually the agency had shown tremendous integrity under Ruckelshaus. But it was not exactly getting stout support from the White House. Signs of what could be expected came in 1972 when the White House set up an advisory committee for EPA. On this committee one could identify the representatives of some of the most actively polluting industries in the nation—the American Iron and Steel Institute, the National Coal Association, the American Petroleum Institute, and the American Paper Institute.

A few months before the 1972 election, Howard A. Cohen, EPA's legislative director, was linked to memos advocating that enforcement of the environmental controls be eased off to help Nixon win reelection. When the memos were uncovered by the press, Cohen was fired—and rehired at the White House.

Finally, if there was any doubt as to where the White House

---

* In 1973 Ruckelshaus was appointed interim director of the Federal Bureau of Investigation, whose pollution obviously needed the attention of a man of his experience. For one thing, he could apply the Clean Air Act to the FBI. Its outgoing director, G. Patrick Gray, had been bad about burning secret documents.

stood, it vetoed the EPA's program for cleaning up the Great Lakes, cut in half the clean water funds, and cut $24 million from the $30 million requested by EPA's solid waste management programs. The environmental budget for fiscal 1974 was reduced to shreds and patches. On September 8, 1973 Nixon declared that the country must retreat from its clean air standards to avoid a fuel shortage. More dirty-burning coal should be used, and less low-sulphur oil. Pressure was put on the EPA to weaken its clean air standards.

And when one considers that the Department of Agriculture is still more interested in growing cotton than in protecting people and wildlife and birds, that the Department of Commerce is still more interested in shipping goods and promoting business than in keeping harbors and oceans free of oil spills, that the Department of the Interior is still more interested in helping miners and cattlemen and lumbermen than in husbanding natural resources for all the people—the EPA seems a slender reed to lean on.

The future of the EPA is also clouded by the record of what has happened to individual bureaucrats who have favored reform and have tried to act accordingly.* In 1970, John F. O'Leary, director of the Bureau of Mines, tired to crack down on coal-mine operators who were violating safety regulations. At one point in his crusade O'Leary told his top staff aides, "The question is, who is running things here—the government or U.S. Steel?" Not long thereafter he got a clue to the answer: he was fired.

Walter J. Hickel, Nixon's first Secretary of the Interior, refused to let the Everglades National Park be ruined by the construction of the world's largest jet airport; he ordered Chevron Oil prosecuted after one of its rigs blew up and polluted the Gulf of Mexico; he proposed a new system of urban parks; he asked the Justice Department to prosecute firms dumping poisonous mercury into public waters; he published the names of fifty polluters previously kept secret; he put whales on the list of endangered species; he proposed banning billboards on the 521 million

---

* President Rutherford Hayes appointed Carl Schurz as his Secretary of the Interior in 1877, and Schurz immediately set out to stop what he called "lumbermen who are not merely stealing trees, but whole forests" from the public domain. After urging the establishment of stiff penalties against lumber companies caught stealing federal timber, he was upbraided by some in Congress, including Speaker James G. Blaine, who damned Schurz's proposals as a "Prussian method" for oppressing honest businessmen. Blaine followed up his denunciation of the Schurz plan by recruiting enough votes to kill the Interior Department's office of timber inspection. By 1920, the honest businessmen had cut four-fifths of our primeval forests.

acres of lands administered by his department; he banned the use of DDT and other dangerous pesticides by agencies within his department.

Of course, Hickel was friendly with industry, too. He supported giveaway grazing fees for cattlemen. He wanted to lay the oil pipeline through Alaska that would probably ruin the tundra around it. And he had other weak points. But by and large he stood up for the people's interests far more than any other Secretary of the Interior had in recent years. So, after being on the job less than two years, he was fired.

In 1971, largely as a result of the aggressiveness of John M. Burns III, a federal prosecutor, Standard Brands was forced to pay a $125,000 fine for polluting New York waterways; Washburn Wire Company also paid $125,000, Transit-Mix Company and Kay Fries Chemicals $25,000 each, and Consolidated Edison $5000. Then General Motors was caught polluting the Hudson River, and Burns wanted to file both criminal and civil suits against the company. Attorney General John Mitchell wanted to let GM off with a civil suit "agreement." Burns said he thought that was no way to run the public's business, so he was fired.

Things just somehow seem to go wrong all the time for the people and the programs that might bring about protection for the public's land and water and air. This is especially noticed by private citizens or local officials who seek federal assistance in fighting the depravations of favored industries. After the notorious blowout of the Union Oil Company well that dumped 230,000 gallons of oil into the Santa Barbara channel in 1969, Marvin Levine, deputy county counsel for Santa Barbara, tried to find some allies in Washington. He said later:

> When I went into this fight to save the Bay from further oil pollution, I was really naive. I thought it was our government—your government and my government—and that it wouldn't lie to us and that it would try to protect the people. Why, it acts like nothing but a major stockholder in the oil companies. Federal officials, the Corps of Engineers, the oil companies operate in league. The government won't even talk to you sometimes.[10]

Not that the federal government failed entirely to act. Although it refused to stop the pumping of oil where oil had been discovered in the channel, it bought back the leases for areas where the oil companies had sunk "dry" holes and established these as "sanctuary" areas. In other words, the government blocked the pumping of oil only where there was no oil to pump—and at the same time reimbursed the companies for their failure.

On February 10, 1971, more than two hundred industrial leaders met with President Nixon and begged him not to implement any antipollution policies that would "disrupt the nationwide market systems" or require them to take corrective actions "at economically intolerable costs." Comforting them, President Nixon gave the industrialists his assurance that they would not be made "scapegoats" in the drive for cleaner air and water, and he further assured them that he did not see "the problem of cleaning up the environment as being one of the people versus business, of government versus business."

If the President had done a little investigating, he might have wondered just what the industrialists meant by complaining about the crushing economic burden of cleaning up their own mess. They have paid very little for the job. Gladwin Hill had written just a few days before the Nixon-industrialists meeting:

> A close look at the available data on pollution control suggests that up to now industry has done a lot more grunting and groaning than suffering. The petroleum industry, for instance, says it spends more than $1-million a day on pollution control and research. The industry's sales run over $60-billion a year. A million dollars is only one-half of 1 percent of a day's income. The steel industry says it is budgeting some $326-million a year for pollution control. That's about 6 percent of the income of just one company in the industry. The inorganic chemical industry grosses about $13-billion a year. Its estimated 1970 waste treatment outlay was $414.5 million— about 3 percent of its gross.[11]

Industry continued to poor-mouth its position, filling business publications with articles headlined "Pollution Laws Closing Plants by the Hundreds" or "A Drive to Find Jobs for Victims of Pollution War." But as of 1973, federal statistics show fewer than 1500 jobs lost because of pollution laws forcing industries out of business.

As for the claimed insufferable burden of updating plants so that they wouldn't suffocate communities or turn water into mudflows, the Council on Environmental Quality came up with statistics that brought industry's complaints into perspective. It disclosed that the national outlay to meet existing air-, water-, and solid waste-pollution control standards would come to only $105 billion for the period 1970–75, and that of this total, industry's share would come to only $28 billion, or an average of about $4.7 billion each year. That is $\frac{1}{150}$ of American industry's annual income. Said Russell Train, chairman of the Council on Environmental Quality, "Industry air and water pollution-control expenditures will generally be less than 1 percent of the value of shipments."[12]

That sort of news comes as no surprise. In 1964, Los Angeles County air-pollution control chief Griswold pointed out that although the auto industry had been complaining about how very much they were spending on air-pollution control, in fact "during the past decade the industry's total investment in controlling the nation's number one air pollution problem, a blight that is costing the rest of us more than $11 billion a year, has constituted less than one year's salary for 22 of their [the auto industry's] executives."[13]

In May 1973, the Council on Economic Priorities disclosed that the worst steel mill offender in the nation was Bethlehem Steel's plant at Sparrows Point on the Chesapeake Bay, which daily dumped "an average of 324 pounds of arsenic and 5,469 pounds of cyanide" into the Bay. It takes "only a few thousandths of an ounce" of either poison to kill a person. Fish could not live within a mile of the dumping grounds. Bethlehem Steel had taken only "token" steps, said CEP, to clean up its pollution. But in this it was showing the same attitude that all steel companies were showing. U.S. Steel's plant at Gary, Indiana, is responsible for 40 percent of that city's soot pollution—spewing out 22,000 pounds of soot and dust an hour.

How much would it cost the steel industry to clean itself up? The Council on Environmental Quality estimates it would cost $2.78 billion to do the job—or about $5 extra for a large rail car containing two tons of steel. But industry officials say they can't afford it. "There's not going to be any free lunch counter," said Duane R. Borst, controller of Inland Steel Company, at about the time when the above embarrassing smudges were being uncovered on Big Steel's record. "The costs for a clean environment have got to be passed on to the consumer."[14]

When one considers such statistics, sympathy for industry's antipollution "burden" seems rather mawkish. Yet sympathy the government has always had in abundance—sympathy and generosity. When the choice is between a clean environment for the public or a free-wheeling market for industry, government has almost always chosen the latter. After acknowledging that the proposed eight-hundred-mile pipeline from the North Slope of Alaska to the southern port of Valdez would inevitably break occasionally and do serious harm to the tundra, and after acknowledging also that there would inevitably be oil spills at the tanker facilities, both types of accidents being dangerous to wild-life and fishlife, the Interior Department nevertheless concluded that the development of oil reserves was "essential to the strength, growth and security of the United States"—meaning the strength, growth, and security of the major oil companies involved—and that therefore the pipeline should be laid. Eventually Congress and the Department of Commerce came to a similar conclusion, despite a special report by Commerce Department scientists warning that a large oil spill could permanently damage the rich fishing grounds of the Arctic and that, furthermore, withdrawing the oil might even cause the North Slope's ice fields to sink.

Still, the federal government is not totally devoid of concern for the public's welfare. If it is not willing to join them in their fight to salvage the land, at least it has been generous enough to supply them with a song for their crusade.* First sung by Burl Ives at a little ceremony at the Department of the Interior, with then Secretary Walter Hickel beaming approval, the song is called "Johnny Horizon," and it goes like this:

Earth, air, sunshine and water
We'd all keep that life support system
A—OK and ready to go. . . .
A gentlemen's agreement
Based on a handshake
Stronger than all the steel and cement
Linking up the whole continent. . . .
We need you to help keep America clean
With Teddy Roosevelt, George Washington, Tom Jefferson
And the rangers and the Wolf Cubs and the Boy Scouts and the
    Girl Scouts
And Johnny Horizon. . . .
What do you do with a beautiful land?
Keep it clean, keep it clean, keep it clean. . . .

That song may not *seem* to have much of a moral, but it actually has. Notice that the Department of the Interior, which is supposed to be the voice of the government's environmental con-science, has assigned as our guides and defenders in this matter three dead Presidents, some kids, and a make-believe character hot off a government publicity agent's typewriter. The people will have to look out for themselves.

* Not to mention a slogan from the Department of the Interior's copyrighted bird, "Woodsy Owl," who advises: "Give a hoot, don't pollute." Doesn't that touch your heart, U.S. Steel?

The Economy: Changing the Rules to Fit the Game, and Vice Versa

*For at least another hundred years we must pretend
to ourselves and to everyone that fair is foul and foul is fair;
for foul is useful and fair is not. Avarice and usury
and precaution must be our gods for a little longer still.
For only they can lead us out of the tunnel
of economic necessity into daylight.*

John Maynard Keynes, "Economic Possibilities
for Our Grandchildren," quoted in Anthony Sampson,
The Sovereign State of ITT

Under the most ideal circumstances, the nation's economy would be extremely difficult to keep in good shape. Under the present circumstances, it is impossible, and will be for the foreseeable future—assuming that by "healthy economy" is meant one in which there is an equitable distribution of wealth, an equitable distribution of taxes, a normal amount of inflation, and virtually no unemployment.

The evidence of failure is piled rather high. The richest 10 percent of the population get 29 percent of the income and own 56 percent of the national wealth; the poorest 10 percent of the

population get 1 percent of the income and keep getting deeper in debt. Indeed, the top of the pyramid is as thinly elite and wonderful as a golden needle: the richest 1 percent of us own 40 percent of the nation's wealth; 1.6 percent of Americans own 82.4 percent of all publicly held stock. Moreover, the income gap between the poorest and richest has nearly doubled in the last twenty years. The average unemployment rate for the last twenty years has been 4.5 percent, but in the last few years—even while economists claimed the nation was "booming"—it has been well over 5 percent and sometimes over 6 percent. The average wage earner has increasingly had to carry the burden of supporting the government. In 1963 the payroll tax accounted for only 19 percent of federal budget receipts from all sources. By 1973 it was accounting for 29 percent. Not only were payroll taxes—the kind of tax that hits the middle-income and low-income worker—rising at a faster rate than personal income taxes—the only kind of tax the wealthy person has to worry about—but they were also rising faster in absolute magnitude. One reason for the latter trend was the ability of wealthy people to find loopholes in the tax law. In 1970—the most recent year for which the Internal Revenue Service has supplied figures—112 American families with incomes above $200,000 paid no federal income tax. Three families with an average dividend income of $2,450,000 paid no federal income tax. Corporations also have a big place in the sunshine of tax favoritism, with billions of dollars in savings as a result of such practices as depletion allowances and business investment credit (meaning, they get tax credit for getting bigger and more profitable). In 1970–71, nine corporations that made a total of $650 million in profits paid no U.S. income tax.[1]

The one insurmountable handicap is the attitude of those who are in a position to manipulate the federal economy. One may substitute the word *priority* for *attitude*, and it comes to the same thing. The primary objective in all recent administrations has been to achieve a "sound dollar" and "price stability." That is, the primary objective has been to "fight inflation."* It is a worthy priority, no doubt, as long as the fight is supported by those persons best able to pay for it and at the expense of those programs that are least likely to be missed. When President Nixon in 1970 vetoed

* Seldom do government economists put this nation's inflationary problem into a global context; if they did, they would lose one of their propaganda weapons. From 1965 to 1970, inflation in the United States averaged 4 percent a year, while in Japan it was 4.7 percent; in Germany, 4.3 percent; in France, 4.6 percent; and in the United Kingdom, 4.7 percent.

$1 billion that Congress had appropriated for education, he claimed that he did so only because that amount was inflationary. Yet in the twelve months prior to his veto, banks had added an additional $1.5 billion to the national debt through higher interest rates on money borrowed by the government—surely as inflationary an expense as spending money for schools—and Nixon had done nothing to blunt the bankers' profits. Subsequently, in 1971, 1972, and 1973, Nixon continued to impound money appropriated by Congress and vetoed programs for education, school lunches, food stamps, job training, housing, and urban improvements as "inflationary," while continuing to put his signature to programs aimed at aiding the big corporations, the big agribusinessmen, and defense contractors that were at least as inflationary. His budget for fiscal 1974 was the most clear-cut evidence of this trend: Nixon proposed slashing $10 billion from "social" programs, to fight inflation, while increasing the defense budget by $5 billion, although for the first time in more than a decade we weren't at war with anyone.

A sound dollar and price stability and controlled inflation have been the goals of government economists because those things are good for big bankers and other businessmen. To be sure, they are good for the general public as well; indeed, they are essential for the person living on a low fixed income (social security, pensions of various sorts). But for many low-income and all no-income Americans (which means the 25 million living in poverty) there are things that take prior consideration to a sound dollar—things, to be exact, like full-time jobs. The typical government economist, however, sees jobs not as something that people want; he sees jobs only as an element that affects the soundness of the dollar. Shortly before his eighteen-year tenure ended as chairman of the Federal Reserve Board (which controls the nation's monetary policy), William McChesney Martin said that it would help if more people were out of work. "A 4 percent level of unemployment is very good," he conceded, "though 5 percent would be better."*

There is another perspective to these priorities. Leon H. Keyserling, an economic adviser to Franklin Roosevelt and Harry Truman, has this to say about it:

---

* Mr. Martin was no more callous than most others who direct the nation's economics and who seem too far removed to hear the growling stomachs of the unemployed. In his 1971 Economic Message to Congress, President Nixon predicted that he would reach "full prosperity without war." Six months later, however, his chief economic spokesman, Treasury Secretary John Connally,

Is a stable price level nirvana? The modern period of most stability in prices (except for falling farm prices) was between 1922 and 1929—which was followed by the biggest depression in our history because, while the price level was stable, wages and farm incomes were rising much slower than productivity. As a result, the nation was getting a terrible distribution of wealth.

The key to a healthy economy is not determined in a phony contest between inflation and deflation (meaning rising or falling prices). A healthy economy is determined by the proper distribution of wealth. And this is something that one rarely hears discussed in Washington these days.

So when the administration's economists say, "We mustn't let the rate of unemployment get too low because that would be inflationary," they are being absolutely criminal. They are saying to the unemployed person who has to support a family on a welfare payment, "You shall be the insurer of Leon Keyserling against his having to pay 1 percent or 3 percent more a year when he buys a third car. If you will kindly remain unemployed, inflation will not be an irritant for the man with money." This is a cruel argument.

Whether a rising price level hurts everybody at the top or everybody at the bottom or everybody in between cannot be determined by saying that a rising price level is bad. It all depends on the content of the programs that are causing the rising prices. If the war in Vietnam causes inflation, that's bad. If the now defunct war-on-poverty causes inflation, that could be acceptable.

In other words, the emphasis should be on real wealth and its distribution. Real wealth is what people use. They don't eat prices. They eat food. They don't live in prices. They live in houses. They don't wear prices. They wear clothes. If a coat today costs what it did in 1957, that doesn't help the fellow on the bottom who can't afford even 1957 prices.

If the extra cost of spreading food and houses and clothes among more people is a couple of additional percentage points of price inflation a year, then it is well worth the cost. If it weren't, you could carry the argument the other direction to the extreme and say we were all better off during the depths of the Great Depression. Then prices were falling and dollars were worth more than ever since. We had the soundest dollar in our history. But who had the dollars?[2]

Keyserling's sentiments are thrown in here simply to show that not *all* economic advisers to the federal government put abstract fiscal theories and the health of business ahead of the

announced that the administration considered even a 4 percent level of unemployment to be an unrealistically low goal. And Economic Council Chairman Paul W. McCracken, who in 1971 defined full employment as 3.8 percent unemployed, had redefined it as being in the 4.5 percent zone. The economists juggle such figures very offhandedly; to listen to them, one would hardly realize that each percentage point in an 80 million labor force means 800,000 *people.*

physical needs of the people. But it should also be added that the Presidents to whom he gave this kind of advice did not always listen.

The concept of fighting inflation has been made to seem such a sacred, patriotic thing that those who advise living with inflation under certain circumstances are often subjected to abuse. The noted economist Paul A. Samuelson is one who has experienced this. He writes:

> Anyone with a good track record in analyzing the post-1950 developments in North America and Europe realizes that the only cure now known for creeping inflation [that is, the cure of a sharp recession] is decidedly worse than the disease itself.
>
> Whenever I write this simple fact, I am subject to a torrent of abuse, quite devoid of rational rebuttal. Such irate rough-handling of the messenger who brings the truth of bad news diverts attention from the important problem of our times: how to devise policies that minimize the unavoidable degree of creeping inflation without sacrificing long-run living standards and work opportunity."[3]

Even if a pro-people, rather than a pro-dollar, attitude prevailed in the White House and in Congress, the maintenance of a healthy economy would be difficult to achieve—in fact, impossible to achieve consistently—because most of the money men in government are an obtuse lot who keep jowling and fussing and seeking to upstage one another with their own pet theories. To them the economy is an esoteric game, and the lives of real people, down at the bottom, do not seem to be involved. They think only in such abstract terms as "bank fluidity" and "Eurodollar trading" and "gold outflow" and "balance of payment" and "fiscal inventory."

Some economists think the economy can best be kept healthy by manipulating fiscal policies: taxing and spending. If there is inflation loose in the land, take some of the money away from the people by taxing them, and don't let so much federal money seep into the economy through government programs. This, as already indicated, was President Nixon's favorite excuse for cutting back on a variety of education, health, and welfare programs. Yet Nixon refused to raise taxes, a mistake Lyndon Johnson had also made when he escalated the war. The result was that while Nixon talked anti-inflationary thrift, he regularly wound up with the biggest deficits in the nation's history: in fiscal 1973 a staggering $40 billion worth of red ink.

Another camp argues that the best way to manipulate the economy is through monetary policies: increasing or decreasing the flow of money at its source, the banks. If there is inflation, crimp the outlet. The less money there is in the banks to borrow and the, higher the price (higher interest) of that money, the less attractive will be the process of borrowing and spending.*

The basic monetary theory is simple, but as applied by the Federal Reserve Board (or, more simply, the Fed) during most of the past generation, it has been a baffling process, accurately described by financial writer Hobart Rowen as "the most controversial and least understood element in the U.S. economic complex. It is now generally agreed that the wide swings in the application of monetary policy in the past few years—from great ease to very tight—have themselves contributed to both inflation and recession in this country. And nobody even now is quite sure of how to manage the potent weapon of money flows and growth."[†4]

(The management of money in the international market is even trickier. In 1971, for the first time in forty-one years, the U.S. dollar was cut loose from gold and devalued. It came as a sharp blow to our pride, but officials indicated that devaluation probably wouldn't have to happen again; then in December 1971, representatives of the big nations of the world met in the Smithsonian Institution and came to an agreement on monetary values. Within seven months the agreement had fallen apart, and shortly thereafter the dollar was devalued again—for a total of about 30 percent.)

Nixon's New Economics

When the fiscalists and the monetarists make an either-or game out of the nation's economy, they simply increase the dark-

---

* Another wing of the monetarists believes that the Federal Reserve Board should decide on a flow of money that increases steadily at a fixed rate to allow for growth in the economy but is not altered to meet emergencies. These theorists—and some of them sit in the highest council seats of government today—believe in perpetual motion; if that perfect rate of flow can be found, they say, then the nation's economy will roll on forever above recession and below inflation.

† Indeed, some economists believe that when the Fed has encouraged interest rate increases (for the purpose, it says, of combating inflation) it has actually increased inflation. Keyserling is among those who hold this view. He argues: "Inflation is a rising price of something that you use. The rising price of steel is more inflationary than the rising price of bananas because steel enters into more products. And since the price of money enters into the cost of just about everything, rising money costs are at the very core of inflation." (Personal interview, August 1971.)

ness that economists normally cast over the operation of government. A foolish fiscal policy cannot be entirely offset if followed by a brilliant monetary policy, and vice versa; there can be no assured control of the economy without taking a number of processes into consideration at the same time. As President Nixon discovered, neither a tight monetary policy nor a thrifty fiscal policy, nor a combination of the two, can be relied on to stop inflation. Putting people out of work and stunting the nation's economic growth won't guarantee a "sound dollar." Wages and prices simply do not respond as they once did to the classic supply-and-demand theory. Unemployment figures kept climbing on President Nixon, but so did the wage levels. Consumers were drawing in their belts, but the price index kept climbing nevertheless.

One explanation for this comes from Dr. Milton Friedman, one of Nixon's advisers: "Once inflation starts, it is built into wage contracts, price lists, interest rates." This is the inflation that results from the *expectation* of inflation. Steelworkers say, "Prices will be 10 percent higher a year from now, so we'll demand a 10 percent increase right now." The accuracy of their prediction is neither here nor there; the very fact that they anticipate higher prices has made them act in such a way as to help bring about those higher prices.

Likewise, prices on some key products also escape the "law" of supply and demand. General Motors does not price its autos according to demand. In fact, if demand for Chevrolets drops, the price of Chevies may climb, for, as is now generally recognized, when a company such as GM runs into a period of slow sales, it will try to compensate for the inadequate volume by getting a higher return per unit through a price increase.

To control wages and prices in a way that is sure to affect the economy in a quick and predictable fashion, an administration simply must be willing to use across-the-board, *direct*, government-imposed wage-and-price controls—something that is offensive to business tories and big labor as well, so the thought of imposing wage-and-price controls, except in wartime, is enough to make the ordinary President tremble. Yet at the same time no President would likely disagree with the logic of John Kenneth Galbraith's statement: "The American economy, whatever wishful analysis there may be to the contrary, is not stable at or near full employment. Wages will always shove up prices and prices will always pull up wages and this spiral will revolve for Republicans and Democrats alike. Moreover, it has been the experience of virtually every other major industrial country that some machinery for wage and price restraint is the only alternative to inflation or heavy unemployment."[5]

This is a truism that Nixon preferred to disregard for the first two and a half years of his administration. But by the middle of 1971 the economic disarray that he had inherited from Lyndon Johnson—especially the inflationarily hot economy triggered by excessive military spending without an accompanying increase in taxes—brought Nixon to an uncomfortable showdown. He had campaigned in 1968 on an economic platform of nonintervention and individual enterprise—a minimum of government restraint on moneymaking and spending. Some of his closest advisers urged him to continue following that policy to the bitter end and to let the snarls and tangles of the economy work themselves out. But others, especially Treasury Secretary John Connally and Arthur Burns, chairman of the Federal Reserve Board, urged at least a temporary controls program, and Nixon ultimately acted on their advice.

Connally, taking the White House microphone to announce the flabbergasting decision (flabbergasting to conservatives, at any rate), said that Nixon had been forced into changing his mind— indeed, about a month earlier Nixon had emphatically stated he would *not* institute wage-and-price controls—because of "an unacceptable level of unemployment, an unacceptable rate of inflation, and the need for a continuing and expanding economy, a deteriorating balance of trade, a very unsatisfactory balance of payments situation, plus a continuing uncertainty and instability in the international monetary markets."[6]

Although that sounds like the coolly logical approach to a problem analytically dissected by humane experts, the long-range appraisal by most observers of what Nixon called his New Economics (and others call Nixonomics) is that, as Professors R. L. Miller and R. M. Williams put it, there was "more politics in Nixon's economics than there was anything else."

Significantly, what finally gave Nixon the impetus to temporarily freeze wages and prices in August 1971 was not public outrage over the fact that retired persons on fixed incomes were being chewed up by inflation, or that unorganized workers were being hurt in the same way. He did it primarily to help the international business interests, the "multinational corporations," whose dollars were being abused in other countries. According to *Newsweek* (August 30, 1971), the very thought that the business giants were hurting would send Nixon into arm-waving spasms of anger: " 'Goddam those so-and-so's,' he'd say, and 'We'll fix those bastards.' "

So he "fixed" the foreigners (he thought) by devaluing the dollar overseas; then, lest this frighten American wage earners into thinking their dollars at home were worth less and thus bring on a new round of pay-increase demands, he froze wages. He had to freeze prices, too, of course, but to make this more palatable to business, he gave it a 10 percent investment tax credit, slapped on a 10 percent import surtax (to keep out the cheaper-than-U.S.-made foreign competition), and singled out the auto industry for a special favor by lifting its 7 percent excise tax. All that razzle-dazzle was prompted to assist the big outfits in their international trading. Not that the man on the bottom was entirely forgotten: he got an income tax exemption that would average out at $10 per person.

That may seem like a somewhat cynical appraisal, but it was widely believed by many knowledgeable observers, and the way that the wage-and-price controls were bungled does seem to justify cynicism. For one thing, Nixon put his economic adviser Herbert Stein in charge of wage-and-price control planning, which was—considering the fact that Stein abhorred the whole idea—about "like putting Polly Adler in charge of a convent," to use the apt appraisal of Robert R. Nathan, who used to advise Presidents on economic affairs back in the Democratic days. Critics pointed out that while Nixon froze the wage earner's income, he did not freeze income from profits, dividends, and interests—a boon to big stockholders and corporations. Critics also claimed that while the wage freeze was easy to enforce, the price freeze was easy to evade.

And they were right. Administration officials admitted it. At the end of the first full year of "controls," the Labor Department announced that wholesale prices had risen at a faster rate than during the last noncontrol year. The Department conceded that wages had risen only 60 percent as fast as prices during the control year. The problem appeared to be that price increase applications from companies with little market power or political influence were being rejected by the Price Commission, while the big companies with plenty of backdoor political clout were getting just about all the price increases they asked for. In one industry that touched nearly every home in the country, the utilities industry, prices were jumping higher than at any time in history—jumps that were, by the way, two to four times the "ceiling" ostensibly set by the Price Commission. While wage earners were held to a 5.5 percent increase, outfits like General Motors were hitting record income levels ($2.16 billion in 1972), and their executives weren't doing so badly either. Ford Motor Company's fifty-one top executives shared $12.9 million in salaries, fees, and other compensations in 1972—up from $11.3 million in 1971. The manner in which the wage-and-price controls were operated did indeed give AFL-CIO President George Meany some foundation for saying that they were "Robin Hood in reverse, robbing the poor to pay the rich."

But as the nation discovered, even some jerry-built controls worked better than none at all. In January 1973, Treasury Secretary George P. Shultz, who had always opposed controls of any kind, happily announced that Nixon was ending all mandatory controls and was replacing them with "voluntary" curbs. He said the White House had a "stick in the closet" and "people who don't comply voluntarily are going to get clobbered." But when it comes to voluntarily abjuring profits, Americans aren't very enthusiastic. The "voluntary curbs" were ignored, and the administration kept the stick in the closet. As a result, as anybody could have predicted, prices rose swiftly: in the first quarter of the voluntary phase, wholesale prices were up at an annual rate of 21.2 percent; farm products went up 37.3 percent. Corporate profits jumped 11.4 percent during the first quarter of voluntary price controls as compared with the last quarter of mandatory controls (which had inhibited profit margins to some extent). As the *Wall Street Journal* pointed out wryly on May 30, 1973, "The price of lumber has gone up so much under Phase 3 that, if the White House had to go out today and buy a new stick to put in the closet, it would cost nearly 23 percent more than in January." In short, the administration—leaving the housewife to deal with the highest food prices in a generation—simply had given up the idea of controlling the economy that way. Everything was back to the good old American method of market cannibalism.

The power to control prices and wages is at least within reach of the people's representatives, just as is the power to regulate taxes and government expenditures. But even if the people could persuade their representatives in the White House and in Congress to start making sense in those fiscal areas, the other principal lever for operating the economy would still be out of reach, and to that extent the people would still be out of luck. The people have virtually no control over the nation's monetary policies.* This most vital power rests in the hands of the Federal Reserve System.

The Power of the Fed

The Federal Reserve System is made up of all privately owned "national" banks, which is to say the 6000 banks chartered by the federal government. The system is divided into twelve parts, presided over by regional Reserve Banks in New York, Boston, Philadelphia, Cleveland, Richmond, Atlanta, Chicago, St. Louis, Minneapolis, Kansas City, Dallas, and San Francisco. Each regional bank has nine directors, of whom a majority are usually commercial bankers. Presiding over the system as a whole is the Federal Reserve Board of Governors in Washington. The board's prime function is to make monetary policy.

On the surface, that sounds like a logical arrangement for a national banking system. But there is one thing about it that is very peculiar—in fact, there is nothing else like it in any other nation's banking system—namely, the private banks literally own the public system. The capital stock of the twelve regional Federal Reserve Banks is subscribed to by the private banks that belong to the system. In other words, they own the system that is supposed to be regulating them. It is as though the Bell Telephone System owned the Federal Communications Commission.† If

* Like everything else said in or about economics, however, this categorical statement must be modified. The people's loss of control is to some extent merely the result of political convenience. Any time it wants to, Congress can take back the constitutional powers over money that it surrendered to the governors of the Federal Reserve System; but to buck the big banks in this way would take courage. Nor is the President so powerless and innocent as he would lead the people to believe. The Credit Control Act of 1969 gave the President authority to regulate the nation's credit. Even though 1970 saw interest rates rise to the most ruinous level in a hundred years, the President made no use of the act. His default was part of a long-established pattern of favoritism of which the Federal Reserve System is simply the most important part; the favoritism surfaced again in 1971 when the only major industry exempted from the price freeze was the banking industry.

† Among those over the years to criticize this set-up was the Commission on Money and Credit (see its Report, published by Prentice-Hall in 1961). In general this commission concluded that the Fed should be set up in such a way as to be much more responsive to the President and much more candid with Congress; it also concluded that the Fed should at least end the *appearance* of conflict of interest in its ties to commercial banks. This commission was very "Establishment" in its composition—it included David Rockefeller, Robert R. Nathan, Marriner S. Eccles, Henry H. Fowler, and Adolf A. Berle, Jr. If even

further evidence of the private nature of the Fed were needed, it could be found in the fact that until 1971 its member banks paid membership dues to the American Bankers Association, one of the most notorious lobbies against public interest programs. This conflict of interest was ended only after repeated demands by some critical congressmen and newsmen.

When one considers that these private commercial banks, whose only purpose in life is to make a higher profit, are in a position to eliminate competition among lending institutions, set interest rates, and direct the public's monetary regimen, it is an unsettling thought.

Briefly, this is the manner in which the Federal Reserve Board juggles the money and credit supply: Banks would either lend or invest every cent that came their way unless they were required to hold something in reserve. The Federal Reserve Board has the authority to say how much its members should hold in reserve. If, for example, the reserve requirement were $2 on hand for every $10 on deposit, and if the Fed decided it would like to put more money in circulation, it could drop the reserve requirement to, say, $1 per $10. This action does not simply free the extra $1; it frees it to the multiple of ten. Whereas the banks previously could lend only $10 for each $2 held in reserve, now they could begin lending $20. When the Fed drops the reserve requirement, it literally gives the banks that much more money to deal with and to profit from. If the Fed, however, wants to tighten the economy, it can simply move in the reverse direction and increase the reserve requirements.

Another method for injecting money into the economy through the banks is for the Fed's Open Market Committee to buy United States government securities from a dozen or so favored dealers, which include big banks and bond houses. If, say, the FOMC wants to put another $1 billion into the nation's monetary pipeline through the Federal Reserve System Region No. 2, it can buy $1 billion in government securities from Chase Manhattan Bank; Chase takes the check from the FOMC and deposits it in the Federal Reserve Bank in New York, and $1 billion thereby goes into circulation. (Conversely, if the Fed wants to take money

---

they concede that the smell from the Fed is so rank that the public may soon begin to notice, it is little wonder that the ideological left damns the Fed as downright oppressive, and the ideological right damns it as conspiratorial (Wall Street Conspiracy genre).

out of circulation, it *sells* securities to its member banks, thus sopping up that much of their money.)*

Looking back over the Federal Reserve Board's history, many would agree with *New York Times* business editor Albert L. Kraus:

> It is no small source of irony that the central banking system has enjoyed indifferent success in helping the government achieve its peacetime goals, full employment and economic growth with stable output and prices, but that it has been an outstanding aid in financing World Wars I and II, Korea and Vietnam. Despite much incantation to the contrary, these successes have been achieved largely by suspending the peacetime goal of stability and permitting more than a modicum of inflation.[7]

It is not difficult for observers such as Kraus to prove their point, for during those periods of the past forty years when a freer monetary policy was most needed to prime the civilian economy— in the 1930s and the 1950s—the Fed notably and repeatedly erred by crimping back. But with wartime, the Fed loosened up again—for cheap money makes it easier for the government to indulge in the deficit financing of its belligerent pastime. Bankers know the public relations value of this course of action; after all, patriotic people might get a bit upset if they saw the bankers putting an excessive interest rate on war budget borrowings. So the bankers, while still earning quite enough, refrain during those emergency periods from their usual gouging, and in gratitude the government does not complain too loudly when peace returns and the Fed again jacks up the price of money for civilian programs.

As it presently operates, the Federal Reserve Board, by being independent of the President and of Congress, is actually a fourth branch of government. The Federal Reserve Board is far more than merely an independent regulatory agency, like the FCC, FTC, and

---

* This bit of papershuffling unnecessarily benefits the private money houses, which earn interest and commissions through these transactions. Chemical Bank of New York took an ad in the *New York Times* (March 21, 1971), which boasted, "Banking Serves Government." It explained that when the federal government needs operating money "it can only acquire funds either by taxing or by borrowing." The bank neglected to mention that there is no reason why the government should not "borrow" from itself, or simply declare the creation of whatever money it needs. This method for obtaining government funds, eliminating the billions in interest now paid to banks, has been suggested for many years; banks ridicule it, saying it would produce only "printing press money," that is, worthless. But in fact money that is "borrowed" through private dealers is no sounder than money the government pulls out of its hat.

ICC, for those agencies must look to Congress for their operational funds, and they are constantly receiving new guidelines and mandates from Congress. Not so the Fed. The funds for operating the Federal Reserve System are exempt from controls of the budget and from controls of congressional appropriations. Operating funds come from assessments on the twelve Federal Reserve Banks and from the interest on the government securities held by the Fed. The General Accounting Office is charged by Congress with auditing all federal agencies, but in practice the Fed is also exempt from the GAO's supervision.

Although the law creating the Federal Reserve System in 1913 did give broad, general guidelines, the Fed is quite free to interpret those guidelines just about any way it chooses. Originally the Federal Reserve System was conceived by Congress merely as a mechanism by which the national banks could operate more smoothly and safely. The nation was tired of bank panics, wipeouts of great hunks of the banking fraternity, which had helped create depressions in 1873, 1884, 1893, and 1907. One reason for the panics was that there was no cooperative way for the banks across the nation to back up one another. The banks in one region of the country might have a shortage of money at the very time when the banks in another region had more money than they could use. The Federal Reserve System of twelve regional Reserve Banks gave all member national banks a place to go for funds to shore up their reserves (although this, as it turned out, was not sufficient to prevent the collapse of the banking system after 1929), as well as offering them a conduit by which checks passing from one region to another could be cleared much faster.

Initially, then, the Federal Reserve System was not seen as a "central bank" in the sense that it would have dictatorial control over the nation's money affairs. The laws giving the Fed that power came in 1933 and 1935, at the very time when the wobbly national banks had the least right to ask the American people to give them any confidence, much less any power to run the show, for the banks had botched nearly everything they had touched in the previous dozen years.

The most potent new power came with the establishment of the Federal Open Market Committee. An unfriendly description of the FOMC, but for all that an accurate one, was given by Congressman Wright Patman:

> The entire structure of the Federal Reserve is designed to help the banks first and the public last. The Federal Open Market Com-

mittee is probably one of this country's most vital and most important institutions. It sets interest rates and determines the supply of money. Yet it is virtually controlled lock, stock and barrel by the banks.

It is really amazing that we have such an institution at the nerve center of a democratic society. The Open Market Committee is composed of the seven members of the Federal Reserve Board and five of the twelve presidents of the Federal Reserve Banks. In practice, however, all twelve presidents of the Federal Reserve Banks participate in these secret Open Market Committee meetings. Here is where the banks move in—right to the center of our monetary policymaking.

Each of these twelve Federal Reserve Bank presidents is selected by a nine-member board of directors. Six of these board members in each bank are selected directly from the commercial banking industry. The remaining three are required to be persons with "tested banking experience." The result is that the Federal Reserve Banks—and in turn the Open Market Committee—are completely dominated by the commercial banking industry. In fact, a recent survey conducted by the [House] Banking and Currency Committee revealed that 84 of the 108 directors are either now, or have been, directors, employees, or officers of commercial banks.

As the system is constituted, only a handful of insiders—perhaps 2,000 to 3,000—have access to the information of these secret Open Market Committee meetings. These are people that are connected with the boards of directors of the various Federal Reserve Banks as well as the employees that attend such sessions. So the meetings are totally secret for everyone except these insiders. They are secret from the President, the Congress—in fact, everyone except the inside banking community.

With this kind of system prevailing, it is not surprising that our monetary policies have fallen into disrepute. It is simply absurd to think that the bankers are going to participate in the Open Market Committee and set policies against their own interests. . . .

The super-secret nature of our monetary policymaking is a grave threat to our entire democratic system. A democracy and its institutions must operate out in the open if they are to maintain their prime strength—public confidence.[8]

Of the Fed's secrecy there can be no doubt. When one considers that it is the public's money that the Fed is manipulating, and that the mistakes its members make will be paid for by the public, it may be somewhat difficult to understand the attitude of Fed Chairman Arthur Burns, who replied to a question of the Congressional Joint Economic Committee: "You know, I'm in the central banking business now. There are some questions on which central bankers cannot speak with freedom." The question that had been put to Burns was not anything relating to national security; it was simply a question regarding the monetary and credit policies that the Fed was imposing on the nation. What was no secret to the ruling circle of bankers must, he insisted, be kept secret from the American people.*

All of this adds up to just one thing: the present operation of the Fed ravages the democratic concept that the credit of the nation is the people's credit—a public resource—and the people should have the right to direct the use of that credit. The banking and monetary system—including the Federal Reserve—is simply a mechanism that the people have set up to handle this credit; a mechanism, not a policy-maker. Policies about the people's credit should be set by the people. But the mechanical device—the Federal Reserve—has taken control from the people.

The Big Banks

When critics like Patman damn the Federal Reserve as a front for bankers, they mean the big bankers, the real pashas of the financial world. There are about 14,000 banks in this country. Less than half of them belong to the Federal Reserve System, but they account for 85 percent of all banking accounts. The kingpin of the whole system is the New York Federal Reserve Bank and its members. No matter who else is on the Open Market Committee, New York is always formally represented.

The Fed's policies largely reflect the wishes of the big banks, which historically have had as little concern for the welfare of the small banker as they have had for the country in general. To illustrate from the most dramatic period, the beginning of the Great Depression: When the banks began to collapse in 1931 under an avalanche of worthless paper—bonds whose prices had gone to nothing and mortgages on property that could not be sold —President Hoover called a secret meeting of the fifteen most pow-

---

* One reason Congress does such a sloppy job in economic affairs is simply that the members, like most of the public, avoid the subject as much as possible and leave the problems of the economic field to the supposed experts. Even the least adept of these professional economists can usually talk circles around a typical congressman, and when the professional is especially crafty he can even intimidate the more knowledgeable congressmen. After Federal Reserve Board Chairman Burns concluded his testimony before the Joint Economic Committee not long ago, the JEC's chairman, William Proxmire, said with awe, "I can describe your performance only like Stokowski playing us as if we were an orchestra, and I feel like someone in the back row playing the cymbals." (Washington Post, February 10, 1972.)

erful men in the banking world, and he laid out a simple and workable plan. The big banks would supply a credit pool for the rickety smaller banks to borrow from, and thus all could stay in business. It was called the National Credit Corporation, but it didn't work because the big banks were not interested in risking anything for the smaller ones. So Hoover talked Congress into setting up the Reconstruction Finance Corporation, funded at $2 billion, to make loans to desperate banks, railroads, and insurance companies. It did a great deal of good for some, but the banks that were helped by it did not react as the theorists had hoped: after *they* had been pulled back from the brink, they refused to risk anything to help pull the general public back from the brink. The transfusion of new blood went no farther than the banks themselves.

After the 1929 crash and its aftermath had wiped out about half the banks in the country, some of the banks that survived, especially the larger ones, found themselves in a splendid position for getting their way. Since nothing had so shattered the public as the banking system disaster, and since the public (including politicians) seemed willing to do just about anything to prevent more of the same, the banks pushed for and got several highly profitable programs with the argument that they were needed to provide a "healthy" financial community.

One law that was passed permitted banks not to pay interest on checking accounts (in fact, to prevent competition, the law *forbade* the payment of interest). There was no good reason for this indulgence then; there is less reason now. According to House Banking Committee records, today more than $225 billion of the deposits of commercial banks are in the form of demand deposits—checking accounts—that bear no interest. The banks use the money for free. In fact, some banks charge depositors for the "service" of handling these funds. If the banks consider it such a burden to handle checking accounts, why do they always lobby so heavily against legislation that would permit savings and loan institutions to offer the same service?

Another important action taken by the banks in the Depression of the 1930s was to set up a price-fixing arrangement. The banks that survived the crash had more money than customers. Most businesses and individuals were too hard-up to take out loans; those who could afford to borrow could "shop around" for their money. Under those conditions, if the law of supply and demand had been allowed to prevail, the price of money would have hit rock bottom. But at that point some of the more ingenious bankers got together and said, in effect: "Why cut each other's throats? Why allow competition to ruin our profits? Let's set a price below which we all agree we won't go." And that's how the prime interest rate came into existence. The prime rate was, and still is, the rate of interest banks charge their biggest and best customers. It is the bargain rate. Everybody else must pay more. Those most able to pay—outfits like General Electric—get the lowest rates; those least able to pay—such as this writer and his readers—must pay the maximum. It sounds like a conspiratorial and unfair arrangement, and it is even acknowledged to be that way by such authorities as George Mitchell, Federal Reserve Board governor. He concluded, "This kind of price fixing inherent in the prime rate contravenes some of the key virtues that we associate with competitive market enterprise."[9]

He could have been harsher and still been exact. He could have said, for example, that the prime rate is a very obvious violation of the antitrust laws, both in the agreement by which it was originally established and in the way it is applied today.

Almost always, when one big bank raises its prime lending rate, the other big banks follow suit within a matter of minutes, or, if they want to make a light effort to preserve the patina of competition, within a matter of hours.

For example, on June 9, 1969, a historic moment occurred in banking history: for the first time, the prime rate was raised more than ½ percent in one step. At 9:16 A.M. Eastern Standard Time, Bankers Trust Company of New York City, the nation's seventh largest bank, announced the new rate of 8½ percent. Thirty-four minutes later, First National City Bank of New York, the third largest in the country, followed suit; within minutes identical increases had been made by other major banks.

An even more impressive act of collusion was stretched over the first eight months of 1973. Between January 1 and August 28, the prime interest rate was raised fifteen times; in the last five weeks of that incredible period, the rate was raised once a week. And on every step of that journey upward, *all* the major commercial banks moved together. At the first of the year, the prime rate was 6 percent; on August 28 it was 9.75 percent—a 62 percent increase in the price of money—the swiftest rise and the highest level ever recorded. (A couple of weeks later a few big banks went to 10 percent, but others did not follow, and so the prime rate continued at 9.75.)

Sometimes after a staggering rise of that kind, taken in unison by the banking fraternity, the Department of Justice will promise to investigate for antitrust violations, but nothing ever comes of it. If the big three auto-makers all jumped their prices by 62 percent in fifteen regular steps over an eight-month period, so as to avoid competition, neither Congress nor the public nor the Justice Department would put up with it. If the Teamsters and the Steelworkers and the United Auto Workers joined in a 62-percent escalation of wages in eight months, they would never get by with it. At the very least, injunctions against the raises would be obtained by the government. Probably Congress would impose a wage ceiling. Unquestionably the Justice Department would sue them under the Sherman Anti-Trust Act. But when the major banks of the country join in concert to increase the price of money by 62 percent— thereby inflating the most essential price in the American economy —for no reason but their own profit, it is passed off by government economists as simply a normal money-market operation and quite in keeping with the free enterprise system. They may or may not be correct in that appraisal, but it is certainly in keeping with the favoritism with which the major banks are accustomed to being treated.

Most irritating of all, when the Federal Reserve launches programs that force an interest raise, or when the major banks lead the way with the approval of the Federal Reserve, it is always done with great piety, in benevolent tones, with the argument that this is being done only for the best interest of the country, that it is being done only because the economy needs "cooling off."

Even the most cynical responses to this line do not seem exaggerated. Galbraith sounded only realistic on this point when he observed: "If anybody else is lobbying for a higher price, we take for granted that they want more dough. But if a banker is lobbying for higher interest rates, this is pure unadulterated righteousness. Everybody else says they want more money, but let David Rockefeller [of Chase Manhattan] speak for higher interest rates, and, boy, that's statesmanship."[10]

Even financial writers who try to keep the cynicism out of their observations have been unable to ignore the bizarre and even ridiculous sales pitches by which the public has been asked to accept higher interest rates. In the midst of the banks' historic rash of interest gougings in early 1969, Edwin L. Dale, Jr., observed in the *New York Times* (March 23, 1969):

> At one moment, the citizen is told that high interest rates are a weapon against inflation. At the next, he reads—from no less exalted figures than the White House Press Secretary and the chairman of

the President's Council of Economic Advisers—that they are the result of inflation. If he is a borrower, and pays the rates, he might think they are a cause of inflation.

Somewhere in between, he gets the idea that high interest rates are the result of something done by the Federal Reserve Board to fight inflation. That seems to make sense until he is told by the chairman of the Reserve Board, and most economists, that the market, not the Federal Reserve, fixes interest rates.

Despite this fast talk (and it is rather fast, for as we have seen, there is no competitive market; the price is simply rigged by the biggest banks), Americans realized something was askew when—during the first eighteen months of the Nixon Administration, a period dominated by the 8½-percent prime interest rates—unemployment climbed 50 percent, unemployment compensation dependency shot up 100 percent, real weekly earnings went down $3.92, and the consumer price index climbed 11.1 points. But banks were showing tremendous profits. Again in 1973 consumers were probably wondering how much of an interest-rate "cure" they could take when they analyzed the situation in August: prime interest rates hit 9.75 percent, consumer prices rose 23 percent, grocery prices climbed a staggering 92.4 percent on an annual adjusted basis (the steepest climb in twenty-six years), while the average wage earner's spendable income *dropped* 1.9 percent. Unemployment hung stubbornly at 5 percent.[11] But bank profits were rolling right along very nicely, and the latest quarterly showing of corporate profits was up 24 percent. As Galbraith put it, "boy, that's statesmanship."

One last, flamboyant example of government favoritism for banks must be given. This has to do with how the banks get to use our tax money, which most Americans probably think goes directly to the United States Treasury. After all, if we are late in paying our taxes, the government levies a fine, so obviously it would seem that the government wants its money right now, and no detours. Right? Wrong. In 1917, the federal government began allowing the commercial banks to hold some of the government's income for a brief time without paying any interest. And after the Second World War, Congress—always a dependable patsy for the banking industry—authorized employers to make payments of withheld income taxes (payroll taxes) by having their banks debit their accounts and credit the Treasury accounts (now known as the Tax and Loan Accounts). Since then this system has been expanded so that the banks may do the same thing for other taxes.

This simply means that the banks get to hold on to the tax deductions until the Treasury calls for them. On a typical day, commercial banks use between $5 billion and $7 billion of federal money (plus another $15 billion or so of state and local taxes), on which they pay no interest at all. In other words, the banks get to use our money, for free, to make loans back to us at interest rates of up to 10 percent or more. Not a bad business.

Opportunities for Reform

Reform of the economic structure is not impossible to achieve in such a way as to greatly improve the position of the middle-income and low-income families; but this is certainly the most difficult reform that the general voting public could attempt to achieve. The reason is simple. Those with the most to lose—that is, those with the greatest share of the wealth—have the most potent weapon in politics: big money. Money buys politicians to protect money, and big money buys more politicians to protect more money.

According to Joseph A. Pechman, an economist at Brookings Institution, using tax loopholes allows 6 million families with incomes under $3000 to get "tax welfare" payments of $92 million (or an average of about $15 per family), and allows 3000 families with incomes over $1 million to get "tax welfare" payments of $2.2 billion (or an average of $733,333 per family).[12] Pechman estimated in 1972 that the government would collect an additional $77 billion that year if it would tax all income at the published rates without exception.

Without exception—that's the catch. The tax statutes are riddled with exceptions. It will not happen in our lifetime, barring a miracle. For if the government were to follow Pechman's simple rule of taxation, wealthy people would have to pay an additional $13 billion a year in capital gains taxes. That may not seem like a very horrifying thought to the average person, but to the wealthy, the capital gains tax is sacred. Former Secretary of the Treasury John Connally once solemnly predicted that if the capital gains tax favoritism were ever done away with, the capitalist system would crumble, and the Western world would succumb to the powers of darkness. That's the way the rich fight to protect their pocketbooks, with all the zealousness of Christian Crusaders attacking the infidel.

Do you think that the depletion allowances that have made special empires out of the oil companies, or the export subsidies that have made multinational corporations uncontrollable could be done away with? Not so, said Nixon's former domestic adviser John Ehrlichman. Before he left in the wake of Watergate, Ehrlichman appeared on the TV program "Issues and Answers" in March 1973 and was asked by ABC announcer Herbert Kaplow: "Are you saying there can be no significant tax reform? There is no combination of loopholes that can be closed that would bring in a significant amount of additional revenue?"

To which Ehrlichman, no doubt voicing the deepest belief of President Nixon and the entire economic brain trust in power at that time, replied, "That is what I am telling you."

If the reform of the banking system is just about as difficult to undertake, at least it is a reform that has not been attempted and defeated quite as often; so it bears a welcome freshness.

One of the most commonplace concepts in other advanced countries is that the central bank should respond, or be made to respond, to the social and economic goals of the government and of the people at large. The central banks in some countries can, and do, actually veto individual bank loans unless the loans fit into the national development program. The Federal Reserve Board and the banking community that it represents have been able to resist the establishment of any such required "social allocation" of credit in this country.

Not all members of the board, however, resist this reform. One member, Andrew F. Brimmer, takes the position that regulating bank loans according to social and economic priorities is the only sure way of achieving a fair distribution of credit during periods of high interest rates and tight money.* Using 1969 as his example, Brimmer recalled that the Fed attempted to curtail the expansion of business, as one of the key steps toward curtailing inflation. To this end the Fed tightened the supply of money, which increased its price. This action temporarily demolished the

* Another board member who sounds like he might be getting in the mood to twist bank arms is Sherman J. Maisel, who in 1971 upbraided the banking community for refusing to grant loans for inner-city projects, thereby "helping to create major social and economic problems of crime, decay and segregation." Sounding very much like Ralph Nader, Maisel accused the banks of shooting for the fast buck in the suburbs, while the inner cities were "tottering on the brink of breakdown and bankruptcy." (Speech to National Conference of Christians and Jews in Omaha, Nebraska, July 11, 1971.)

housing industry and crippled many small businesses; but big business and big industry, which can absorb and pass along even the highest interest rates, went right on expanding just as rapidly as ever. The twenty largest international banks and the sixty largest regional banks felt hardly any monetary restraint, he said, for they could tap funds outside the normal channels (for example, they could borrow dollars from European sources). And their largest customers felt no restraint on either borrowing or expanding. The Fed's ostensible "control" of the money market to fight inflation was a failure where it was needed most—at the highest levels of finance—and it had an unnaturally devastating effect at the levels that had least resilience to economic retrenchments.

Brimmer's recommendation was to set a sliding schedule for the requirements of reserves, depending on the type of loans. That is, the Fed could require a low reserve or zero reserve for loans in high-priority fields, and it could set high reserves for low-priority loans. (That's the way Mexico, for example, does it.) If the banks played along with the government's social goals by lending to the right places—say, to hard-pressed local government or to the housing market—they wouldn't have to keep so much of their money out of circulation, in reserve, and it would pay them to make that kind of loan. However, if they insisted on pumping money into the expansion of big corporations, they would be forced to keep large reserves on hand and out of circulation. Says Brimmer, "Any array of loan priorities could be adopted and the reserve requirement scaled accordingly—depending on the changing needs of public policy."[13]

Fed Chairman Burns, like his predecessors, has opposed this concept. Repeatedly he has testified before congressional committees that the most valuable support the Fed can give to social priorities is to stick to its business of maintaining a "sound" dollar. When proposals similar to Brimmer's have begun to gain headway in Congress, Burns personally has launched a lobbying counteroffensive to undermine them, using the scare tactics that have succeeded so far for the Fed majority and their banker allies—that is, the argument that to allow the social needs of the country to determine the distribution of credit would be to "undermine the dollar," to "debase the dollar," to "involve the Federal Reserve Board in politics" (as though it isn't already), and to introduce a new and dangerous element of socialism into the national economy.

Typical of this sentiment was the testimony of a high official with the Mortgage Bankers Association who appeared before a Senate banking subcommittee to comment on the proposal that banks be required to take a certain percentage of the pension fund and trust fund monies they manage and invest it in the housing market at especially low interest rates. He said he was dead set against it, because if bankers allowed Congress to set the precedent of pinpointing credit for housing—which he admitted was in a sorry condition—then "we may be requiring" banks "to invest in air pollution" efforts. What makes that so horrible to contemplate? For the elite bankers who now control the nation's credit, any surrendering of their control to public interest is unthinkable.

But the big banks are not content simply to maintain their own aloofness to social issues; they are also adamantly against the government's setting up any separate credit source for "need" loans. In the last few years, several members of Congress have introduced legislation that would create a "National Development Bank"—a nonprivate banking establishment authorized not only to guarantee loans made by conventional lending institutions but also to make direct loans at low interest to finance low- and moderate-income housing, public facilities, and the kind of high-risk business ventures (as in slums) that most banks turn away. The proposed lending agency would be capitalized with $1 billion in stock subscribed by the federal government, and it would be authorized to lend twenty times that amount. This kind of money source would be a godsend not only for outfits such as public housing corporations but also for state and local governments that in recent years have had to postpone countless worthy projects because they simply could not afford to meet the high-interest demands of the ordinary commercial lender.

Obviously, this proposed government bank would not really be in competition with the commercial banks because it would be assisting customers that the commercial bankers would not be doing business with anyway. Nevertheless, the bank lobby has successfully kept this proposal from getting very far in Congress.

There are other reform proposals that make good sense. The government should strip the banks of some of their needless subsidies, starting with the no-interest checking accounts. Even a modest 2-percent interest on the $225 billion banks hold in checking accounts would put $4.5 billion into the depositors' pockets—including the pocket of the federal government, which at the present time is one of those luckless depositors.

Most important of all, the Fed itself should be restructured in such a way that its governors are directly responsible to the people's elected representatives in Congress and the White House. That can hardly be considered a radical idea when even *Fortune* magazine, the capitalists' favorite light reading, says that "the concept of the Fed as an independent body, within but not of the government, clearly needs to be modified in a period when Presidents are actively trying to guide the economy with closely coordinated fiscal and monetary policies."[14] That's *Fortune*'s way of saying, and quite rightly, that considering the Fed's spotty record, there would be little to lose if it were stripped of its independence and transformed into a political instrument through which the people could make their own mistakes.

Reforms of any nature—whether they relate to the management of the public's money or to the management of the banking system—are not likely to get far, considering the power of the bank lobby. The lobby's presence in Washington is felt in the traditional manner—through a group of lobbyists who go around buttonholing congressmen. Charls Walker, Undersecretary of the Treasury during Nixon's first term, gained his first fame as the chief lobbyist for the American Bankers Association. He transformed the ABA lobby from a stuffy "educational" organization into a crack outfit that (in the proud words of the *American Banker* newspaper) "is a force to be reckoned with on all legislative issues affecting financial institutions."

The ABA has a 320-man staff, of whom between 35 and 40 are employed in the "governmental relations" falange. Only 8 are actually registered as lobbyists, but the ABA takes a quaintly narrow view of lobbying. According to the ABA's executive secretary: "If I call one of our members and say to him, 'Call up Congressman Smith and tell him how you want him to vote on this piece of legislation'—that is lobbying. But if I call up a member and say 'Here is a piece of legislation and this is what we think about it'—that is not lobbying."[15] Under whatever guise it goes, the lobbying of the bankers costs more than $2 million a year by the ABA's own estimates and includes such refinements—so Patman claims—as detailed dossiers on the personal lives and whims and weaknesses of all members of Congress.

But that kind of pressure is insignificant—as is the blatant effort to buy votes through campaign contributions from the Bankers Political Action Committee, which in 1972 reported giving money to thirteen members of the Senate and House banking committee—compared with the pressure on Washington politicians from the sheer financial massiveness, the Great Presence, of the banking industry. Commercial banks control more than $800 billion, or almost 60 percent of all the assets in all the financial institutions in the country.

Even more awesome is the reality that this financial mass is controlled by a small number of banks that usually appear to be unified in their goals. In 1967, the House Banking and Currency Committee made a detailed study of the holdings and interlocking relationships of forty-nine of the nation's largest financial institutions—the first extensive survey of the concentration of banking power completed in this generation. The committee found that these forty-nine banks held 5 percent or more of the common stock of 147 companies listed in the *Fortune* Directory of the 500 largest United States industrial corporations.

"Interlocking directorship situations between these 49 banks and the corporations listed on the Fortune 500 largest industrials list is even more substantial," the committee report continued. "These banks hold a total of 768 interlocking directorships with 286 of the 500 largest industrial corporations in the United States. This is an average of almost three directorships for each corporation board on which bank director representation is found."

So when the elite of the banking community make their wishes known to Washington, it is apparent to all within earshot that they speak not merely for bankers but for the most powerful level of *all* industry. Seventy-five percent of the commercial bank deposits in the metropolitan New York City area, which is the financial capital of the country, are held by six banks. It is this kind of concentration, greater today than ever before but even more frightening because it has been of such long duration, that gives the following warning a special piquancy:

> The great monopoly in this country is the money monopoly. So long as that exists, our old variety and freedom and individual energy of development are out of the question. A great industrial nation is controlled by its system of credit. Our system of credit is concentrated. The growth of the nation, therefore, and all our activities are in the hands of a few men who, even if their actions be honest and intended for the public interest, are necessarily concentrated upon the great undertakings in which their own money is involved and who, necessarily, by every reason of their own limitations, chill and check and destroy genuine economic freedom.

This is the greatest question of all, and to this statesmen must address themselves with an earnest determination to serve the long future and the true liberties of man.

If one's response to that is more one of hopelessness than encouragement to do battle, one may perhaps be forgiven, for it was said by Woodrow Wilson more than fifty years ago—before the big bankers had perfected their seizure of the government's monetary program through domination of the Federal Reserve System.

The Press, Propaganda, and Enforced Ignorance

Well, when you come down to it, I don't see that a reporter could do much to a President, do you?

Dwight Eisenhower

Judging by what has usually occurred, Eisenhower was correct to think that a President need worry very little about what a reporter, a mere mouse in the White House corner, could do to him. But as President Nixon discovered, perhaps *two* reporters are a different matter. Two young reporters, Bob Woodward and Carl Bernstein of the *Washington Post*, were largely responsible for uncovering the Watergate scandal—a reporting achievement that Ben H. Bagdikian correctly appraised as "the greatest political news story of our time."

In the last few years the press has had a number of flamboyant victories. At the height of the India-Pakistan confrontation in 1972, for example, at a time when the United States was pretending to be neutral, a transcript of a secret meeting at the White House between Henry Kissinger and other Nixon advisers was leaked to columnist Jack Anderson. This transcript showed that in fact the United States was "tilting" its influence and assistance on behalf of Pakistan, a revelation that greatly embarrassed the administration.

The press also has uncovered a number of secret military ventures. Top Air Force officers were caught authorizing illegal bombing raids over North Vietnam and making fake reports of their activities. A couple of years after the press revealed the massacre by U.S. soldiers of 347 Vietnamese civilians at the hamlet called My Lai 40, the press found out about another massacre of 155 Viet civilians by U.S. soldiers that the Pentagon had tried to cover up.

And of course there was the revelation of the "Pentagon Papers," those documents leaked by Dr. Daniel Ellsberg that showed step-by-step how the United States became enmeshed in a hopeless war. It was the most important leak of confidential government documents in our history.

Inspiring as these few victories may be to the newsmen who cover Washington, most of them would agree that they are susceptible to misinterpretation. Victory is not a way of life with the Washington press corps.

Shortly after the Pentagon Papers came to light, CBS commentator Bernard Kalb asked Maxwell Taylor, "Well, what do you make, General, of the people's right to know when decisions of this dimension [getting into and escalating the Vietnam war] are taken?" Taylor replied: "I don't believe in that as a general principle. You have to talk about cases. What is a citizen going to do after reading these documents [the Pentagon Papers] that he wouldn't have done otherwise? A citizen should know those things he needs to know to be a good citizen and discharge his functions —not to get in on the secrets which simply damage his government and indirectly damage the citizen himself."[1]

It is interesting to note that Taylor, former chairman of the Joint Chiefs of Staff and also a former Ambassador to Vietnam, was selected by President Kennedy to be one of his closest advisers in foreign affairs. A liberal President is just as likely as a conservative President to suppress information. Most officials, military and civilian, at the top of the federal hierarchy share the belief that the government should tell the people only enough to make them step along briskly and discharge their "functions" for the state.

By and large those who hold to that grim doctrine are successful in forcing the press to operate within its borders. The press and the government are not equal adversaries; the government frustrates the press at almost every turn. The moral of the *New York Times'* printing of the Pentagon Papers was only that the press is free to print what it can get by luck and stealth, not that it is free to get all that the public should know. The auxiliary value of the Pentagon Papers was as a reminder to realists of just how little information the press normally gets from the government. "There are really two levels at which the press operates in Washington," said Richard Dudman, chief of the *St. Louis Post-Dispatch's* Washington bureau. "Mostly we operate at the level at which the scenario is done by government p.r. flacks. When something like the Pentagon papers comes along, you suddenly get a swift look at reality—at what's really going on in this town,"[2] most of which, tucked safely away in files all over town, neither the press nor the public will ever know about.

The manipulation of the press has been a hallmark of every administration in recent years. The federal budget openly lists more than $160 million as earmarked for public relations programs to make the government look good, and the true figure is probably much higher. HEW alone reported a 1973 p.r. budget of $20 million and a stable of 1200 public relations flacks cranking out the HEW good tidings. In September 1973, HEW Secretary Casper Weinberger vowed that he would cut his department's public relations budget by $20 million, or what he called 77 percent, with the pious explanation that "this is money that could be spent better in programs to reach the poor, the aged, and the infirm."[3] Spectators might have had more confidence in Weinberger's promise (1) if it hadn't been so plain that a very fast shuffle was going on (that is, just a few months before, the official HEW line was that $20 million was 100 percent of the budget, but here was Weinberger admitting it was only 77 percent), and (2) if his avowed concern for the poor, aged, and infirm had not been somewhat marred by the announcement in August that HEW had in fact spent $1.8 billion less than Congress earmarked for the poor, the aged, and the infirm during the preceding year. An end to puffery is always being promised by the bureaucracy, and that promise is itself the kind of puffery best guaranteed to win space in the press. In the same season as Weinberger's promise, the General Accounting Office was disclosing that the other giant puffery machine, the Pentagon, had failed to list

$48 million in public relations expenditures during fiscal 1972 and fiscal 1973.

The hope for digging beneath this surface of puffery and secrecy rests with 2400 or so reporters. But of these no more than a couple of hundred have the ability or the time (or the support of their employers) to cope with the federal politician's complex wiles. Although this elite group constitutes what is undoubtedly the finest capital press corps in the world, it is far too small to do the job that needs to be done.

The Patriotism
of Press Industrialists

The almost hopeless odds against these reporters is to a great extent the fault of the press industrialists who hire them. Most of the Washington press corps represent newspaper and television companies that are corporately comfortable and defensive of the status quo. Press industrialists do not believe, ordinarily, in hiring tough reporters to make "their" government uncomfortable or to stir the rabble to suspicions that perhaps things should be put in different hands. The First Amendment has been good to the lords of the press, it has put great wealth next to their skins, and they are going to show their gratitude by employing reporters who are content to write about the positive side of government—about contracts for new dams and about auto safety awards.*

* A notable recent exception is Mrs. Katherine Graham, publisher of the *Washington Post*. Mrs. Graham herself has often been tolerant of the stupidities of her favorite politicians. But in the case of the Watergate investigation the Nixon crowd handled her wrong. They publicly insulted her, and they insulted her paper. Clark MacGregor, then in charge of Nixon's reelection campaign, called the *Washington Post*'s stories about the White House's involvement in Watergate "malicious." White House counsel Charles Colson said the *Post*'s stories were "fantasy, a work of fiction rivaling only 'Gone With the Wind' in circulation and 'Portnoy's Complaint' for indecency." Former Attorney General John Mitchell complained to *Post* reporters Woodward and Bernstein: "All that crap! You're putting it in the paper? It's all been denied. . . . Good Christ. That's the most sickening thing I've ever heard." And he signed off the phone call, according to Bernstein, by warning that before the Nixon Administration was through, "We're going to put a certain part of your publisher's anatomy through the wringer." Additionally in private, Mrs. Graham was receiving personal insults and threats.

Enough was enough, and she decided, she says, "either I go to jail, or they go to jail."

Seldom do reporters get to benefit from such a wholesale declaration of war by a publisher.

If the press industrialists felt otherwise, the head count of their hirelings, for one thing, would be very different. There are only about a dozen reporters assigned full-time to find out how the Pentagon is spending $80 billion a year and how it is running the lives of 3 million servicemen and several million civilian employees (counting the industries supported by the military). Of newspapers west of the Appalachian Mountains, only one, the *Chicago Tribune*, assigns a full-time reporter to that mammoth beat. Only two newspapers—the *Washington Post* and the *New York Times*—assign as many as two reporters to it. Since President Kennedy's time, the Pentagon has been increasingly difficult to cover; the bureaucrats throw up new hurdles all the time. For a decade reporters have been unable to make appointments on their own and to interview officials privately. They must be "escorted" to the interviews by a Pentagon hireling, and the interview must be "monitored" by a third party. No publisher, and certainly no group of publishers, has been known to protest this restrictive procedure.

The Freedom of Information Act was passed in 1967 to permit the press to sue the government to obtain information wrongfully suppressed; as of 1971, not one publisher had used the law. Since then, several dozen have used it, but that's hardly a tidal wave of activity. Aside from the element of stinginess (lawyers cost money), there is a solid philosophical reason for such restraint. The bigwigs of any administration and the press industrialists understand each other. The patriotism of press industrialists is no different from that of any other group of industrialists, which means that their idea of serving the country is to defend all aspects of private enterprise and all necessary commercial imperialism, including the politicians who serve these best. In this regard, some scholars of American journalism contend we have retrogressed. Ben H. Bagdikian believes:

> All serious people in the news business have read about the dramatic rise of the pioneers in popular journalism, Hearst, Pulitzer, and E. W. Scripps. What most of us have forgotten is that they were persistent and enterprising protectors of the ordinary man against the status quo, against insensitive governments, utilities, and corporations.
> Today the news corporations are eminently respectable. The thousands of journalistic outlets served by the corporate descendants of Hearst, Pulitzer, and Scripps would never run the stories and editorials their founders ran; some because they are not good stories and editorials, but also because they would be too radical and would sound too hostile to corporate leadership.[4]

Publishers and politicians may have their squabbles,* but they see eye to eye on basics, such as making money and living the good life and shunning what is loosely called "radicalism." The Nixon Administration and the broadcasting companies squabble like old marrieds, but behind the cash register they find true love. As *New York Times* television critic John O'Connor has said with only slight exaggeration, "Everyone knows the networks operate from a base of undiluted greed."[5]

Any administration does big and little favors for the broadcast industrialists. It was journalistic chic to make the trip to China with Nixon, so he allowed a number of network front office big shots to go along disguised as "technicians." (There were a limited number of seats on the press planes, and all of these were supposed to be taken up by authentic newsmen or cameramen or broadcast technicians, not corporate biggies.) Network officials jump to do favors in return. In early March 1973, CBS abruptly postponed *Sticks and Bones*, a powerful and controversial drama about a blinded Vietnam war veteran whose mother, resenting his angry view of the war, encourages him to kill himself with a razor, after which his body is put in a black plastic bag and is last seen on top of a row of garbage cans. CBS claimed it backed down under affiliate station pressure, and the affiliate stations claimed they had been pressured by the Nixon Administration, which did not want the drama interfering with the fanfare surrounding the return of the prisoners of war. Whatever the reason, the broadcasters played along with the politicians.

* In 1969, in Montgomery, Alabama, Vice President Agnew denounced the "concentration of power" that was developing in the newspaper field because of the increasing number of monopolies. Yet in 1970, against the advice of the antitrust division of its own Justice Department, the Nixon Administration threw its weight (successfully) in support of legislation that allowed many newspapers to engage in monopolistic practices with total immunity from antitrust laws. As the top politicians and the barons of the press agree, politics is politics and business is business.

Agnew's constant pretense, continuing well into Nixon's second administration, that "the press" was picking on the Republican administration was something of a farce. Shortly before Nixon's landslide reelection in 1972, *Editor and Publisher* reported 548 daily newspapers for Nixon and 38 for McGovern. By circulation, it was 17,532,436 for Nixon; 1,468,223 for McGovern. In twelve states, there wasn't a single Democratic newspaper. Regarding the Nixon-Agnew complaints of being unloved by the press, Clayton Fritchey observed in the *Los Angeles Times* (September 15, 1973): "Apparently having more than 93 percent of the nation's newspapers in his corner was not enough for Mr. Nixon. It is, of course, possible to get 100 percent but only under certain kinds of government."

Throughout the summer of 1973 the Watergate hearings were shown, live, over network television. But the White House insisted that "most" Americans weren't really that interested in the scandal and that the press was overplaying it. Perhaps because CBS was sympathetic to the White House's complaints (or perhaps only because it wanted to return to its regular soap opera fare), shortly after Congress convened following its summer recess four freshmen representatives were interviewed by Walter Cronkite to get what he described as "a cross section" of opinion on what the voters back home were thinking. How keen, for instance, was their interest in Watergate? Each of the congressmen said his constituents had very little interest in Watergate. In fact, they said, the voters back home thought the Senate investigations of the scandal to be "nonsense."

But each of the congressmen chosen by Cronkite for the CBS television interview was a conservative Republican.

Tit for tat. In 1973 the administration pushed legislation that would give television and radio stations a much longer lock on their licenses and would make it much more difficult for their licenses to be challenged by "public interest" groups. The legislation would also prevent the use of "media concentration" (a newspaper owning a television station) as a basis for challenging a license. This, of course, would help dozens of owners, but outstanding among those is the *Washington Post*, whose two Florida television stations had been challenged on the grounds of media concentration as recently as 1972.*

Of the fifty largest cities in the country, twenty-three are served by monopoly newspapers, many of which also own at least one local television station and a potpourri of other corporate ventures; one must not expect them to be too interested in stories

* One might wonder—despite the Watergate revelations that the *Post* led the way in publishing—if the animosity between the *Post* and the Establishment was quite so intense as some pretended. After all, the *Post* is quite smooth about showing courtesies to the people of the Establishment. When Chief Justice Warren Burger appeared at his front door with a gun (some say it was a pistol, some say a shotgun) to greet two *Washington Post* reporters, the newspaper's executive editor, Benjamin Bradlee, decided not to print a word about that startling apparition. Top People, after all, should hide each other's dirty linen so far as is possible. Thus, too, when the Supreme Court declined to take a case in the summer of 1973 in which a woman was suing Arthur O. Sulzberger, publisher of the *New York Times*, in a paternity suit (he had already paid her $41,000 in settlement), neither the *Washington Post* nor the *New York Times* printed a word about it.

exposing corporate skulduggery.* Tom Wicker of the *New York Times*, who has an unusually sensitive conscience for an editor, asks:

> Why has it been left mostly to people outside the press to raise the great issue of consumerism in America? Until Ralph Nader came along and began making challenges . . . little of this was done. I was one of a long line of reporters hired by the *New York Times* Washington bureau to look into and cover the regulatory agencies. I can name at least eight reporters who have been in our bureau who were hired precisely to do that, and the only one who has ever done it is the man who is there now.[6]

If publishers were compelled to disclose all their financial operations the public would be better able to understand why publishers act the way they do, and why they require no more from their reporters than they do. If it is desirable that the public be told that Senator Russell Long, chairman of the Senate Finance Committee, became a millionaire through his oil holdings and might be influenced by this, it would also be desirable for the readers of the *Los Angeles Times* and other newspapers owned by the Chandler family to know that the Chandlers also own oil wells, book publishing companies, lumber companies, television stations, enormous land and farming interests, and have been directors of Santa Fe Railway, Kaiser Steel, Pan American World Airways, Safeway Stores, Security First National Bank, and Buffum's department stores—and conceivably might have been influenced from time to time as a result of these holdings.

The Hearst empire includes not only a chain of newspapers and magazines both here and in Britain, and radio and television

---

* Not only have the sins of business in general been overlooked by the press, so have the particular sins of certain business-oriented politicians and their friends. Perhaps the *Washington Post* felt a somewhat proprietary relationship with LBJ because Philip Graham, the late publisher of the *Post*, had a backstage part in the maneuverings that ended with Johnson's accepting the vice-presidential nomination in 1960. In any event, for two years before Johnson left office, the *Post* knew that LBJ's friend Robert Anderson, former Secretary of the Treasury and former Navy Secretary under Eisenhower, had benefited by several hundred thousand dollars (estimates of the bonanza vary, some ranging as high as one million dollars) in a deal with Texas oilmen. Subsequently Anderson did these oilmen a favor by helping to write the oil import program in such a way as to put about one billion dollars a year into the pockets of favored oil companies. A pretty good news story by anyone's measure. But a full detailing of Anderson's oil deal at that time would have been an embarrassment to Johnson, so the *Post* held off and did not run the story until Johnson had been out of office for two years.

stations, but also water and power companies, paper pulp companies, vast real estate in New York and San Francisco and elsewhere, book publishing houses, movie companies, and wire syndicates.

When the Scripps-Howard newspaper chain stoutly opposed federal legislation that would have benefited trucking companies, its readers might have been better able to judge the quarrel if they had known of the many close ties between Scripps-Howard and the railroad industry.

The "patriotism" of the press, especially at the top management level, has also been shown in a willingness to withhold criticism of the war policy, no matter how disastrous it was.* When the press did criticize the government it usually was for not being militarily aggressive enough or "security-conscious" enough, or for paying too much attention to the advocates of disarmament or the advocates of negotiated peace.

In mid-1973 Congressman Les Aspin (D., Wisconsin) revealed that the Columbia Broadcasting System had been involved in the bombing of Southeast Asia under a contract with the Air Force. The contract called on CBS to transmit aerial reconnaissance photos from Southeast Asia to the Pentagon. Over the previous two years CBS had earned $1 million from this contract—small stuff in the total earnings of that corporation, but could it not prove, as Aspin suggested, "potentially compromising" to CBS's news organization? And did it not show where the corporation's heart lay in terms of the war business?

Wicker has admitted the "failure of the American press" to "adequately question the assumptions, the intelligence, the whole idea of America in the world—indeed the whole idea of the world— which led this country into the Vietnam war in the 1960s. It is commonplace now, when the horse has already been stolen, to examine those assumptions. But where were we at the time we might have brought an enlightened public view to bear on that question?"[7]

Richard Harwood, a *Washington Post* editor, also acknowledged in 1971—when it was much too late to matter—that his newspaper went along willingly with the bureaucratic assumptions leading up to the war and "parroted those assumptions" and, in effect, "helped paint the administration into a corner." The news-

---

* There were a few notable exceptions. The *Chicago Tribune* opposed the early commitments in Vietnam, and the *St. Louis Post-Dispatch* opposed the war all the way.

paper followed this course not only out of ignorance and laziness but because badmouthing the North Vietnamese regime fitted "the postwar assumptions of the *Post* and the *Times* relative to the Cold War and 'collective security.' "[8]

After the 1967 march on the Pentagon, Laurence Stern, then national editor of the *Post*, complained in his column of the "ugliness" of the demonstration and dismissed the march as of no consequence. "It is doubtful," he wrote, "whether yesterday's protestors could account for more than a few small niches on a Gallup or Harris poll."

Perhaps that was true. But if so, it made all the more curious the fact that the *Post* assigned thirty-nine reporters to cover the Pentagon protest, and the *Washington Star* assigned thirty-two reporters to it, when the *Post* assigns only two reporters and the *Star* only one to cover the Pentagon on a day-to-day basis. There is probably a moral somewhere in that ratio: Washington's two hometown papers considered an ad hoc grouping of peace demonstrators fifteen and twenty times more necessary to watch for misadventures than they considered the war machine, which consumes three-quarters of the federal budget and which drew the protestors together in anger for two days.

When Senator Ernest Gruening on March 10, 1964, delivered the first speech in the Senate advocating a pull-out of our troops in Southeast Asia, neither the *Washington Post* nor the *New York Times* printed a word of his message. Reviewing this remarkable failure in 1971, Jules Witcover of the *Los Angeles Times* observed:

> This single incident tells much about the performance of the Washington press corps in covering the Vietnam war. It represents not simply the misreading of the significance of a single event; more critically, it pinpoints the breakdown of a cardinal principle of newsgathering, especially early in the war: pursuit of all points of view.
>
> While the Washington press corps in those years diligently reported what the government said about Vietnam, and questioned the inconsistencies as they arose, too few sought out opposing viewpoints and expertise until very late, when events and the prominence of the Vietnam dissent no longer could be ignored. Gruening and other early dissenters from official policy in and out of the Senate attest that they found very few attentive ears among Washington reporters in the early 1960s.[9]

Aside from being pro-war by neglect throughout all the years of the Vietnam build-up, the press was also pro-war in the contents of its stories and airwaves programs.

Of the 1967 CBS documentary "Vietnam Perspective: Air War in the North," Dr. Erik Barnouw noted that while it ignored the horrors of guava bombs and napalm it "was full of administration rationales, punctuated with marvelous shots of hardware in action and the rhapsody of roars that went with it. It referred to civilian deaths, but 'civilians are always killed in war,' said the narrator."[10] Michael Arlen concluded in his *New Yorker* review that the tone of this documentary conveyed the feeling that "CBS is another branch of the government, or of the military, or both."

From the beginning, the Nixon Administration, knowing the networks' flashpoint of fright, bore down heavily and was rewarded with network self-censorship. Vice President Spiro Agnew damned the networks publicly for being too liberal, and Senator Robert Dole, chairman of the Republican National Committee, denounced them for being not only too liberal but too "antiwar." A few days after Agnew got in his first licks, Washington was besieged by a crowd variously estimated at from 250,000 to 500,000 people. "It was one of the largest crowds in the history of the United States," FCC Commissioner Nicholas Johnson observed later, "and everyone was there, it seemed, except the President and the network newsmen. They had blacked it out. Picking up the spirit of the times, ABC Sports banned halftime coverage of the Buffalo-Holy Cross football game because it had to do with the 'controversial' subject of peace but provided a nationwide audience for the chairman of the Joint Chiefs of Staff to say a few words on behalf of war at the halftime of the Army-Navy game."[11] But no network could match CBS for its patriotism: it blanked out the face of Abbie Hoffman because he appeared on a talk show wearing a shirt made from the American flag, and censored Carol Burnett's request that her audience send peace letters to Coretta King.

Individual members of the Establishment press who did reach for opposing viewpoints were sometimes persecuted by their colleagues. In 1967 Harrison Salisbury, an assistant managing editor of the *Times*, became the first "Western" correspondent allowed to visit North Vietnam. His dispatches were as fair and accurate as possible, considering that his travels within the country were circumscribed and that much of the information he received came from Hanoi officials who were trying to put the best face on their side. Salisbury reported that, contrary to government claims, our planes were killing and wounding many civilians and destroying their homes.

A number of influential segments of the press in this country immediately questioned Salisbury's patriotism.* The *Washington Post* discredited his casualty figures because they corresponded with those found in a "Communist propaganda pamphlet" (the *Wall Street Journal* later charged that the Pentagon planted that story with the *Post*). William Randolph Hearst, Jr., wrote that the Salisbury-type stories reminded him of the treasonable broadcasts of Lord Haw Haw and Tokyo Rose during the Second World War. Crosby Noyes, foreign editor of the *Washington Star*, denounced reporters such as Salisbury for their "utter lack of identification . . . with what the government defines as the national interest." Chalmers Roberts of the *Washington Post* called Salisbury an "instrument" of Ho Chi Minh.

Publishers and editors have shown themselves so willing to be the handmaiden of the government that officials have quite naturally come to think of not only publishers and editors in that way but reporters too. Irritated by surprisingly tough questions from one newsman, Secretary of State Dean Rusk interrupted a news conference to ask angrily, "Whose side are you on, anyway?" President Kennedy sometimes asked, without blushing, that newsmen exercise self-censorship. Johnson frequently implied that newsmen who veered from simply printing administration handouts on the war and on foreign policy were "aiding the enemy."

Seldom have federal politicians had to be so grumpy as that to get cooperation at the publisher's level, for most publishers get their patriotic kick stifling brink-of-war stories, or stories showing that what the "Commie enemy" claimed was an undercover conspiracy on our part was, indeed, an undercover conspiracy. In November 1960, Carey McWilliams, editor of the *Nation*, learned that the next issue of *Hispanic American Report* was to contain an article by Ronald Hilton, then director of Stanford's Institute of Hispanic American and Luso-Brazilian Studies, in which he reported that the CIA was training Cuban exiles at a hidden base in Guatemala. The "secret" was well known to Guatemalans, according to Hilton, as was the purpose of the training.

McWilliams phoned Dr. Hilton for further details and wrote an editorial for the November 19 issue of the *Nation* in which he outlined the upcoming cloak-and-dagger adventure and urged that the rumor "be checked immediately by all U.S. news media with correspondents in Guatemala." The *Nation* sent seventy-five proofs

* For more on this, see James Aaronson, *The Press and the Cold War* (Indianapolis: Bobbs-Merrill, 1971).

of that editorial to the major news centers of New York, including the wire services and the *Times*, with no results. April 7, nearly five months after the *Nation's* editorial, the *Times* printed its own account of the pending military experiment, but by this time it was too late to reverse the disastrous chain of events leading to the Bay of Pigs. And even in its April 7 story, the *Times* withheld information it had on the involvement of the CIA and the nearness of the invasion date.

After the debacle, it was discovered that the *Miami Herald* had also withheld a story of the pending invasion—written and set aside at about the same time the *Nation* was trying to alert the press—and that the *New Republic* had written an exposé one month prior to the invasion that was killed by the publisher, Gilbert Harrison, at the request of the White House. The *Times*, the *Miami Herald*, and the *New Republic* obviously saw themselves as an adjunct of the government and as a supporter, through silence, of government propaganda, for the State Department was issuing lies on the hour in an effort to hide the gambit.

As it turned out, the press's patriotism was as stupid as the government's policy-making. Even Kennedy admitted it, telling Turner Catledge, then the *Times'* managing editor, "If you had printed more about the operation, you would have saved us from a colossal mistake." Perhaps it was even more colossal than Kennedy realized. Observers both within and without the government (Walter Lippmann among the latter) have seriously proposed that one reason Kennedy stepped up our intrusion into Vietnam was to prove that just because he had bungled the Cuba thing didn't mean he should be considered a "push-over."[12]

How to Keep a Reporter Down

When the Washington press corps isn't being sold out by management, and when it isn't being opiated by star-spangled orthodoxies, and when it isn't being cannibalized by envious peers, and when it isn't exhausting itself chasing politicians who are out of town on four-day weekends and bureaucrats who are out of the office on three-hour lunches, there are still other handicaps.

Secrets and more secrets.   In the eyes of the antipublic bureaucrat or politician, the best technique for keeping information secret is to achieve this end without actually denying public access to it. One method is to charge exorbitant fees for copies of certain material. Many documents that reporters—or any other citizens, for that matter—are interested in are much too long and complex and voluminous to read right on the spot. It's the kind of stuff that a reporter needs to take back to the office and mull over for hours to see just what it contains. To get it out of the government office means, of course, buying a copy—and that's where the crafty government official ups the price tag in order to turn the reporter away. The Maritime Institute has been known to ask $12,000 for information about ships bought by the government from private owners. It's quite common for bureaucratic agencies to charge as much as $1 a page for duplicating public documents, enough to freeze all but the most uncommon curiosity. Congressman Wayne Hays of Ohio, angered because newsmen were going to the congressional bookkeeping offices and discovering what extravagant salaries congressmen were paying their favorite secretaries, at first ordered that such information only be released at $1 a page. When that didn't inhibit snooping newsmen, he got such information placed off limits entirely.

But the most impressive device for keeping the public from finding out what's going on is simply the rubber stamp that transforms ordinary information into "Secret" or "Confidential" or "Eyes Only" or some other cloak-and-dagger pigeonhole. The mentality behind this gimmickry is, of course, most elaborately displayed at the Central Intelligence Agency. Congressman Edward I. Koch of New York tells of attending a breakfast with other freshmen congressmen at the CIA when Richard Helms was its director. "It was a very good breakfast," Koch recalls, "on gold service no less, and afterward Mr. Helms said to us in a friendly way, 'Gentlemen, this is the only time you'll ever have to ask questions about our work, so ask.' " Whereupon Koch asked two simple questions: What was the CIA's budget? How many men were employed by the CIA? Helms responded, "These are two questions I can't answer."[13]

In 1971 a study of the Defense Department, the State Department, the Atomic Energy Commission, and the National Aeronautics and Space Administration showed that just the mechanism of stamping documents "Secret" and maintaining them in some sort of hush-hush condition costs the four agencies $60 million a year.

Probably more than 90 percent of the papers in the State Department are classified. In the Pentagon, estimates of the classified documents are roughly (such guesses have to be rough) in the range of 200 million pages, some of the classified documents going back to the Civil War. Documents marked "Secret" are the commonest thing in town. It has reached a point of total absurdity, as brief glimpses behind the curtain show. In 1973 the United States Information Agency declassified seventy-seven "highly sensitive" studies that included such red-hot documents as "Opinions and Values of Egyptian Students in West Germany" and "Media Habits of Spanish Intellectuals."[14]

It used to be that "Top Secret" was as secret as one could get in Washington. But the inflamed imagination of the bureaucrats changed that. A White House aide, acting on orders from Nixon to try to straighten out the absurdities of the classification system, poked around in the files for eighteen months and found thirty-eight security classifications that supposedly designated conditions more secret than top secret. As for the written instructions he received from the President at the time he went to work on the project, that innocent document was stamped with forty-five security classifications. If government officials took that designation seriously, and if they were able to maintain an effective security lid on all secrets, the press might as well go out of business. But, as Congressman F. Edward Hébert said with considerable exaggeration, "I don't think you can keep a secret in Washington if you told it to your mirror." Things aren't that loose, but there is enough laxness of security to at least give the impression of news "coverage."

The fact is, however, that very few of the secrets are obtained by the press through its own digging. Most of the important ones (including, of course, the Pentagon Papers) are handed to the press. Officials who believe that it is in the best interest of the country to divulge what their colleagues want to keep hidden, officials who are in a policy dispute with their boss or others in government, officials who are seeking revenge—these are common sources of secrets.

Robert Walters, a *Washington Star* reporter, puts the "drama" of digging for secrets in this perspective:

> Investigative reporting to a great extent is a fraud, and newspapers and the public should realize it and start from there. When the Department of Justice wants to go out after a guy, it has subpoena power, it has task forces of unlimited numbers, it has the FBI which can walk into any bank in the country and flash a badge and a warrant and say, "Let's see this guy's account." Newspapers have none of that. More often than not they have one guy working on a story. And if it's a really big deal they have three or four or five, but almost never more than that. So it's *not* investigating.

The *New York Times* says that Neil Sheehan's "investigative reporting" got the Pentagon papers. Actually, as everybody knows, Daniel Ellsberg got unhappy and *dumped* the stuff on the *Times.* Which is fine. But that's how newspapers get most of their best stories, not by investigative reporting. We shouldn't foist off on the public the idea that our reporters are out getting stuff that *nobody* wants them to have. Somebody, somewhere, wants you to have it before you'll get it.[15]

It is no accident that columnist Jack Anderson is surfeited with classified information, nor is it any special credit to his industriousness. The reason people in and out of government leak information to him is that his column is syndicated in seven hundred newspapers across the country. Nor is it accidental when the *Wall Street Journal* winds up with the best leaks on insider trading among Penn Central executives, or that the *Washington Post* and the *New York Times* get the most fulsome leaks regarding State Department and Pentagon policies. These things are the result of the basic law of leak physics: secrets always seek the outlet of greatest impact.

Why aren't more leaks addressed to the *New York Daily News,* which has the largest circulation in the country? Because a big circulation does not always mean a big impact. Very few of the 2 million people who read the *Daily News* are among Washington's policy-makers. The *Washington Post* and the *New York Times* are must reading for policy-makers in the Pentagon and State Department, so that's where foreign affairs and military leaks get impact.

Two dangers accompany the leak system. First of all, it makes the press extremely vulnerable to being used—"used" in the sense that it becomes a tool for self-serving politicians and bureaucrats.

Every year just before the deadline for filing income taxes, a raft of newspaper stories appear that are designed to frighten the taxpayer into paying up promptly. The stories don't appear by accident. They are planted by the Internal Revenue Service. When the fright stories began to be published in the spring of 1973, the *Wall Street Journal* explained:

> The IRS's motive in promoting stories of tax fraud investigations isn't a general desire to keep the public well-informed. Rather, the articles are the IRS's way of instilling fear in potential tax cheats that they might live to regret any misdeeds. An internal IRS policy manual that recently became available to the *Wall Street Journal* spells out detailed procedures for seeking optimum news coverage

of IRS enforcement activities. The IRS calls this coverage "deterrent publicity."[16]

One sidelight of the Watergate scandal revealed a bogus "leak" that did not quite succeed. White House aides put together a phony State Department cable allegedly showing that the late President Kennedy had been guilty of complicity in the murder of President Ngo Dinh Diem of South Vietnam. Then the White House aides got in touch with William G. Lambert, a well-known reporter for *Life* who had worked with government officials on other leaked information. This time, however, the leak didn't smell quite right to Lambert, and he didn't use it. Those who work closely with the White House are not always so lucky.

Stewart Alsop recalls writing a piece for the *Saturday Evening Post* on what he called "Kennedy's Grand Design," in which he quoted President Kennedy directly as saying, in reference to the Soviet Union, "we might have to strike first." He submitted the article for Kennedy's editing, and not only did the President read it, but so did McGeorge Bundy and Pierre Salinger. They approved the article. But later, when the Russians became outraged by this threat, the White House brigade pretended innocence. "There was a hell of a row about it at the time," says Alsop. "I never have been able to make up my mind whether I was being used or not. I still have the suspicion that I was used. And I still feel it is a bad thing for a journalist to submit his copy to anybody, including the President."[17]

Columnist Tom Braden, who was a high official in the CIA in the late 1940s and early 1950s, says one of the most adroit uses of the press was in setting up the CIA. The way he tells it, General William J. ("Wild Bill") Donovan, head of the wartime Office of Strategic Services, wanted to get President Truman and Congress to make the OSS a permanent organization. He put together a public relations outfit to start turning out propaganda about how heroic that spy outfit had been and how swell it would be if it were a permanent thing. "I worked on the project," says Braden. "I was back from Europe waiting to get out of the Army. I sat there and wrote reams of stories about the secret OSS operation in Europe. As fast as I'd finish with a secret document, Donovan would de-classify the information. The newspapers were absolutely full of our stuff. By the time you got through reading the *New York Times, and* the *Readers Digest, and* the *Saturday Evening Post, and* you saw the movie they got Corey Ford to make—the

OSS, which had been nothing but a couple of paragraphs in Drew Pearson's column, became the hero of World War II. It was all a calculated effort through the press."[*18]

The second major danger of the leak system is that if a newspaper gets some of its most potent news by being favored as the conduit of an administration, officials will inevitably begin to feel that that newspaper is a part of the administration. And very often the favored newspapers act as though they reciprocate the feeling. It isn't unusual for favored reporters to do some writing on the side for politicians who slip them information. This risky habit goes back at least to the days when Colonel George Harvey was earning $75,000 a year as the chief editorial writer of the *Washington Post* at the same time he was writing speeches on the sly for Presidents Harding and Coolidge. Sometimes it was difficult to tell the speeches from the editorials, and vice versa.

Washington columnists, few of whom have much enthusiasm for digging up material on their own, are notoriously used for political leaks. Indeed, most of the columnists depend for their living on leakers, and sometimes they become as jealous as schoolgirls at a dance when rival columnists are chosen for the favored leaks. Thus when Jack Anderson disclosed secret White House transcripts showing the duplicity of our government during the India-Pakistan confrontation in 1972, columnist Joseph Kraft, who likes leaks just as much as Anderson, pouted and complained about how "the man who leaked the stuff . . . has done this country a disservice."[19] Such prissy feuding does little to advance the cause of vigorous journalism.

An auxiliary corruption, seldom noticed by the public but widely felt in the Washington press corps, is a corruption of the spirit of competition. The interplay of the top Eastern newspapers with the government discourages some of the excellent reporters whose only sin is in working for newspapers of the "wrong" geography. If reporters for the non-Eastern elite press are unable to open doors because of their lack of status, to that degree—and it is a serious degree—the size of the Washington press corps is effec-

---

* As will happen, these leaks were combated by counterleaks. J. Edgar Hoover, who feared that Donovan's outfit would compete with the FBI, leaked to the *Chicago Tribune* copies of Donovan's memos to the White House, and these were written about in such a way as to make it seem that Donovan had in mind setting up a super-spy network on the *domestic* scene. Hoover's leaks were not able to prevent the establishment of the CIA, but they were successful in blocking Donovan from heading the new agency.

tively reduced, and its power is effectively cut. By favoring the *Washington Post* and the *New York Times*, as they do, federal officials have (although probably not by design) dealt a blow to the rest of the press corps.

Thomas Ross, head of the Washington bureau of the *Chicago Sun-Times*, the nation's fifth largest morning newspaper, says:

> Frankly, even in this administration, which supposedly is having a blood feud with the Eastern Establishment press, that's the only press they read and that's the only press they seem to think exists. When they want to leak a story, my feeling is that they still leak it to the *Times* and the *Post*. I can't recall once in the fifteen or so years I've been in Washington that I've been used for a calculated leak by the government. Anything which I've got, I've got by blood, sweat, and tears.
>
> Consistently we produce three, four, five times a week an important story out of this bureau that is not produced by the *Times* or *Post*. The usual pattern is that the story will sit in the *Sun-Times* until somebody points it out to the *Times* and *Post*, and then they will write it and at that point it becomes an important story. Until that point, it might as well not have been written—so far as Washington is concerned.
>
> I have worked on stories where I felt I had it exclusively, and I was laboriously building up details, and then when I felt I was approaching the point where I could sit down and write it, the next day I would see it all laid out in the *Times*, although I had had a sense from personal conversations with that [*Times*] reporter that he hadn't known anything about it the day before. One often assumes that the decision was made (in government) to lay it out in the *Times* in a way they wanted it laid out.[20]

With variations, Ross's sentiments are repeated by many good reporters in Washington.

The backgrounder.   Of the same genre as the leak is the "backgrounder" or the "don't quote me" session, which can be employed either in a massive press conference or on an individual basis. The only requirement is that the spokesman remain anonymous.

These sessions, if not abused, can be highly useful to newsmen because they enable officials to speak candidly without feeling that they will be pounced on by their colleagues or the public the next day and lacerated for their views. Given the justifiable timidity of most politicians and public officials when discussing controversial topics, off-the-record interviews are a necessity.

All the same, they are extremely risky. If they benefit the official by not subjecting him to abuse for telling the truth, they also benefit the official by not subjecting him to abuse for lying or misleading. If he is of a mind to do so, he can use the off-the-record interviews as a way to peddle his pet theories, improve his own public image, tout a program, spitefully undermine his opponents in government, and propagandize for dangerous foreign policies—and do this without revealing what he is up to.

On this point James Reston has written (probably from experience):

> The power of the President to use the free press against itself is . . . very great. If, for example, an influential columnist or commentator criticizes him for landing 23,000 Marines in the Dominican Republic to put down a rebellion, it is very easy for him to call in several other carefully selected commentators and give them the detailed argument for landing the Marines. He has all the vivid facts of the situation, and if he wants to put them out, he does not have to announce them himself. Other reporters will be perfectly willing to accommodate him, even though they know they are being used to knock down the story of a colleague.[21]

In January 1964 newsmen on hand at the Texas White House were told in a background news conference that President Johnson would absolutely be unable to hold the next federal budget below $100 billion. And that's the way the reporters wrote their stories, attributing their information only to "a high White House source."

A few days later Johnson submitted his budget to Congress. It was for $97.7 billion. Recalling that incident, *Newsweek*'s White House reporter, Charles Roberts, wrote unhappily, "That was a breathtaking $3 billion to $4 billion under what the President and his aides had held out as an irreducible minimum. *Voilà!* Mr. Johnson looked like a fiscal Houdini—and the press, which had been used, looked ridiculous."[22]

One method of handling the background session is that employed by Richard Dudman of the *St. Louis Post-Dispatch*, who does not have a high regard for information obtained in this way and believes the public should get a clue to the self-serving motivations of the officials who hold the backgrounders. Dudman usually writes it this way: "A high official who refused to be identified because he did not want to be held accountable for his remarks indicated that he wanted reporters to write," etc., etc., with the background information following.

The best, and simplest, remedy for the backgrounder was discovered by the *Washington Post* in December 1971. With the flash of common sense that sometimes passes for genius, its editors decided they would no longer participate in backgrounders.

This decision came about when Nixon's foreign adviser Henry Kissinger, while flying back from the Azores on the President's jet, sat down with a five-member "pool" of reporters representing another eighty-eight newsmen who were traveling on two separate planes and chatted with them about Soviet-American relations. He asked the reporters to identify him in their dispatches only as "a White House official" or "the White House." But the *Post* refused to go along with this ritual. It identified Kissinger as Kissinger, arguing that "almost one hundred newspaper reporters knew who was speaking; the Russians knew, and also the Indians, and before the night was out anybody in town with the slightest interest in the question would know, so why not the readers of the *Post*? . . . Is this a game a newspaper ought to be playing?" The *Post* answered no, and its managing editor vowed publicly "to get this newspaper once and for all out of the business of distributing the party line of any official of any government without identifying that official and that government."[23]

The shouts of anguish from the White House and accusations of betrayal from official Washington continued for weeks. But some who had been in and out of the White House experience and could view it with objective hindsight agreed that the *Post* had taken the right step. Among these was Bill Moyers, former press secretary to President Johnson and later publisher of *Newsday*, who commented in the *New York Times* (January 6, 1972): "The backgrounder permits the press and the government to sleep together, even procreate, without getting married or having to accept responsibility for any offspring. It's the public on whose doorstep orphans of deceptive information and misleading allegations are left, while the press and the government roll their eyes innocently and exclaim: '*non mea culpa!*' I know. I used to do a little seducing myself. The objects of this chase—members of the Washington press corps—were all consenting adults." (When Nixon's press secretary, Ron Ziegler, was told what Moyers had said, he remarked: "That's the way he used it. It's not the way we use it. If that's the way he used it, that's very interesting." The deep crust of sanctimonious piety does not begin falling away to reveal candor until one has left the White House.)

Delays and more delays. Although Washington is headquarters for the most centralized major government in the world, a reporter seeking data that could embarrass the bureaucracy may discover that the government has become suspiciously decentralized as soon as he places his question. "Oh, *that* information," he will be told, "isn't in this office. The only place you can get that is in our regional office in Atlanta," or Denver or Jacksonville or Chicago—anywhere away from Washington.

The regulatory agencies often tell reporters that they do not keep data on such things as travel expenses, costs of investigations, complaints from consumers, or the sales volume and profits of corporations accused of breaking the law. Even if it is evident on the face of it that they are lying, what is a reporter going to do about it?

For instance, some government agencies and businesses regularly engage in illegal bugging of offices and homes and tapping of telephones. When these violations are discovered, they are supposed to be reported to the Federal Communications Commission. When Curtis B. Plummer, the FCC's chief of the field engineering bureau, was asked by reporters how many illegal bugs and taps are found each year, he said the FCC doesn't keep such statistics. Later, confronted with evidence showing that in fact the agency does keep the data, Plummer simply shrugged, said okay, so the figures are kept, but "it's none of the press's business."

In that kind of a situation, how can reporters fight back? If convinced that the agency does in fact have the data being sought, they can sue under the Freedom of Information Act to have it produced.* But this technique is extremely time-consuming and uncertain, at best.

The consumption of time is (next to secrecy) a government's best way to keep the press at bay. Many topics are too timely to survive a long delay.

Immediately after the *New York Times* began printing the Pentagon Papers, Lloyd Norman, *Newsweek*'s Pentagon reporter, asked the Department of Defense for a list of the names of people who had been disciplined over the years for violating security laws. The DOD began mumbling excuses, and Norman snapped back: "Don't you guys know, by God, who in your organizations have committed serious violations of security? I'm not talking about the piddling stuff where somebody forgets to lock his safe. I mean

---

* The true value of the Freedom of Information Act was demonstrated in an ironic fashion when Congress convened in 1971. The House Government Operations Committee, which wrote the Freedom of Information Act, voted to bar the press and public from its organizational meeting, and Representative John E. Moss, author of the 1967 law that is supposed to open the flow of information from the executive branch, was among those voting for secrecy. That's the prevailing attitude in Washington: let the free access to information begin somewhere *else*.

serious stuff, where somebody has taken documents out and given them to somebody." For the next two weeks the Pentagon information officers kept telling him that the stuff was being compiled; then, three weeks after he had made his request, they changed their story and said, sorry, they didn't have the information after all. They suggested he go to the Justice Department.[24] From the bureaucrat's position, the delay had served its purpose: even if he could have obtained the information, by that time the story was dead.

The exception trap.   The Freedom of Information Act is supposed to make all important government material available to "responsible" people. The key exceptions to this law are information that might endanger the national security or foreign policy and information that would give away "trade secrets" or financial information (proprietary information) relating to private industry doing business with the government.

Lockheed Aircraft overspent by $200 million in the building of the giant C–5A Galaxy transport. Where did the extra costs come from? Where did the money go? Was Lockheed siphoning off defense money into nondefense work? The Joint Economic Committee of Congress attempted to get answers to these questions from the Pentagon, but the Pentagon refused to make public the data needed to develop the answers on the grounds that this was Lockheed's proprietary information—that is, a "trade secret." Congress later guaranteed a $250-million loan to Lockheed without being supplied this or any other information to indicate what sort of risk Congress was taking with the people's money.

The "trade secret" ploy is one of the most abused maneuvers approved by the Freedom of Information Act. Consumer advocate Ralph Nader points out:

> First of all, there is no way to determine what a trade secret is. In California, pesticide information sought by migrant workers is considered a trade secret by the Department of Agriculture in California. It thinks that if the migrant workers are told how much is applied per acre, this would be telling competitors. The more I look into the trade secret area, the more I realize that it isn't a trade secret between competitors—they know all about it—it's a trade secret against consumers or against the public. The classic example of this is the trade secret in pollution. Companies don't want to tell the federal government how much they're dumping into the rivers and lakes and into the air because it would be a "trade secret." Now, a trade secret in lethality is going a little too far.[25]

Sweet talk and threats. For newsmen, sweet talk and little favors, pats on the head and a swim with Himself, are much more dangerous than threats. Could the *Washington Post* view the LBJ claque with the same critical objectivity after Johnson appointed one of the paper's editors to be ambassador to the UN? How critically could Jack Bell, chief political writer and chief of the Senate staff for the Associated Press, view the career of Senator Everett Dirksen of Illinois after Dirksen wrote a highly laudatory foreword for Bell's book *The Presidency: Office of Power*? Could the Hearst papers be quite as objective about President Kennedy after he used one of their top reporters as his personal go-between in negotiations with Haiti and after he gave such favored treatment to one of the Hearst reporters, Marianne Means, that her good fortune became the topic for a *Time* magazine article? Kennedy's canny friendships with the most influential journalists was legendary. "I always had the feeling," says columnist Rowland Evans, "when I was writing about President Kennedy that he was standing right there behind me, watching the words come and waiting to bore in. No question about it, friendship with a President can be a burden on a reporter's professionalism."[26]

It is the problem of the reporter who gets caught up in the swirl of the officialdom he is supposed to be watching, the reporter who thinks he is important because he had lunch at a posh restaurant with a top-echelon politician, the reporter who gets by with calling Senator Edward Kennedy "Teddy"—it's acknowledged to be one of the most crippling of professional diseases.

"When a reporter falls for the messiah complex," says Jerry Greene, chief of the *New York Daily News* bureau, "and when his complex combines with that of a bureaucrat who thinks he is important, Christ, you need a shovel to clean the room. Send a young reporter to the White House and let him indulge in a Presidential trip or two and he isn't worth a damn for six months. He gets on a first-name basis with these clowns, he gets to indulge in fancy drinks and big hotel rooms that he couldn't otherwise afford, and he's wiped out."[27]

The old-timers are just as vulnerable to the chummy syndrome. Mingling with the mighty does something to them. They operate from the Olympian heights, and they perceive the rabble below through the heady fog that comes from being on a first-name basis with Henry Kissinger. They associate with the people who are making the news in a cordial backroom atmosphere, and amidst the laughter and clinking of glassses they begin to see things the way their sources see them.

A certain amount of probing and criticism is tolerated in this arrangement. A top official will allow newsmen who are close and friendly to disagree within accepted limits. Even to criticize him within accepted limits. That's part of the game. But the official sets the limits—and to this extent his reporter pals are corrupted. The reporter who must cover one beat regularly or cover one congressional delegation is subjected to what are perhaps even more relentless demands to string along. Robert Walters elaborated:

> You get invited to the agency's parties. Not that the bureaucrats are consciously trying to co-opt you. They just want to get to know you better and make you feel more kindly toward them. But then if you get into a shoving match with them over some story, you get the stick instead of the carrot. You not only don't get invited to the parties, what's more important you don't get invited to the background briefings. The same goes for reporters covering for Wyoming or Nebraska or Connecticut papers at the Capitol. It becomes a totally symbiotic relationship.
>
> If you go to enough congressional parties and talk with enough drunk administrative aides and legislative aides, you sure enough find out quick where a senator's faults are, which special interests he's responsive to, and how they repay him. But it's suicide to the hick reporters if they write it. Their congressional offices just cut them off with no more tips on what's going to happen. I don't know of any cases where that's actually happened, but I know that small newspaper reporters fear it, and they just won't write tough stories about the politicians they regularly cover for exactly that reason.[28]

Johnson thought he knew how to coddle and threaten the White House press corps. He gave 374 individual interviews in his first fifteen months of office (by comparison, Nixon gave none), and he thought surely the press must love him as a result; when he found out it didn't, he tried other methods. On one occasion the White House press plane was mysteriously diverted to a field other than the one the President's plane had landed at, and the newsmen were left to catch up with him any way they could. Some had to hitchhike aboard a garbage truck. A reporter who wrote about Johnson as a "people eater"—meaning one whose ego and demands devoured those around him—was told he would not get to speak to Johnson again until he had written a nice story to cancel out the other. Occasionally, a White House reporter who was dictating a story on the telephone would be startled by Johnson's breaking in on the line and criticizing something the reporter was telling his home office. He had been eavesdropping.

Pique, even presidential pique, seldom has the frightening effect on the press that officialdom desires. Except, of course, with the television and radio networks. They are, of all the news media, the most easily frightened. Panic is a normal condition for them. They have their excuses, but they are only excuses. Bill Monroe, one of Washington's editors for NBC, argues that their fears are justified because the Federal Communications Commission, which has life and death powers over all radio and television stations, "has a Democratic majority when a Democrat is in the White House and a Republican majority when a Republican is in the White House. So it is a board with a certain political tone to it that is guiding television editors on certain decisions in areas where no government body would dare tell newspaper editors what to do. Under these circumstances, is television a free element of a free press? No, it is not. Where it gets FCC guidance, it is a captive of seven men who owe their jobs to the White House."[29]

If ever a fear was based on the flimsiest hypothesis, this one that hovers around television business offices certainly is. None of the hundreds of TV stations—neither those owned by networks, nor those owned by others—has ever lost its license because of its news coverage. But the very thought of risking one of those golden licenses for something as transient as a hard-hitting news story turns the corporate heart to Jell-O. And as long as this is true, the politicians of the day will take advantage of it.

The big boys in government are beginning to play rougher. Leslie Whitten, who helps Jack Anderson write his column, was arrested in 1973 by the FBI and charged with receiving, concealing, and retaining three boxes of government documents. The government later dropped the charges because, as the FBI agents knew very well at the time of the arrest, the documents had been stolen by somebody else, and Whitten, in fact, was on his way to return them to the FBI. The government sleuths were simply harassing the press.

One of the most publicized jobs of harassment occurred in late 1971 when the White House asked the FBI to investigate CBS correspondent Daniel Schorr. He had recently made a number of TV appearances with news breaks that embarrassed the administration. One of these newscasts had even prompted President Nixon to publicly call him a liar. On the pretext that it wanted to offer Schorr a job, the White House unleashed the FBI agents on his trail—interviewing all the top officials at CBS, asking (but not getting) to see his personnel file, interviewing neighbors and friends—

seriously interfering with Schorr's professional and private life. Of course, there was no job awaiting Schorr, nor was any ever offered.

Unhappy about the success of some newsmen in uncovering stories that the administration wanted to keep hidden, President Nixon in 1971 personally approved setting up a special group of secret police nicknamed "the plumbers" to plug news leaks. Their techniques, again approved by Nixon, included tapping several newsmen's telephone lines. CBS White House correspondent Dan Rather's home files were burglarized—and he, with good cause, suspects it was an official job.

When several newspapers began printing the Pentagon Papers, the Nixon Administration obtained a temporary injunction prohibiting the newspapers from continuing to publish these documents. For fifteen days that restraint was in effect before the Supreme Court lifted the ban. The press claimed a victory, but in fact it was a chilling defeat: for the first time in our nation's history American newspapers had been restrained by a court order from printing the news. "Even though the restraint lasted only for 15 days," said Harding Bancroft, executive vice president of the *New York Times*, "an extremely unfortunate precedent has been established."

The Public Broadcasting Corporation, the stepfather of educational television, had allowed so many controversial—and innovative and truly educational—programs to go on the air in recent years that the Nixon Administration began to look on it as a mouthpiece for the enemy and cut its financial water down to a trickle. It was easily done: the President simply vetoed a $155-million appropriation. To make ends meet, and to try to make peace with the White House, PBS dropped several programs unpopular with the administration, including the highly original but somewhat iconoclastic "The Great American Dream Machine."

Lies and more lies.   Most officials tell the truth most of the time, but their record for veracity drops off dramatically when questions begin touching important nerve centers. Furthermore, it is an operational rule to expect all officials to lie or play ignorant when to do otherwise would be to inconvenience themselves or to disturb their work. Given the character and perspective of most politicians and public officials, it is probably natural that they act in this way. Their first objective is to survive in office, and they feel that the best way to survive is to duck criticism, to shift the blame to others, to sidestep hot issues, to always have a cartload of excuses and alibis ready in case of emergency. This is simply the protective coloration of the official animal—chartreuse, combining the natural hues of ambition and fear.

Examples of lying are so numerous, especially in foreign affairs, that reporters often despair of having it otherwise and ask only that the lies be flamboyant ones that make good copy. No modern President supplied more of that type than Johnson did.

One of his most elaborate falsehoods was spun in an effort to win public support for his invasion of the Dominican Republic. On April 23, 1965, there was a revolt in that country. When President Johnson sent in the Marines, newsmen intimately familiar with the workings of our State Department and with the situation in the Dominican Republic wrote that our fighters were sent to prevent a communist coup. The State Department denied this, and so did President Johnson, both insisting that the only reason Marine and Army personnel were sent to the Caribbean nation was to protect American citizens living or visiting there. To make his point, President Johnson told a news conference on May 5 that "there has been almost constant firing on our American Embassy. As we talked to Ambassador Bennett [on the phone], he said to apparently one of the girls who brought him a cable, he said, please get away from the window, that glass is going to cut your head, because the glass had been shattered, and we heard the bullets coming through the office where he was sitting while talking to us." By June 17, Johnson had really warmed up to the subject: he held another news conference in which he further explained his intervention: ". . . some 1,500 innocent people were murdered and shot, and their heads cut off, and as we talked to our ambassador to confirm the horror and tragedy and the unbelievable fact that they were firing on Americans and the American Embassy, he was talking to us from under a desk while bullets were going through his windows and he had a thousand American men, women, and children assembled in the hotel who were pleading with their President for help to preserve their lives."

None of this was true. William Tapley Bennett, Jr., who had been the ambassador under siege, later told reporters that no bullets came through his office, nor did he take cover under his desk, nor were there any beheadings, nor were any American citizens harmed—or even threatened. In fact, the only two American citizens hurt during the revolt were two newsmen shot down without provocation by our own Marines.

For marathon lying, or at least blinking at the truth, President Nixon probably holds the record. For a ten-month stretch after the Watergate burglary, Nixon either personally or through his aides denied that he or his White House staff was aware of, much less privy to the preparations for, the whole complex of political skulduggery known collectively as Watergate. He also denied for ten months that the White House had participated in a cover-up of the scandal.

Finally, when the pretense obviously could be kept up no longer, Nixon's press aide announced that all previous denials were "inoperative"—as nice a word as was ever concocted to wipe out ten months of false information.

Nixon was also loose with the truth in foreign affairs. On his instructions, the Air Force indulged in 3630 secret bombing sorties over Cambodia during a fourteen-month period in 1969 and 1970. After this took place, Nixon told Congress that "we have respected Cambodia's neutrality for the past five years." He sent a faked report to Congress to support this claim and to hide the bombing raids. Not until 1973 did the truth come out.

One of the more candid fellows to pass through government in recent years was Arthur Sylvester, Assistant Secretary of Defense for Public Affairs under Kennedy and Johnson. His two most famous declarations were (1) "The government has the right to lie," and (2) "Look, if you think any American official is going to tell you the truth, then you're stupid. Did you hear that?— *stupid*."[30]

Sylvester made the second statement after reporters had caught Defense Department officials lying again, and he was arguing that it was no big deal. Stinging him to this outburst of candor was one of the smaller victories achieved by the Washington press corps. Even the small ones are counted, however, because victories of any kind are scattered, spasmodic, often incomplete, always costly in time and sometimes in money. Although the capital's newsmen are outwitted far more often than they outwit, they have done enough to make this the Era of the Press. Never before have newsmen had such a profound impact on government. Far more than most Americans probably realize, the foreign policy and most certainly the economic and social reform policies of the past dozen years have been shaped by names that many people in Peoria have likely never heard of: Jack Nelson, Robert Walters, Richard Dudman, Nick Kotz, Walter Pincus, Seymour Hersh, Carl Bernstein, Bob Woodward, Judith Randal, William Greider, Mary Russell, Mike Causey, Fred Zimmerman, to name a few of the newsmen who, even on their off days, have been zealous enough to make politicians blush and bureaucrats sweat and all to promise that they will reform at least a little.

New Power
to the People,
Maybe

*The common denominator in any definition of pressure groups
is interest; if the interest is* special *or* vested,
the pressure is venal, but if the interest is public,
*the pressure is benevolent. "We call them 'interest groups'
when we are feeling clinical," writes historian Clinton Rossiter,
" 'pressure groups' when we are feeling critical, and 'lobbies'
when we are watching them at work in our fifty-one capitals."*

William Safire, The New Language of Politics

For most Americans, making a distinction be-
tween the phrases *special interest* and *public interest*, between
pressure group and *lobby*, is the kind of gamesmanship that
belongs to a more leisurely age. Americans have become much
more casual about language, and much more intense about their
needs. They don't care what the political activity is called, as long
as it produces results that pay off well in their lives. Lord Acton's
most famous remark—that power corrupts, and absolute power
corrupts absolutely, refers to a corruption that the typical American

need not fear will tempt him. What he should be more reasonably concerned with is the opposite and just as accurate truism—that lack of power corrupts, and absolute lack of power corrupts absolutely. Arrogance is no more corrupting on one end than desperation on the other.

When William Kunstler, the famed civil rights lawyer, took the position that "nothing will change anything in this country until the people go into the streets" (meaning nothing as simplistic as throwing stones and molotov cocktails, but getting deeply and personally *involved*) he spoke for one side in the most significant and lasting tension in a democracy: some are trying to spread power over the widest possible base, others are trying to gather it into the hands of a select few. At its worst—and it often does seem to vacillate between two worsts—this is a choice between broad incompetence and narrow venality, venality in the sense that the public trust is perverted to benefit the "right people."

One reason some of the more boisterous populists have turned to matches and axes and dynamite for their political expression may be that the voting route, and dependency on politicians and bureaucrats, seems so futile. Since it took six years under the Highway Beautification Act to get one billboard removed through official channels, it does seem rather reasonable—whatever the morality of the action—for a band of University of Michigan students to make midnight forays with axe and saw and topple dozens of billboards. More legitimate shortcuts have wide public support.

Statistics show why people are beginning to release their political feelings and find their political heroes outside the traditional channels of politics. Thirty-nine million adults did not vote in 1960. Forty-three million did not vote in 1964. Forty-seven million—40 percent of our eligible voting-age population—did not vote in the 1968 presidential election. The slump continued in 1972: sixty-two million people, about 45 percent of the electorate, stayed home in an election shaped by negative reactions. ABC commentator Harry Reasoner correctly appraised the 1972 election as presenting most voters with the choice of "whether they were more depressed by Nixon than scared by McGovern." Were the stay-at-homes the most eloquent citizens, after all?*

* George Will, Washington editor of the *National Review*, makes a meritorious proposal on this point: "I think a word should be said on behalf of those who do not vote because they intelligently decide against it. We must accept no philosophy which does not let us respect the little old lady who, when asked whom she intended to vote for, said: 'I *never* vote. It only encourages 'em.' " (*Washington Post*, January 19, 1973.)

The feeling of inefficacy is, rather naturally, followed by a feeling of political lethargy. If there is little that the public can do to shape national affairs, why fill the head with the raw material of those affairs—no matter how jazzy they may be. In mid-1973, after the first two weeks of television coverage of the Senate investigation into the Watergate scandal, CBS reported that the mail from its viewers showed only 27 percent supporting the expensive live coverage, 30 percent denouncing it as a crude anti-Republican plot, and 24 percent calling it a bore. (The other letter-writers didn't make enough sense to categorize.) Thus 54 percent of those feeling strongly enough about the coverage to write to the network would have preferred not to know what was going on.

That may not be a fair sampling of the national attitude, but it is accurate enough to suggest that the political field has become dangerously overgrown and tangled with weeds. Is an informed and energetic electorate still possible?

They've heard all the pep talks of democracy, and now they're hearing them again. John Gardner:

> What difference does one vote make? It can make a lot. In most elections, those who fail to vote could have changed the result had they gone to the polls. For every vote in Richard Nixon's plurality over Hubert Humphrey in 1968, 150 people did not vote. The 1960 presidential election was decided by less than one vote per precinct. In 1962, the governorship of Minnesota was decided by 91 votes out of more than one million cast. The outcome of the 1968 U.S. Senate election in Oregon turned on four-tenths of one percent of the 814,000 votes cast. Local races—for mayor, for city council, for school board—have sometimes been decided by a single vote.[1]

The persuasiveness of that argument depends very much on convincing the people that there is a significant difference in how the opposing candidates could perform and would want to perform. With recent national elections and many state elections fresh in their minds, that is something the people will not easily be convinced of.

Even among people who are not extremists of either right or left, there are profound doubts, for example, that the Republican party stands for conservatism and that the Democratic party advocates more than a very cautious liberalism (although it unquestionably did a generation ago). The moguls of Big Labor and Big Industry move back and forth across the demilitarized zone, like Red Cross units carrying money-plasma between the supposedly warring parties. The same George Meany who walked the

White House rose garden paths with Lyndon Johnson is, a couple of years later, swinging his deals at the Burning Tree Golf Course with Richard Nixon. Meanwhile, the working stiff is left to figure out how he fits in. (Only after the Watergate scandals made daily headlines was Meany embarrassed into ending his dalliance with the GOP.)

And what about the right-winger? Where is his candidate? He had thought that Nixon promised no détente with Communist China, no devaluation of the dollar, no more deficit spending, no arms deals with Russia. But if those were the things Nixon promised the right wing, it got snookered. And if he was not the right wing's candidate, who could be? Congressman John Ashbrook of Ohio tried to fill the role in 1972, but he got no publicity and less campaign money. And who, in the last half-dozen presidential elections, has been the candidate of the small farmer? The small businessman? The lower–middle-class American or the fixed-income American who cannot bend to economic fluctuations?

Even if there were national candidates who promised to champion the causes of the average American, there is little historical evidence to show that majority votes have had a decisively creative hand in the biggest issues. As Frank Trippett, the political writer, pointed out in *The Intellectual Digest* (December 1972):

> None of the major changes in our society took place because of elections. Take the Volstead Act—both its passage and its repeal—take women's suffrage, or the coming of the New Deal. Nobody "voted in" the New Deal. Fiscally, Roosevelt's 1932 platform was conservative. He accused Herbert Hoover of spending too much.
>
> Just as nobody "voted in" the New Deal, the New Deal government didn't "govern out" the Great Depression it strove so hard to overcome. That particular social ailment was cured only by the enormous production effort demanded by World War II—which also was scarcely a consequence of popular mandate.
>
> Examples of the irrelevance of elections to crucial tides and events are easy to turn up. What may be the biggest social event of the last 20 years—the outlawing of racial segregation in schools—resulted from nobody's vote or election. And elections hardly started the related black liberation or civil rights movement.
>
> No election stopped it either. It was stopped by the Vietnam war, which students generally credit with also wrecking the economy.
>
> So what carried us into a big undeclared war? Did anyone vote for Lyndon Johnson to start it? Obviously not. And who would have voted for Richard Nixon to keep it going except someone with foreknowledge that his fervent promise to stop it was hollow?

This is a point made by many astute political writers. William Chapman of the *Washington Post* notes that the most important events of Nixon's first administration—his visits to China and Russia, his prolongation of the war in Vietnam and the invasion of Cambodia, his attempt to radically upgrade the welfare policy, his institution of wage-and-price controls—could not possibly have been foreseen by the voters in 1968. Chapman also points out that other actions that affected almost every household in the United States— such as raising the price of milk—were generally *not* brought about by the expression of preference on the part of the voters or even by the expression of their representatives in Congress but by an administrative wave of the wand. As Chapman concludes: "The point isn't that these decisions were good or bad, fair or arbitrary. The point is that busing and milk prices and wars are the things people worry about but can't seem to influence. An accumulation of these experiences, over a period of time, produces a widespread feeling of political inefficacy."[2]

But even if the riptides of history have responded more often to the influence of the moon than to the influence of the voters, that hardly gives politicians the right to treat the electorate with such contempt.

Campaign Conmanship and Political Propaganda

Many polls have been taken to show voter indifference; no studies have ever been done of voter intelligence. But it could not possibly be as low as the politicians seem to assume, judging by the quality of their campaign propaganda. During the 1972 presidential campaign, a number of "surrogate candidates"—so-called because they spoke for Nixon by proxy—accused Democratic candidate George McGovern of unpatriotic treachery simply because he proposed reducing the military budget by $20 billion. Even with the reduction the Pentagon would have been left with enough money to maintain a standing army, update its air force, and keep handy twenty times the number of nuclear arms needed to blow up any potential enemy nation. During the 1970 campaign, advertisements placed in sixty-one newspapers accused eight Democrats —Senators Joseph Tydings. Edmund Muskie, Gale McGee, Joseph Montoya, Harrison Williams, Lawton Chiles, John Tunney, and Adlai Stevenson III—of being "extremists" and "radicals." Most of the men on the list would qualify only as the most orthodox kind of liberal; not one is in the slightest degree radical. The advertisements were paid for by the Republican National Committee and approved by the White House.

The quality of the content of political propaganda is quite in keeping with the witless extravagance of the propaganda budget. In the most extensive study of campaign spending ever undertaken, the Citizen's Research Foundation of Princeton found that the total bill for all races in 1968 was at least $300 million.[3] (Since secrecy is the chief characteristic of campaign spending, it took the Citizen's Research Foundation nearly three years to put together its findings, and even then they were incomplete.) In only four years, campaign spending had jumped 50 percent. The costs of the 1972 election are estimated to exceed $400 million. Nixon managed to raise at least $60 million—according to the best calculations and guesses available to the General Accounting Office a year after the campaign had ended—while challenger McGovern was collecting about $21 million. Nixon's top 154 backers gave that much.

The campaign spending law that Congress passed in 1971 did not take effect until April 7, 1972, leaving the incumbent administration in a position throughout 1971 and the spring of 1972 to shovel in funds with its high-pressure brazenness. Much of Nixon's funds were raised by "assessing" wealthy individuals, especially corporate executives, a certain amount of their income—a kind of tithing to that old-time religion called *quid pro quo*. Could there perhaps have been a connection between, say, the $100,000 that officials of the American Ship Building Company gave Nixon in 1972 and the $5 million the company was trying to collect from the government in cost overruns? Or a connection between the oil industry's $5 million contributions to Nixon's 1972 presidential campaign and the price and tax favoritism by which the Nixon Administration further enriched the oil industry.

The voter is free to let his one-dollar contribution compete for the attention of the politician who is being distracted by the enormous slush funds provided by wealthy businessmen, industrialists, big unions, big corporations. Although some seats in the House of Representatives can still be won, or held on to, with a campaign fund of $25,000, and although one can still win a Senate seat from a sparsely settled state like South Dakota with no more than $150,000, since the postwar advent of television it is also becoming commonplace for a House seat to cost half a million dollars and a Senate seat to cost $5 million. Let the "average voter,"

whoever that may be, try to buy a noticeable pile of chips in that game. National politics has become the domain of financial kings.*
There are other ways to conduct campaigns. The British prohibit the purchasing of television time for political advertising. Each major party in Britain is allotted free time. Former Federal Communications Commissioner Nicholas Johnson suggested something of the same sort for this country; he would require radio and TV broadcasters to reserve one-third of their prime evening time for what he calls "non-common-denominator programing"— interesting stuff, perhaps even important stuff, something hopefully that touches existence a bit more solidly than "All in the Family." Some of this time would be sold and some given away to politicians during campaign periods. The rest of the year, politics might even be presented on a more realistic level than what one columnist called the "Hunt the Radiclib Game," which requires the voter to believe that the allegations that "Senator A raised money for Candidate B, who spoke at the dinner of Organization C, which gave $25 to the Panthers' Defense Fund, proves that Senator A is a transvestite traitor to flag and country."

Granted, simply having such programs on the air will not guarantee that the public will watch them, but there is considerable evidence that many people would watch almost anything—even political programs—rather than turn the machine off. In any event, it would give the voter a choice he does not now have: whether or not to learn something about those windy fellows who are spending more than $250 billion of his money in Washington.

If at present the rhetoric has little variety, one reason is that there is so little real competition. In many races there is none at all. In 1970, according to the National Committee for an Effective

---

* Money does not mean *everything*. Some of the biggest spenders in Senate races in 1970, as, for example, Norton Simon in California and Richard Ottinger in New York, didn't make it. Also, a Federal Communications Commission survey in New York in 1970 showed that in fifteen New York congressional races the candidate who spent the most for radio and television advertising lost the election. In 1972, John Kerry lost his congressional race in Massachusetts to Paul Cronin, a Republican, while outspending Cronin $279,746 to $171,414. In Arizona, congressional candidate Jack Brown spent $318,254 and lost to Republican John Conlan, spending $154,662. In California, Roger Boas, Democrat, spent $266,760 in his congressional race but was beaten by William Maillard, $148,550. And in one of the most celebrated contests, challenger Allard Lowenstein spent $285,475 and yet failed by a wide margin (28 to 53.9 percent) to unseat Congressman John Rooney of New York, who spent only $110,054.

Congress, there were 402 members of the House of Representatives running for reelection, and 279 were unopposed in the primary. That's 69.4 percent. Two years later, 385 were running for reelection, and 247 were unopposed in the primary: 61.4 percent. Only thirteen of those running for reelection in 1972 lost, and three of the losers were running against other incumbents because of redistricting. This study emphasizes the lack of intra-party competition in the primary because in some sections of the country, notably the South, if the incumbent gets past the primary without competition then he gets a free ride back to Washington; the opposition party seldom shows up with any strength in the general election. From 1950 to 1970, 88 percent of committee chairmen in the House came from essentially one-party districts.[4]

Where there is a choice, there will be, sooner or later, change of some kind, and the *availability* of change is an important prerequisite for peace in the streets. Or at least that's the opinion of The National Commission on the Causes and Prevention of Violence. The commission warned in its report: "To resist necessary and healthy change in today's America is to invite social tumult. . . . Our history is filled with examples of the powerless determined to bring their grievances to a just hearing."[5] Irving Howe, in *Beyond the New Left*, claims that it was the presence of Eugene McCarthy and Robert Kennedy in the 1968 campaign that kept the streets quiet. As long as those two were in the race, the young radicals and liberals turned away from violence and stayed with standard electoral politics, he says. But when Kennedy was killed and McCarthy was eliminated at Chicago, "moods of despair swept across the campus and the New Left could transform these moods into disillusionment with liberal politics in particular and the idea of liberalism in general." And out of this disillusionment came "a strange mixture of Guevarist fantasia, residual Stalinism, anarchist braggadocio, and homemade tough-guy methods"[6]— everything from campus rioting to blowing up Bank of America branches to dynamiting one of the men's rooms in the United States Capitol.

The New Electorate

But flying bricks and falling plaster eventually become as boringly nonproductive as politics of no choice. So when the Twenty-sixth Amendment to the Constitution was ratified in 1971 (enfranchising eighteen-year-olds), many young people decided to give standard politics one more chance and began registering and organizing in droves. Many, however, stayed away from the registration office and did not vote. They were, in short, typical citizens—or a bit atypical in being even more lethargic.

There had been, of course, much speculation about what the new vote would mean. After all, it could have had a significant impact. If it had been carried to its ultimate, there would have been another 25.7 million men and women in the eighteen to twenty-four age group going to the polls in 1972 who had never voted before (11 million in the eighteen to twenty category, and 14 million in the twenty-one to twenty-four age group who were too young to vote in 1968).

The ideological and partisan direction of the new vote had been a matter of keen interest. In January 1971, pollster Louis Harris took three separate surveys that added up to this picture of the differences in attitudes between persons eighteen to twenty years old and persons over fifty:[7]

	Those in favor	
	18–20-year-olds	Over 50
Spend more on pollution control	90%	75%
Help blacks achieve equality faster	60	41
Get all U.S. troops out of Vietnam by the end of 1971	76	52
U.S. and Soviet Union should explore space jointly	75	48
Increase federal programs to help the poor	70	55
Approve desegregation of schools now	60	47
Student protests are healthy sign	54	21
Rate Nixon good-excellent	39	51
College corrupts students on drugs and pornography	38	63
Abolish welfare and make recipients go to work	37	47
College presidents too lenient with protesters	34	69
Rate Agnew good-excellent	27	47

That looked like a sizable generation gap, but other surveys narrowed it. The American Council of Education, after questioning 169,000 college freshmen, concluded that few were "far out" (only one in twenty described himself as "leftist" or "rightist"). The Gallup poll in 1971 found that only 7 percent of college students viewed themselves as "far left" and only 17 percent as "right" or "far right," while the great majority classified themselves as moderate progressives (30 percent "left" and 41 percent "middle of the road").*

Of course, neither partisan nor ideological labeling means very much in a practical sense unless it is translated into the ballot. And as it turned out, the new "wave" of young voters didn't produce a very loud surf. Fewer than half (48 percent) of the eighteen to twenty age group voted in 1972—about 15 percent less than the population as a whole; of the total 25.7 million in the eighteen to twenty-four group, only about 12 million voted, again less than half. The division between Democratic and Republican turnout in the youth vote was just about 50-50. Consequently, as the Census Bureau pointed out at the time, the youth vote had no impact on the presidential election.

Polls showed that the young voter on campus was subject to the same pendulum swings that beset his elders. As the nation drifted slightly to the right, so drifted the campus electorate. In 1973 a new study conducted by the American Council on Education, polling 188,900 freshmen, showed that about two-thirds viewed themselves as "middle of the road" or "conservative," while fewer than one-third called themselves "liberals." Questioned on specifics, the students backed up their new conservatism rather consistently: one-fourth believed that a college has a right to ban extremist speakers; one-third would give college officials the right to "clear" student publications; and almost one-half felt that colleges have been too easy on student protesters. Self-interest prevails on campus, as elsewhere. With the end of the military draft, many students were immediately deradicalized.

People's Lobbies

As might be expected, many who desire reform most zealously are beginning to withhold their support from either major party and are putting their faith in ad hoc organizations of "the people" themselves—people's lobbies.

* Polls of that sort mean little unless those being polled are willing to play the game of self-categorization. Doubtless, many of the young, seeing where that kind of senseless labeling has taken their elders, were rather lukewarm to the questioning. After all, is a person to be considered "liberal" or "conservative" if he is offended by the building, with federal highway funds, of a four-lane driveway for a Jones & Laughlin steel plant in Illinois when the federal government cannot even meet its school lunch obligations?

On campuses, there seemed to be at least as much interest in supporting public-interest research and advocacy groups as there was in supporting political candidates. By the beginning of the spring term, 1973, more than 350,000 college students had enrolled in these public-interest research groups (called PIRGs, a Ralph Nader program). More to the point, they were contributing money to hire full-time scientists, lawyers, and community organizers for the consumer and environmental fights. Around the nation, PIRG units could claim credit for forcing the U.S. Forest Service to stop the timber-cutting in the Boundary Water Canoe territory along the Canadian border; uncovering fraudulent advertising in Oregon; spotlighting the harmful effects of new highway construction in some areas of Vermont; filing a lawsuit, which the Massachusetts attorney general joined, to overturn state procedures for setting utility rates; working with Missouri labor unions for stiffer enforcement of occupational and safety laws.

Both on and off campus, the phenomenon of tougher citizenship is cropping up, sometimes in the most unlikely places, and in all degrees of rebelliousness. In Alabama, a fishermen's organization sued 216 companies, the Secretary of the Army, the director of the Corps of Engineers, and the Alabama Water Improvement Commission for polluting their streams so much that the bass had fled. In Kentucky, residents of the eastern part of the state were, after several years' lull, beginning to break out the guns again to chase away the strip miners. True, it came from a feeling of desperation, not exultation or power. When Warren Wright of Southern Mountain heard the bulldozers were coming back, he got his gun, saying: "I had to make up my mind whether to go up that hill. I knew what the consequences could be. Once you go up there you can never back down or they've got you forever." He went, and neighbors went with him.

In the mid-1950s the highway lobby sold Memphis, Tennessee, officials on the idea of building an expressway through the middle of Overton Park, a 342-acre area that was regionally famed for its wildlife, its zoo, and its oak-hickory forest. But neighbors of the park, led by Ms. Anona Stoner, now in her seventies, fought back with lawsuits. So stubborn and persuasive were they that in January 1973, as his last act as U.S. Transportation Secretary, John Volpe ruled that the park-killing expressway was a lousy idea and would not get the $18 million subsidies necessary for its completion.

Citizens living near the north branch of the Chicago River

became so appalled by its condition that they forced the U.S. Army Corps of Engineers to lay aside its boondoggle work for the moment—no small victory in itself—and help them clean up the river. By mid-1973 it was done. Their success could be physically measured in the 3,720,000 pounds of man-made rubbish they had dredged from the river, including 1000 shopping carts, 150 picnic tables, an automobile, a station wagon, a complete telephone pole with four cross arms, 12 wheelbarrows, 2 motorcycles, 30 bicycles, dozens of wagons, 4 pay telephones, a full barrel of beer, parking meters, a traffic light signal with pole, a cattle tank, air conditioners, traffic signs, railroad ties, tires, steel fencing and snow fences, a flag from the seventh hole of a golf course, a sofa, chairs, beds, bed springs, refrigerators, hot-water tanks, gas stoves, washers and driers, a hub from a wagon wheel (antique), lawn mowers, 2 rowboats, dead animals, a military bayonet, and an assortment of guns. At one point on this earth, man had begun to dig his way out of his own filth.

In Connecticut, a citizens' tax revolt had put some politicians in fear of their personal safety; a special session of the legislature was called in an effort to smooth things over. In Portland, Oregon, homeowners and conservationists were successfully stalling the construction of a jetport on the shore of the Columbia River. The nationwide conservation movement was drawing so much participation from politicians, heartfelt or otherwise, that former Congressman Richard L. Ottinger observed wryly: "Unanimity raises the danger of a new kind of pollution—a form of pollution that may be the greatest threat of all—political pollution. It could undermine all the concern that has been focused and mobilized in this new movement. When you find Nixon, Rockefeller, and Reagan on your side, you know you're in trouble."[8] That go-to-hell attitude was no front. Many had it. Giving up her job as chairwoman of the New York State Consumer Protection Board, Betty Furness cited the hopelessness of trying to deal with a legislature and said, "I think there is a great deal to be said for the Ralph Nader approach—to stand outside and holler at everybody." When Fred Harris quit the U.S. Senate in 1973, he set up a public-interest group aimed at reforming tax laws. When George Romney quit the Nixon Cabinet in 1973, he also said the system wasn't meeting the problems, and he wanted eventually to set up a public-interest group to goose the politicians.

Standing outside and hollering in Washington were all sorts of specialty outfits—antiwar, antidraft, for fair taxation, for women's liberation, for more money for cities, antipollution of all sorts, for modernizing Congress, for auto safety, for mine safety, for legal abortion, for prison reforms—the list is a long one. Some, such as the National Urban Coalition, the National Committee for an Effective Congress, and Common Cause, are big and well financed, while other lobbies can hardly afford a Xerox machine.

If publicity is any measure, the most potent of the new flock of lobbies is Common Cause, founded in 1970 by John Gardner, former Secretary of Health, Education, and Welfare and former president of the Carnegie Foundation. In 1973 Common Cause claimed to have 220,000 members. Because of his weighty Establishment background, and because of the Establishment source of funds on which Common Cause had to rely (including Ford Motor Company, Time Inc., Amalgamated Bank of New York, Allied Chemical Corporation), many thought Gardner would run a useless organization that would prove to be little more than an adjunct to the normal political machinery. He did better than that. And if talk counts, he does talk like a maverick. "People," he says, "have a wholly unrealistic notion of the power of the President or of any elected official. If you replaced 10 percent of the officials with the best people in the country, which would change a lot [of office-holders], and got the best possible President, it would still make very little difference toward fixing the things that are wrong. By the time they are elected, they've had to make their deals and the man is molded to the system. . . . To make the system work, you've got to be a little outside, on the sidelines."[9]

Common Cause puts out a slick, well-researched newsletter lobbying for the toughest issues before Congress, and the language of the lobbying pitch is often anything but moderate. Some congressmen belittle Common Cause's efforts, claiming that the letter-writing campaigns it initiates in target congressional districts are anything but persuasive. But other congressmen concede they are influenced.* For the last several years, beginning in 1971 and continuing into 1974, Common Cause has been suing both major political parties for election law violations. Representative Wayne Hays, chairman of the committee that drafted the new law requiring the filing of campaign contributions by a certain deadline, was

---

* Some congressmen belittle letters from any source. But those are the fellows with the safe districts and the monolithic states. More would understand why Senator Clinton Anderson of New Mexico changed his position on the SST. At first he supported it, but when his desk piled up with anti-SST letters he shifted from yes to no.

one candidate who had failed to obey that law. When Common Cause called this to the press's attention, Hays immediately used his authority to increase the price of Xerox copies of the official reports from ten cents a page to $1 a page. It was another technique to keep records of campaign contributions away from the public, for no private citizen and few public-interest groups could afford to pay that price to get the hundreds of thousands of sheets involved in a survey. Common Cause sued the Clerk of the House and forced a rollback to the old ten-cent price. No small victory.

In short, the courts have been rediscovered by the militant reformers. Changes that would take years to push through a reluctant Congress have sometimes been achieved in months through the courts. This recourse has given the people's lobbyists a bright new cockiness, the kind heard in a speech by Victor Yannacone at Michigan State University in 1970. Representing the environmental section of the American Trial Lawyers Association, Yannacone (who handled some of the landmark antipollution cases himself) reminded and urged the students:

> This land does not belong to General Motors, Ford, or Chrysler; this land does not belong to Consolidated Edison, Commonwealth Edison, or any other private investor-owned utility company; this land does not belong to Penn-Central, B&O, C&O, Union Pacific, Southern Pacific, or any other railroad; this land does not belong to American Airlines, United Airlines, TWA, or any common carrier; this land does not belong to Minnesota Mining and Manufacturing Company, Minneapolis Honeywell, IBM, Xerox, Eastman Kodak, Polaroid, or any other company marketing technological marvels; this land does not belong to International Paper Company, Scott Paper, Boise Cascade, Weyerhaeuser, Crown Zellerbach, or any other paper products company; this land does not belong to United States Steel, Bethlehem Steel, Inland Steel, Crucible Steel, or any other steel company; this land does not belong to Anaconda, Kennecott, Alcoa, or any other nonferrous metal company; this land does not belong to any soulless corporation!
>
> This land does not belong to the ICC, FPC, FCC, AEC, TVA, FDA, USDA, BLM, Forest Service, Fish and Wildlife Service, or any other federal or state alphabet agency!
>
> This land does not belong to the President of the United States, the Congress of the United States, the governor of any state, or the legislatures of the fifty states. This land belongs to its people. This land belongs to you and this land belongs to me.
>
> Don't just sit there like lambs waiting for the slaughter, or canaries waiting to see if the mine shaft is really safe. Don't just sit around talking about the environmental crisis, or worse yet, just listening to others talk about it.
>
> Don't just sit there and bitch. Sue somebody!

All across the country the bright, militant pro-people lawyers are doing just that. More important than whatever substantive successes these attorneys achieve is their demonstration that success is not always dependent on being backed by a great deal of wealth or a powerful industry. They have proved that one man—if he is sharp enough and stubborn enough—can oppose the whole Establishment and win.

This was the great lesson passed on by Ralph Nader. Nader has become such an institution himself that people tend to forget that when he first took the measure of Detroit in his book *Unsafe at Any Speed,* in 1965, he was known only among the most limited circle of safety buffs in Washington. He had no standing in the world of science or letters, and the publisher that put the book out had never had a successful book on the market before and had never had a profitable year. Even after the book became a best-seller, it still took Nader a couple of years of hard plugging to become even tentatively established as *the* consumer advocate. To be sure, he got important assistance from the Washington press corps, which took a liking to the tough young man, and he eventually got the financial backing of several wealthy businessmen, but for the most part Nader's achievement was a tour de force of individual determination. To a nation grown accustomed to thinking that nothing less than a committee could have an impact on government, this was inspiration indeed.

Like all successes that begin with the "purity" of the individual and spread into organizational efforts, Nader's work by 1973 had some mild signs of corporate disease itself. He sat at the top of an empire of organizations—Center for Study of Responsive Law, Center for Concerned Engineering, Clearinghouse for Professional Responsibility, Public Citizens Inc., Professionals for Auto Safety, Aviation Consumer Action Project, Action for Blue-Collar Workers, Corporate Accountability Research Group, Consumer Action for Improved Foods, Center for Auto Safety, Public Interest Research Group, Fishermen's Clear Water Action Project, among others—for which he gives public relations direction, selects the personnel, solicits the subsidies, and acts as symbol. But the actual research and writing of reports is mostly left to gung-ho young people, few of whom have either Nader's talent or his concern for precision, accuracy, and balance. The work they do has been important, but none of it has compared with the work Nader did when he was starting out, working alone. And none of the legislation to which the Nader followers have contributed has had the impact of the auto safety legislation that Nader's book was largely responsible for passing. That in itself is monument enough to the work of one man, as evidenced by the fact that between 1966 and 1973, 36 million motor vehicles had been recalled by the auto makers as "unsafe."

Unfortunately, Nader's stardom as consumer advocate drew away much of the attention that should have been given to a number of other young attorneys. They got some headlines, but not what they deserved. John Banzhaf, for example, at the ripe old revolutionary age of twenty-seven, forced the television networks to surrender time worth millions of dollars for the running of anti-smoking ads. In fact, Banzhaf is the lawyer who forced cigarette ads off TV and radio.

Weren't the cigarette companies urging Americans to participate in a debatable activity? And didn't the Federal Communications Commission, under its "fairness doctrine," require that the networks present both sides of controversial questions? Banzhaf sat down one night at his home in the Bronx in New York City and addressed these questions to the FCC in a three-page letter. That was the simple way it began.

Eventually, the FCC agreed with him and issued orders to the networks to give up a "significant amount" of time for the presentation of antismoking ads. This ruling cost the networks about $75 million a year in broadcast time. And partly because the antismoking ads—prepared by the American Cancer Society and the American Heart Association—were so devastatingly effective, the smoking commercials were banned from the air entirely as of January 1971.

By one measure, Banzhaf's victory was something of a miracle. After all, who would suppose that an unknown lawyer could dash off a letter to one of those impervious government agencies and wind up not only getting its cooperation but crushing a corner of Madison Avenue? But the moral of the story, or at least the moral that Banzhaf and his type of attorney would convey, is that the accomplishment should not be thought of as a miracle; it should be considered as an object lesson in the fact that the average citizen, if he knows how to use it, has more power at his disposal than he imagines. Banzhaf says:

> We are having trouble with young people, because they are convinced that they can't beat the system. So either they withdraw via drugs, or they turn to extralegal activities, taking to the streets, burning and rioting and bombing. I'm trying to show them that

with many problems something can be done within the system. If I can win against the billion-dollar cigarette lobby, if Ralph Nader can take on the auto companies and win, if my students on a part-time basis can take on the ad agencies, the Federal Trade Commission, the Federal Communications Commission, the retail credit associations—it shows there are untapped resources within the system that the young can try.[10]

By "my students" Banzhaf meant those studying under him at the George Washington Law School in Washington, D.C. He teaches primarily through experience—urging students to find some governmental or corporate villain to sue. The student crusaders are fond of acronyms. SOUP (Students Opposing Unfair Practices) petitioned the Federal Trade Commission to make the Campbell Soup Company quit putting marbles in its soup for TV commercials. The marbles forced the "alphabet" pieces to the top and made it look as if there were more of them than actually existed. Since then, the company has quit the practice.

Without instruction, the average citizen is not equipped to handle complex legal battles with government agencies or with large corporations. There is no handy-dandy kit to instruct an outraged citizen on how to sue Gulf Oil Company, say, for advertising clean restrooms and then not supplying them. But collectively, pooling their resources, any beleaguered group can afford a good lawyer and a court fight.

Probably the most amazing court fight waged by citizens' groups this generation was in the effort to prevent the construction of an oil pipeline from the northern to the southern coast of Alaska, a distance of about eight hundred miles. The poorly financed citizens' organizations lost the fight, but when one considers that they kept it going for years in a powerful way, despite the bitter opposition of the largest oil companies in the world, plus the opposition of the Nixon Administration and a majority of the members of Congress, the achievement begins to take shape.

The oil companies are Standard Oil, British Petroleum, Atlantic-Richfield, Mobil, Phillips, Union, and Amerada Hess. That's a corporate gang of such muscle as to make most citizens' knees turn to water at the thought of bucking them. But when they started to build the trans-Alaska pipeline, citizens' groups—The Wilderness Society, Friends of the Earth, and the Environmental Defense Fund —filed suit to stop them. The conservationists based their suit on the National Environmental Policy Act of 1969, which requires the federal government to justify the exploitation of federal lands with an "environmental impact" statement showing that a project balances out on the side of public good. The oil companies argued that America needed the oil. The environmentalist organizations argued that the pipeline would cross earthquake-prone territory and numerous rivers, risking land-spoiling spills and harm to fish and wildlife. When the oil reached a south Alaska port, it would then be carried by tanker to the United States. The environmentalists argued that there were bound to be many harmful spills en route.

Losing in the courts, the oil companies finally had to ask Congress for special legislation to get them off the hook and to salvage their multimillion-dollar investments in Alaska. But the fight was so brutal it was not likely that the oil companies would treat their Alaskan terrain as frivolously as they might have done otherwise.

One of the public-interest groups in that lawsuit, the Environmental Defense Fund, is worth special mention as an example of how the movement is growing. When the EDF came into being in 1967, it consisted of two people—Victor Yannacone and Charles F. Wurster, a chemist at the State University of New York. From a modest beginning (they were just trying to get a mosquito control board to stop spraying DDT on Long Island) EDF has grown to an influential body of interlocking interests. Today it can call on several hundred scientists and dozens of attorneys across the country to help prepare its cases.

So impressive was the work of these public-interest law firms the Internal Revenue Service announced in the autumn of 1970 that it was suspending their tax exemptions and might do so permanently. Why? Some observers thought the answer was rather plain. The *Washington Post* editorialized:

> The impact is clear. Since many of the firms take cases for which there is no pay, they must rely on grants and gifts; but since the IRS now says the donations are not tax deductible, the water is cut off. Benefactors will look elsewhere to give their money. . . . Who is behind it? . . . It is no secret that major corporations, already buffeted by tight money, a bear market and strikes, feel harassed by court cases in anti-pollution and consumer areas. . . . Business interests may have sent an SOS to the Nixon administration, saying in effect, get the kids off our backs.

But it didn't work. The public outcry against the action was so great that two days after the temporary suspension went into effect, the IRS reversed its pronouncement.

An Aroused Public

Confrontations of this sort would seem to indicate that the conscience and the aspirations of some elements of the electorate are beginning to have a sharp impact on those who run the government. They are having the same impact on that part of society that supports the Establishment: George Washington University tried to deny tenure to Banzhaf and would have succeeded except once again the public's opposition embarrassed the authorities into relenting. The reaction of officials is sometimes awe and often fear —fear that the people themselves may be within reach of the levers of power. Suddenly there has arisen the specter of an electorate that believes politics is too important to leave to the politicians— or at least too important to leave to the same old politicians under the same old conditions.

Suddenly a crusading spirit seems to have seized a significant element of the electorate. It would be too optimistic to call this spirit widespread, but at least there is no doubt about its existence.

It has even sent a tremor through the ballot box. Gone now from the Washington scene is Philip J. Philbin. Before the election of 1970, few members of Congress would have believed that Phil Philbin would ever be defeated. He had been in Congress for fourteen terms, serving with total lack of distinction but doing the little favors that a politician believes endear him to his constituents. He was the No. 2 Democrat on the House Armed Services Committee, and he would be chairman of that powerful committee today if his constituents had not turned him out. But they did, ending the old routine that found him daily entering the House chamber, bidding his colleagues good day, selecting a soft seat, and promptly falling asleep. Congress is full of hacks, but occasionally the electorate throws one out. When it is done to the Philbins, men who are just one step away from the topmost positions of power, it is an object lesson to the congressmen who remain. According to the *New York Times*, "the day after Philbin was beaten, a colleague who used to sleep in the next seat during House sessions showed up in the chamber with a yellow pad and pencil and, bright-eyed, took notes."

Gone, too, as the result of public impatience is Representative George Fallon of Maryland, once chairman of the powerful Public Works Committee and darling of the highway lobby. The electorate in 1970 also threw out Congressman Samuel N. Friedel, chairman of the House Administration Committee, an old ward-heeler who loved to take junkets around the world and find government jobs for his cronies and for cronies of cronies. He was a waste of time, and despite the fact that he was powerful in his way, the electorate had the final word.

Some really dramatic public expulsions occurred in 1972. Representative John L. McMillan, seventy-four, who for twenty-four years had been dictator of city affairs in the District of Columbia (as chairman of the House District Committee), was voted out by his South Carolina constituents. Naturally, he blamed the newly aroused blacks for this act of political "disloyalty." An even greater fall from power was that of Representative Wayne Aspinall, seventy-five, Colorado Democrat, who more than any other man in the previous dozen years had been responsible for shaping the use of land and water in America. This power came with his chairmanship of the House Interior Committee. Unfortunately for the nation, he had used his power on behalf of the big lumbering companies, the cattle barons, the big commercial looters of the public's mining resources. He considered conservationists "a lunatic fringe." Fortunately, the conservationists had the last word, but it had taken them twenty-four years to get rid of him. His 1972 race was only the second time in those two dozen years that Aspinall had had to face opposition in the primary.

These changes did not come about by accident. For the last few elections, several public-interest groups have compiled lists of congressmen marked for "extinction" and then sought—through publicity campaigns and contributions to opposing candidates—to bring this about. The National Committee for an Effective Congress, for example, targeted nineteen congressmen for what it called "Operation Cowpasture." The committee poured nearly a million dollars and lots of publicity into their opposition. Fourteen of the nineteen left Congress—seven by retirement and seven by defeat. Aspinall was on the NCEC's list. Another citizens' group, Environmental Action, had a list called the "Dirty Dozen." Five of the twelve congressmen named were defeated. Aspinall was on that list, too. To qualify, a congressman was judged horrible according to his position on thirty-one votes.

The citizens' groups forced some politicians to come around to their point of view. Senator Lee Metcalf of Montana, who had previously been in favor of letting the strip-mining companies have their way without restraint, reversed his position to win the backing of environmentalists; it was just as well that he did, for he won reelection by only one-half of 1 percent of the vote. Senator Gordon Allott of Colorado, who had drawn the opposition of environmentalists, lost by about 1 percent. Obviously, these intense minority groups are beginning to make their weight felt on special issues.

Among the most encouraging offshoots of the public's arousal has been the decline in awe for institutions and institutional figures. For half a century J. Edgar Hoover dominated the federal cop scene in such a way as to make the FBI sacrosanct. Then in 1972 he died, and the agency's reputation began to fall apart. His successor, Patrick Gray, admitted burning incriminating records at the bidding of a White House hired hand. Also, as the Watergate scandal unfolded, some of Hoover's antics came to light. One of his former top aides charged that Hoover had, at various Presidents' requests, spied on the sex life of opposing politicians. Hoover was also accused by the same former FBI official of using his files for political blackmail. Press and congressional investigators began to discover that the agency itself was just as weak and just as fallible as any other section of the bureaucracy, if not more so.

People are also once again learning to treat the President as something less than a demigod. The presidential bungles and lies in conducting the Vietnam war and in covering up the Watergate scandal helped give the electorate the strength of healthy skepticism. When Senator Eugene McCarthy challenged President Johnson in the New Hampshire primary of 1968, the public had been startled; but when Congressmen Paul McCloskey and John Ashbrook challenged Nixon for his party's nomination, there was no shock effect. It was generally viewed as a healthy, revitalizing act of normal intra-party rivalry. In the period from 1966 to 1968 nice people didn't publicly talk about presidential lies—they talked about the "credibility gap." Three years later, thanks in great part to the printing of the secret Pentagon Papers, the word *lie* gained new acceptability. Although the gentlemanly big-city press tried to maintain decorum, the grass-roots press was again using the language of the man in the street.*

Why, so fresh is the new breeze blowing across Washington that newsmen who used to blush and demur when made aware of the little human vices of our leaders are now discussing them with open merriment. When House Speaker Carl Albert, after an inter-

---

* Consider this from the Charleston, West Virginia, *Gazette* (June 18, 1971): "The most shocking and painful disclosure of the McNamara-inspired study of how America was suckered into Vietnam is that the leader Americans honored so overwhelmingly in 1964 with their confidence, respect and ballots was a liar, a jingoistic bully, a scheming scoundrel, and an exquisite example of Plato's contention that democracy can sink to the level of asses and people stalking the streets together."

lude at a Washington saloon, bounced his car off two vehicles, the press gave full attention to the escapade of this gentleman who is second in line for succession to the Presidency. *Parade* magazine, the Sunday supplement, began fielding questions from the public about such things as "the greatest womanizers in the U.S. Senate in the past 30 years" (some of the notables mentioned: Lyndon Johnson, Edward Kennedy, Eugene McCarthy, George Smathers, Estes Kefauver, Birch Bayh, Henry Jackson). For the *Washingtonian* magazine, columnist Jack Anderson cataloged congressmen by name under such headings as "Dirty Old Men: The Greying Gallants," "Jack Daniel's Safe Driving Award: But I Just Had One," "Slippery Fingers and Bulging Pockets: Caught Redhanded in Unsavory Deals," and "The Godfathers: Friends in the Mob." Happily, the overinflated balloon is beginning to leak in many places.

The Pentagon still rules the budget roost, but for the first time since the Second World War the complaints from an abused public have forced the government to concede the waste and corruption within the military arena. It was the outpouring of public sentiment after the Cambodia invasion in 1970 that forced Nixon and the Pentagon to promise not to send American troops elsewhere in Southeast Asia. They might break the promise on the sly, but at least it must be on the sly—or in defiance of the law. It was the constant critical attention of the public-interest lawyers and some of the more ingenious newspaper reporters that forced regulatory bodies like the FTC and FPC and FDA to show some stirrings of life in recent years. It was the pounding from the environmentalists that began to turn the government around on the enforcement of pollution laws. It was the hooting and jeering from the public that forced Congress to make the first reforms in its operation that had been made in a generation.

If, as some say, a dangerous Establishment has developed outside the normal electoral channels, the people are learning to challenge this force on its own extra-electoral grounds—picketing, marching, demonstrating, pressuring, threatening, suing. Above all else, the people's lobbyists have become masters of publicity and counterpublicity. As means for permanent reform, their techniques may leave something to be desired. But while the machinery of government is being repaired, the people will just have to go on innovating. Government is problem-solving, and if the problems are not solved swiftly enough by officials chosen for the job, then the people—intemperate, illogical, disorganized, and flighty though their techniques may be—must ultimately lead their own leaders.

Notes

Foreword

[1] Quoted in *Washington Post*, June 2, 1973.
[2] Quoted in *Washington Post*, September 21, 1973.
[3] See, for example, Gallup poll, reported in *St. Louis Post-Dispatch*, June 17, 1973.
[4] Reported in *Washington Post*, April 23, 1973.
[5] Quoted in *Washington Post*, February 11, 1971.
[6] Stewart Alsop, *Newsweek*, April 6, 1970.
[7] Quoted in Mary Blume, "Walter Lippmann at 80," *Washington Post*, May 31, 1970.
[8] Quoted in John Neary, *Julian Bond: Black Rebel* (N.Y.: William Morrow, 1971).
[9] Stokely Carmichael, *Stokely Speaks* (N.Y.: Random House, 1971).
[10] Quoted in *New York Times*, June 28, 1970.

Chapter One

[1] Associated Press, December 23, 1972.
[2] Marquis Childs, November 17, 1972, syndicated column.
[3] Excerpt from "The Presidency," TV broadcast on WNDT, October 15, 1968.
[4] Quoted in Saul K. Padover, "The Power of the President," *Commonweal*, August 9, 1968.
[5] Excerpt from "The Presidency."
[6] Reported in *New York Times*, August 5, 1973; *Newsweek*, August 20, 1973.
[7] George E. Reedy, *The Twilight of the Presidency* (N.Y.: New American Library, 1970).
[8] Reported in *Newsweek*, August 20, 1973.
[9] Reported in *New York Times*, February 2, 1973.
[10] Padover, "The Power of the President."
[11] Reported in *Washington Post*, January 8, 1973.
[12] Hugh Sidey, *Life*, May 19, 1972.
[13] Quoted in *ibid.*
[14] Quoted in *Foreign Policy*, 8 (Fall 1972).
[15] Hans J. Morgenthau, "Congress and Foreign Policy," *New Republic*, June 14, 1969.
[16] *Progressive*, May 1973.
[17] Morgenthau, "Congress and Foreign Policy."
[18] Edward S. Herman and Richard DuBoff, *America's Vietnam Policy* (Washington, D.C.: Public Affairs Press, 1966).
[19] Excerpt from "The Presidency."

[20] Arthur Schlesinger, Jr., "The Limits and Excesses of Presidential Power," *Saturday Review*, May 3, 1969.
[21] Quoted in *Foreign Policy*, 8 (Fall 1972).
[22] *The Pentagon Papers* (N.Y.: Bantam Books, 1971).
[23] Reported in *Time*, August 14, 1964.
[24] Arthur F. Burns, *Business Cycles in a Changing World* (N.Y.: Columbia University Press, 1970).
[25] Quoted in Adam Yarmolinsky, *The Military Establishment: Its Impacts on American Society* (N.Y.: Harper, 1971).
[26] Henry Steele Commager, "Presidential Power," *New Republic*, April 6, 1968.

Chapter Two

[1] Colonel James A. Donovan, *Militarism, U.S.A.* (N.Y.: Scribner's, 1970).
[2] Colonel William H. Neblett, *Pentagon Politics* (N.Y.: Pageant Press, 1953).
[3] Adam Yarmolinsky, *The Military Establishment: Its Impacts on American Society* (N.Y.: Harper, 1971).
[4] All quotes from *U.S. Farm News*, March 1971.
[5] Quoted in *Congressional Record*, June 13, 1973.
[6] Reported in *ADA Legislative Newsletter*, April 1, 1973.
[7] Quoted in Robert Sherrill, "The War Machine," *Playboy*, May 1970.
[8] Sanford Rose, "Making a Turn to a Peacetime Economy," *Fortune*, September 1970.
[9] Quoted in *The Nation*, August 7, 1972.
[10] Quoted in *Federation of American Scientists Newsletter*, March 1973.
[11] Quoted in Sherrill, "The War Machine."
[12] Reported in *New York Times*, March 15, 1972.
[13] Quoted in *Foreign Policy* (Summer 1973).
[14] Quoted by Clayton Fritchey, June 16, 1973, syndicated column.
[15] Reported in *New York Times*, January 19, 1973.
[16] Richard F. Kaufman, *The War Profiteers* (Indianapolis: Bobbs-Merrill, 1970).
[17] Reported in *Congressional Record*, May 16, 1973.
[18] Bert Cochran, *The War System* (N.Y.: Macmillan, 1965).
[19] David Wise and Thomas B. Ross, *The Invisible Government* (N.Y.: Random House, 1964).
[20] Reported in *Washington Post*, April 11, 1973.
[21] Quoted in *Washington Post*, May 20, 1970.
[22] *Congress and the Nation, 1945–1964: A Review of Government and Politics in the Postwar Years* (Washington, D.C.: Congressional Quarterly Service, 1965).
[23] Reported in *Washington Post*, June 11, 1973.
[24] Sidney Lens, *The Military-Industrial Complex* (Philadelphia: United Church Press, Pilgrim Press; Kansas City, Mo.: National Catholic Reporter, 1970).
[25] Quoted in *Congressional Record*, April 18, 1973.
[26] Reported in *The Defense Monitor*, September 8, 1972.
[27] Reported in *ibid.*
[28] Reported in *Washington Post*, April 4, 1973.
[29] Senate Foreign Relations Committee's hearings on extension of the Military Sales Act, March 24, 1970.
[30] Donovan, *Militarism, U.S.A.*
[31] General Nathan F. Twining, *Neither Liberty Nor Safety: A Hard Look at U.S. Military Policy and Strategy* (N.Y.: Holt, 1966).

Chapter Three

[1] Arthur Schlesinger, Jr., "The Limits and Excesses of Presidential Power," *Saturday Review*, May 3, 1969.

[2] Interview with Ronald Steel, quoted in *Congressional Record*, March 29, 1973.

[3] Speech delivered at Oxford University, January 21, 1973.

[4] Quoted in *Congressional Record*, June 29, 1973.

[5] Quoted in Emmet John Hughes, *The Living Presidency* (N.Y.: Coward, McCann & Geoghegan, 1973).

[6] Quoted in *ibid.*

[7] Quoted in *Washington Post*, June 6, 1973.

[8] James David Barber, *The Presidential Character* (Englewood Cliffs, N.J.: Prentice-Hall, 1972).

[9] Quoted in Theodore H. White, *The Making of the President 1968* (N.Y.: Atheneum, 1969).

[10] Quoted in *Washington Post*, March 2, 1973.

[11] Interview with Dan Rather on CBS-TV, January 2, 1972.

[12] Reported in *Washington Post*, August 1 and 6, 1973.

[13] Quoted in *Washington Post*, August 8, 1971.

[14] Excerpt from "The Presidency," TV broadcast on WNDT, October 15, 1968.

[15] Quoted in Barber, *The Presidential Character.*

[16] Don Oberdorfer, *Washington Post*, August 15, 1971.

[17] Quoted in *New York Times Magazine*, January 7, 1968.

[18] Quoted in *Washington Post*, February 4, 1973.

[19] Richard J. Whalen, *Catch the Falling Flag: A Republican's Challenge to His Party* (Boston: Houghton Mifflin, 1972).

[20] Quoted in *Washington Post*, July 1, 1973.

[21] Whalen, *Catch the Falling Flag.*

[22] Quoted in *Congressional Record*, July 12, 1973.

[23] Quoted in *Washington Post*, February 4, 1973.

[24] Walter Hickel, *Who Owns America?* (Englewood Cliffs, N.J.: Prentice-Hall, 1971).

[25] Harold Ickes, *The Secret Diary of Harold Ickes: The First Thousand Days* (N.Y.: Simon and Schuster, 1953.)

[26] Quoted in Robert Sherrill, *Gothic Politics in the Deep South* (N.Y.: Grossman, 1970).

[27] Quoted in Sam Houston Johnson, *My Brother Lyndon* (N.Y.: Cowles, 1969, 1970).

[28] Personal interview, November 1966.

[29] *Smithsonian Magazine*, March 1972.

[30] Hughes, *The Living Presidency.*

[31] Robert B. Semple, *New York Times*, January 21, 1973.

[32] Quoted in *Washington Post*, July 24, 1973.

Chapter Four

[1] Stewart Alsop, *The Center: People and Power in Political Washington* (N.Y.: Harper, 1968).

[2] Quoted in *Congressional Record*, March 22, 1973.

[3] Tom Dowling, *Washington Star-News*, May 14, 1973.

[4] Richard Bolling, *House Out of Order* (N.Y.: Dutton, 1965).
[5] Personal interview, January 1971. See also Robert Sherrill, "92nd Congress: Eulogies and Evasions," *The Nation*, February 15, 1971.
[6] Warren Weaver, Jr., *Both Your Houses. The Truth About Congress* (N.Y.: Praeger, 1972).
[7] Fred Harris, "The Senate Can Be Reformed," *Washington Post*, July 11, 1971.
[8] Quoted in *Washington Post*, July 11, 1971.
[9] Democratic Study Group Special Report, "The Seniority System in the U.S. House of Representatives," February 25, 1970.
[10] Bolling, *House Out of Order*.
[11] Hearings before House Subcommittee on Agricultural Labor of the Education and Labor Committee, April 6 and 7, 1973.
[12] Quoted in *Human Events*, September 29, 1973.
[13] Quoted in *Congressional Record*, April 6, 1973.
[14] Quoted in *Congressional Record*, March 22, 1973.
[15] Mark J. Green *et al.*, *Who Runs Congress?* (N.Y.: Bantam Books, 1972).
[16] Personal interview, December 1969. See also Robert Sherrill, "L. Mendel Rivers: King of the Military Mountain," *The Nation*, January 19, 1970.
[17] Bolling, *House Out of Order*.
[18] Quoted in *Washington Post*, January 18, 1971.
[19] Quoted in *ibid*.
[20] Richard L. Lyons, *Washington Post*, August 1, 1971.
[21] Personal interview, September 1970. See also Robert Sherrill, "Who Runs Congress?" *New York Times Magazine*, November 22, 1970.
[22] Quoted in *Congressional Record*, March 22, 1973.
[23] Democratic Study Group Special Report, "Serving the Public in Secret," July 6, 1970.
[24] Personal interview. See also Sherrill, "L. Mendel Rivers: King of the Military Mountain."
[25] Personal interviews, Summer 1969.
[26] Quoted in *Congressional Record*, April 19, 1973.
[27] Reported in *Washington Post*, April 1, 1972.
[28] Reported in *New York Times*, February 12, 1971.
[29] Reported in *Washington Post*, December 28, 1970.
[30] Reported in *New York Times*, April 11, 1971.
[31] Common Cause financial report, September 1973.
[32] *Ibid*. Also *Congressional Record*, April 6, 1973.
[33] Personal interview. See also Sherrill, "Who Runs Congress?"
[34] Robert Sherrill, "The Instant Electorate," *Playboy*, November 1968.
[35] V. O. Key, Jr., "Public Opinion and the Decay of Democracy," *The Virginia Quarterly Review*, Autumn 1961.
[36] Representative W. L. Hungate, reported in *Washington Post*, April 29, 1971.

Chapter Five

[1] Personal interview, May 1968.
[2] Reported in *Washington Post*, November 1, 1970.
[3] Seymour Martin Lipset, "Private Opinion on the Polls," *New York Times Magazine*, August 30, 1964.
[4] James W. Prothro and Charles M. Grigg, "Fundamental Principles of Democracy: Bases of Agreement and Disagreement," *The Journal of Politics*, 22 (1960).
[5] Herbert McClosky, "Consensus and Ideology in American Politics," *American Political Science Review* (June 1964).

6 Carl Brent Swisher, *The Supreme Court in Modern Role* (N.Y.: New York University Press, 1958).

7 Sam J. Ervin, Jr., and Ramsey Clark, *Role of the Supreme Court: Policymaker or Adjudicator?* (Washington, D.C.: American Enterprise Institute for Public Policy Research, 1970).

8 Samuel Krislov, *The Supreme Court and Political Freedom* (N.Y.: Free Press, 1968).

9 Quoted in Louis Heren, *The New American Commonwealth* (N.Y.: Harper, 1968).

10 James E. Clayton, *Washington Post*, November 10, 1970.

11 Abe Fortas, James Madison Lecture at the New York University Law School, March 29, 1967.

12 Ervin and Clark, *Role of the Supreme Court: Policymaker or Adjudicator?*

13 Adolf Berle, *The Three Faces of Power* (N.Y.: Harcourt Brace Jovanovich, 1967).

14 McClatchy Broadcasting Interview, reprinted in *New York Times*, June 27, 1969.

15 Alexander M. Bickel, *The Supreme Court and the Idea of Progress* (N.Y.: Harper, 1970).

16 Quoted in Robert H. Bork, "The Supreme Court Needs a New Philosophy," *Fortune*, December 1968.

17 Burke Marshall, *Federalism and Civil Rights* (N.Y.: Columbia University Press, 1964).

18 Ramsey Clark, *Crime in America* (N.Y.: Simon and Schuster, 1970).

19 Bork, "The Supreme Court Needs a New Philosophy."

20 Philip Kurland, *Harvard Law Review*, 78 (1964).

21 Quoted in Julius Duscha, "Chief Justice Burger Asks: 'If It Doesn't Make Good Sense, How Can It Make Good Law?'" *New York Times Magazine*, October 5, 1969.

22 *Washington Post*, July 1, 1972.

23 Tom Wicker, *New York Times*, July 2, 1972.

24 Quoted in *Washington Post*, July 3, 1972.

25 John P. Frank, *Marble Palace: The Supreme Court in American Life* (N.Y.: Knopf, 1961).

26 Fred Graham, *New York Times*, March 7, 1971.

27 Quoted in *New York Times*, February 3, 1973.

Chapter Six

1 Barry Goldwater, speech on Senate floor, July 14, 1970.

2 Quoted in *Washington Post*, June 19, 1973.

3 Quoted in *National Journal*, March 3, 1973.

4 Quoted in *Wall Street Journal*, September 30, 1970.

5 Nader's press briefing for Public Interest Research Group's report, "The Spoiled System," reported in *Washington Post*, June 18, 1972.

6 Reported in *Washington Post*, August 13, 1972.

7 Quoted in *Wall Street Journal*, March 17, 1972.

8 Quoted in *New York Times*, March 5, 1972.

9 Reported in National Farmers Union *Washington Newsletter*, April 14, 1972.

10 Reported in *Congressional Record*, May 22, 1973.

11 Charles Frankel, *High on Foggy Bottom* (N.Y.: Harper, 1969).

12 Quoted in Marriner S. Eccles, *Beckoning Frontiers*, edited by Sidney Hyman (N.Y.: Knopf, 1951).

13 Quoted in *Washington Post*, May 30, 1972.

[14] Quoted in *Washington Star-News*, June 11, 1973.
[15] Quoted in *Newsweek*, August 21, 1972.
[16] Personal interview, October 1970.
[17] Adolf Berle, *The Three Faces of Power* (N.Y.: Harcourt Brace Jovanovich, 1967).
[18] GAO study released April 24, 1973.
[19] Reported in *Washington Post*, March 29, 1972, and April 23, 1972.
[20] Reported in *Coal Patrol*, 20 (February 1972).
[21] Quoted in *New York Times*, December 30, 1969.
[22] Quoted in *Congressional Record*, March 8, 1973.
[23] Quoted in *Washington Star-News*, March 28, 1973.
[24] Quoted in *Washington Post*, February 16, 1972.
[25] Associated Press story by G. David Wallace, July 25, 1971.
[26] Reported in *Washington Post*, February 25, 1972.
[27] Lawrence Laurent, *Washington Post*, July 5, 1968.
[28] Quoted in *New York Times*, August 8, 1971.
[29] Philip Elman, speech before American Bar Association meeting in St. Louis, August 1970.
[30] *Ibid.*
[31] Ralph Nader, Introduction to Morton Mintz and Jerry S. Cohen, *America, Inc.* (N.Y.: Dial, 1971).
[32] Quoted in *New York Times*, April 2, 1972.

Chapter Seven

[1] Melvin J. Grayson and Thomas B. Shepard, Jr., *The Disaster Lobby: Prophets of Ecological Doom and Other Absurdities* (Chicago: Follett, 1973).
[2] Colman McCarthy, *Washington Post*, April 20, 1972.
[3] Bill Kovach, *New York Times*, June 10, 1973.
[4] Joseph Morgenstern, *Newsweek*, May 24, 1971.
[5] Norman Pollack, ed., *The Populist Mind* (Indianapolis: Bobbs-Merrill, 1967).
[6] Peter Barnes and Larry Casalino, *Who Owns the Land?* (Berkeley: The Center for Rural Studies, 1972).
[7] First Annual Report of the Council on Environmental Quality (Washington, D.C.: Government Printing Office, 1970).
[8] William O. Douglas, "The Public Be Damned," *Playboy*, July 1969.
[9] Reported in *New York Times*, April 15, 1973.
[10] Personal interview, February 1970.
[11] Gladwin Hill, *New York Times*, January 10, 1971.
[12] Quoted in *New York Times*, June 4, 1972.
[13] Quoted in *Washington Post*, January 26, 1970.
[14] Quoted in *New York Times*, May 27, 1973.

Chapter Eight

[1] Philip M. Stern, *The Rape of the Taxpayer* (New York: Random House, 1973).
[2] Personal interview, August 1971.
[3] Paul A. Samuelson, column in *Newsweek*, May 21, 1973.
[4] Hobart Rowen, *Washington Post*, January 14, 1970.
[5] Quoted in *Washington Post*, February 11, 1969.

⁶ Quoted in Roger Leroy Miller and Raburn M. Williams, *The New Economics of Richard Nixon* (N.Y.: Harper's Magazine Press, 1972).
⁷ Albert L. Kraus, *New York Times*, October 23, 1969.
⁸ Wright Patman, speech to the Public Affairs Forum of the Harvard Business School, February 9, 1970.
⁹ George Mitchell, St. Louis Federal Reserve Bank *Review*, May 1966.
¹⁰ Quoted by Patman, speech at Harvard Business School.
¹¹ Reported in *Wall Street Journal*, September 24, 1973.
¹² Cited in Stern, *The Rape of the Taxpayer*.
¹³ Andrew F. Brimmer, speech to the San Francisco Bond Club, April 1, 1971.
¹⁴ Juan Cameron, "The Fed on the Firing Line," *Fortune*, December 1968.
¹⁵ Quoted in *New York Times*, January 10, 1971.

Chapter Nine

¹ CBS Morning News with John Hart, June 17, 1971.
² Personal interview, July 1971.
³ Quoted in *Christian Science Monitor*, September 15, 1973.
⁴ Conversation, July 1971.
⁵ John J. O'Connor, *New York Times*, June 10, 1973.
⁶ Tom Wicker, "The Greening of the Press," *Columbia Journalism Review*, May/June 1971.
⁷ *Ibid.*
⁸ Richard Harwood, *Washington Post*, July 27, 1971.
⁹ Jules Witcover, "Where Washington Reporting Failed," reprinted in *Congressional Record*, February 2, 1971.
¹⁰ Dr. Erik Barnouw, *The Image Empire: A History of Broadcasting in the United States*. Volume III: From 1953. (N.Y.: Oxford, 1970).
¹¹ Quoted in *Washington Post*, March 28, 1971.
¹² Victor Bernstein and Jesse Gordon, "The Press and the Bay of Pigs," *The Columbia University Forum*, Fall 1967.
¹³ Quoted in *New York Times*, May 21, 1973.
¹⁴ David Wise, *The Politics of Lying: Governmental Deception, Secrecy and Power* (N.Y.: Random House, 1973).
¹⁵ Personal interview, July 1971.
¹⁶ Reported in *Wall Street Journal*, March 7, 1973.
¹⁷ Personal interview, July 1971.
¹⁸ Personal interview, June 1971.
¹⁹ Quoted in *Washington Post*, January 9, 1972.
²⁰ Personal interview, June 1971.
²¹ James Reston, *The Artillery of the Press* (N.Y.: Harper, 1967).
²² Charles Roberts, "Fearsome Antagonist," *The Nation*, October 24, 1966.
²³ Quoted in *Washington Post*, December 17, 1971.
²⁴ Personal interview, June 1971.
²⁵ Quoted in *New York Times*, January 24, 1971.
²⁶ Quoted in Stewart Alsop, *The Center: People and Power in Political Washington* (N.Y.: Harper, 1968).
²⁷ Personal interview, July 1971.
²⁸ Personal interview, July 1971.
²⁹ Bill Monroe, speech at KMTV Dinner, Omaha, Nebraska, January 18, 1971.
³⁰ Quoted in William McGaffin and Erwin Knoll, *Anything But the Truth* (N.Y.: Putnam, 1968).

Chapter Ten

[1] John Gardner, Common Cause *Report from Washington*, 1, No. 1 (November 1970).

[2] Quoted in *Washington Post*, January 30, 1973.

[3] Reported in *New York Times*, June 20, 1971.

[4] Mark J. Green *et al.*, *Who Runs Congress?* (N.Y.: Bantam Books, 1973).

[5] *Rights in Conflict*, The Walker Report to the National Commission on the Causes and Prevention of Violence (N.Y.: Bantam Books, 1973).

[6] Irving Howe, ed., *Beyond the New Left* (N.Y.: McCall, 1969).

[7] Louis Harris poll, reported in *Washington Post*, January 10, 1971.

[8] Richard L. Ottinger, speech at Sarah Lawrence College, April 22, 1970. Reprinted in *Earth Day—The Beginning* (N.Y.: Arno Press, 1970).

[9] Quoted in *Washington Post*, May 17, 1971.

[10] Personal interview, May 1970.

Index

Estuaries Preservation Act (1968), 244
Eurodollar trading, 261
Europe, Cold War and, 42–44; Soviet Union and, 45
Evans, Rowland, 308
Everglades National Park, 251
Evins, Joe L., 130
Excise tax, 265
Executive Office of the President, 204. *See also* White House
ExIm Bank, 67–68

Fairlie, Harry, 16
Fairness doctrine, 218
Fallon, George, 333
Family Assistance Plan, 85–86
Farkas, Ruth, 146
Farms, splitting up of, 126*n*.
Farm subsidies, 126
Fascell, Dante, 34
Fascism, native, 159; power crisis in, 79
Favors, presidential, 100–01
FBI (Federal Bureau of Investigation), ix, 175, 207, 299, 310–11, 335
Federal Aviation Administration, 127*n*., 210
Federal Communications Commission, 204–05, 215, 217, 267, 296, 306, 310, 321, 330; "fairness" doctrine of, 218*n*.
Federal Corrupt Practices Act (1925), 128, 143–44, 146
Federal Election Campaign Act (1971), 145–46
Federalism, bureaucracy and, 193–96
Federalist, The, xvi, 10, 19
Federal Open Market Committee, 270
Federal Power Commission, 146, 195*n*., 205–06, 215, 222, 336
Federal Reserve Board, 37, 93, 195*n*., 259, 262, 267–69; reforms in, 278–80
Federal Reserve System, big banks and, 272–76, 282–83; as "central bank," 270; power of, 267–72
Federal Trade Commission, 205, 222–24, 331, 336
Federal Water Pollution Control Act (1948), 244
Federal Water Quality Administration, 245, 246*n*.
Federation of American Scientists, 54
Fellmeth, Robert, 215
Fertitta, R. J., 55
Fifth Amendment, 163
Finch, Robert, 202, 213
First Amendment, 115, 158, 164, 185, 187, 288
First National City Bank of New York,

274
Fiscal policy, monetary policy and, 263
Fish, mercury concentration in, 231
Fitzgerald, Ernest, 18, 49
Fitzhugh, Gilbert W., 197
Flag Salute Cases, Supreme Court and, 165*n*.
Flammable Fabrics Act (1967), 216–17
FMC Corporation, 216
F-111 plane, 50
Food and Drug Administration, 212–13, 217, 222, 336
Food for Peace Program, 66
Forbes, 235
Force, justification for, 160
Ford, Corey, 301
Ford Foundation, 59
Ford, Gerald, xii, 15, 96, 144
Ford Motor Company, 10*n*., 11*n*., 247, 266, 327–28
Foreign Affairs, 42
Foreign policy, arms peddling and, 67–69; "collective security" in, 19; Kissinger and, 30; President's role in, 18–31; State Department and, 29–30
Foreman, Ed, xvi
Forest lands, depletion of, 232–33, 238–40, 251*n*.
Forest Service, U.S. *See* United States Forest Service
Formosa, arms sale to, 68
Forrestal, James, 62
Fortas, Abe, 169
Fortune, 281
Fourteenth Amendment, 167–68, 188; "equal protection" clause in, 170
Frankel, Charles, 203
Frankfurter, Felix, 163, 165*n*., 167, 176–77, 181
Frank, John P., 186
Freedom, institutionalized, 166
Freedom of Information Act (1967), 289, 306–07
Freeman, Orville, 135
Free press, 158–60, 164, 185; Supreme Court and, 174
Free speech, 155; Supreme Court and, 174
Free world security gap, 57–58
Friedel, Samuel N., 333
Friedman, Milton, 263
Friends of the Earth, 331
Fulbright, J. William, 24–25, 34, 74, 116
Furness, Betty, 326

Gaines v. Canada, 178

Long, Russell B., 116, 126, 292
Look, 228
Loory, Stuart H., 28n.
Los Angeles, pollution of, 230, 254
Los Angeles Times, xii, 290n., 292, 294
Louisville Courier-Journal, 216
Loyalty oaths, 174
Lubell, Sam, 84
Lung cancer, smoking and, 218n.
Lyons, Richard L., 136

MacArthur, Douglas, 40, 45n.
McCarthy, Colman, 228
McCarthy, Eugene, 74, 322, 335–36
McCarthyism, 168, 174
McCarthy, Joseph R., 73, 173, 175
Machiavelli, Niccolò, 94
McClelland Air Force Base, 133
McClellan, John, 115, 127
McClendon, Sarah, 65
McClosky, Herbert, 160
McClosky, Paul, 335
McCormack, John, 121
McDonald's Hamburgers, 224
McDonnell Douglas, Inc., 145
McFall, John J., 125
McGee, Gale W., 116, 238, 319
McGovern, George, ix, 25–26, 47n., 50, 51n., 53, 80, 98, 145, 316, 319
McGrory, Mary, x
McKellar, Kenneth B., xvi
MacKenzie, John P., 186
McKinley, William, 9
McMillan, John L., 334
McNamara, Robert S., 45, 49, 71–73, 335n.
McReynolds, James C., 186
McWilliams, Carey, 296
Maddox, U.S.S., 36
Madison, James, xvi, 6, 9
Mafia-linked companies, 220
Magnuson, Warren G., 116
Magruder, Jeb Stuart, 4
Mahon, George, 114, 135–36, 141–42
Mail service, deterioration of, 221n.
Making of Justice, The (Clayton), 169
Malaysia, arms sale to, 68
Manley, John F., 133
Mansfield, Mike, 34, 111
Manufacturing Chemists Association, 246
Mao Tse-tung, 30
Mardian, Robert, 200
Mare Island Navy Shipyard, 133
Marine Corps Association, 49
Marine Corps League, 49
Maritime Institute, 298
Marshall, Burke, 176
Marshall, George C., 75

Marshall, John, 177, 186
Marshall Plan, 46
Marshall, Thurgood, 100
Martin, William McChesney, 259
Massachusetts Institute of Technology, 54
Mather Air Force Base, 133
Means, Marianne, 308
Meany, George, xii, 266, 317–18
Medicaid, 122n.
Medical care, for aged, 121–22
Medicare, 122n.
Mellon, Andrew, 115
Mercury pollution, 231, 246n.
Meridian Investing and Development Corporation, 234
Metcalf, Lee, 210n., 334
Methrotrexate, 217
Metromedia News, 64
Metropolitan Life Insurance Company, 197
Miami Herald, 297
Michigan State University, 328
Michigan, University of, 316
Middle East, arms peddling to, 70
Migratory Labor Commission, 122
Mikva, Abner, 113
Military budget, realities of, 52–55; waste in, 60
Military-industrial-political complex, 45n., 46n., 48–55
Miller, R. L., 264
Milligan, Lambden P., 161
Mills, Wilbur, 102, 114
Miners, land exploitation by, 235–36
Minneapolis Honeywell Company, 328
Minnesota Mining and Manufacturing Company, 328
Minnesota Newspaper Association, 209
Miranda decision, Supreme Court and, 178
MIRV missiles, 54
Missile gap, Soviet Union and, 57–58
Mitchell, George, 274
Mitchell, James P., 210
Mitchell, John N., x, 94, 187, 252, 288n.
Mitchell v. United States, 178
Mobil Oil Company, 331
Model cities grants, 130
Monarchy, fear of, 8–9, 18
Monetary policy, fiscal policy and, 263; inflation and, 261–62
Money costs, inflation and, 262n.
Money management, in international market, 262
Money monopoly, 282–83
Monroe, Bill, 310
Monroe Doctrine, 26